Our

Edited & annotated by

Nancy Tystad Koupal

Landlady

L. FRANK BAUM

UNIVERSITY OF NEBRASKA PRESS *Lincoln & London*

© 1996 by the
University of Nebraska Press
All rights reserved
Manufactured in the United States of America

First Bison Books printing : 1999
Most recent printing indicated by the
last digit below:
10 9 8 7 6 5 4 3 2 1
Library of Congress Cataloging-in-Publication Data
Baum, L. Frank (Lyman Frank), 1856–1919.
    Our landlady / L. Frank Baum : edited and
    annotated by Nancy Tystad Koupal.
          p.   cm.
    A collection of the author's 1890–91 "Our
landlady" columns originally appearing in the
Aberdeen Saturday Pioneer.
    Includes bibliographical references and index.
    ISBN 0-8032-1221-6 (cl.: alk. paper)
    ISBN 0-8032-6156-x (pa.: alk. paper)
1. United States — Social life and customs
— 19th century — Fiction.   2. City and
town life — South Dakota — Aberdeen —
Fiction.   3. Satire, American — South Dakota
— Aberdeen.   4. Aberdeen (S.D.) — Social
life and customs.   I. Koupal, Nancy Tystad.
II. Title.
PS3503.A923097   1996
813'.4 — dc20   95-32094
CIP

CONTENTS

✺ ILLUSTRATIONS

 **PREFACE**

Since 1900 and the publication of *The Wonderful Wizard of Oz*, L. Frank Baum's life and writings have been scrutinized for clues that would unlock the meaning of this enduring American fairy tale. Overlooked in the search have been the author's South Dakota writings, most of which appeared in a rare newspaper, the *Aberdeen Saturday Pioneer*. As a consequence, biographical and critical studies have sketched rather than studied Baum's literary and political apprenticeship on the western frontier. From the sparse data, scholars have then generalized about the nature of Baum's western years and writings, leading to the chronic mistakes concerning the author's life and politics that mar most critical and interpretive discussions. This annotated edition of the author's 1890–91 "Our Landlady" columns makes the most significant portion of Baum's western writings available to readers and attempts to correct some long-standing misconceptions about the author's experiences in the West.

Only cursory or heavily clichéd references to Baum's three years (1888–91) in South Dakota occur in many scholarly treatments of the author's work. A standard discussion usually takes up a paragraph or, at best, a page. It includes the information that he came west as a storekeeper, failed, and then took over a newspaper, which likewise failed. Often added to these bare bones is a mention that he wrote the satirical "Our Landlady" series and experienced firsthand the agrarian unrest that took place in the area at the time. On these bald statements alone, critics have "documented" Baum's sympathy for the farmer and, in fact, have metamorphosed the author himself into an agrarian radical or Populist to support a reading of *The Wonderful Wizard of Oz* as a political commentary. As I quickly found out when I began reading his newspaper, however, Baum considered himself a traditional Republican, and his view of the farmers' problems was often as critical as it was sympathetic.

Scholars less interested in politics have tended to emphasize other stereotypical concepts of Baum's frontier experience. Assuming that his description of Kansas at the beginning of *The Wizard* is actually a stand-in for Dakota, they have concluded that Baum's western years must have been bleak, isolated, and deprived — akin to the well-known experiences of Hamlin Garland a few years earlier. In this scenario the local townspeople become country bumpkins, yokels, rubes, and other stereotypes of rural Americans. This concept has been especially prevalent in popular treatments. For example, the N B C made-for-T V movie *Dreamer of Oz* (1990), based on Baum's life, "re-created" an Aberdeen,

South Dakota, that resembled hillbilly heaven, complete with gun-toting rustics and pigs wallowing in the streets. In reality, the Aberdeen of 1888–91 contained a sophisticated population of easterners and foreign-born immigrants. Although its streets were indeed unpaved, its business district boasted electric street lights and some of the first telephones west of New York City.

Perhaps the most obvious clue that the research behind the NBC movie had come from the standard generalizations about Baum's Dakota years could be seen in the distance: at the end of the fictional Aberdeen's main street loomed a mountain range. The first biography of Baum (Frank Joslyn Baum and Russell P. MacFall's *To Please a Child*, published in 1961) offered readers the misinformation that Aberdeen's citizens had been drawn by the 1876 Black Hills gold rush, and few have questioned the idea since. The real Aberdeen, however, was platted in 1881 — five years after the rush began — and was situated in the flat James River Valley over three hundred miles northeast of the Black Hills. Its boomtown days resulted from the fields of golden wheat that surrounded it on all sides. Nevertheless, the misconception about its relationship to the gold rush persists, appearing even in the better-researched 1994 BBC documentary *In Search of Oz.*

Furthermore, the BBC production shows that even when researchers look more closely at Baum's life in the West, their sometimes skimpy knowledge of the history and region still causes them to make mistakes in sorting fact from fiction. One scholar dismissed the entire concept of the *Wizard of Oz* as a political commentary, claiming that Baum never even mentioned the Populists in his newspaper even though Populists were agitating all around him — a "fact" apparently gleaned from the standard generalizations. What the critic did not recognize in his reading of the *Aberdeen Saturday Pioneer* was that the Populists of 1890 were not yet going by that name. In Baum's era, they were known as Independents, and Baum wrote about them frequently.

Clearly, if the dialogue about Baum's politics and other ideas is to progress, his South Dakota years must be better understood and explicated. An understanding of his Republicanism, his western boosterism, his active social life on the northern plains, and his disappointments can add richness and depth to the national discussion about the works of this important American storyteller. Context and knowledge of the time period can also give fuller appreciation of a controversial aspect of Baum's Dakota writings that has surfaced in recent years. Both in textbooks and the popular press, Baum has been berated for racism toward American Indians. His statements about Indians come from one source only: two *Aberdeen Saturday Pioneer* editorials written in the middle of the

1890 Indian scare that culminated in the death of Sitting Bull and the killings at Wounded Knee. Although one cannot ignore these bitter editorials, our understanding of Baum's humanity — and our own — becomes more complete when we recognize the historical events and local hysteria out of which his remarks came.

To illuminate Baum's time in South Dakota and his South Dakota writings, the weekly satirical column "Our Landlady" is an ideal means. Not only does the column offer insights into Baum's politics and thought; it also provides a powerful literary lens through which to view the urban frontier of a century ago. Like other American authors, Baum used local settings and characters to focus on the larger human condition. As a result, a close study of "Our Landlady" not only explodes generalizations about Baum and South Dakota but offers the reader an entertaining social and political history of American town-building in the late nineteenth century.

When I first started on this project, I was struck by the fact that (like the critics) South Dakota librarians and historians always mentioned L. Frank Baum as an early resident and state author, but (also like the critics) most could tell me nothing about him or his works beyond the *Wizard of Oz*. I found it puzzling that people were willing to claim someone who had gained nothing visible from South Dakota and apparently given nothing in return. For them, Baum was only an impressive statistic. Once I began to work with the columns, however, it became clear that librarians and statisticians had been right to claim him as a native son. The state had contributed a wealth of experiences and impressions to Baum, and he, in turn, had given South Dakota his time and talent and a remarkable literary persona, Mrs. Bilkins. Through the weekly diatribe of Baum's alter ego, the hopes and trials of the citizens of a fledgling prairie state took on rich dimensions. To bring this bounty to book form, however, has required years of research and writing that could not have been done without the help of others.

The South Dakota Humanities Council got the ball rolling with two small research grants that enabled me to travel to Aberdeen to use the resources of the Alexander Mitchell Library and the Dacotah Prairie Museum. David Rave, the head librarian at the Alexander Mitchell Library, opened the library's valuable Baum collection to my unrestricted use. Without the access he allowed me, this book truly could not have been what it is. The fragile nature of the original file of the *Aberdeen Saturday Pioneer* demands that it be locked away to ensure its preservation. A microfilm copy exists, but because the original text on highly acidic paper is beginning to fade, the camera missed punctuation marks and other characters. To guarantee an accurate text for this book, Rave allowed me to proofread my copy, ever so carefully, against the original text.

Merry Coleman, director of the Dacotah Prairie Museum, also accommodated my special research needs, lending me copies of the unmicrofilmed *Aberdeen Evening Republican* and facilitating the research that turned up many of the pictures of Aberdeen businesses that complement the text. I also thank the staff of the George Arents Research Library at Syracuse University, who made it so easy to use the L. Frank Baum Papers there. Karen Zimmerman, head of the Richardson Archives at the University of South Dakota, provided generous help in accessing the large WPA Writers' Project Collection. Not least, I wish to acknowledge my debts to former South Dakota State Archivist Linda Sommer and former South Dakota State Historical Society Director J. R. Fishburne. Without the willing cooperation of these two professionals in my home institution, I could not have embarked on this research effort.

The debt I owe to the many scholars who have preceded me in researching Baum and his works, the history of South Dakota and the region, the history of woman suffrage, Wounded Knee, and prohibition, among other things, is acknowledged in the long list of sources that make up this book's bibliography. In addition, I offer special thanks to Michael Patrick Hearn, who has cheered me on and supplied information and documents from his personal collection and research. Other colleagues who have offered moral support and assistance when I most needed it are William C. Pratt, Ruth Ann Alexander, Jay D. Vogt, Sally Roesch Wagner, and Michael Gessel. To one and all, many thanks. I acknowledge the previous appearance of a greatly condensed version of the introduction in the *Baum Bugle* in 1992; of a small portion of the discussion of Baum's fantasy columns in the *Great Plains Quarterly* in 1989; and of brief sections of the discussion of the 1890 political scene in *Montana, the Magazine of Western History* in 1990.

In the early stages of this project I had no idea that it would ultimately demand so much time, eating up vacations and consuming my thought processes. People with day jobs, children, and a spouse should approach such projects with more caution than I did. To my staff, Jeanne Kilen Ode and Laura Ries, I offer thanks for their encouragement and thoughtfulness. From my husband, William G. Koupal, and daughters Alyssa and Kristen I received an unstinting and abiding faith in my ability to do the job I had set myself. For them, however, thanks are not really enough. I also offer apologies for my abstraction and promise herewith to return to the late twentieth century, leaving the 1890s behind — for a while.

Our Landlady

Long before *The Wonderful Wizard of Oz* (1900) brought lasting fame to L. Frank Baum, the tall author with a handsome mustache and dancing eyes was already the talk of the town in Aberdeen, South Dakota. Baum had come west in 1888 to make money in the retail business and stayed to make fun of his fellow entrepreneurs as editor of a weekly newspaper. It was an exciting time for a keen observer with a wicked wit and a gift for making people laugh at themselves. South Dakota had joined the Union on 2 November 1889, and the new citizens had political appointments, capital location, railroads, failing wheat crops, woman suffrage referendums, and loopholes in the prohibition laws, among other things, on their minds. In a newspaper column titled "Our Landlady," Baum employed satire and humor to prod his readers along the paths of honor as they juggled private and public values in the creation of state and community.[1] Although the columns are all but forgotten today, Baum's weekly "Our Landlady" offerings caused embarrassed gasps and howls of amusement when they appeared in 1890.

Baum learned to express himself in print at an early age. Born in Chittenango, New York, on 15 May 1856, he spent his childhood amid wealth and luxury. His father, Benjamin Ward Baum, who had made his money in the Pennsylvania oil fields, bought his son a printing press in 1870 when the aspiring young author expressed an interest. Fourteen-year-old Lyman Frank Baum — who disliked his first name and preferred to be called Frank — and his younger brother Harry established a monthly newspaper, the *Rose Lawn Home Journal*, a successful job-printing business, a literary newspaper, and a stamp-collecting journal in the next few years. In his late teens Frank Baum reportedly worked as writer and editor for newspapers in New York and Pennsylvania. By 1878 he had worked a year in a family retail business and was then raising (and writing about) purebred chickens on the family estate near Syracuse. He next took up acting and, in 1882, added playwriting with a musical comedy titled *The Maid of Arran*, written under the name he was then using, Louis F. Baum. For the next couple of years he wrote plays and toured with his own theater company.[2]

During his theater years Baum met and married Maud Gage, the youngest daughter of feminist thinker Matilda Joslyn Gage. With his wife's first pregnancy in 1883, the author left the stage, going into another Baum business in Syracuse. A change in the family fortunes, however, led Baum to seek greater opportunities in the West. In the fall of 1888, he left the East Coast permanently, going first to Aberdeen, Dakota Territory. Out on the newest frontier Baum ran a store and then a newspaper before moving to Chicago, where he spent a few weeks working for the *Chicago Evening Post*. He then took a job with a wholesale crockery house, ultimately becoming a traveling salesman. In 1897 he started a magazine for window dressers and began to write and publish children's books, beginning that same year with *Mother Goose in Prose*. Three years later the George M. Hill Company brought out his masterpiece, *The Wonderful Wizard of Oz*. In 1902, with Baum as lyricist and Paul Tietjens as composer, the *Wizard* became a Chicago and then New York hit musical. Baum's career as an author was at last assured. From 1900 until his death, he wrote thirteen more Oz tales and more than fifty other books, using at least seven pseudonyms. In a final move he settled on the West Coast in 1910, taking up residence in Hollywood, California, where he transferred his interest from the theater to moving pictures until his death on 6 May 1919.[3]

It was back in the summer of 1888 that Baum made his first move toward the West and his future. Although his production of the *Maid of Arran* six years earlier had been a critical success, and his acting and singing had been acclaimed, the play and those that followed were financial failures. With a family to support, Baum left the theater circuit at the end of 1883 to work with Baum's Castorine Company of Syracuse, New York, a family concern that manufactured axle oil, paste, and grease.[4] By the end of July 1888, however, both the business and Baum's interest in it had faded, and he could find nothing to warrant his "wasting any more years of my life in trying to boom it." Further, he wrote his brother-in-law, the competition in the crowded East "keeps a man down" because "for one house needed, twenty firms are in business." He concluded bleakly, "In this struggling mass of humanity a man like myself is lost." Baum confessed that a June 1888 trip to Dakota Territory, where his wife's brother and sisters were doing well in the Great Dakota Boom, had given him "western fever." In Dakota, Baum decided, "opportunities are constantly arising where an intelligent man may profit," and he determined to go west.[5]

Established in 1861, Dakota Territory had not begun to prosper until the railroads arrived in the 1870s. The discovery of gold on the territory's western edge in 1874 fueled public interest, but good weather and excellent wheat crops provided the incentive that brought immigrants to the eastern tier of counties in the late 1870s and early 1880s. With the railroads to bring in settlers and take agricultural products to market, Dakota was booming by the time Baum became interested. Brown County, in the northeastern corner of what would become South Dakota, had some 12,000 settlers by 1885 and almost 17,000 five years later. In the center of the county lay Aberdeen, platted in 1881 and located where three railroad lines crossed. Its three to four thousand inhabitants promoted the "Hub City" as a burgeoning distribution center, the next "metropolis" west of Chicago and Minneapolis. A large proportion of these town-builders were business and professional people, including an incredible seventy-four lawyers (suggesting that competition in the West could also be a bit overwhelming).[6]

The atmosphere in Aberdeen in 1888 was one of boosterism and excitement. Lawyers, real estate brokers, bankers, doctors, and business owners of many types had relocated from the East, Midwest, and South. A colony of forty or more had migrated from Baum's home area of Syracuse and Fayetteville, New York. Some came to make quick money during the boom, but others settled permanently, taking up claims, gambling that Aberdeen would grow and prosper. Speculation in land, building construction, and attempts to gain political jobs and community stability through procurement of appointments and territorial institutions kept the lawyers, bankers, and real estate men busy. Railroads, elevators, lumberyards, flour mills, and a cigar factory provided work for engineers, clerks, teamsters, and other laborers, as did several wholesale grocery, dry goods, and readyprint businesses. In 1888 Aberdeen's future looked bright as the Brown County homesteaders, both old-stock Americans and foreign-born immigrants, continued to produce good wheat crops, and community boosters challenged "the admiration of the bread-eating world" in their promotional literature.[7]

Among the settlers participating in this enterprise were Maud Gage Baum's only brother and her oldest sister from Fayetteville, New York. T. Clarkson Gage had been one of the original settlers of Aberdeen and now, with two other New Yorkers, ran a successful general store, with a branch business about fifty miles north in Ellendale. He and others had also established the Aberdeen Building and Loan Association, which financed the construction of more than two hundred homes in Aberdeen between 1881 and 1888. Maud Baum's sister, Helen Leslie Gage, and Helen's husband, Charles Gage, invested in property throughout the area and owned store buildings on Aberdeen's Main Street. About seventy miles north on the Milwaukee Road in what would become North Dakota, Maud's other sister, Julia Gage Carpenter, had homesteaded near Edgeley, where her husband, Frank, also worked as bookkeeper for a major agribusiness concern.[8] When he visited his wife's relatives in June 1888, Baum had found Aberdeen's potential as a railroad hub to be impressive. "I feel," he wrote to Clarkson Gage, "as though Aberdeen is destined one day to be a good city, and it *may be* a metropolis. It seems as though it [is] not too late to throw my fortunes in with the town, which appears to me to be only in its infancy."[9]

Baum came into this new country with the intent of starting a "Bazaar" to sell fancy goods, camera supplies, books, toys, and sporting equipment. In his judgment, the town-builders of Aberdeen looked prosperous enough to support a store modeled on the Fair (a Chicago department store) but "on a much smaller scale" and geared to local tastes. Bringing with him a small printing press, he planned to promote the store "by genuine Yankee enterprise in advertising" and by starting camera and sporting clubs "to render such goods popular." Baum also proposed to "wholesale holiday & fancy goods to dealers in the small towns about Aberdeen," and he had genuine hopes that the town could eventually support some of his other interests and make his fortune. "I could," Baum wrote Clarkson Gage, "work up the Stock Co. to build an Opera House, and take the management of it. And I could be on the lookout for opportunities to invest."[10]

Renting a frame building on Main Street from his sister-in-law Helen Gage, Baum opened Baum's Bazaar on 1 October 1888. The next day the local newspaper declared that "Mr. L. F. Baum" had demonstrated "in a very short time that he possesses to an enviable degree the push and enterprise necessary to the western business man." Complimenting the storekeeper on his "artistic" and "elegant" displays, the paper reported that nearly one thousand people attended the opening, at which each woman received a box of "Gunther's celebrated Chicago Candies."[11] In keeping with the plans he made before leaving New York, Baum advertised aggressively in the local press, displaying the wit and humor that would cause generations of children to love him. In mid-October, for example, he announced that he had just received a new "Poetry Grinder" which, when cranked, ground out verse in praise of his inventory. The final stanza concluded:

> You're sure to find just what you mind,
>   The bric-a-brac so rare.
> The baskets light, the jewels bright,
>   The flowers so fresh and fair,
> And then the toys for girls and boys
>   Are surely. . . . .

(Here the machine got stuck, and on taking it apart it was found so full of enthusiasm that we were obliged to send it to one of the old-fashioned up-town stores to enable it to ooz out.)[12]

To stimulate interest in his stock of sporting equipment, Baum joined with other young Aberdeen businessmen in organizing a baseball club in the spring of 1889. The proprietor of Baum's Bazaar emerged as secretary of the Hub City Nine, and each edition of the daily newspaper carried his advertisements for Spalding Sporting Goods. Baum also chaired the executive committee of the newly formed South Dakota Baseball League, and correspondence and travel associated with these positions occupied him throughout the summer. After his team secured the territorial championship, the businessman turned his attention back to Baum's Bazaar in October, announcing his readiness to deliver goods anywhere in Brown County and boasting that he was already shipping Gunther's candies via railroad to all surrounding towns.[13] On 2 November he "issued his annual fall catalogue and holiday guide of the many attractions" at the Bazaar. The catalogue's six hundred items led a newspaper to remark, "Baum is nothing if not metropolitan."[14] Two weeks later the businessman opened "a branch bazaar at Webster," a small town about fifty miles east of Aberdeen.[15] Advertising the branch as "Santa Claus' Headquarters," Baum claimed businesses in "Webster, Aberdeen, Grand Forks."[16]

Despite the grandiose statements, the entire enterprise soon proved insolvent. Baum had left New York state with little ready money, and his Aberdeen business was undercapitalized from the beginning. Borrowing from friends in the East and from a local bank, he had gambled that the business climate generated by the Dakota boom would repay his investment. Unfortunately, stiff competition and uncontrollable circumstances dictated otherwise. Shortly after the 1888 opening of Baum's Bazaar, its stock of holiday goods went down with the *Susquehanna* in Lake Huron, forcing Baum to reorder hastily before Christmas.[17] Competing businesses took full advantage of the delay, bragging that "the sinking of a barge" had not affected their stock.[18] Baum seemed to recover from this mishap by spring 1889, when trade appears to have been brisk, but his inattention to business during the baseball season may have caused him to overlook other impending trouble. By August 1889 hard times had hit the Great Plains. A year earlier, wheat farmers had harvested a bumper crop that found good grain markets throughout the world, but in 1889 the crops failed, and international markets fell. By November, farmers and townspeople had little to spend on sporting equipment, fancy crockery, and elaborate holiday goods. Baum's willingness to sell on credit and his unwillingness to keep adequate books or to collect rigorously from customers compounded his difficulties.[19]

On 1 January 1890 the Northwestern National Bank of Aberdeen, which held a chattel mortgage of $550 against Baum's stock at Aberdeen and Webster, closed the business down. Baum told the newspapers, "The matter is simply a temporary embarrassment and I hope to effect a settlement in a few days."[20] On 18 January, Helen Leslie Gage bought "the stock and good will" of the business for $772 at a foreclosure sale and reopened within the month as the H. L. Gage Bazaar.[21] Years later, she remarked that Baum had "let his taste run riot in his choice of the eastern markets" and had set up a store "too impractical" for the time and place.[22] Scaling down the inventory and gearing the enterprise to the hard times, she managed to run the business with moderate success for the next twelve years.[23] Her brother-in-law, meanwhile, searched for alternative employment.

His journalistic background led the thirty-three-year-old Baum to the newspaper profession. Like any frontier community of the period, Aberdeen boasted many newspapers — two dailies, three regular weeklies, and at least four special-interest weeklies. The area also supported two readyprint and printer's supply businesses. Consequently, Aberdeen was home to a large number of journalists, printers, and typesetters, and by 1889 the Aberdeen Typographical Union's Local 224 had also been organized there. In this era, political parties and pressure groups deemed it necessary to the vitality of party or movement to have their own newspapers to plead the cause and ensure their influence. Journalistic endeavors based more or less on business principles also found it necessary to endorse candidates and garner patronage, since some form of public favor — such as the city printing — was important to economic survival. The competition this situation created made it difficult for newspaper publishers to flourish financially and created a wide-open, unrestrained style of journalism.[24]

In his search for alternatives, Baum applied to the *Aberdeen Evening Republican*, where crotchety, Virginia-born C. Boyd Barrett published both a daily and weekly edition that endorsed the Democratic Party and, in 1889 and early 1890, had the benefit of doing the city printing. Undoubtedly, Baum also applied to the Daily News Company, a group of Republican business and newspaper men who published the *Aberdeen Daily News* and a weekly *News* edition, which functioned as the official county newspaper. Job printing of pamphlets, programs, business cards, and other items provided a large source of income for Barrett, for the Daily News Company, and for the other weekly, the *Dakota Pioneer*. Special-interest newspapers included the *Dakota Ruralist* (the state Farmers' Alliance paper) and the *Aberdeen Appeal* (the official organ of the state Women's Christian Temperance Union). Both the Catholics and the Presbyterians published state newspapers from Aberdeen, as well. Ultimately,

Baum bought or leased the weekly *Dakota Pioneer*, which fellow Syracuse transplant John H. Drake had established in 1881 as one of the first newspapers in town.[25] Renaming it the *Aberdeen Saturday Pioneer*, Baum moved into the brick Excelsior Block and embarked on a venture which, although it would fail within fifteen months, would leave behind a remarkable literary legacy.

From the first issue on 25 January 1890, the *Aberdeen Saturday Pioneer* set itself apart from the other newspapers in town. Although Baum used boiler plate, or readyprint copy, for more than half of each eight-page issue, he also endorsed the Republican Party, published locally produced reports on the Farmers' Alliance, carried syndicated columnists Bill Nye and Thomas Nast, and editorialized with great intensity. More important, he commented urbanely on thoughts and ideas of the day and wrote humorous columns that displayed the creative talent of the man who would ultimately conceptualize America's most enduring fairyland.[26] His greatest achievement during this period was the forty-eight "Our Landlady" columns that appeared weekly (with a few exceptions) from 25 January 1890 to 8 February 1891. In these, Baum employed satire, fantasy, broad comedy, and verse to entertain and criticize his fellow Aberdonians. He commented outrageously on the absurdities of human nature and, like other American authors, used local settings and characters to focus on the larger human condition as it played itself out in one American community.

The scene for the columns was a boardinghouse, representative of the rows of such accommodations that led off from Aberdeen's "three blocks of business," said one of Baum's contemporaries, and "sheltered the town's disproportionate population of transients and unattached, at four and five dollars a week."[27] Another early resident recalled that "the hotels, or boarding houses, of those early days were the gathering places of the young people, for various harmless amusements."[28] In charge of Baum's fictional establishment was Sairy Ann Bilkins, familiarly known as "Our Landlady." Baum's love of puns and characterizing names can be seen in her name, since "bilking" the boarders would be expected of a landlady of Mrs. Bilkins's ilk.[29] She and her three steady boarders gathered weekly, usually around the supper table, where the conversation was dominated by the malapropian and semiliterate landlady. A widow and busybody with a social conscience, Mrs. Bilkins shared her weekly observations in a rustic Yankee dialect that bespoke her lack of education and proper upbringing. Her boarders, all male, were much better educated, or so their dialectless speech and proper grammar suggested. They included the cigar-smoking colonel, for whom Mrs. Bilkins harbored a poorly hidden passion; Tom, the store clerk whose rent was always in arrears; and the kindhearted doctor, who was a soft touch for a sob story.

In creating the series, Baum followed, in part, a formula set down by Oliver Wendell Holmes in a feature he began for the *Atlantic Monthly* in 1857. The first twelve of his monthly columns became famous when published in 1858 as *The Autocrat of the Breakfast-Table*, which has been mentioned elsewhere as a possible model for Baum's column.³⁰ Holmes's work was set in a Boston boardinghouse, but the main speaker in that establishment was a learned, witty, and class-conscious New England gentleman who shared his observations with the more doltish residents. Baum inverted the formula, allowing the almost invisible landlady of the Holmes columns to come out of the background and become the spokesperson. "Our landlady," Holmes had written, "is a decent body, poor, and a widow, of course; *celè va sans dire*. She told me her story once; it was as if a grain of corn that had been ground and bolted had tried to individualize itself by a special narrative."³¹ Much of this description fits Mrs. Bilkins, as one would expect, since Holmes was pointedly suggesting that such boardinghouse keepers were ubiquitous and undifferentiated members of society — whether in Aberdeen, South Dakota, or Boston, Massachusetts.

Another and perhaps more immediate model for Baum was a column that had appeared for a brief time in 1884 in his hometown newspaper, the *Syracuse Standard*. The first installment was headlined "Table Talk about Electric Lights. What 'Our Landlady' Thinks about the New Fangled Notion" (1 March 1884), and the last was "The Landlady and Society. She Gets Interested in the Published Records of Fashionable Events" (30 August 1884). Like Baum's 1890 Aberdeen landlady, this New York state boardinghouse keeper held forth in front of her lodgers on the doings of the city council, local politicians and businessmen, and social activities. Indeed, there are enough surface similarities between the two sets of columns to make one speculate that Baum himself may have provided the *Syracuse Standard* with its landlady series. If they were indeed products of the same pen, however, the first was but a pale precursor of the later series.³²

In giving voice to a landlady, both the unknown Syracuse writer and Baum were following earlier literary models. A homespun female character who commented sagely yet only partially literately and in regional dialect on the things going on around her was a device that had appeared in the newspapers since Frances M. Whitcher introduced the "The Widow Spriggins" in a Rome, New York, paper and "The Widow Bedott's Table-Talk" in the *Saturday Gazette and Lady's Literary Museum* in 1846. A year later, Benjamin Shillaber created his Mrs. Partington for the *Boston Post*.33 Perhaps Whitcher's Widow Bedott provides the closest model for Mrs. Bilkins, since both characters are widows and unashamed man-chasers,34 but Shillaber's briefer vignettes of Mrs. Partington, also a widow, seem closer to the type of humor Baum employed. Like Shillaber's "Oracular Pearls" from Mrs. Partington, the "Our Landlady" columns quickly sketch a small, frequently hilarious domestic scene in which the atmosphere is part of the fun, and the humor sometimes hinges on a malapropism or pun of which the speaker herself is innocent. Mrs. Bilkins differs, however, in that she is not just a commentator but often part of the larger community action, as her efforts in soliciting for the missions (15 February 1890) or in running for mayor (8 March 1890) illustrate.

During Baum's theater years he may have encountered such female rustics through dramatic adaptations. For example, David R. Locke (writing under the pen name Petroleum V. Nasby) had adapted Whitcher's collected work, *The Widow Bedott Papers* (1856), for the stage in 1879. The four-act comedy, *Widow Bedott, or a Hunt for a Husband*, featured actor Neil Burgess as the widow. A year later Burgess brought out his own version, *The Widow and Elder: A Farcical Comedy in Three Acts*, which played in New York state theaters, as did his *Vim*, a version of Marietta Holley's Samantha Allen books which he produced in 1883, with revivals as late as 1888.35 Given Baum's interest in the theater, he would certainly have been aware of Burgess's highly successful works, and his "Our Landlady" columns display a propensity for the slapstick and broad comedy aspects of farce. Baum rarely forgets to entertain his audience, and such antics as Mrs. Bilkins's bombastic embrace of the colonel (29 March 1890) and the disastrous milking of the cow Klokettle (19 July 1890) suggest the comic theater's methods of getting a laugh.

Baum's Sairy Ann Bilkins is something different from any of the New England models, however. Preeminently, she is a western landlady who keeps a roominghouse on the frontier, where social conventions are less constraining and polite society has some rough edges. Her boarders, too, though more refined, are representative of the local scene and responsive to it. A summer of drought and stagnating business, for example, has Mrs. Bilkins attempting to stir up some enthusiasm among her lodgers on 2 August 1890. "Rustlers," she remarks, "don't know what dull times is, it's only such perfeshional men as you, doc, or such loan agents as the colonel, (as hain't had nothin' to loan in six months) or sich worthless clerks as Tom, who spends his time waitin' fer the customers as don't come, that finds times dull. The farmer what's harvestin' has to rustle after he cuts one stalk o' wheat to reach another 'afore he loses sight of it." In their closeness to the frontier and its realities, Baum's characters are firmly rooted in the western milieu of the early 1890s, where loan agents like the colonel were taking bad risks on drought-stricken homesteads, for example, and store clerks like Tom (and Baum before him) could not afford to pay their rent.

In spite of hard times, the Dakota frontier at the dawn of statehood was an exciting time and place — if you were willing to "rustle." Baum and his fellow Aberdonians were conscious of the fact that they were creating a brand-new state and its institutions, setting down policies and values for several generations to come. In the literary persona of Mrs. Bilkins, Baum fashioned both an eager participant in the adventure and a commentator on the activities of others. During South Dakota's first year of statehood, Mrs. Bilkins would investigate the liquor laws, participate in municipal and county political campaigns, and attend various social functions, to name just a few in her wide range of civic activities. She likewise would express herself emphatically on everything from prohibition, woman suffrage, the quality of local leadership, and the failings of farmers, railroads, and local and state politicians to an overpaid school superintendent, rival newspaper editors, the 1890 Indian scare, and the location of South Dakota's capital. By the end of the year she would be as well known in the community of Aberdeen as Baum himself.

With South Dakota's entry into the Union on 2 November 1889, a number of political processes were automatically set in motion. Two of these were frequent topics at Mrs. Bilkins's table — the prohibition law and the suffrage referendum. The constitution of the new state, adopted in October 1889, contained a prohibition clause, and one of the first duties of the new legislature in the session of 1890 was to enact enforcement laws. The buying and selling of liquor became illegal in the state on 1 May of that year. Baum's editorials were staunchly in support of the social experiment — precisely, it turned out, because it *was* an experiment and one that he expected to fail because it was too likely to hurt the local economy of frontier towns such as Aberdeen. Hence, he called for rigid enforcement so that supporters could be convinced once and for all that it was detrimental to the business climate of the new state.[36]

In "Our Landlady," Baum displayed a slightly different attitude, poking fun at the sillier ramifications of the law, such as druggists' inability to sell vanilla and other extracts or grocers' to sell brandied peaches (22 March 1890). Quite obviously, too, Mrs. Bilkins and her boarders were not teetotalers, and their antics frequently revolved around the various loopholes in the law or other dodges that allowed them to imbibe despite the legal restrictions. In this context, Baum made one of his finer comments on the inconsistencies of politicians. His 19 April 1890 column related that the boarders celebrated the election of the Republican ticket for city government by coming home falling-down drunk, a condition apparently common to a good many of the party's loyal Aberdeen supporters on election night in spite of the party's strong prohibition stance. Each boarder apologized to Mrs. Bilkins for his behavior and stressed his usual restraint. " 'Very true,' replied our landlady, 'an' I don't bare no grudge, for it's the fust time I ever knew one o' you to touch the firewater, but it strikes me that it were a queer way to celebrate the 'lection of a law and order administration.' "

Baum's satirical humor is likewise apparent in his treatment of the woman suffrage issue. The new constitution required the first legislature to submit to the male voters at the next general election (4 November 1890) the question of whether or not women should be allowed to vote. Signaling the trouble the cause would encounter that year, the legislature first held a vote to determine whether or not it should actually do as the constitution directed. Rightness prevailed, and the legislature submitted a bill for a general vote.[37] Editor Baum and Mrs. Bilkins were unqualified supporters, and throughout the year the columns alluded to various suffrage personalities and happenings.

Both nationally and locally, 1890 proved an extremely interesting year in the history of woman suffrage. At the national level the American Woman Suffrage Association and the National Woman Suffrage Association merged to become the National-American Woman Suffrage Association. This merger met a less than cordial reception in some circles. Baum's mother-in-law, Matilda Joslyn Gage, broke completely with the new organization over philosophy and methodology. Claiming that organized religion was the largest impediment to women's rights, she formed the Woman's National Liberal Union, a radical antichurch organization. Shrugging off this desertion, the National-American Woman Suffrage Association chose the South Dakota suffrage law as its most important and attainable goal of 1890. Early in the year it dispatched Susan B. Anthony to take over the campaign, thereby incurring the ire of many local suffragists but especially of Marietta Bones, who had been vice-president for South Dakota in the old National organization. During the merger, Anthony had rudely dismissed Bones from that post; in response, Bones publicly accused Anthony of embezzling funds earmarked for the state campaign.[38] The South Dakota struggle was off to a rough start.

Baum, who became secretary of the Aberdeen suffrage organization in April 1890, was highly critical of the adverse press coverage the Anthony and Bones feud attracted. Because Matilda Joslyn Gage lived with him and Maud much of the time, and both Anthony and Bones visted his home, Baum knew the inside details of the quarrel and understood the philosophical disagreements involved. Although he tended to endorse his mother-in-law's point of view, he did not pick sides in the Anthony and Bones struggle. Instead, he chided both women for their want of sympathy and failure to compromise.39 Editorially, he focused on the philosophical arguments for suffrage, supporting it at every opportunity. On 26 April 1890, for example, he devoted three full columns to the topic, concluding, "If our politics are to be masculine forever I despair of the republic." His consistent and vigorous championship of women's rights led the rival Democratic newspaper and others to criticize the *Pioneer* as a "ring organ" in pursuit of public patronage from the suffragists.40 Baum's belief in women's rights and abilities appeared to be genuine, and he anticipated a time when women in government would dictate "a pure and just political policy that will be impossible to refute and difficult to improve upon."41

While Baum was filling his editorial columns with considered arguments in support of suffrage, his landlady took a more direct approach. Not a great thinker, she simply appropriated the privileges of a fully equal woman: she ran for mayor, attended the Republican convention as a proxy delegate, and acted the part of a responsible, though bombastic, citizen. She allowed that "it's the conceit o' men as is the biggest stumblin' block ter universal sufferin' o' women" (15 March 1890), but she did not let that stand in her way. In these instances, Mrs. Bilkins was Baum's quintessential "western woman," without "nonsense or false pride," who went ahead and did what had to be done. In Baum's view, which is apparent in both the *Aberdeen Saturday Pioneer* and his Oz novels, the women of the West did not wait for men to do things for them.42 That did not mean, however, that they were not naive or exceedingly gullible when political deals were afoot. Baum clearly thought the women were making bad political judgments in the summer and fall of 1890 when they appeared to join forces with the newly formed Independent Party, and he ridiculed their mixed motives and naiveté (18 October 1890).

The advent of this third party provided yet another ingredient in the highly charged political atmosphere of 1890. The South Dakota Farmers' Alliance, an agricultural pressure group, and the Dakota Knights of Labor, a workers' organization, joined forces that summer in an attempt to relieve the financial burdens of farmers who were at the mercy not only of nature but of national and international market conditions. Railroad and elevator companies, in turn, attempted to manipulate the situation to their advantage, and the new party looked to government for such solutions as the subtreasury bill, railroad regulation, and antimonopoly legislation.[43] Baum's understanding of the farmers' debt problem can be seen in his columns of 5 April and 3 May 1890, for example. In the latter a fictional farmer, asked whether or not he has dependents, answers: "Well, there's them Hail Insurance agints, an' the Machine men, an' the Elevaitors, an' the Loan agints, an' the Prohibition speakers an' singers an' the preachers, an' lots more. What'll they do if I don't git a crop this spring?" Clearly, however, Baum considered farmers responsible for some of their own problems, and he accused them of being too acquisitive, buying unnecessary machinery on credit in the hope that next year's crops would pay off the debt.[44] His ambivalent attitude thus lends a cutting edge to his humorous discussions of the "Dakota farmer."

The political marriage between the Farmers' Alliance and the Knights of Labor — first called the Independent Party — would become a national phenomenon called the People's or Populist Party in the next two years, and some critics have suggested that Baum allegorically critiqued the new party and national leaders in *The Wonderful Wizard of Oz* ten years later.[45] In this respect, it is important to note that Aberdeen was central to South Dakota's and the nation's burgeoning third-party movement. Both the farmers' and the workers' groups maintained their state headquarters there in 1890, and the official papers of their organizations carried Aberdeen datelines. Aberdonian James H. Kyle, who would become one of the first Populists elected to the United States Senate, stood for state senator from Brown County on the Independent ticket that fall and won. During the legislative session of 1891, the South Dakota lawmakers elected Kyle to the national body. Likewise, the 1890 Independent candidate for governor, Henry L. Loucks from nearby Deuel County, would become president of the National Farmers' Alliance and Industrial Union (the Southern Alliance) in 1892.[46] Baum's opinion of Loucks's Populist philosophy is apparent in his columns of 26 July and 11 October 1890.

Baum's 1890 editorials portray the Populists as misguided fellow Republicans who, lacking the sophistication and know-how to solve the country's problems, suggested solutions that would ultimately prove worse than the problems themselves. The editor insisted that their right to form a third party must be respected, but he also predicted that before long the farmers would return to the G O P, which they had traditionally supported in Dakota — and within ten years, of course, most did.[47] In "Our Landlady," Baum initially discussed the doings of the new party through the metaphorical language of secret elopements and romantic entanglements, as in the 12 July 1890 column; this treatment seemed to suggest that the party could be snickered at and ignored. By 18 October the columnist was taking the defectors and their questionable partnership with the suffragists much more seriously. The Independents, Baum now implied, had duped the suffragists into supporting a shaky third-party movement in a quid pro quo that had no substance. The column mirrored the actual situation: many suffragists had thrown their support to the party, but the Independents had failed to give their unqualified support to suffrage.[48] In the end the Independents won the Brown County election and (through cooperation with Democrats) the United States Senate, but suffrage lost resoundingly — and suffrage was the cause for which Baum and Mrs. Bilkins cared most deeply (note particularly the column of 1 November 1890).

In addition to the author's support for women's rights and his skepticism about the Populist Party, his columns reveal some other concepts that would later figure in his novels. One interesting example is his lack of sympathy for organized religion, an attitude he shared with his mother-in-law. Baum's wife participated regularly in Episcopalian church and social functions, and Baum himself was active in the theatrical fund-raising events of more than one denomination, but his editorials and other features in the *Pioneer* — most notably a semi-regular column titled "The Editor's Musings" — made clear that he was not "an earnest Christian."[49] Instead, like Matilda Joslyn Gage, Baum was skeptical of the claims of organized churches, professing instead a respect for Theosophy, a philosophy that joined "the dissatisfied of the world, the dissenters from all creeds" who were "searchers after Truth." The sect embodied "an eager longing to penetrate the secrets of Nature — an aspiration for knowledge we have been taught is forbidden."[50] The Theosophists' attention to occultism and the mysticism of eastern religions appealed to Baum, and he discussed such topics frequently in his newspaper. Critic John Algeo has found that Baum actually joined the Theosophical Society in 1892 and has suggested that *The Wonderful Wizard of Oz* can also be read as a Theosophical allegory.[51]

In "Our Landlady," Baum's unorthodox attitude toward traditional religions is lightheartedly reflected in his willingness to tease and criticize specific clergymen, especially over their stance on the prohibition laws. A more total lack of respect for clergy is straightforwardly stated in the 7 June 1890 column, where the landlady manages to sum up her position on organized religion in one overlong sentence: "A pusson as never goes to church can't realize the fun there is in stayin' away, an' somebody's got to support these ministers what is gittin' thicker an' thicker every day, or else they'll be obleeged to work fer a livin', an' religion will be at a standstill." Although this column entertains rather than preaches, it reflects Baum's belief that churchgoing was a matter of "policy and fashion" rather than "intelligence and nobility."[52] Yet though many of Baum's columns are devoted to satirical comments on national, state, and local politics and cultural thought, some are meant merely to entertain, displaying slapstick elements, outrageous puns, and other wordplays.

Two additional types of columns should be mentioned as well. First, the 24 May 1890 column is a fine example of Baum's sure comic touch in exploring the general frailties of human nature and how they work themselves out in the American system. The setting is still Dakota, but here Baum focuses on the business practices and human attitudes apparent in a small town that could clearly be anywhere in the rural United States. After a week of drenching rains had temporarily relieved the drought, Mrs. Bilkins naturally expected good spirits to reign among farmers but encountered the opposite attitude. When she asked why, a complainer enlightened her: "Ye see, we've been growlin' about the dry so long that this here rain were a kind of shock to us, an' did'nt leave us nothin' to growl about. An' if we was fools enough to yell hurray! — the ground is wet! — the crops is growin'! — the country's saved! — an' all that rubbish, the people as we've been owin' so long would be arter us wi' sharp sticks to pay up. The only salvation fer a man as is in debt is to yell 'hard times' no matter what happens."

Second, in his last columns Baum turned to the future and began to guess what might happen to Aberdeen and America in the years to come. These sketches from 27 December 1890 to 8 February 1891, more fantasy and science fiction than satire, offer us an unparalleled opportunity to examine various influences on and patterns in Baum's fiction writing. The author created his most delightful fantasy for the 3 January 1891 issue, the story of Mrs. Bilkins's visit to the "Great Downditch Farm." The immediate inspiration for this column came from two articles that appeared in the rival *Aberdeen Daily News* on 16 and 30 December 1890. In the first, "The Wonderful Updyke Farm," the writer created a promotional daydream in which the James River Valley of the Dakotas had become a fertile and booming paradise through irrigation. The Updyke farm, a prototype of this future, was a modern marvel where lights and heat were run by electricity supplied through a water wheel attached to an artesian well. This futuristic fantasy world, elaborately detailed, probably owed its inspiration to Edward Bellamy's popular utopian fantasy *Looking Backward* (1888), as did one of Baum's later columns (31 January 1891), but the use of artesian wells for both irrigation and electricity also appears to have been something South

Dakota promoters were hoping to demonstrate in a scale-model exhibit for the 1892 (postponed to 1893) World's Columbian Exposition.[53]

In Baum's hands, however, the material became something else — something that bears his distinctive trademarks and displays his ability to turn American scenery, concepts, desires, and themes into humorous American fairy tales. Edward Wagenknecht in *Utopia Americana* (1929) was the first to point out that Baum's fairyland of Oz was uniquely American and to note that Baum's "fancy plays about and transforms not things that he has seen but things he has read about."[54] This transformation is exactly what is taking place in the 3 January 1891 column, where farmer Updyke becomes Downditch, who once employed the "inferior" Updyke. Whereas Updyke's use of electricity had practical agricultural applications (farmers could plant, cultivate, and harvest electrically), Downditch's foreshadows future amusements (such as movie theaters) before moving on to aspects that suggest Baum's own peculiar fantasy world of the Oz novels. Downditch, who shrugs his shoulders and smiles electrically, reminds the reader of such later creations as Tik-Tok of Oz or the Wizard himself.

Fictional characters such as Aesop Downditch, which Baum sometimes created to interact with Mrs. Bilkins and her three boarders, were rare. Much more frequently the columnist employed local people as dramatic actors in his satirical, slapstick, and fantasy columns. Baum might disguise an individual slightly, using puns such as "grin and barrett" to refer to his archrival C. Boyd Barrett, or "the moody man" to denote Aberdeen mayor Robert Moody. Most often, however, the mayor, an alderman, or some other local figure appeared without disguise. Once introduced, the individual could be central to the point or merely supply background texture — as does suffragist "Mary Etter Bones," who metamorphosed into "Vice-President o' South Dakota" for the 8 March 1890 column.

By tying the columns firmly to the landscape and commercial interests of South Dakota and using actual names when speaking of druggists, lawyers, bankers, or hotels and businesses, Baum kept the local community involved and interested. In the final line of the Downditch column, for instance, Mrs. Bilkins said, "This 'ere establishment is a goin' to have a artesian well with electricity attachments, if it takes every dollar I've got in Hagerty's to sink it." Baum could have concluded this pleasant fantasy with a general reference to funds "in the bank," but he had a much more subtle irony in mind. Since October 1890, Frank J. Hagerty's bank had been closed because of uncollectible loans to bankrupt farmers. Nobody in Aberdeen could withdraw anything from this establishment, and all Baum's readers were aware of that fact. The columnist may have been trying for a painful laugh from those who shared Mrs. Bilkins's plight, or, possibly, he was attempting to show his faith in the bank's eventual reopening. If so, his confidence was misplaced, for within two weeks the press was forced to announce that the bank had definitely failed and would not reopen.55

There is still another way of looking at the ending of the 3 January 1891 column: it could be considered a body blow to a man who was already down. In other words, Hagerty could have taken it personally, as could any of the many people Baum included in his columns. Generally speaking, most Aberdonians appeared to take his ribbing with good humor. Baum's niece, who lived in Aberdeen all her life, recalled being told that "when the *Pioneer* was delivered to its subscribers, there was a grand rush to read it to see whom Mrs. Bilkins had good naturedly ridiculed. . . . I never heard it said that these people were offended."56 Still, Baum's satire could be cutting and sometimes too close to home for the targets to remain unaffected. The author himself knew that he often scored a hit. As the doctor told Mrs. Bilkins on 16 August 1890, "You interest yourself too much in other people's business . . . to be very popular. A good many of your criticisms have leaked out, someway, and if you ever hope to change your name, you will have to be more careful."

In the unrestrained journalistic practices of the day, negative responses could be nasty and extremely personal. C. Boyd Barrett, who took exception to Baum's criticism, retaliated with a vicious attack in his own newspaper, calling Baum a "creature" with a "slimy tongue" who did not pay his debts and who, as secretary of the town's baseball club, had embezzled money from the team.57 When Baum suggested in two columns (3 and 17 May 1890) and a pointed editorial (14 February 1891) that the school superintendent was overpaid, students began to write letters to rival editors, calling the *Pioneer* publisher a "public nuisance" and "a traitor to the best interest of the city and its children."58 Baum was forced to defend his position in various editorials.59

Baum's frequent criticism of the fire department brought letters to the rival *Aberdeen Daily News* in the winter of 1890–91. Signed "Truthful Zeke," these letters playfully suggested that Mrs. Bilkins be assigned to the fire department to right the wrongs of the place.60 Editor Baum took umbrage at the slur on his landlady, retorting: "We would simply suggest that T. Zeke skip the articles by 'Our Landlady,' which occupy only a small space in a paper chock full of newsiness, and if he then thinks two cents a copy too high a price for the *Pioneer* he can invest his money in a dime novel and so get some real good out of life. For we shan't desert Mrs. Bilkins without some more substantial kick from our subscribers."[61] Mrs. Bilkins herself responded to criticism in a similar fashion on 16 August 1890: "If folks don't like my style they needn't listen to me."

With these and other uncomfortable exchanges, the defeat of the Republicans in November, the trouncing of the woman suffrage amendment, and the worsening business climate (Hagerty's bank failure was a good indication of the economic hard times), Baum seemed to lose heart at the end of 1890. Early in 1891 he began to have health problems, and the *Pioneer* often carried a notice that asked readers to excuse its deficiencies because the editor was either ill or out of town.[62] The "Our Landlady" columns ceased to appear after 8 February, and on 4 April the *Aberdeen Daily News* announced that Baum had taken a position elsewhere and would retire from the *Pioneer*. Abandoning drought, privation, and an unprofitable newspaper, Baum moved on to Chicago and, ultimately, a successful writing career.

He left behind him an almost forgotten legacy in the files of the *Aberdeen Saturday Pioneer*. In spite of their humor and importance to Baum's later writing, the "Our Landlady" columns are virtually unknown. There are two reasons for this neglect. First, only one file of the *Aberdeen Saturday Pioneer* is known to exist, and even this copy has one issue missing. Housed at the Alexander Mitchell Library in Aberdeen, South Dakota, the paper has only recently been microfilmed to permit increased usage.[63] Most researchers have relied on a rare booklet titled *L. Frank Baum's "Our Landlady,"* which was compiled and annotated by the South Dakota Writers' Project in 1941. This 46-page publication reprinted thirteen of the forty-eight columns and, in the process, aptly illustrated the second reason why they are little known and used. Making almost no attempt to recreate the Dakota background against which the columns were originally written, the 1941 booklet devoted most of its three-page introduction to a sketch of Baum's later career. Although the project workers originally intended to print all forty-eight columns virtually unedited, money for paper and other supplies and services ran short, and the editors chose "only columns which satirized the town and the times or provided identification of places and people known locally."[64] The resulting publication offered a smattering of annotations to deal with the many local, state, and national names and places that Baum used but made some mistakes in assigning identity.

In one case, however, the Writers' Project was remarkably thorough. One of the compilers contacted Maud Gage Baum, who signed an affidavit attesting that all the "Our Landlady" columns had been written by her late husband.[65] Having documented Baum's authorship, the editors and annotators nevertheless proved lamentably lax in providing a reliable text. Errors in wording crept in, and parts of Baum's original text were lopped off when annotating proved difficult or the compilers did not understand the punch line (as in the 3 January 1891 column). Such editing may actually have improved the comic timing of a sketch or two, but it sacrificed the texture and historical richness of the original.

In this edition, all the extant columns appear in chronological order. The text is complete, and editorial revisions have been limited to the regularization of quotation marks and apostrophes. Spelling errors have been quietly corrected only where they represent obvious typesetting lapses, such as a u for an n or insufficient leading between words. To deal with the historical context, two features have been added. First, each column is preceded by an introductory section that sketches the pertinent 1890–91 news events for that week and provides other historical or literary background as necessary. Second, a glossary of names and places has been appended to supply information about items in the columns that may not be immediately recognizable.

With these aids to guide them, readers will discover that Baum's vignettes build upon one another and that the landlady's character develops over time. They will also come to know and enjoy some of the real people who appear repeatedly in the columns. Baum poked fun often enough, for example, at the Episcopalians and a certain Episcopal missionary that we can almost share the cleric's blushes when he inadvertently votes for woman suffrage in November 1890. Harder for modern audiences to appreciate are the stereotypical attitudes displayed toward women and American Indians. Despite Baum's commitment to women's rights and toleration for diverse political and religious creeds, he was still a man of his times, and his language and humor reflect attitudes prevalent in the 1890s. In portraying Mrs. Bilkins, however, Baum appears to have reinforced some of the stereotypes about women in order to undermine them. Something similar occurs in his 6 December 1890 caricature of an Indian chief, producing an essentially sympathetic, albeit satirical, portrait of an Indian leader.

In the end, Baum's skill as a storyteller ensures that no matter what the subject matter or distance in time and values, readers of the columns will find themselves caught up in the community's high hopes for the new state, personal dreams of success, and the unyielding reality of drought and privation. As such reality ceased to be funny, Baum turned his attention to the future, weaving an idiosyncratic vision of a twentieth century that combines scientific progress and the wizardry of Oz: interactive phonographs, airships, cinemas, and whimsical gadgets to meet every desire. Modern readers will find Baum's final columns strangely prophetic and not at all surprising, coming from the creator of America's own fairyland.

"Our Landlady"

She Remarks Emphatically on Some Timely
and Truthful Topics

25 January 1890

With the failure of the 1889 wheat crop in southern Dakota, parts of the new state were experiencing extreme destitution by January 1890. Prairie fires and subzero temperatures compounded the problem, and not far from Aberdeen, in Mellette, four people froze to death because they could not afford fuel. Storekeepers were refusing all credit, Baum reported on 1 February, adding, "Only by charity can the people be fed." Because of the need to maintain favorable press on the frontier, where each town needed continuing infusions of eastern capital and new settlers, the newspapers were reluctant to expose the situation. Some of them branded as false the reports of suffering that "leaked out." Although claiming that the accounts of privation were "wantonly exaggerated," Baum did not attempt to hide the situation, blaming it on the drought and "the improvidence of farmers during preceding years of plenty."

In Aberdeen, a fashionable epidemic of *la grippe,* or Russian influenza, also troubled inhabitants, and Baum lapsed into poetry on 25 January to illuminate the problem:

> Now when a man doth catch a cold
> Or feel a pain oft felt of old
> He whines aloud, with trembling lip —
> "God help me! I have got la grippe."

No matter what the condition was called, it could become pneumonia, which was not a laughing matter, and deaths had been reported in the region.[1]

Baum's inaugural "Our Landlady" column found the boardinghouse keeper determinedly cheerful in the face of hard times and sickness. She confined most of her comments to the hapless city council, which was, Baum reported, hiring people to dig "through the frost and snow to fix a huge post at each of the four corners of the streets." These posts, he pointed out, would not remain in place once the ground thawed, making the expense of placing them "both injudicious and unnecessary." It was time, the landlady suggested, to economize.

"It beats all," said our landlady, as she threw down the plate of pancakes and wiped the turner on her apron, "it beats all how hard the times really is. There's no end to the sufferin', right here in our own neighborhood — excuse me, colonel, but your a butterin' of that cake the second time! Why, only yesterday a poor woman from the country was beggin' the grocery man to trust her for a pint o' kerosene, and he wouldn't let her have it. It made my heart bleed, that's what it did, and if any o' you boarders had a paid up lately I'd have gin it to her myself."

Here Tom looked rather red, and said hastily, "But Mrs. Bilkins, she might have been an impostor."

"Nonsense," replied the landlady, moving the syrup out of the colonel's reach, "the country people hain't got a cent — nor the city ones neither for that matter! Even the hotels is economizing. Don't it look bad for Al. Ward to eat at the Sherman House and Jim Ringrose go sneakin' down to Ward's for lunch?"

"Mrs. Bilkins!" cried the colonel, "are you trying to starve us? Let me tell you ma'am, that I for one won't be economized on. Fetch on the cakes!" The landlady darted a wicked look at him and retired to the kitchen.

"The times are bad," said the doctor, thoughtfully, as he removed the grounds from his coffee, "any one would think the prevailing epidemic would help my business, but it don't. Nine out of ten who declare they have la grippe are impostors, and the other one suffers tortures rather than pay for a prescription because he thinks the deseas[e] isn't fatal.

"That's false economy."

"Economy!" shr[ie]ked the landlady, reappearing with the hot cakes, "everybody's economizin'! What do you think o' Nat. Wendell's chewin' both ends of his toothpick, and Frank Beard blackin' of his own boots, an' Skip Salisbury refusin' to shake for the cigars, and Cholly Brockway's stayin' at Columbia three weeks rather than pay the fare home to see his girl? There's economy for you!"

The colonel picked his teeth with a ruminating air.

"If," said he, "I had any money, I too would economize. But it's impos[s]ible to economize on nothing."

"Why, gentlemen;" continued the landlady, sitting down across the arms of the baby's high chair, and waving the empty pancake plate with the air of a newly elected speaker to a brand new House, "why see how the uncommon council is economizin'! Ain't they hired a lot o' poor men to plant sign posts in the snow, so as to keep them from starvin' and obligin' the city to bury 'em?

"Ain't they cut down poor Major Barrett's printing bill to $1700, when they might have gin him five thousand? And he such a nice, pleasant gentleman, too! I declare it's too aggravatin'! But economy must begin somewhere, and why not with the uncommon council — hey?"

But the boarders had quietly stolen away, and the landlady having wiped the mouth of the syrup jug with her finger, put it in her mouth (the finger, that is) and retired to the kitchen in a triumphant mood.   PETE[2]

She Re[m]onstrates on the Giddiness of Church Socials

1 February 1890

In the second issue of the *Aberdeen Saturday Pioneer*, Baum began his social reporting with an examination of the church groups that were responsible for Aberdeen's rich social life. Each church, he noted, had a young women's group that organized social events in order to raise funds to help the poor, furnish the altars, and build the churches. "What a man would give grudgeingly [*sic*] if approached by a subscription committee (or would not give at all, perhaps)," Baum observed, "he hands over [to the women] with a grin of delight, for the fair matrons and damsels have contrived means to give him genuine pleasure in return."

On 21 January the Young Ladies Guild of Saint Mark's Episcopal Church launched its 1890 series of socials with a supper party and dance at Samuel H. Jumper's residence, where the men "bought" their dinner partners. The young women, disguised with drapes and veils, were auctioned off to the highest bidders in order to furnish Saint Mark's with a pipe organ. The following week the guild held a progressive euchre party at which the men each bought a string protruding from behind a closed door for fifty cents; the young woman at the other end of the string was his card partner for the evening. The same week, the Presbyterian Gleaners, who were raising money for "pulpit furnishings," announced that they would inaugurate their social season with a "weight social" at which the young men would purchase their supper partners at fifty cents per one hundred pounds. The women, whose names the men would draw from a hat, would be weighed in the presence of their buyers. To help along a good cause, the Gleaners would "surreptitiously hang horseshoes amongst their hoop-skirts, or put rocks in their pockets," Baum hinted. The social docket of the week of 1 February also featured a "bonnet social," a "feet social," and numerous luncheons, coffees, and dances. Since the frontier town contained more men than women, the male "extras" at these events consoled themselves with lemonade and other refreshments.

Going the rounds of this circle of young people was the 1888 vaudeville tune "Down Went McGinty." In verse after verse, an irrepressible Irishman named Dan McGinty underwent a stanza of misadventures before the chorus began with the line "Down went McGinty to the bottom of the wall," or "jail," or "hole," or "sea." The following example offers the best clues to the meaning of the punch line of Baum's 1 February column:

> Down went McGinty to the bottom of the jail,
>
> Where his board would cost him nix and he stay'd exactly six,

They were big long months he stopp'd for no one went his bail,
Dress'd in his best suit of clothes.3
Had the well-dressed Irishman stayed a week with Mrs. Bilkins?

"When I was young," remarked our landlady, picking a gray hair out of the butter and laying it on the edge of the plate to tempt our appetites. "When I was a gal, they didn't have such goin's on at the church sociables."

"That must have been before my time," said the colonel, ignoring the icy regard of a scorned woman's eyes turned full upon him.

"To what do you refer, ma'am?" asked Tom unwarily, meaning to avert the coming storm.

"Why to these goin's on about buyin' gals at auction, as if they was so many slaves at the market! It's outrageous, that's what it is, and oughten ter be allowed in a christian country!"

"But the girls didn't seem to object," suggested the doctor, eating a crust without spreading it.

"Oh, no, the gals didn't object!" acquiesced the landlady, elevating her nasal appendage; "the girls nowadays is too highty-tighty for anything. Why they're actually goin' to be weighed 'afore the men folks, I hear, and bought for so much a pound! Think o' that, gentlemen!"

"Nothing very improper in the thought, I'm sure," said the Colonel, helping himself to a pickled onion to remove the taste of the stewed prunes from his mouth. "It's only a little matter of fun, Mrs. Bilkins, and if the young ladies don't object I don't see why you should."

"I don't! Let 'em ruin their chances of gettin' married if they want to. Who'd marry a girl as was weighed 'afore the whole world? And at a church sociable, too! What can the ministers be thinkin' of?"

"They probably dream of the church debts being paid and are content," quoth Tom, sotto voce.

"These gals," continued the landlady, car[e]lessly wiping her forehead with the doctor's napkin, "are probably all designing women, and are doin' their best to catch onter the fellers. Poor Skip's gone crazy over 'em they say, and Mutz and Peepo can't hardly wait for the next sociable to spend their money. And Harvey Jewett went to try and stop the doin's at Gilmore's and make 'em behave proper, and Harry Marple went to help him do it, and they was the two biggest fools o' the lot and almost fit each other to see which could buy the first string with a gal hitched onto the tother end of it! I declare it's enough to make me want to move to Columbia!"

"Don't do that!" exclaimed the colonel, with a startled look, but further remark was cut short by the entrance of the new boarder.

"I'm sorry to say, Mrs. Bilkins," said the new-comer, suavely, "that important business calls me out of town. I have been here just a week. Please accept this check in payment; any one will cash it for you. Good day ma'am!"

He was gone, and the landlady turned the check over and murmured

"I hain't got my glasses here. Colonel, will you give me the money on this 'ere thing?'"

The Colonel glanced at it, got very red, and left the room without a word. She handed it to Tom, but he merely looked at the signature and walked away with a low whistle. The doctor did not wait, but softly made his exit, and the landlady, looking after them was struck by a sudden thought. She rushed to the window and held the paper close to her eyes. It was a check, right enough, and regularly drawn, but the signature was both mysterious and portentious:

"Dan McGinty."   PETE

. . . .

She Goes to a Ball and Lets a Cat out of the Bag

8 February 1890

> The third Young Ladies Guild social featured a dance at a home in West Hill, Aberdeen's most exclusive residential district. "If any stranger had popped in on the gathering of young folks," Baum reported, he "would have imagined he had intruded into a veritable 'Fairie land.'" The young women had "crashed and cleared" the double drawing rooms, entry, and dining hall for dancing and had conveniently placed a "supply of a popular temperance beverage which was liberally patronized." The guild's "own personal, private and exclusive orchestra," a three-piece band of local talent (violinist, cornetist, and pianist), provided the music. Prominent among the dancers were the town's many bachelors and unmarried women, one of whom, apparently, was Mrs. Bilkins.

✿ "Yes," acknowledged our landlady, fanning her hot and florid face with her apron, "I do feel a little rocky today, colonel, and that's a fact. You see, everybody has to have a little recreation, though it's the first time in seving year as I've tripped the light fantastic myself."

"Been to a party, ma'am?" asked the doctor, picking a china button out of the gravy.

"Well, this were more like a ball," replied the landlady, smiling broadly; "an' a reglar out 'n outer it was, too! The music played reglar tunes, it did, and every onct in a while, when the boys stopped yellin', you could hear it as plain as day, an' — "

Here Tom interrupted the discourse with a cry of agony, and rushing to the window he carefully extracted something from his jaws with many facial contortions.

"What is it, Tom?" asked the doctor, expectantly.

"A pin!" groaned the unfortunate boarder, holding it up in full view; " 'twas in the mashed potato."

"Madam!" cried the Colonel, severely, "you will oblige us by looking a little closer after your wearing apparel. It's my turn next, and I hav'nt the least doubt but I'll strike a corset in the horseradish or something equally as bad. We're not kickers, Mrs. Bilkins, — far from it, — but in the future be a little more particular!"

"Dear me, gentlemen," exclaimed the landlady, aghast; "I'm orful sorry, but I'm that flustrated today that I can't account for nothin' as happens, nohow! Disserpation is so a tryin' to the nerves!"

"True," acquiesced the doctor, mildly, "but you haven't told us who was present at the ball."

"No — an' I must!" returned the landlady, brightening, "for they was a real swell crowd, I can tell you. There was me in my red gownd, an' Miss Smithers' hired lady in a black an' brown balmoral, an' Miss Jenkyns the dressmaker in a green perlice, an' a hired lady from West Hill in a yaller an' blue striped jersey, an' — "

"Never mind the ladies, Mrs. Bilkins," broke in Tom, more to try if his jaw would work than because he was interested.

"An' there was two other ladies there, too," continued the landlady, with much satisfaction, "but I did'nt hear their names, for no one interduced 'em: an' one wored a scarlet plush all embroidered up the side, an' — "

"But who were the gentlemen?"

"Oh, there was Jay Gould, an' — "

"Who?"

"Well, they called him Jay, anyhow. And he was a daisy, too, and swung around Miss Smitherses hired lady till she most fainted. An' then there was Dill-ole-man — "

"Who?"

"That's what they called him. An' a feller named Toothpicks, an' a lot more o' the swell boys. But I guess some on 'em was nervous, for I heerd Jay Gould — or whatever his name is — say to Toothpicks, "Oh lor'! if they ever know as we've been here!" So I guess they must have some wives to home, or some gals as they didn't bring, anyhow. Don't go, colonel, you haven't had your pie yet."

"What kind is it?"

"Mince, Colonel."

"H'm. And the mince meat — did you buy it — "

"Oh, I made it myself this blessed mornin'."

"Very well, Mrs. Bilkins," returned the colonel, as he took his hat and coat from the stand, "I'm not very hungry, anyway, and in view of your being so flustered today I believe I'll forego the pleasure of the pie."

And the doctor and Tom, with resigned looks, followed his example, while the landlady, gazing wistfully after them, remarked:

"There's no great loss without some small gain — it'll do for tomorrow, anyhow."   PETE

· ·

She outdoes Nellie Bly and Makes a Trip around Aberdeen in 72 minutes and 6 seconds

15 February 1890

> Nellie Bly was the pen name of Elizabeth Cochrane, a reporter for the *New York World*, who had started around the globe on 14 November 1889 in an effort to circle it faster than the fictional Phileas Fogg of Jules Verne's *Around the World in Eighty Days*. Aberdonians followed her voyage in the pages of the *Aberdeen Daily News*, which announced on 26 January 1890 that the intrepid young woman had "girdled" the earth in exactly seventy-two days, six hours, and eleven minutes. In his 15 February parody of Nellie Bly's trip, Baum satirized the foibles of his fellow editors, as well as those of local lawyers and businessmen. More pointedly, however, he swiped at the purposes and methods of women's missionary societies. The Aberdeen Methodists and Presbyterians sponsored women's groups that met for weekly teas and solicited money for foreign and domestic missions, but their direct appeal for funds was far less successful than the more entertaining methods of the young women's organizations. In 1890 the Presbyterian missionary society, for example, made $89 for the missions, while the more social women's groups brought in $348 for church furnishings.4 Mrs. Bilkins's solicitation on behalf of the women of "Africanistan" suggested some of the problems of the door-to-door approach.

❧ "Good heavings," cried our landlady, with a two-for-a-nickel look on her face and a sigh that burst her apron strings: "if I ain't done up then there never was a critter as was!"

"You do look tired," agreed the colonel, as the boarders gathered around the tea-table, "been excercising, ma'am?"

"Exercising!" snapped the landlady, indignantly, "well I should say so! Why that 'ere bold female named Bly warn't a patch on the way as I had to flummux around this blessed arternoon! You see our church serciety appinted me a c'mittee fer to get subscriptions to supply the poor heathen women in Africanistan with hairpins, an' tonight I've got to report, an' I had'nt done a single thing towards gettin' a penny o' money together to report with. An' so I says to myself, why if them tarnal fools o' men go to these church sociables an' pay a dollar or two a night fer just amusement, they'll be willin' to give me a few pennies fer the poor heathen wimmin in Africanistan. An' so at nine minutes arter four o'clock I sot out on my errant o' mercy, an' I had ter git back in time to git supper, and you can better believe it was quick work."

"Mrs. Bilkins," interrupted the doctor mournfully, "will you kindly tell me what this stuff is in the tea?"

The landlady looked surprised, and the colonel and Tom, as men will, instantly tasted their tea to see what was wrong.

"It's plaster!" screamed Tom, while the colonel sank back and gasped that he was poisoned.

"Nothing of the kind!" sniffed the landlady, angrily, as she peered into the cream jug, "it's just my clear starch as I mistook for the milk, that's all, an' considerin' the flurry as I were in it ain't to be wondered at!"

"Certainly not, ma'am," quoth the doctor resignedly, "but if you will acco-modate us with a little lacteal fluid instead we shall be greatly obliged."

"And the pickles, ma'am, have a strong odor of kerosene," complained Tom.

"Oh, that's nothin'," protested the landlady, "I must ha' set the dish right under the hangin' lamp, an' the blamed thing will leak ile in spite of all I can do. Try another piece, sir; that one might ha' caught it all."

"But did you get any subscriptions?" asked the colonel, when harmony was finally restored.

"Well, you see I thought as I'd do it thorough," replied the landlady, settling back in her chair and picking her teeth reflectively with the carving fork, "so an' I started in at the Northwestern bank buildin'. The lawyers was busy. I found Johnny Adams a settin' with his feet on a high desk an' recitin' Pat. Henry's speech in a tremblin' voice; and Georgie Jenkins practisin' short-hand with a type-writer, an' Judge Crofoot an' Phil. Skilman a argufyin' as how far the sun were from the moon, an' — "

"Did they give you anything?"

"Nary cent. Johnnie he felt fer a nickel an' could'nt find it, an' Georgie he said as practisin' short-hand had made him short, and the Jedge he said excuse me a momint an' he went outer one door, an' Phil says excuse me fer a momint an' he went outer a nuther door and I waited some time and they did'nt come back, so I excused myself an' went down an' saw Major Barrett. An' he says as how he was just makin' a new bill fer the city printin' and I'd have ter wait til he collected it, and then he opened the 'cyclopedia fer to write his editorial an' I took the hint an' left. An' I stepped inter Al. Ward's an' he said if I wanted a mince pie fer the heathen, ter take it along, but as fer hairpins he did'nt go a cent on 'em. But I knew Al's pies was tew rich fer the heathen's blood. And I went up to the Dakota Bildin' and Loan assassination an' found Gena Jewell a scribblin' L.J. on the blottin' paper an' not a penny to be got outen' the whole crowd. An' then I met Sill an' he said as Slosser were kickin' on payin' him because he'd a hurt Fred Kile's feelin's what edits the Warner Schoolboy's Bugle an' because Billy Kid thinks as he's too fresh an' he knows hisself that he ain't, an' so I did'nt get any money there. An' Billy Paulhamus, as I come to next, said he's jest sent Susan B. Anthony a diamont necklace fer a birthday present and he hain't no spare cash. An' I met Sam Vroom, as is makin' sich a reckerd as the brittle statesman of Columbia, an' he'd spent his last cent fer a crowbar fer the boys to kill snakes with at ther county seat. An' Dave Strauss wanted to figger out how many women there was in Africanistan as had hair, an' how many hair pins it took to each head, an' how much hairpins was a gross an' how much it would cost to supply each woman, an' it took so long I came away an' left him. An' Ed. Randall said if it was guage pins it might interest him, but hairpins did'nt. An' Harvey Jewett wanted to know what kind of a snap it would be to send Dill out there with a cord o' clothspins, an' Scott wanted me to cash a wheat check an' pay him the balance, an' then I looked at the clock an' saw I'd just time to skip home an' git supper, an' when I got here I found I'd been gone jest seventy two minits an' six seconds, an' I'd been all round the town. I can almost sympathize with that Bly gal."

"And how much did you get?"

"Nary cent. But I've one satisfaction, anyhow," she continued, with a sigh, "I've a did my duty; and if the heathens in Africanistan want hairpins arter this, why, they can rustle for 'em themselves!"

. . . .

She Insists on Her Boarders Keeping Lent,
With Indifferent Success

22 February 1890

Since the Young Ladies Guild social at Samuel H. Jumper's house on 21 January 1890, the people of Aberdeen had been in a perfect "swhirl" of social activity, which reached a crescendo just prior to Ash Wednesday (19 February). Baum, whose wife was active in Episcopalian women's groups, poked fun most comfortably at the activities of that denomination, which provided the grist for Mrs. Bilkins's remarks on keeping Lent. Beyond this gentle ribbing, however, Baum did not use his "Our Landlady" column to criticize the townspeople for their almost frenetic social activities as drought and hunger threatened the welfare of the community at large. Conversely, rival editor C. Boyd Barrett commented sarcastically in the *Aberdeen Evening Republican* of 15 February that ministers could be "glad of one thing . . . that the immigration commissioner in his next report can tell the misinformed people of the east how a Dakota city can bear itself up gaily under the depressing influences of short harvests, dull trade, scanty clothing and scarcity of the necessaries of life." On 21 February he also insinuated that "certain newspapers in the city" dwelt too much on dancing and not enough on religion.

Baum responded quickly. "Any matter of religion," he remarked on 22 February, "lies between our God and ourselves; any matter of society or dancing is properly consigned to the columns of our paper. Pecksniffian theology as applied to a daily journal has never yet proved a howling success." Barrett condemned "Aberdeen people for dancing while there is so much suffering in Dakota," said Baum, "evidently considering that it makes the poor farmers hungrier, and forgetting that these same society people are the ones who have contributed most liberally toward relief for the unfortunate." Baum concluded that "merry hearts" did more good in the world than "elongated visages or soured and discontented religious sentiments," and he and Mrs. Bilkins did their part to keep people smiling.

🌱 "I suppose," said the landlady, furtively eying an ink-stain on the carpet and smoothing the ample wrinkles out of her ample gown with her ample hands, "I suppose, gentlemen, as you're all good 'Piskipalians."

The doctor colored, and answered, "I frequently attend that church, and — yes, I may say that I am an Episcopalian."

"Ever sense that Jumper sociable!" remarked the landlady, sarcastically.

"I myself feel strongly drawn to that excellent — would you call it religion? or sect? or — "

"Call it the Guilded Clique!" chuckled the landlady, to the Colonel's no small confusion.

"And Tom — "

"I was brought up in the tenets of the church," replied that languid young man. "I don't know what the tenets were, but I was brought up in 'em."

"Then they was probably red flannels an' diapers," answered the landlady, absent-mindedly, while Tom turned to the photograph of Susan B. to enable him to regain his self-possession. For poor Susan has always possessed herself.

"Therefore," says the landlady, with a smile of satisfaction, "you are all 'Piskiples. Of course you'll keep lent."

The boarders looked at each other in surprise and uneasiness.

"I think I shall deny myself something," remarked the colonel; "I shall either smoke nickle cigars instead of imported ones or take to a pipe. I haven't dicided which."

"And I," said the doctor, cheerfully, "shall economise on horse feed. My mare has really had to[o] liberal an allowance of oats lately. What shall you do, Tom?" and they all looked curiously at the dyed-in-the-wool Episcopalian.

"Oh, there is one course of denial which I always follow," says this interesting youth. "I deny myself postage stamps and write to all my friends on postals. It's inconvenient, ye know, but the lenten season must be duly observed."

The landlady smiled an Act III. Scene III smile, for the climax was approaching, and led them without a word to the dinner table.

"Mrs. Bilkins," said the colonel, when all were seated. "I am a little rushed today, as I have a client awaiting my return to renew a note. Please fetch on the dinner."

"The dinner," replied the landlady, trying to repress a fiendish look of triumph, "is on. This is ash We'nsday. Most landladys who has 'Piskiple boarders has nothin' but ashes fer to eat today, but I ain't that sort. Good 'Piskiples, as 'tends the Guild socials so reglar, mustn't be starved, altho' they should be incouraged in them tenements o' the church as Mr. Tom were brought up in. So I've got some nice mush an' milk for you, and if your conscience don't prick you, — fall to an' eat hearty!"

The boarders were conquered. They turned their hollow eyes and mouths and pink suffused brows upon the mush, and naught save the rattle of the spoons against the bowls broke the ominous silence which was the only thing that had reigned in Aberdeen since winter set in.

"I once knew a woman," remarked the colonel at last, spitefully, "so mean that she put holes in her fried-cakes to economise."

"Did she die a horrible death?" asked Tom.

"She did."

[T]he landlady was unmoved.

"And an old woman with whom I boarded chopped her hash so fine that she had to press the atmosphere over the platter to keep it from floating in the air."

"That was in lent," beamed the landlady, good-naturedly.

Here the doctor distinguished himself.

"One good thing about this season," said he, "is that boarding house keepers never ask you for any money, because they know it's lent!"

Mrs. Bilkins turned pale, and left the room abruptly, while the boarders made the best of their meagre fare and started for town in a brighter mood.

The landlady looked after them through the crack in the kitchen door.

"It'll be a heap o' savin' just now, this lent business; but I'm afeared," with a sigh tha[t] came from the darns on the heels of her socks, "I'm afeared they'll more n' make it up at Yeaster!"

. . . .

She Gets a Letter from her Brother in Harriman that Nearly Breaks up the Establishment

1 March 1890

Continuing drought and slow trade were making Aberdeen businessmen uneasy, especially as they anticipated a new prohibition law that threatened some businesses and would close others. Investment opportunities in other states began to look good, and the newspapers consistently reported on the travels of prominent land speculators. The *Aberdeen Daily News* paid particular attention to Ralph L. Brown, who was touring the southern states and telegraphed back on 22 February that he had found "a gap in the mountains [of Tennessee] and saw a chance for real estate investment." His Aberdeen friends wired him $15,000 to purchase land in Harriman, where the East Tennessee Land Company proposed to build a new mining and manufacturing center. A scheduled auction of town lots on 26 February led five eager Aberdonians — Samuel H. Jumper, Henry S. ("Hank") Williams, Fred C. Beard, Frank A. Brown, and James Ringrose — to board the train for Harriman. "Jumper," the *News* announced on 23 February, went along "to furnish the money, Williams the cards [cinch was the favorite betting game], Beard the revolvers, Brown the prayers and Ringrose the w — ater." The men promised to send "their Aberdeen admirers complete telegraphic reports of their progress in getting richer." The first wires indicated that prices were high. "From the way sales are running," the *News* announced on 28 February, "it is safe to say that Aberdeen men are enthusiastic spectators and not heavy buyers." Such news pleased hometown boosters like Baum, who regarded "foreign investments" as detrimental to the continued health of Aberdeen.

"Mrs. Bilkins," gasped the Colonel, in amazement, "what does this mean? You've actually given us tenderloin steak for supper!"

"Dear me!" cried the landlady, "is it possible I'm that flustered? — but never mind! Eat it an' welcome, for tonight I give ye all warnin'!"

"Warning!" quoth Tom, "warning of what?"

"To go away — to find another boardin' place, for this 'ere old ranch ceases to exist termorrer!"

The boarders turned their wondering eyes upon the landlady. There she stood, her round face red with excitement, and wringing her hands convulsively together as she nodded her head at them as if it was worked by a Keely motor.

"May I ask," remarked the doctor, in a voice he strove to render calm, "may I ask, ma'am, where you are going?"

The landlady's agitation increased. "To Tennessee!" she managed to reply at last. For a moment there was dead silence.

"Harriman?"

The landlady nodded.

"This is Jim Ringrose's work," remarked Tom, tragically, "he's jealous of your reputation, ma'am. You'd better give up the idea and stick to Aberdeen."

"No such thing!" returned Mrs. Bilkins, indignantly. "Do you s'pose there's nobody there 'xcept from Aberdeen? My brother's there, gents, an' he's a writ me a letter about it, an' he says it's a wonderful openin' fer a hotel. If ye'll jest listen, I'll read it to ye."

"By all means," acquiesced the doctor, leaning back and picking his teeth, while the landlady drew the precious document from her bosom with trembling hands, adjusted her glasses, and began:

"I asked the boys from Aberdeen if they was lookin' fer a fust-class hotel, 'cause they was still carryin' their gripsacks, and one on 'em pulls me aside an' says:

" 'My fren',' says he, 'is this here a prohibition state?'

"An' I says, 'ole hoss,' says I, 'you're welcome to do anything in Harriman but pray.' An' he turned to a fine lookin' man as was tryin' to get a cork out o' a bottle an' says:

" 'Hank, what'd I tell you? It'll take longer'n this ter git the Brown Brothers grip on Harriman! Drink 'arty!' An' they did. An' another, he says:

" 'Where'll we sleep, Jim?' and the feller he spoked to wiped his mouth an' says:

" 'Fred,' says 'e, 'less buy a claim an' sleep on that.'

" 'Claim!' says the Bared boy, 'why these 'ere ain't claims, — they's lots.'

" 'Then,' says a pleasant-faced gentl'man what they calls Jump, 'then,' says 'e, 'less buy a lot of em!'

" 'This won't do,' says a'nuther wot looks like a preacher, 'we've got to go to a hotel.'

" 'Hotels,' says a solemn feller with his han's in his vest pockets, 'must be patronized. I've got one on my han's now.' But I didn't see nothin' on his han's but warts. Then they all agrees, an' ses to me to lead 'em to the best hotel in town. An' away I goes. There ain't but one, an' it can't feed more'n a hundred people a day, an' there's anyhow 5000 here, an' so I tole 'em.

" 'Jest give us a chance to put our names on the register,' says the hansom man, 'an' we'll russle fer the vittles! I hain't lived in Columbia all winter fer nothin'.' An' so I takes 'em to the hotel an' manages to get their luggage put in a corner o' the wash room. There was six gripsacks, — little ones, a champaigan basket marked 'Fred. Bared,' a case o' beer marked 'me an' ringrose's,' an' a big jimmyjohn marked 'Free-fer-all.' There was a little package marked 'poison' in big letters, and writ on with a ledpencil was 'Comps of Al. Ward — Somethin' to make the boys think o' home.'

"After a while I got 'em a room, an' they called me up an' asked what I thought of Harriman fer an investment.

" 'Fust class,' says I. 'I've a knowed it fer twenty year. It's a nice gap in the mountains, which is the only place as a railroad can get through — if it ever takes it into its head that it wants to get through at all. It's also the only place as a cyclone can get through, an' that gets through pretty lively oncet in a while an' blows every shanty in Harriman down the other side o' the mountains. But I ferget, gentlemen; I promised the estate agent as I wouldn't mention that.'

" 'Boys,' says one feller, 'if my wife knewed I was in danger o' cyclones, she'd go crazy. Ye see,' he says, turnin' to me, 'we don't have high winds in Dakota.'

"Then the hansom man asked what lots was bringin'. I told him 'bout a thousan' dollars each. Then they looked at each other an' wanted ter know if ye could buy a quarter of a lot.

" 'No,' says I, 'but yes can buy as many lots as ye want to.'

" 'Less buy a lottery ticket,' says Jump.

"But they didn't anser.

"They jest asked me to go out and see what I could buy an option on one little lot fer.

"Now, my dear sister, I write all this to let ye see how high the excitement is. You can make dollars here where ye could cents in Aberdeen. Come right along, an' bring all yer friends."

The landlady's trembling voice ceased, an' looking up she asked triumphantly,

"What do ye say to that, gentlemen?"

"Go!" replied the colonel, dejectedly, "go by all means."

"I've half a mind," said the doctor, timidly, "to go with you!"

"What would it cost?" asked Tom, catching the excitement.

"Well," replied the landlady, "my brother mentions that. He says: 'If any more Aberdeen ducks want some o' this pudden, and want ter know how much money it takes to invest in Harriman, you can show 'em this slip o' paper, which I picked up on the floor of the room the Aberdeen boys hangs out in. He probably dropped it by mistake, as it looks like a expense account.' Read it, colonel," added the landlady. The colonel took it and read as follows:

"Railroad ticket	$96.25
Sinch	11.00
Sleeper	1.50
Cigars	1.00
Sinch	16.50
Lunch	.10
Refreshments	12.00
Sinch (a bad one)	51.00
Cigars	2.00
Refreshments	2.00
Sinch	17.00
Refreshments	1.50
Lent Ringrose	10.00
Sinch	9.00

Lunch	.05
Sleeper	2.00
Cigars	2.25
Lent Brown	15.00
Refreshments	14.00
Hotel Bill	16.00
⅛ interest in one outside lot . . .	125.00
Total	835.15

SUMMARY

Bro't from Home	$1000.00
P'd out as above	835.15
Got left	164.85
Will cost to get back	100.00
Total outlay	93[5].15
Probable value of Lot	200.00
Profits	735.15"

The colonel finished amidst a dead silence, which was broken by a rap at the door.

The dirty-faced messenger boy had a telegram for Mrs. Bilkins. She read it, sighed deeply, and handed it to the colonel. It ran as follows:

"Stay where you are. The bottom may drop outen this thing an bust suthin'.

JERRY"

"That's my brother," said the landlady mournfully, "an' his jedgement is usually good. Gents, what'd ye like fer a Sunday dinner?"

In spite of Baum's satire, at least one of the Aberdeen speculators did make a tidy profit in Harriman. James Ringrose purchased a lot for $2,500 and sold it twenty minutes later for $3,200. Of the travelers, Frank and Ralph Brown and their silent Aberdeen partners were the big spenders, paying over $33,000 for only thirteen lots. The prices, as the early telegrams had indicated, were beyond the reach of most Aberdeen men as individuals. Only Ringrose, Jumper, and Williams purchased lots in their own right.[5] Still, those who invested modest amounts hoped for a good return on their joint investments, and Baum found them a source of further humor and satire. On 29 March he penned the following squib at the expense of Aberdeen realtor Carril M. Coe:

C. M. Coe is anxious to know,
How high Tennessee land is advancing.

He owns three-quarters of an inch or so,
An his worries are something entrancing.

In the same issue Baum's longer poem "Aberdeen's Pride" suggested that the deplorable condition of the town's opera house could be blamed on the fact that Aberdeen's financial capital — and its civic pride — was now invested in Tennessee.

. . . .

She Dabbles in Politics and Aspires to a Great Office

8 March 1890

For weeks the Aberdeen newspapers had been anticipating the 15 April municipal election and the party caucuses that would precede it. The Republican *Aberdeen Daily News* attacked the Democratic city council, as well as the city auditor, engineer, and printer, accusing them of numerous improprieties, including overspending on civic projects. The *Aberdeen Saturday Pioneer* contributed its share of scathing editorials, and, not incidentally, the ongoing feud between Democrat C. Boyd Barrett, city printer and editor of the *Aberdeen Evening Republican*, and Republican Baum flared up again. On 4 March, Barrett advised Baum "to be careful in fooling with the buzz saw. . . . There are governors, bankers, corrupt politicians, individuals whom the editor of the *Republican* has treated with the utmost kindess but in an evil hour they tried to down him, and now some of them are wandering exiles on the Pacific coast, some are in southern climes. . . . It is well to leave the buzz saw alone, Mr. Editor."[6] The next day the *Aberdeen Daily News* ridiculed the editorialist's diatribe, dubbing him "Czar Buzz-saw Barrett." Understandably, this incident featured heavily in Baum's 8 March column, but the sketch also took aim at political posturing and the lack of Republican leadership. So far, the G O P had been unable to find a man willing to run for mayor against incumbent Benjamin Stearns. Berating the prominent city men for their reluctance, Baum concluded on 15 March, "The hour will find the man, and the man will be ready to sacrifice some personal inclinations for the benefit of his fellow citizens." Until that time, however, Mrs. Bilkins would have to supply the leadership in Aberdeen.

🌹 "Yes," said the landlady, as she pep[p]ered the hash and tasted of it to see if it was right; "Yes, I'm a gettin' some political aspersions into my head, an' don't see as why I shouldn't run fer office as well as any other citizen o' this here Yernited States."

"But," said Tom, opening the tightly stopped holes in the salt shaker with a toothpick, "woman is not yet enfranchised, you know."

"The[y] ain't, hey?" retorted the landlady, glaring upon him, "I guess if Mary Etter Bones is good enough to be Vice-President o' South Dakota, Sairy Ann Bilkins is good enough fer mayor o' Aberdeen!"

"What!" exclaimed the doctor, aroused from his brown study of the hash, "do you then aspire to the Mayorality?"

"Why not?" answered the landlady, raising her eyebrows in surprise, "ain't I as good as Ben Stearns?"

"Undoubtedly, but — "

"And ain't Major Burke promised to 'lect me if I'm nomernated, an' will give him the city printin' to start his new paper, an' — "

"If you're nominated he might," interrupted the colonel, who is a thorough politician, "but no democrat, man or woman, who works against B. S. Barrett, can hope to secure the nomination for anything."

"Pooh," sneered Mrs. Bilkins, drawing herself up proudly, "I berlong to the oppersition, I does, an' I've got the wimmin to back me up. I've a writ to Mrs. Alice Pickeler to gimme her support, and the Bugle is to be my official organ."

"Well, even a hand-organ is better than no organ at all," remarked the doctor, "and I'm glad to see you so powerfully supported. Of course, so far as I'm concerned, I've helped support you so long that I won't go back on you now."

"Nor I," chimed in the others.

"Thanks, feller citizens an' boarders," said the landlady, majestically, "all I needs now is L. C. Dennis an' the Rhines votin' machine to carry me through to the Mayor's cheer."

"And with the new newspaper to back you, you have a brilliant career in prospect," remarked the doctor. "I suppose the paper will be conservative?"

"Oh yes," replied the landlady. "The editor agrees not to send nobody awanderin' broken hearted on the face o' the yerth because he just fooled with a buzz-saw. An' he agrees not ter call no mean names nor fill up his paper with bills o' fare a week old because he can't get news. An' he'll print pamphlets fer church societies at five minits notis an' take 'em back agin with a smilin' face. All he asks is the city printin' at the highest market price, an' the reports o' Butler's Signal Service an' seven subscribers to carry him through to fortune."

"But who are your other supporters?" asked Tom.

"Why, there's Tom Nolan and Jim Davis, as is both overworked, an' are aching for some soft snaps, an' there's Al. Ward who wants ter supply the city pies, an' there's Miss Jones who says she's liberal enough to support anything but her stockings, an' there's Chollie Fisher that wants me to stand by him for the treasurership, because he feels easiest when he's a handlin' money, an' there's Mat Stroupe who thinks he can beat me if he runs agin' me, an' there's Billy Paulhamus who allus supports everybody to make hisself solid, an' there's Skip Salisbury who says he'd like to support a woman fer a little while an' see how it feels, an' there's Zach Spitler who says he wants to tackle something excitin', an' there's C. N. Harris who says he can control his own vote an' — lots of others!'"

"With such a backing," said the colonel with a sigh, "you ought to win."

"I shall," said the landlady confidently, "but as it's a long time 'afore the caucus I believe I'll go down town an' buy a case o' strawberries to do up. It ain't quite the season, but they're plenty in town I hear,7 an' if I'm agoin' to be mayor o' this here berg, I won't have no time this summer to monkey over cannin' fruit, fer my time'll be tuk up with water main extensions an' lookin' up them seven subscribers fer the new paper!'"

. . . .

She Worries over Seed Wheat,
and Gets Lectured by the Boarders

15 March 1890

In 1888, Aberdeen businessmen had formed a commercial group called the Aberdeen Club, voting to build a $5,000 clubhouse and to lobby the legislature in support of railroads. Baum called the group a "sawdust-stuffed concern" that wallowed in its expensive quarters while the town's opera house and civic pride fell into disrepair.[8] Suddenly, on 20 February 1890, this moribund group took notice of the hard times and petitioned the governor to hold a convention to study the farmers' need for affordable seed grain for spring planting. To everyone's surprise, Governor Arthur C. Mellette responded immediately, authorizing the club to issue a call for a convention.

Held on 3 March in Huron, the seed wheat convention determined that twenty-one South Dakota counties desperately needed over 500,000 bushels of wheat at a value of over $500,000. The governor had already signed legislation that would enable counties to buy seed grain and sell it to impoverished farmers on credit, waiting until harvest for payment. One-fourth of the money was to be raised "by the issuance of warrants by counties benefitted, the remainder to be donated by other counties and contributions from outside states," Baum's newspaper reported on 8 March. To obtain the rest, Mellette and a commission of delegates (including Aberdonian John H. Drake) left to solicit funds in Minneapolis and Chicago and to talk to railroad and elevator companies.

In Brown County the elevators appeared to hold ample seed, but money to draw it forth was missing. The county commissioners prepared to issue warrants. Within days, problems arose. Was the law that allowed counties to issue credit constitutional? Many observers warned that until the issue was resolved potential buyers for the warrants were not likely to emerge.[9] In that case, Baum editorialized on 15 March, wealthy Aberdonians should stand security for the warrants, because the city's "men of means" would be "men of means no longer" if the farmers went out of business.

As a mayoral candidate, Mrs. Bilkins took notice of these events, and the 15 March column featured club members (Hagerty and Jewett), convention delegates (McGlachlin and Hagerty), and a commission member (Drake). Still, the strongest statement in this vignette concerns not seed wheat and hard times but an issue much closer to Baum's heart — woman suffrage. In editorial after editorial, Baum supported universal suffrage, remarking on 1 February 1890, for example, that Americans as a people "must do away with sex prejudice and render equal distinction and reward to brains and ability, no matter whether found in man or woman." Mrs. Bilkins shared his conviction, but the boarders displayed typical male attitudes.

"Oh, dear," exclaimed our landlady, as she sank into a chair and gasped for breath, "I've a most made up my mind to give up tryin' to be a public woman."

"What's happened now?" queried the doctor, stealthily wiping his plate with his napkin before helping himself to the cutlets.

"Why, I'm bothered to death about this seed wheat business," she replied, growing calmer before the gaze of the sympathetic boarders.

"You see, I knew very well that the gov'ner hadn't appinted the proper folks to look arter it, an' I decided that unless I took the matter inter my own hands the poor farmer's might whistle fer their seed. So I goes out an' sees cap. Hauser, an' asks him what he thinks about sellin' them 'air warrants. An' he says, says he, 'missus, the tea what we grows in Injy on me an' some other folkses plantations, beats the world.' And so I left him an' met Jedge Drake, an' I says, 'Jedge, what'll we do about seed wheat?' an' he answered, sayin', 'what do you s'pose I know about it? What's seed wheat got ter do with apintments?' an' he kissed his hand an' left on the fust train fer Pierre. An' then I came across Dight. McGlachlin, an' he tole me as how there was more wheat in the elevators than would plant two such states as South Dakota. But, says he, 'it takes money, ma'am, to git it out.' An' I called on the komishner of emigrants an' he said that if some rich folks like me would put up the kerlateral that the wheat would pop out'er them elevators right inter the farmers' hands. 'I'd put up some securities myself,' says he, 'but I'm a poor man as can't afford to run the chances.'

"An' Harvey Jewett said, that the club had a done their duty an' called the convention, and decided ter issue warrants, an' now if anybody wanted ter make them warrants sell, the rich folk could jest write their names on the back of 'em. An' so I come home discouraged an' — Great heavings!" she exclaimed, "I've lost my weddin' ring!"

"Don't get excited, ma'am," remarked the colonel. "I think I've found it," and he fished out a discolored band from the gravy.

"There!" cried the landlady, "I've growd so poor worrittin' over other people's business, that I can't keep even my rings on, an' arter this I'll jest mind my own business an' let other people mind mine."

"Bravo!" yelled Tom, "now you are getting sensible. I've felt like home without a mother ever since you got to running over the town, and my chum Clayton Thompson got stuck on the printing business. But if you'll look after me in the future, I'll — I actually believe I'll pay something on account."

"Hm!" said the landlady.

"My dear Mrs. Bilkins," remarked the doctor, "Tom is right. In a certain sense we are your family, and a woman of family should not meddle in public affairs."

"Hm!" said the landlady.

"Your kind heart," said the colonel, "leads you to meddle in affairs that should be left to the sterner sex. Now you're a better cook than politician, or anything else, and you should devote your energies to those talents that the Lord has given you."

"Hm!" sniffed the landlady, as the boarders filed out; "it's the conceit o' men as is the biggest stumblin' block ter universal sufferin' o' women! But let 'em talk. They'll find I know my business — yes, an' everybody else's, too!"

. . . .

She Discusses the Disadvantages of Prohibition, and Invents a New Method of Baking Pies

22 March 1890

The first stock of goods for sale in Aberdeen had been a keg of whiskey, a fact that illuminates why town fathers both welcomed and dreaded the advent of prohibition. By mid-March the state legislature had finally succeeded in passing an enforcement law for the state's constitutional prohibition clause that would go into effect on 1 May. The act, drafted by former Hub City resident William Fielder, had 156 amendments appended before passage, many of them directed toward regulation of druggists. In an attempt to leave liquor available for "medicinal, mechanical, sacramental and scientific purposes" without creating a drugstore saloon, the law provided that a pharmacist could be granted a permit for the selling of liquor or liquor-based medicines but first had to put up a $1,000 bond. A county court also had to judge the validity of a petition signed in his behalf by twenty-five "reputable free-holders" and twenty-five "reputable women," who certified to the good character of the applicant and his fitness for the business. Drugstore owners across the state were insulted, and Aberdeen's nine druggists signed an agreement not to take out permits. Baum chided them for their folly, suggesting that either state agents or doctors would take over the business if pharmacists did not comply.[10] Besides, he added on 22 March, the grocers were in a worse predicament because they could no longer sell anything with a liquor base. He then sent Mrs. Bilkins forth to sample the attitudes of affected merchants.

"These is terrible times!" sighed our landlady, as she brushed the dust off the butter with her finger tips and tasted the milk to see if it was sweet. "All the town is riled up as if you'd stirred 'em with a stick like you would a hasty puddin'."

"Anything wrong?" queried the colonel, helping himself to the soup.

"Everything!" declared our landlady. "If Bill Fielder had only knowed what a damage he was doin' this town, he'd never a thunk up all them hard measures to prevent his feller-citizens from gettin' drunk. I've been tradin' a little this mornin', an' I went inter Scott's store for some borax, an' you orter heered him talk! He says he can't sell patent medicines without a license, because they all hez alcohol in 'em. 'I'm goin' ter quit the town,' sez he. So I didn't buy the borox, as I wasn't goin' ter patronize anything but home instertutions, and I goes over to Lacey's, an' Doc he says — 'Them prohibish fellers is pritty hard on our perfeshin, but so long as they lets us sell Soda water with a wink in it I guess we'll pull through.' An' then I goes over to Narregang's — that ain't no druggist nor no loan agent nuther, cause he don't belong to nary gang, — an' he says, 'Why ma'am, they'll arrest a feller fer smilin' after the fust o' May, because it's agin' the law to be in good spirits!'"

"Great Scott!" yelled the doctor.

"Oh, it wasn't my joke," said the landlady, complacently.

"It wasn't that, Mrs. Bilkins. It was this confounded hairpin in the soup. I've run it twice through my tongue and broken off a front tooth."

"What, your new tooth?" asked Tom, sympathetically.

The Doctor scowled upon him in silence, and the landlady proceeded briskly: —

"But the drug fellers ain't a patch on the grocery men fur bein' riled. Harry Olwin is as much put out as the electric lights on a dark night, cause he can't sell lemon extract any more. 'Ye see, ma'am;' sez he, 'they might as well a took the bread and cake out o' my family's mouth as to perwent our a sellin' extracts. Them extracts,' he sez, pointin' to a row of 'em, 'only costs us four cents a bottle, an' we gets 35 cents for 'em because it's pretty close to sell 'em fer a quarter. Now if they'd a forbid our sellin' sugar, who'd a kicked?' 'I would!' sez I, an' I came away. Teek Gilmore inter Beard an' Gage's was lookin' as mad as the city Auditor when he gits showed up in the papers. 'Lay in your stock o' pickles before the fust o' May, Mrs. Bilkins,' yells Teek, 'fer they've decided as vinegar is intoxicatin', an' can't be sold without a license. What on earth can we put our spare water into when the vinegar barrel's gone?' 'Try reducin' the molasses with it,' sez I sourcastically, an' I left him pullin' the hair outer Frank Beard's head in great handfulls, he was so mad. Clayton Thompson was just sendin' a boy down to buy Roache's old sign that reads 'all these goods at your own figgers,' when I stepped in. He wanted it to put on his brandy peaches, he said, because they must be closed out 'afore May fust. 'I don't know what the folks will do,' sez he with a care-worn air, 'when they've got to buck agin' the loss o' the wheat crop and brandy-peaches at the same time!' I ansered, 'but perhaps you can git Frank Hagerty to take 'em off your hands, seein' as they're marked — ' "

A horrible racket coming from the direction of the kitchen, here interrupted her.

"Fire!" shouted the boarders in unison, and followed by our landlady they all rushed into the kitchen.

Everything there appeared to be in its usual disordered condition. Mrs. Bilkins sank panting into a chair, while the colonel slipped his revolver quietly back into his hip-pocket.

"What could it have been?" asked Tom, as he wiped his forehead with a trembling hand and a pocket-handkerchief.

"I know!" suddenly cried the landlady, and going to the stove she opened the oven door and drew out an alarm-clock!

"You see," she explained, "I had them pies a-bakin' an' I knew if I got talkin'

I'd ferget all about 'em, an' so I just sot the alarm to let me know when they was done, — an' forgot all about it!"

"Mrs. Bilkins," said the colonel, with marked disapproval, "some day you will over-reach yourself in one of these ingenious contrivances, and lose either your life, or your boarders — or both!" and followed by the others he walked angrily away.

"I don't care," muttered Mrs. Bilkins, as she blew on the clock to cool it, "it were a good scheme anyway, — an' the pies is done to a turn!"

. . . .

She Makes a Terrible Mistake and Quotes a Proverb

29 March 1890

> Since Ash Wednesday on 19 February, social activity in Aberdeen had been largely confined to missionary teas, women's coffees, and club meetings. "Lent," Baum reported on 22 March, "is being very generally observed among the Episcopalians and Roman Catholics. It seems easy for many people to practice denial in Dakota this year." In contrast to the large pre-Lenten socials, quiet house parties of four or six young people were now the norm. During this subdued time, Mrs. Bilkins's thoughts, like those of the other single people in town, turned to romance.

Our landlady sat in the kitchen peeling some genuine green apples for pies, and as she dextrously separated the outer cuticle with the old razor that was the only visible relict of the late Mr. Bilkins, her thoughts wandered into figuring the cost of each apple and how much would go into a piece of pie and whether she could really afford to feed her boarders on such a luxury at the present rate of board. And then, glancing at the razor, she thought of the late Mr. B. and sighed as she remembered her lonely condition, till woman-like — widow-woman-like, we mean — she begun wondering when the fairy prince would come to her and awaken her into new life with a lover's kiss, saying "Sairy Ann, loved one, you shall never keep boarders more while your Alphonso lives to work his fingers to the bone to dress you in silks and satins!" The razor lay idle upon her knee now, and our landlady wiped her eyes and nose on her apron and gazed dreamily out of the window.

"Madam!"

It was the colonel's voice that aroused her. He had come to see if he couldn't get his dinner a little earlier than usual as he was going out of town for a day, but seeing how startled she was, he controlled the natural severity of his voice, and coming to her side he added — "My dear Mrs. Bilkins, I have a proposal to make to you."

Undoubtedly her previous train of thought had slightly turned our landlady's head.

A light of rapture shone in her eyes; the pan of apples flew right over the colonel's head — the razor just skipping his cheek — and a large apple paring wound around his nose and buried its point in his right eye, while to cap the climax to his surprise Mrs. Bilkins threw herself with a loud scream of ecstacy into his arms.

The colonel has been through many wars, but this was a coup-de-main for which he was wholly unprepared.

He gave a groan and sat down abruptly upon the floor, Mrs. Bilkins falling upon his lap and retaining presence of mind enough to pin down both his arms in a warm and hearty embrace, while she stuck the knot of hair she wore on the top of her head plump into the colonel's open mouth.

For a moment nothing could be heard but the babble of Mrs. Bilkins' endearing words, for the colonel was struggling for breath and buried under the weight of a good 300 lbs.

Then the door suddenly flew open, and Tom and the doctor stood upon the threshold.

For one instant they stood horror-stricken, and then they wickedly burst into a roar of laughter, while the one eye the colonel could see out of glared angrily over the top of Mrs. Bilkins' head, and the landlady, impervious to interruption, murmured

"My sweet, sweet colonel — I've a prayed for this hour to come an' I knew all the time as you loved me as I love you an' no knife can cut our love in-two, my own lovey dovey — "

"Excuse us," said the doctor, in his gentle voice. "We were unaware that a love-scene was going on here, and finding no dinner ready, we — "

The colonel made a superhuman effort and rolled Mrs. Bilkins from his lap; then he sprang to his feet, pulled his dripping hat out of the water barrel, and with a cry of rage that sounded like a naughty cuss-word tore out of the back door and disappeared.

Tom attempted to assist Mrs. Bilkins to her feet, but she pushed him aside and rising unaided she cried

"There, you've a found out our little love affair most as soon as we found it out ourselves! I don't care fer my part but the colonel seems a little riled."

"He does, indeed," said Tom.

"May we congratulate you?" asked the doctor.

"To be sure ye may!" answered the landlady, holding her breath to see if she couldn't blush, "now set right down here, an' I'll git dinner an' tell you all about it at the same time. Ye see this here lenten season is jest the time fer love-affairs. There ain't no parties, an' the boys an' gals jest keep company, and after the season o' Lent is gone there allus comes a season o' keeps, when marryin' an' givin' in marriage is in order. In Aberdeen a gal ain't in style if she ain't going ter be married after Yeaster, or ain't got a diamond ring ter show, anyhow. I can count more'n twenty couples as is parin' off, and the colonel and I jest thought as we'd be in style. He hain't give me no ring yet, but," she added reflectively, "he ain't had a chance!"

"I think he has gone for one now," said Tom.

"Well, anyhow," said the landlady, "you can't keep no secrets in a boardin' house, so it's just as well you found it out. The colonel ain't young, ner hansome, ner rich, an' he owes me nine weeks board, but love is blind, they say, an' he's a man, anyhow, and'll pertect me if he knows what's good fer hisself! But there — dinner's ready. Excuse my flustration, gentlemen, fer a perposal allus knocks a woman silly — even when she expects it!"

The two boarders ate their meal in dismal silence. They were full of awe and horror, and there was an air of mystery about the affair which puzzled them.

As they finished, a messenger boy strolled lazily in with a note for Mrs. Bilkins.

"Please read it, doctor," she asked, excitedly, "it's from the Kernel, but I'm that flustrated I could'nt find my glasses in a week!"

" 'My dear madam,' " read the doctor, " 'I simply wished to propose to you that you gave me a lunch before dinner so I could catch the train, as I am obliged to be out of town for a day. But as it is, I have gone without it, so don't trouble yourself.' "

A hushed silence pervaded the room, during which the doctor was afraid to look at the landlady, and Tom was afraid to look at the doctor.

At length the former remarked quietly as he fitted his napkin into its pewter ring,

"There's many a slip twixt the cup and the lip."

"An' there's as good fish in the sea as was ever pulled out'n it," quoted our landlady bitterly.

"For my part," said Tom to the doctor, as he closed the front door behind them, "if the colonel ever tries to put on any more airs, I shall just call him 'the Landlord!' "

"Men," remarked Mrs. Bilkins, as she walked into the kitchen and kicked the cat for eating the soup, "men is all deceivers, an' allus was. I won't git a husband — not jest now — but I'll get them nine weeks board if it takes a leg!"

. . . .

She Tells Why Farmers Should be Happy and Displays Remarkable Forethought

5 April 1890

On 29 March, Baum announced that the county commissioners, headed by Elias H. Alley, had issued warrants and procured enough seed wheat for the needy farmers of Brown County. The grain, purchased locally from such firms as Van Dusen & Company and Bagley and Cargill, would cost the farmers sixty-five to seventy cents per bushel after harvest, and each farmer would get a maximum of seventy-five bushels. Complaints about the bushel limit were already coming in, and Baum remarked that those "able to have more land broken will be able to procure additional outside aid." His landlady and her boarders explored the kind of assistance they were likely to receive.

Even though Baum clearly sympathized with the debt problems of Dakota farmers,[11] he blamed them, as well as the drought, for their problems. A successful year on Dakota soil, he wrote on 1 Feburary 1890, had "unsettled" the frontier farmers, and "they plunged into all sorts of extravagance. They bought expensive harvesters on long credit, and left them standing in the fields to be ruined by sun and frost. . . . They lived better than they ever dreamed of doing in the old life, bought expensive goods, extravagant table luxuries, and spent their money down to the last cent." These practices left them "penniless, deeply in debt and totally unprovided for" when a "short crop struck." Not surprisingly, the profligate tendencies of Dakota farmers received their share of ridicule in the following sketch, but Baum ended it on a lighter note, ribbing the local merchants about the inflated prices of eggs as Easter Sunday (6 April) approached. Grocers had stocked up on the "hen fruit" because, Baum wrote, "every well disposed citizen will feel it obligatory to eat more eggs for breakfast [on Easter] than are good for him, doze tranquilly at church, . . . and consume the biggest dinner of the year." Anticipating both the appetites of boarders and the cupidity of merchants, Mrs. Bilkins planned ahead.

🌹 "Yes," said our landlady, as she buttered the toast with a strange compound she scraped from an old teacup, "yes, it's a splendid mornin', an' one that reminds me of my childhood's days."

"I have heard," said the doctor, tapping his boiled egg with his knife, "that in the beginning of the present century the weather was very delightful."

Our landlady looked puzzled, and glanced at the colonel, but the colonel's eyes sought his plate. He has been very quiet since his adventure of last week.

"The farmers," continued Mrs. Bilkins, "is in splendid spirits. They say the ground is as damp as an infant and will plow like new cheese. An' old Wiggins he perdicts a flood in the Jim river valley, an' every farmer in the land is happy, from Jena Jewell to ole Hick inbotham, for they expects a big crop — anything wrong wi' that egg, doctor?"

"Chickens," remarked the doctor, meekly, pushing aside his egg-cup, "should be broiled for breakfast — not boiled in the shell; and permit me to state that I consider it wicked to cook so young a fowl at all."

"Dear me," exclaimed our landlady, "what a fraud them grocers is, and so near Yeaster, too! Try another — do!"

But the doctor took a mature doughnut instead, one that he was well enough acquainted with to believe it entitled to vote under the universal suffrage bill.[12]

"It's all very well for the farmers to feel good," said Tom, "but where are they going to get the seed to sow?"

"Pshaw!" replied Mrs. Bilkins, "that don't worry 'em. Ain't they got ole man Alley to look out fer 'em? Why, my cousin Jim were jest the destitutest man in Brown county, an' now he goes about grinnin' like Fred Wallace, he's so happy. He went to Alley, as is pullin' the strings down ter Bagley's elevator, an' he says, 'C'mish',' says he, 'I'll take them 75 bushel o' wheat as is comin' to me.' An' the C'mish' had him sign a paper swearin' to everything excep' that his soul were his own, an' gin him the 75 bushel. An' then he goes to a private grain dealer, an' mortgages his stock fer another seventy-five bushel, an' then he goes to the bank and mortgages his farm fer enough money to buy a team o' horses, an' then he hired a boy fer his board to do his plowin'; an' now he's all fixed, an' is hangin' around the Senate waitin' fer a machine man ter sell him a new harvester, a threshin' machine, a hay baler an' a stump puller on time an' take his notes fer security. Oh, my cousin Jim is a reglar Dakota farmer, an' don't you fergit it!"

"He is a Jim dandy," said the doctor, gravely.

"But what will he do when his notes come due?" asked Tom.

"Do? why give 'em all the wheat he's got an' put a new mortgage on his stock fer the balance an' a new mortgage on his farm fer enough to see him through the winter. What do s'pose he'll do?"

"And how long can he keep this up?"

"Well, he's been a farmer here fer seven year, an' he's better off today than he ever were. The fust year he got in debt he worried so his wife hed to lock up the razor an' the 'rough on agents,'[13] but now he lets the agents an' the banks worry, an' he lives happy an' contented."

"The banks," remarked the doctor, "own half the farms in the State."

"Mebbe they do," replied Mrs. Bilkins, "but they can't work 'em, an' so they let the farmers raise the crops for 'em. It ain't the farmers as is worryin' about the crops, it's them as holds the mortgages. But termorrer's Yeaster, ye know, an' I'd like to know as how you gentlemen'd like yer eggs cooked."

"I," said Tom, "will have a few boiled, a few fried, and a few roasted on the coals."

"An omelet," said the colonel, "will do for me."

"If they are fresh," the doctor replied, remembering his late encounter, "I'll have mine scrambled, dropped on toast, and frizzled."

"Oh, they're fresh," declared our landlady.

But when they had gone down town she repaired to the attic and drew out an old box apparently filled with salt, but from which she fished enough soiled looking eggs to fill her apron.

"Some of 'em rattles a mite," she said, holding one to her ear, "but I guess they'll do. Them boarders thinks as they can bust this establishment jest because it's Yeaster, but I remembered Yeaster day last Summer, when eggs was six cents a dozen, an' there won't be any bust on my plate — not if I knows it!"

. . . .

She Aspires to Rival Ella Wheeler Wilcox and
Concocts Another Scheme

12 April 1890

> Perhaps in response to Baum's lambasting of city leadership, a few good men had come forward to run for mayor of Aberdeen. Among Republicans, a three-way race developed between hardwareman August Witte (pronounced "witty"), bank president Robert Moody, and printer Frank Wilder, who represented, respectively, antiprohibition, prohibition, and labor interests. A city convention on 12 April settled the question, with Robert Moody emerging

as the Republican candidate for mayor amid a show of party unity, a conclusion Baum punningly alluded to in the third paragraph of the following column.

Opposing Moody in the citywide election would be Benjamin Stearns, Republican alderman and mayor, who had led Aberdeen's largely Democratic city government for most of the preceding twelve months. A pharmacist and patent-medicine manufacturer, Stearns was at odds with the prohibition proponents of his own party. Hoping to attract similarly disaffected Republicans, he and others, mostly Democrats, called for a "People's ticket" to be generated in "citizen's caucuses" rather than Democratic ones.[14] The ploy did not work. After the city convention, proponents of the People's ticket "in true democratic style" moved to the saloons to ratify their action, the *Aberdeen Daily News* reported as it continued to link the ticket with the Democrats and criticize its ties to the saloons and liquor dealers.[15] The fact that the city administration under Stearns and Democratic auditor Major F. Howe had been liberal in public works programs also gave the newspapers a pocketbook issue on which to attack the incumbents. As the 15 April election approached, Baum urged his readers to "wage aggressive warfare . . . against pocket-liners, tricksters and mugwumps."[16] Mrs. Bilkins wasted no time in doing so.

🌹 "Yes," said our landlady, "times has been pretty lively this week, an' all because o' this political business. But it's all turned out pretty well."

"How's that?" asked the doctor, as he scraped the lard off his toast and carefully buttered it.

"Why, you see the witty man is feelin' kind o' moody, and the man as was wilder than he was is tamed down a bit, an' the moody man is a feelin' quite witty an' comfortable, so you see it's all turned out for the best."

"You seem to have sifted the matter pretty thoroughly," said Tom.

"Not I," replied the landlady, after extracting her false teeth, and wiping them on her apron, "I have too much to do siftin' my ashes an' flour to tackle anything else, but at politics I won't take a back seat for anybody. Them boobies that want to run things themselves says as a woman ain't got no head for politics, but I know different. Now I've jest writ a political dockyment that I think will most paralize that air People's Ticket o' theirs, an' I'd like to have you gentlemen read it an' see if it would'nt win more votes than Cholly Howard will for alderman."

"Why, it's poetry," exclaimed the doctor. Our landlady blushed, and the doctor passed it over to the colonel.

"Poetry," said the latter, "was never my forte. Here Tom, read it."

The landlady tittered and became so confused that she put salt into the colonel's second cup of coffee instead of sugar. "Listen," said Tom, and read as follows:

> Hurrah, hurrah! the time is nigh
>   When every honest voter
> Can lift his bugle voice on high
>   An' praise artesian water!
>
> The saloonists they has got to go —
>   The boodlers too is beaten.
> They're punkins that has rotted so
>   They ain't fit ter be eaten!
>
> Poor Major How can advertise
>   "A closin' out sale" on the square.
> He'll go to England, and surprise
>   His rich relations there.
>
> We won't be taxed more than we're worth
>   To pay for water mains
> That's buried in the frozen earth
>   And irrigate our lanes.
>
> On Tuesday how the Dems. will holler
>   When their defeat they learns,
> An' Moody's took 'em by the collar
>   An' gently kicked their Stearns!

"Very good, very good!" cried the doctor, "I didn't think it was in you, Mrs. Bilkins."

"Oh, it were," said our landlady modestly. "It came out kinder by jerks, but it's out, an' I expect it'll have its influence on the 'lection."

"It can't fail to," said the colonel, gravely, "and I'm glad to find you are a good republican."

"Oh, as for that," replied Mrs. Bilkins, "I'm like Clarence Becker, an' looks to see which side my bread is buttered on. An' as I ain't no fool, it's buttered pretty thick for Bob Moody, an' that's a fact. — But what's the matter, colonel?"

"I don't know," replied the veteran, in a voice whose calmness contradicted the uneasy look upon his face, "I simply reached out my leg under the table, and I'm afraid — I've put my foot in something."

Mrs. Bilkins looked startled.

"Dear me!" she said, "what can it be?"

The colonel slowly swung around in his chair and lifted his right leg above the level of the table. At its extremity was a lady's bandbox, and the colonel's foot was completely hidden in its interior.

Our landlady gave one look and a scream and decided to faint — but she changed her mind instantly, and seizing her precious band-box she jerked it from the colonel's boot and burst into a flood of tears.

Now nothing breaks the colonel up so much as a woman's tears, but experience is a dear teacher, and he dared not comfort her. He simply thrust his hands deeply into his trousers pockets and whistled.

The doctor was more gallant; he removed the cover of the wrecked band-box and withdrew the remains of Mrs. Bilkins' last pride and glory — her Easter bonnet!

"I declare!" said Tom sympathetically, "it's too awfully bad."

"But how did it come there?" asked the doctor.

"What is it?" demanded the colonel, begin[n]ing to be frightened.

"What is it, you brute?" sobbed Mrs. Bilkins, in terrible anger, "why it's my Spring bonnet, as I bought of Miss McDonald only the Saturday 'afore Yeaster, an' everybody said as it were the prettiest hat in the whole town, yes, an' the cheapest, too, an' I put jest two week's board inter it an' now the colonel's put his foot inter it an' it's busted wuss nor the Peoples' ticket!" and she sobbed again, and wiped her eyes on the doctor's napkin. And the colonel heaved a deep sea sigh and drew two shining gold p[ie]ces from his pocket and laid them on the table.

Silently the boarders withdrew and left our landlady alone with her sorrow.

But when they were gone she ceased crying and pocketed the gold pieces with a grim smile.

"The Kernel, he'll make more'n that on 'lection day," she said, "an' it's only right to make him divide. But lor' bless the fool! the bonnet ain't hurt much. Miss McDonald said as it would stand no end o' bangin', an' after I've had the feather dressed an' the ribbons pressed a-bit it'll look as good as new. Of course when I put it there I hoped the doctor'd be the one to step in it, 'cause he's so soft-hearted. But the scheme turned out pretty well as it was. A woman," she continued, as she gathered up the bits of butter from the various plates and smoothed it all in shape again in the butter dish, "a woman has no business to keep boarders unless she understands human nature, — an' I jest flatter myself as Mrs. Bilkins does!"

She Lectures the Boarders for Unseemly Conduct and Feeds Them a Green Apple Pie

19 April 1890

In the 15 April city election Republican Robert Moody received 563 votes to Benjamin Stearns's 312. Mimicking his landlady, Baum broke into poetry on 19 April, crowing,

> The mugwumps all before us fell
> And democratic sighs do heave.
> The "People's Ticket" has gone to — well
> All that remains is a "ticket of leave."

That the victory had been "a clean sweep" of the ticket from top to bottom had become apparent by six o'clock on election evening, Baum reported, and by eight the "popular enthusiasm burst all bounds and high carnival reigned supreme. The band came out, a broom brigade was formed and each of the newly-elected officials treated to a serenade, while the happy citizens yelled themselves hoarse with rapture." Mrs. Bilkins's comments suggested that the jubilant Republicans also indulged in one of the vices they had so lately accused their Democratic opponents of wallowing in.

"Well, yes," said our landlady, "we're gettin' settled down to work agin. But I never did see such highfalutin' doin's as you boarders indulged in last Tuesday night. Now that you're sober minded agin, I might as well tell the truth."

"I'm sure, Mrs. Bilkins," exclaimed the doctor, "that I behaved myself with the utmost propriety. I was quiet as a mouse."

"Quieter," said our landlady, with sarcastic emphasis. "When Cholly Wright brought you home in a hack at midnight, with your feet stickin' out of one winder an' a new broom outer the other, you couldn't wiggle. It wasn't till the next mornin' as you told me about the glorious victory, an' how Frank Brown hired you to celebrate for him because Frank Hagerty wouldn't let him celebrate for hisself; an' how you shook han's with Cholly Howard so many times that the las' thing you remembered was Cholly leanin' agin' a telegraph pole and bobbin' his arm up and down like it was a pump handle — although he was the only pusson within two blocks; an' how you had the foresight to buy me a new broom to pay me for pullin' off your boots an' puttin' of you to bed."

"Very true," assented the docter, boldly; but he blushed furiously, and ate a piece of Mrs. Bilkins' corn-starch cake without a grimace.

"Bosh!" exclaimed our landlady: "I ain't no fool, doctor. But I don't complain, because I raked in three new brooms that night. You see while I were a puttin' you to bed I heard a strange noise, so I goes inter the Kernel's room and finds a new broom tucked up in the Kernel's bed. I didn't know what to make of it then, but when I went down into the kitchen I found the Kernel leanin' up behind the kitchen door. 'Who are you?' says I. 'Hush,' says he, 'I'm the new broom, but don't make a noise or else you'll wake the gallant Kernel, as is upstairs abed an' fast asleep!' So I had ter get him to bed. An' just as I were a comin' down stairs I heard a sorter scratchin' on the front door. An' so I opened it and Tom fell inter the hall an' another new broom hit me right over the nose."

"I'm sorry, Mrs. Bilkins," said Tom, "but you must excuse me. It only happens once in a lifetime."

"Very true," replied our landlady, "an' I don't bare no grudge, for it's the fust time I ever knew one o' you to touch the firewater, but it strikes me that it were a queer way to celebrate the 'lection of a law and order administration."

"Oh, that's all right," said Tom, "Charlie Howard — "

"I don't care nothin' 'bout Cholly Howard," interrupted the landlady, severely, "an' if Bob Moody's ever elected agin I'll make you all sign the temperance pledge before 'lection or else I'll close this here boardin' house 'til further notis. You ain't eatin', Kernel — try them turnips."

"No thank you," said the colonel, "I'm too happy to eat."

"Humph!" rejoined Mrs. Bilkins, "I don't see as my grocery bills is any less since 'lection. But I know some folks as ain't happy, although when I met the Majah today he were wearin' a sickly smile on his face an' a grease spot on his vest. 'Grin an' barrett, Majah,' says I. 'I'm a doin' it,' says he. An' he toddled away like an old man with the rheumatiz. I was almost sorry for him, for some folks do say as he's in his second childhood. Green apple pie, doctor?"

"If you please."

"Just see how the times has improved under republican rule. Why, Thompson & Kearney has reduced their tea to twenty cents a pound, there's eleven buildin's goin' to be built right away; the *News* has come out for republican principles, and it's reported as Narregang set up the cigars to a man as he had just sold a dime's worth of ipecac to for forty cents. The Fair man is sellin' three postage stamps fer five cents, the saloons is bein' turned into shoe-shops, an' Taubman has took two drinks o' water. Anything wrong with that pie, doctor?"

"Nothing especial," he replied, meekly, "except that perhaps the under crust is a little burned, and the upper one a little too raw, and you forgot to take the string out of the dried apples you stuffed it with. But it don't matter."

"Some boarders," soliloquized our landlady a half hour later, as she cleared away the dishes, "is too particular for anything. But when women has their rights the men can keep the boardin' houses, an' we'll see then who is the biggest kickers.[17] But it don't matter, as the doctor says, for after all, Moody is elected, an' I b'lieve my poetry had suthin' to do with electin' of him!"

. . . .

Her Experiences in Attempting to Photograph a Baby, and the Severe Mental Strain that Ensued

26 April 1890

> Spring had come to Aberdeen, and more important, it had rained in the county during the week. Everyone was feeling "croptious," to use Mrs. Bilkins's term, as the prospects for planting season began to look good. "The photographers and gasoline stove men and lemonade vendors and house painters are the busy people now-a-days," Baum noted cheerily on 26 April. The young women in town had descended on the local photographer's apartments, the *Aberdeen Daily News* reported on 20 April, and about this time the Baums also took their four-month-old son, Harry Neal Baum, down to J. Q. Miller's studio for his first portrait. The following column may immortalize the experience.[18]

🌾 "Tell you what, gen'lmen," said our landlady, as she leaned over to turn the doctor's coffee and dropped a tea-lea[f] off her front hair into the cup, "I'm just about tuckered out, an' there ain't no more starch in my back-bone than there air in a dish rag."

"Why, when I saw you down town this morning," said Taub,[19] fishing a tack out of the prunes, "I thought you looked remarkably fresh."

"So I might, this mornin'," acknowledged our landlady, sadly, "but that ain't now. You see my niece 'Raldy come to town this mornin' an' brought her baby, because she said the weather were so croptious that she wanted his pictur' took. So she helped me git the breakfast dishes out of the way, an' then we dressed the baby in his best duds an' took him down to the pictur'-taker to be tooked."

"I sympathize with the child," remarked the doctor, sadly, as he eyed the dark lumps in the mashed potatoes.

"Well, you won't," snapped our landlady, "when you've heerd all my story. Well, we got him to the gallery, an' washed his face, an' smoothed his gownd, an' brushed his hair — which is only a little red fizz — an' the fust thing we knew he begun to cry. An' jest then the pictur'-taker he yells 'fetch him along,' an' we fetched him along a bawlin' like a hired girl for the water-man when he's a half a mile away.

" 'Now, then,' says the pictur'-taker, 'stop his yellin'.'

" 'That's werry easy to say,' says I, kind o' riled by all the noise, 'but it ain't so easy ter be did!' Nor was it. A little thing will set a baby a cryin' but a yoke o' oxen won't stop him if he wants ter howl it out. We shooed him, an' cuddled him, an' tossed him in our arms, but he would yell. We couldn't stop him short o' chokin' the brat, an' it weren't wuth while ter do that. An' jest then Taub he comes in ter have his pictur' took 'afore he begins ter git thin on artesian water, an' he says, 'I'll quiet the baby,' says he. So he took him on his knee an' says 'there, there!' to him about fifty times, an' the more he says 'there' the more the little cuss yelled. An' Taub he said he had a engagement an' he went away. An' then Hiram Pratt he comed in wi' a draft, an' the pictur'-taker hed business on a suddent in another room an' Hiram he says 'I know what'll stop his yellin',' says he, so he got down before him an' sung: 'A Grasshopper sat on a sweet pertater bush!'

"An' the kid he just whooped her up fer glory an' Hi forgot the draft an' dropped out.

"An' then Cholly Howard he came in ter be took fer a picter to hang in the council chamber, an' he says 'why don't you stop that brat?'

" 'Stop him yourself,' says I, fer I were nearly crazy with the racket. So Cholly he whistled ter him, an' sing'd ter him, an' chucked him under the chin, an' patted him on the back, but he screeched so much louder that I most hoped he'd bust a blood-vessel an' quit it. An' finally Cholly he wiped the sweat off his face an' says, 'If that were my brat I'd hoss-whip him!' an' 'Raldy she gets mad at that an' shied a nussin'-bottle at his head an' he went away cussin'.

"By that time my nerves was so unstrung I wanted ter yell myself, but there weren't no chance ter be heard while that six-months old baby held the fort.

"Jest then Johnny Waterman comed in with a rose in his butting-hole an' a smile on his face, an' he sat down, an' blushed, an' got up agin, an' smiled an' says to me 'what's wrong?'

" 'That!' says I, pointin' to the baby that was a whoopin' of 'er up wi' his eyes shut an' his mouth wide open.

"An' Waterman he looked at him a minnit, an' then went up an' pulled a pin out from under his arm (that were a stickin' in the poor baby all the time) an' the infant he quit his racket an' looked up an' smiled!

" 'How did it come there?' says I.

" 'I put it there to hold back his dress,' says 'Raldy, 'but oh, sir, I bless ye a thousan' times! You must have lots o' babies yourself for you know jest what ter do!' An' the pore feller blushed like a girl, an' I had ter tell her he weren't even married — not yet.

"But the whole thing broke me up so I had ter take a dose o' the baby's soothin' syrup to quiet me."

"Very sad," remarked the colonel, extracting a morsel of egg shell from his custard pie; and the other boarders looked sympathetic.

"But did you get his picture taken at last?" asked Tom.

"Oh, yes," replied Mrs. Bilkins, "an' he looks jest like a cherub, an' as if he'd never knowd what a pin were, nor ever even learnt how to cry. But the next time I goes with anyone to have a baby's picter tooked, you can put me down fer a born fool, an' no mistake!"

· ·

She Discourses on Many Topics and tells how
Alley deals out the Corn

3 May 1890

In this column Baum commented satirically on all the news of the preceding week. First, his landlady noted that Hulburt's Hippocynagon, an animal show that specialized in dog and horse tricks, was giving parades each day at noon to advertise its evening shows. Mrs. Bilkins then reiterated editor Baum's opinion that Aberdeen was overpaying its school superintendent at a salary of $1,800 when Sioux Falls paid only $1,500 and Huron $1,100.[20] "There are numbers of energetic, capable young men thoroughly competent for the position," Baum remarked, "who would gladly accept [$1,200] and be willing to earn it, too." Next in line for the landlady's attention was the State Land Company, a real estate syndicate that Frank Brown and other Aberdeen businessmen had created to invest in Huron, a town they were booming for permanent capital of South Dakota.

The bulk of the column comprised another commentary on the problems and foibles of Dakota farmers, who were continuing to receive seed and feed under the provisions of the state seed wheat commission. In mid-April, County Commissioner Elias H. Alley had begun dispensing forty bushels of corn for every work team a needy farmer owned. Predictably, townspeople grumbled that farmers who did not really deserve or need feed were receiving it. In support of Alley, the *Aberdeen Daily News* pointed out that the commissioner "knows his business and undoubtedly understands all the circumstances and conditions much better than those who criticise." All the same, some who did not need help would undoubtedly apply, the *News* noted.[21] Taking the cue, Baum let his landlady explore the issue for his readers.

Finally, Mrs. Bilkins noticed that the publisher of the *Aberdeen Saturday Pioneer* had offered a five-dollar prize to the subscriber who sent him the best poem on Spring. The landlady's attempt fit right in with the thirty entries that Baum received, some of which were "the veriest rot imaginable — some won't even rhyme — and such are unworthy even the scrap basket."[22]

"There ain't no use a talkin'," said our landlady, as she faced the boarders and threw out her arms so suddenly that two of her dress buttons popped off with pistolic reports — one going into the soup and the other into the doctor's left eye — "there ain't no use o' talkin' about hard times, for the times ain't hard a bit! Whenever you see a dancin' bear in the streets an' a dog show a paradin' around you can know as times is more flush nor otherwise!"

"But people feel rather poor, nothwithstanding," hazarded the doctor, meekly, as he placed a damp handkerchief over his eye to prevent its swelling.

"They don't neither!" retorted Mrs. Bilkins, fiercely. "People as feel poor don't pay a old codger eighteen hundred dollars a year to sup'intend their schools, as could'ent earn eighteen dollars ahoein' pertaters! Poor people ain't so extravagant as all that!"

"I'm surprised, Mrs. Bilkins," observed the colonel, severely, "to hear you speak in so rabid a manner. You shock me extremely."

"Well, p'raps I were a little hard," responded Mrs. Bilkins, more calmly, "but it just makes me mad. Real estate can't be bought for love or money in Aberdeen, an' our business men has to go to Huron to work up a boom. That shows Aberdeen ain't in the soup — if my butting is!"

"But the farmers at least are poor," said Tom, reflectively.

"Ah, the farmers!" she retorted, "p'raps they do feel ruther light in the pocket. But the farmers has kept us all goin' so fur, an' as soon as they gets another crop they'll keep us goin' agin. The only thing that bothers 'em now is to get feed. Now my cousin Jake he went down to ole man Alley's yesterday to git some o' that free corn that he heerd the spring robins brought back with 'em.[23] An' ole Alley he says, 'I don't know whether you can git any corn or not;' says he, 'we give the corn to them that's done their full duty in trying to farm Dakota dust.'

" 'Well,' says Jake, 'that's me.'

" 'Got any hosses?' says Alley.

" 'Six,' says Jake.

" 'Got any feed?' says Alley.

" 'No,' says Jake, 'I put green goggles on my hosses an' feed 'em shavin's an' they think it's grass, but they ain't gittin' fat on it.'[24]

" 'What 'come o' yer feed?' says Alley.

" 'All gone, an' my money was spent 'afore I got round to buyin' any more.'

" 'How much wheat did you raise?' says Alley, takin' a apple out o' his pocket an' eatin' of it.

" 'Two thousan' bushels,' says Jake.

" 'Any flax?'

" 'Flax didn't do well,' says Jake, 'only got 350 bushel.'

" 'Well,' says Alley, 'you can't have no corn nohow. A man what raises $1,400 wuth o' wheat an' $400.00 wuth o' flax can buy his own feed.'

" 'No he can't,' says Jake, 'when there's so many dependin' on him.'

" 'Got any children?' says Alley, puttin' the core in his pocket to give to the poor children.

" 'No,' says Jake. Then Alley gits mad.

" 'Young feller,' says he, 'you can't work me.'

" 'I ain't tryin' to,' says Jake.

" 'Who's a dependin' on you?'

" 'Well, there's them Hail Insurance agints, an' the Machine men, an' the Elevaitors, an' the Loan agints, an' the Prohibition speakers an' singers an' the preachers, an' lots more. What'll they do if I don't git a crop this spring?'

" 'Oh, pshaw!' says Alley, takin' a chew o' gum, 'what's them fellers got to do with your crop?'

" 'Not much raisin' it,' said Jake, 'but a heap to do wi' the spendin' o' the harvest money. Guess you don't know much about Dakota farmin',' says he, 'but I tell you what, ole man, when you've paid your hail insurance notes — losses or no losses — an' bought a few supplies, an' paid Narre four per cent on what you've borrowed, — it eats a big hole in the harvest, an' then a feller comes along an' says the country's goin' to the devil unless Ralph Brown's circus is kep' goin' and so I subscribes to the circus tent an' temperance songs an' that makes another hole.

" 'Then Miller has to have McCormick's note paid to keep his boss outer the poor house, an' Hoit and Mack an' the rest o' the gang say the wheat's full o' dirt and hes got to be docked, an' there goes more holes. Last year I divided up my crop amongst 'em an' was glad to get away alive — an' feelin' that anyhow I'd done my share to'ards supportin' "Mollie an' the baby" an' the rest o' 'em. Say — be I a goin' to git that corn?'

" 'Why, yes,' says ole Alley, at last, 'I guess as your entitled to it. But be very careful o' them twenty bushels o' corn,' says he, 'for it cost Bach, an' Hoit an' Drake a heap o' trouble to git, an' I don't know but what Mellette wishes it never had been growed.' So after all that chin music Jake gits jest six dollars wuth o' feed.

"I hain't sent no spring poetry to the PIONEER, but when I think o' the poor farmers I feel like sayin'

> All flesh is grass,[25]
> All grass is hay!
> We are here tomorrow
> An' gone today!"

. . . .

She Gives Away the Initiation Ceremonies of the United Workmen And has a Fruitless Search for the Chief of Police

10 May 1890

Among the twenty new candidates admitted to the Ancient Order of United Workmen on Wednesday evening, 7 May 1890, was editor L. Frank Baum. The following Saturday he poked fun at the secret initation rituals that men of the 1890s practiced in fraternal societies such as the United Workmen. Founded in 1868 in Meadville, Pennsylvania, the order's slate of local officers included a Grand Overseer and a Grand Inside Watchman. Like many other orders, the United Workmen borrowed many of their secret activities from the Freemasons, who were also well represented in Aberdeen. Baum spoofed the ceremonies of these groups here, but the geography of his famous fairyland of Oz would later recall the more serious ritualistic imagery of the period.[26] In addition to their secret activities, such organizations served various purposes. The Ancient Order of United Workmen provided life insurance at low cost to its members, a benefit that drew Baum and other South Dakotans of meager means to its ranks. It also contributed money to charitable causes, such as the seed wheat fund.[27] The fact that it limited its membership to men put it in contrast to the Knights of Labor, another workers' organization that was gaining prominence in Aberdeen and South Dakota at this time.

Although the Knights of Labor had started in Philadelphia in 1869 as a secret society for skilled laborers, in 1890 it welcomed workers of both sexes and all occupations and skill levels. Aberdeen hosted the headquarters of the state assembly as well as three local assemblies. The organization had recently started its own newspaper; in fact, one of Baum's employees, Chris M. Sweitzer, left to become its business manager. Politically aggressive, the Dakota Assembly of the Knights of Labor had convinced South Dakota's first legislature to create the Department of Labor and Statistics. Aberdonian Frank Wilder, the Knights' state master workman, became the first labor commissioner, headquartering the department in his hometown. Unlike the Ancient Order of United Workmen, which excluded women, the Knights of Labor supported such causes as woman suffrage, temperance, and child labor laws. It may seem strange that Baum mentioned two seemingly disparate organizations in a single column, but they did share common roots. Both labor unions and fraternal lodges were late nineteenth-century responses to the excesses of industrial capitalism and the rapid changes taking place in American society.[28]

Baum moved the reader's attention from one organization to the other through a fictional search for newly appointed Chief of Police John Jewett, who was unnamed in the column and clearly unknown around Aberdeen. A teamster with the Saint Croix Lumber Company, Jewett belonged to the Knights of Labor, and his appointment as police chief culminated a political deal: Frank Wilder had withdrawn his name from Aberdeen's mayoral election a month earlier and, in return for Wilder's sacrifice, the Republicans had promised the Knights one of the appointed city offices. Robert Moody, the new mayor, now had to pay this debt but had trouble making good on the promise. In the city council meeting of 5 May 1890 the newly elected aldermen objected to the relatively obscure Jewett's nomination as chief of police, giving him the office only "very grudgingly" after young Charles Howard called for a second vote.[29] The council's reluctance had not escaped the notice of Mrs. Bilkins and her fellow Aberdonians.

"There's one thing certain, genl'men," remarked our landlady, as she blew down the spout of the coffee-pot to clear away the grounds, "if you can't manage to get in a little earlier nights this 'ere boardin' house'll git a bad name, an' business will be ruined! Now where was you, Tom?"

"I!" exclaimed that gentleman, taken by surprise and blushing violently, "I was calling on Miss — Miss — on a lady, in fact."

"Then she didn't have a paternal sire," continued Mrs. Bilkins, severely, "or he'd a sent you home 'afore midnight. Now colonel — "

"My dear madam," he interrupted, "I was studying art; — drawing, in fact — "

"Humph!" exclaimed our landlady, "them sort o' artists make a good many chips. I'm onto you all right, colonel, an' I do hope you'll win enough to pay up last month's board."

The colonel was squelched.

"For my part," began the doctor, but Mrs. Bilkins interrupted him contemptuously,

"Oh, you're always out wi' a patient! I know you, too! The worst men in the world to keep an eye on is the doctors, for you never know where to find 'em. But I'm glad o' one thing, an' that is none o' you was in that horrible crowd as joined the United States Workmen last night."

"The what?" asked the colonel.

"The United States Workmen, I said! Oh, I know all about it. They had twenty fellers to be initiated last night, an' everyone o' 'em got more nor he bargained for, I guess. Why the way they abused that poor Fletch is enough to break up the whole order, an' is a disgrace to a civilized community!"

"Did he ride the goat?" asked the colonel with suspicious interest.[30]

"Naw! he didn't ride no goat! You can't foolish me, Kernel, cause I ain't no fool. Miss Smithereses hired gal were there when they brought poor Fletch home, an' in his wild wanderin's he let the whole secret out."

"What did they do to him?"

"Why they put a black-cap over his head an' nearly hung him, an' then they made him walk a barb-wire fence in his stockin' feet, an' then they tossed him up in a blanket an' put him head fust into a water barrel!"

"Good gracious!" exclaimed Tom, in horror, "It's a wonder it didn't kill him."

"So it were. But that wasn't the wust of it. They asked him what he'd like to buy fer the boys, an' Fletch, when he could get his breath, said 'nothin'!' So they got out a big wheel like the wheel o' a water-mill an' it had spikes all over it. An' they took poor Fletchie an' tied him onter the wheel like he were Mazeppy, an' then the Chief Bulldozer says sweetly

" 'What'll you buy, Fletch?'

" 'Nuthin',' says the miserable wictim.

"An' then they took hold o' the crank an' turned the wheel over once, an' the

spikes hurt like blazes, an' when the Chief asked him agin 'what'll you buy?'
Fletch he give in an' whispered

" 'Pop!'

" 'Pop's no go here,' says the torturer, 'turn him over agin!'

"By that time the wictim's eye-balls was layin' over his specks an' he offered
to buy ice cream.

" 'Too cool,' says the torturer, an' they turned him over agin.

"Then Fletch says that if oysters and champagne were any objects he would
be pleased to buy 'em for the crowd, an' so they took him off the wheel, all
bloody an' wounded, an' sent him home in a hack."

"Dreadful!" exclaimed the doctor, but he winked at the colonel nevertheless.

"An' Fletch's friends are wild for vengeance," continued Mrs. Bilkins,
earnestly, "an' the fust thing they started to do was to find the chief o' police
an' have the whole gang arrested. But they couldn't find him anywheres, an'
so I [told] 'em I'd go out and find him myself. So I meets one o' our leadin'
politicians, an' I says

" 'Who's the new chief o' perlice?'

" 'Dunno,' says he, 'it's a man I never heerd of.'

" 'Go-long!' says I.

" 'Go-long yerself,' says he, 'an' find him if ye can.'

" 'I will!' says I, but I didn't know what a job I had on my hands.

"One feller he said as he heard it were Harvey Jewett, but I knew better.
I went into all the stores, but some had fergot his name and some had never
heard it, an' some said as it were a subjec' they didn't care to speak on. An'
there lay poor Fletch all the while, sufferin' an' unavenged!

"Jest then I meets Jack Cavanaugh, an' he says the Chief was in to see him
a minit before to ask what the handcuffs was used for. So I goes out an' meets
another feller who said the chief was lookin' for a number 2 caliber revolver to
carry in his hip pocket, an' so I gave up in despair an' went to Mayor Moody.

" 'What do you want?' says he.

" 'The chief o' perlice,' says I.

" 'Hain't the people got through wantin' the chief o' perlice, yet?' says he.

" 'I hain't,' says I.

" 'Go to the knights o' labor,' says he, 'I'm busy,' an' he turned away an' went
on figgerin' up the cost o' a campaign.

"Someone told me that there were three or four knights o' labor in the town,
but they was hard to find, so I give up the job an' went home, an' if poor Fletchie

is ever goin' to get avenged [on] some one someone else'll have to find the chief o' perlice."

. . . .

She Investigates the Original Package Deal
With Doubtful Results

17 May 1890

The state prohibition law had gone into effect on 1 May, but two weeks later a United States Supreme Court ruling on similar liquor laws in Iowa undermined enforcement in South Dakota. Considering the issue to be the regulation of interstate commerce and therefore under the jurisdiction of Congress, the Supreme Court ruled that "intoxicating liquors of any kind may be carried into any State hereafter and sold, provided that the parcel in which it was originally placed be not broken, and this regardless of State regulations and interdicts," Baum reported on 17 May. The railroads, it seemed, could carry and sell liquor in South Dakota as long as it remained in its "original package," and the state's jurisdiction did not begin until " 'the importer has so acted upon it that it becomes incorporated and mixed up with the mass of property' in the State." Aberdeen residents were confused about the nature of original packages, or "originals," and the newly elected city councilmen and State's Attorney Edward T. Taubman publicly worried over the legality of such things once they had arrived in town.

In other news, the city council was entertaining a proposal from the Northwestern National Bank to "take city warrants drawn on all active funds for the running and contingent expenses of the city at their face value to the amount of $3,000" for the first year in return for the city deposits. This proposition "to place city warrants at par," the *Aberdeen Daily News* reported on 9 May 1890, came "upon the heels of the recent depreciation under democratic misrule."

🌿 "I'd like to know," declared our landlady, as she set the beefsteak on the table and sharpened the carving knife on a scythe-stone, "which o' you boarders hes been tryin' to git this establishment in trouble?"

The boarders cast a unanimous look of astonishment and righteous indignation at Mrs. Bilkins, and said nothing.

" 'Tain't no use, genl'men," she continued, shaking her head 'til her hair settled carelessly over her left ear, "I've got the matter in black an' white, an' I'll have it out o' yer if it comes as hard as a wisdom tooth in the forceps o' a green dentist. Listen to this," and she unfolded a piece of paper majestically, while the boarders glanced uneasily at one another, and Tom got white, and the Colonel red, and the Doctor salmon-color. Mrs. Bilkins read out, in her best equal-rights voice, the following:

"'My dearest sister,' — that's the way he allus calls us — 'I regret to state as it hes comed to my knowledge that one o' your boarders hes been receivin' of a 'riginal packidge. The laws o' this here State must be upheld at any sacrifice, an' I advise you to inwestigate the matter to oncet. — Elder Burdock.'"

For a moment there was silence.

"Why do you call him that?" demanded the Doctor, feebly.

"Elder? Oh, I s'pose because he's older'n you'd think he was to hear him talk. Now, then, what have you got to say for yourselves?"

"Nothing!" protested the boarders, with one voice.

"To tell you the truth," continued our landlady, in a slightly mollified voice, "I didn't know when I got this 'ere dockyment what a 'riginal package was. But where ignorance is bliss it's better to find out, an' so I goes on a inwestigatin' tower. The first man I see was George Jinkens. He's my lawyer, because he never sends up a bill. 'Georgie,' says I, kinder smilin', 'what's a 'riginal packidge?'

"'Ma'am,' says he, throwin' aside a paper where he was figerin' on his school tax with a eighteen hundred dollar Supt. to pay, 'ma'am, when I were a boy, it were a prize packidge, what cost a nickle 'afore you could bust it an' take a brass ring outen its insides, with pink candy stuck all over it. No thanks — the infermashun is free!'

"But it's jest as well to be sure, so I went to my seconk best lawyer — that's Taub.

"'What's a 'riginal packidge?' says I.

"'A 'riginal packidge,' says he, 'is a necessity in South Dakota.' That warn't no answer at all, but knowin' he charged high fer sich legal opinions, I went over to Frank Brown's and asked him.

"'A 'riginal packidge,' says the great man, lookin' me square in the eye, 'is a invention of the devil!'

"That unsettled me, so I tackled Ira Barnes. He was eatin' pop-corn outen a bag an' he says,

"'I'm kinder outer politics, Mrs. Bilkins,' says he, 'an' don't like to be tackled on sich subjec's. But I'll give ye a parable. This here bag were a 'riginal packidge a minit ago, but now,' says he, as he blew it up and busted it, 'it's a wuss inwestment than city warrants at par.'

"August Witte kinder smiled when I put the question to him.

"'Mrs. Bilkins,' says he, 'you yourself are the most 'riginal packidge what I knows of!'

"That made me mad, an' I give him a cast-iron look of virtuous indignation an' lit out.

"As I walked down the street musin' on the fact that I seemed to know as much as anybody else did, the Rev. McBride come along an' overtook me.

"'Parson,' says I, brightenin' up, 'what's a 'riginal packidge, anyhow?'

"He looked up an' down the street, an' then drew me inter a doorway an' pulled a queer little wooden case from his pocket.

"'Mrs. Bilkins,' says he, wi' tears in his voice — at least it seemed as if his mouth was waterin' — 'some idjut has insulted me by sendin' me this little 'riginal packidge by mail! — it don't hold but two ounces — but o' course that's too much for a man as ain't thirsty. But if that's the size o' the 'riginal packidge deal, you can put me on the side o' prohibition.'

"'Is it licker?' says I, reachin' out my hand in holy horror.

"'Don't touch it,' says he, puttin' of it in his pocket, an' stuffin' a handkercher over it; 'yes, it's licker, an' only fit for folks as ain't well. I'm goin' to keep it fer Doc. Diefendorf when he gets under the weather. If you put quinine in it, it ain't so very bad.'

"So I comed home to dinner, an' if it's true as any o' you boarders hes got a 'riginal packidge in yer possession, I want ter know it."

"Not I," said the Colonel, stoutly.

"Nor I."

"Nor I," repeated the others.

"Well, I'm glad to hear it," replied the landlady, looking wistfully out of the window, "for I should have considered it my duty to confisticate 'em an' keep 'em for poor Doc. Diefendorf. — But I see a copy o' the Reprint blowin' about in my back yard, an' I must go an' take it away, for I see by the papers that Street Comiss'ner Lewis has ordered the citizens to remove all rubbish from their premises!"

. . . .

She Raises the Price of Board, but Lowers it Again Through Stern Necessity

24 May 1890

Throughout the month but especially from 17 through 24 May, rain, snow, and hailstorms gave promise that drought conditions had lifted. On 23 May, a tornado blew the roofs off buildings, but the next day editor Baum penned a long poem in praise of the weather, "In Hoc Signo Vinces!" It contained this optimistic passage:

> Oh, the wet, the elegant wet!
> Continue to arrive, my pet.
> All of our troubles we'll now forget,
> Over the crop we'll cease to fret.
> Who cares now if we are in debt?
> We'll get out again in the fall, you bet!

Such enthusiasm was not shared by all.

"Board is riz," said our landlady, decisively, as she slammed the plate of muffins on the table with such force that the colonel's hand made a nervous dive toward his hip pocket before he recovered himself.

"It seems to me," remarked the doctor, in a mild tone, "that it has fallen."

"May I ask," demanded Tom, forget[t]ing in his agitation to butter his gingerbread, "may I ask why you announce that board has risen?"

"For oblivious reasons," returned Mrs. Bilkins, with dignity. "Ye see this rain has altered the complecshun o' affairs in Dakota, an' sot trade on its proper level. I stayed in the house all day Tuesday, while the rain poured down, an' got as grumpy as a councilman who thinks o' suthin' to say jest after the motion has passed; an' so when the sun come out Wednesday I thought I'd take a trip down town an' see how folks felt. Well, the fust man I see, I says

" 'Fine rain we had.'

" 'Yaw,' says he, 'but not near enough.'

" 'P'raps that's so,' thinks I to myself, an' jest then I met another feller.

" 'Elegant rain we had,' says I.

" 'Good enough,' says he, 'what there were of it. Only wet half a inch down!'

" 'No!' says I.

" 'Yes!' says he.

"Well, I felt a little staggered. Jest then I met a friend o' mine as is a farmer.

" 'How's crops?' says I.

" 'Pritty fair,' says he, 'if it were'nt so dry. This drouth is killin' us!'

" 'But it rained all day yesterday, like blazes,' says I, gittin' a little riled.

" 'Yes, so it did,' says he, 'but it'll take a week o' sich rains to start the crop any.'

" 'Look here,' says I, 'I may look like a fool, but looks is deceivin'. So you jest tell me what you're a drivin' at, or else don't never come to me for no more cold vittles.'

" 'Well,' says he, lookin' around to see as nobody heerd, 'the facts is just these. Ye see, we've been growlin' about the dry so long that this here rain were a kind of shock to us, an' did'nt leave us nothin' to growl about. An' if we was fools enough to yell hurray! — the ground is wet! — the crops is growin'! — the country's saved! — an' all that rubbish, the people as we've been owin' so long would be arter us wi' sharp sticks to pay up. The only salvation fer a man as is in debt is to yell "hard times" no matter what happens. They say as we're croakers, but as long as we can keep 'em skeert, the better it'll be fer us. See?'

"Well, as I ain't blind, I told him I did, an' I walked on coagulating on the frailties o' human natur'. An' when I met any one I'd say

" 'Nice rain, eh?'

"An' if he said it din'nt amount to much, or anything of that kind, I knew as he were in debt, an' respected his lilachelishness.

"But when I went into the stores to trade there was a different story to hear.

" 'Beautiful rain!' says the groceryman, rubbin' his hands. 'Want some o' them nice taters? Only sixty cents a bushel.'

" 'But they was fifty cents Monday,' says I.

" 'But it's rained,' says he, 'an' if I only had a heart like a grindstone I'd charge a dollar. But my greatest failin' is bein' soft-hearted!'

"I thanked him fer bein' so easy an' went inter a dry-goods store to buy a new apron.

" 'Some o' that six cent caliker,' says I.

" 'Certainly,' says he, 'but it's eight cents now.'

" 'Why?' says I.

" ''Cause it's rained. Now some men,' says he, 'as has cast-iron bowels o' compashun, would a charged ten, but I ain't built that way.'

"I offered him six cents and he took me up.

"It were just so in the shoe store. They wanted a dollar fer a pair o' rubbers, but o' course they took a quarter when I got mad. This gittin' mad I find saves me lots o' money.

"Well, the price o' beef is goin' up too, an' now there's a prospect fer crops it's safe to bet as flour'll be on the rise — 'specially when it's in the sponge — an' so I've jest made up my mind to raise the price o' board in this here tavern a dollar a week all around, an' you can pay it er skip — jest as you like!" And Mrs. Bilkins went into the kitchen and slammed the door.

The three boarders eyed each other aghast.

Then the doctor jumped up and followed our landlady into the kitchen.

"Mrs. Bilkins," he began, in a choked voice, "I feel that I can't part with you, and yet I'm barely able to pay the old price. It's all right to raise on the others, but I'm sure you'll let me stay at the old figure. Here's a week in advance."

"All right, doc," replied our landlady, tying the money into a corner of her apron, "you can stay, but the others'll have to put up."

Now the doctor had scarcely gone when Tom stuck his head in, and seeing her alone, advanced confidently to her side.

"My dear Mrs. Bilkins," said he, "you see I am fixed rather differently than the others, and can't afford to pay more. But here is last week's board and a dollar on this week's. Of course if I could afford to pay as much as they can, I'd do it with pleasure, but I can't. Is it all right?"

"It's all right," responded our landlady, tying the money into another corner of her apron, with a sigh, "but don't say anything to the rest."

"Of course not."

A half hour later Mrs. Bilkins found the colonel finishing his cigar on the front stoop.

"I am very sorry to say," he remarked, in a voice shaken with emotion, "that I shall have to leave you. My finances won't permit any high-priced luxuries such as a rise in board. I did think that you and I were too old friends to be parted by a dollar a week, but it seems I was mistaken. By the way, here's a couple of dollars on my account."

"Kernel," said Mrs. Bilkins with a huskiness in her voice, "I'm sorry as I hurt yer feelin's. If I'd a thunk you'd a took it this way I wouldn't have said nothin'. But ye see a woman as talks as much as I do can't help offendin' somebody. Like Marthy's Mary Ann, I never opens my mouth but what I puts my foot in it. But I mean well, so nobody must mind what I say! You just stay along at the old price, but don't let the others know as I've relented."

"I won't," said the colonel, brightening, "but stay — I'd forgotten that I shall need a little change this afternoon. Could you lend me a dollar?"

"Cert'nly," replied our landlady, briskly, as she handed over the shiner, and then she watched his stately figure go down the street and whispered

"That 'air dodge about a rise worked fust rate. It ain't no use keepin' boarders unless you understan' how to make 'em shell out. Of course I didn't git much outer the colonel, but I've got 'em all skeert, an' they'll be more prompt in the future. That rain were good fer the crops, but it were'nt so bad fer landladies, neither!"

. . . .

She Manufactures Hash and Gives the Boarders a few Pointers on the Aberdeen Guards

31 May 1890

In mid-April twelve "daughters of old soldiers" formed themselves into the Aberdeen Guards as an auxiliary of the Grand Army of the Republic. The young women announced that they would "endeavor to keep alive the fires of patriotism and hold in steadfast remembrance the defenders of the country in 1861–5."[31] For six weeks the women practiced in secrecy for their first performance on 28 May. Dressed in red skirts, blue waists with gold braid trim, and red forage hats, they drilled with lances topped with red flags. Frances ("Fannie") Hauser, the daughter of Captain John H. Hauser, acted as troop captain. "Much curiosity has been expended as to how well a body of young ladies can be taught to drill," Baum confided three days later, "but even their most confident friends were agreeably surprised at the precision of their manovuers [*sic*], the accuracy of their movements and their erect and soldier-like bearing." Concluding that the "idea of a female band of Lancers was unique and happy," the editor predicted that "we shall derive much pleasure from the various exhibitions they promise us." In fact, Baum found the spectacle of women soldiers so curious and delightful that female armies appeared in his writing throughout his career, starting with this 31 May column. The best-known later examples appear in *The Marvelous Land of Oz* (1904), which features both General Jinjur's Army of Revolt and the Army of Glinda the Good. Although the uniforms and weaponry of Glinda's army more closely recall those of the Aberdeen Guards, General Jinjur and her jaunty and irreverent army of chattering girls most nearly resemble Baum's caricature of Captain Fannie Hauser and the female lancers of Aberdeen.[32]

"You men folks," said our landlady, as she returned to the chopping-bowl after scaring two strange dogs away from the water-pail, "must feel like pritty small pertaters."

"Why?" queried the colonel, who was waiting, with the others, for the advent of the matutinal meal.

"Oh," replied Mrs. Bilkins, carelessly throwing the end of a beefsteak, a piece of bologna, a bit of pork-chop, and a small chunk of fried liver into her bowl, and w[ie]lding the chopper vigorously between each word of her sentences, "them Aberdeen Guards kinder knocks the spots off'n anything you men folks kin do. Now, the time was when the Amazons was celebrated throughout the world as the fiercest lot o' sodjers to tackle there was, an' the men folks was skeert to go near 'em, an' them 'air Aberdeen Guards is built on the same promisin' lines. I tell you, nobody need be 'feered fer the country's safety while them Aberdeen gals is aroun' to see things slide like they orter."

"I didn't attend their exhibition the other night," said Tom, looking hungrily at the chopping-bowl.

"Well, yer missed a great sight. I were there, an' I tell ye what, it was inspirin' an' no mistake. When the curtain rolled up an' a sharp voice yelled 'For'd mush!' there comed a sudden silence. The little patterin' noise to be heered was the enemies o' their country shakin' in their boots, an' the gurglin' sound what broke the stillness were the hearts o' the patriots leapin' inter their throats. Well, on comed the fierce an' furious warriors, their lances glitterin' an' their gum tucked temporarily under their tongues. Not one o' them thunk anything about their back hair, not one paid any attention to the fit o' the coattails on the sodjer in front o' 'em! Every one was thinkin' of their country's enemies an' how they'd like to scratch their eyes out. The men stopped figgerin' on how to bulldoze the assessor and yelled till they was red in the face. The women took out their sour-drops from their mouths and screamed hurray! The old veterans looked ashamed o' theirselves and kinder sorry as they had come, an' the kids was too tuk aback to even yell 'rats!' Cap. Hauser — now I don't mean the old 'un, but the young 'un, who could show her dad some tricks in sodjerin', an' don't you fergit it! — put the G[ua]rds through their paces with business-like celery. They marched by ones an' twos, an' fours an' eights, an' they would a marched by sixteens, only there warn't enough of 'em to do it. The Cap. she watched 'em like a tiger, an' when one o' 'em allowed their gum to roll over her tongue the ossifer would cry 'I's right!' which meant as she was correct in her bet that they couldn't all keep the tooty-frooty quiet till the parade was over. An' then they'd blush an' look at the gal on the end as though they all suspected her, till the Cap skeert 'em out o' it by yellin' 'Front!' ter intimate as she'd call the bell-boy in a twinklin' if they didn't let that end gal alone. I guess they hates bell-boys by the way they minded her."

"But is this Aberdeen Guard only for show?" enquired the doctor.

"Not much!" responded our landlady, as she rolled the hash into little wads between her hands and dropped them into the frying pan. "They's organized so that the standin' army can be discharged. This is gen'ally understood. One man enquired if they had any navy, thinkin' that model essablishment might be abolished too, but the cap'n shook her head an' after a minit's thought replied that they all chewed gum an' left the navy to the men folks. This organization hain't fer show — it's fer business. O' course they was peaceable enough Wen'sday night, but each one has got a spear of Gossamer steel, with a flag near the end o' it. In a fight with their country's enemies they'll just run this spear through the foe's insides, wave the flag when it comes through, and let the lifeless body slide off'n the handle. There's a automatic arrangement in the handle that cuts a notch every time a body slides off, to show how many heart's blood has been took, and the gal as has the fewest notches in her lance handle after a battle has got to set up the ice cream fer the whole lot. Then there's a piece o' flint on the handle o' the lance, besides, and they can point their spears at the foe, an' when the flash o' their eyes runs down the handle it strikts a streak o' lightnin' from the flint an' the steel spear-point, as is guaranteed either to kill or cure a traitor to their country. The one who uses up her ammunition fust is entitled to a box o' caramels. They're all single, these Guards, and is likely to stay so till they gets married. They're all kinder pritty to[o]. I heard that one o' them has a beard, but I didn't see nothin' but smooth faces. They're pritty spry, and walked as if the[y] hadn't had no kitchen work to do for a week. You can bet one thing, and that is that these gals will make their mark 'afore you hears the last of 'em, even if they has to do it with their lead-pencils.

"But breakfast's ready, genl'men, so be lively. 'Tain't nothin' but hash, to be sure, but you ain't likely to git no fish bones in yer throat, an' that's one comfort!"

. . . .

She Tackles Religion and Gives Her Ideas of the Sunday Enforcement Law

7 June 1890

Baum announced on 7 June that the American Sabbath Union was to hold its state convention in Mitchell, South Dakota, on 24 and 25 June and outlined the speaking dates of national organizer Wilbur F. Crafts. The object of the convention was promotion of better Sabbath observance. Addressing an Aberdeen audience on 26 June, Crafts would stress "the necessity of better legislation to secure Sunday rest for laborers." Baum reported two days later that the lecturer "would like all government business, such as mail service, etc., discontinued on Sunday, which would prove a serious obstruction to many business interests." While Crafts hoped thereby to emancipate mechanics and laborers from work one day a week, Baum suggested that the movement's effort to unify church and state made the measure "wholly unsafe." Current laws were already adequate, he wrote, for "there is no manufacturing or industrial labor actually required in any part of the United States where the men are unwilling to perform it." The landlady, however, had her own interpretation of Sabbath legislation.

"I see by the papers," said our landlady, as she took a speck out of the milk-pitcher with her thumb, "that the church folks is to have a conwention to obleege folks to observe the Sabbath."

"So I see," replied the colonel, turning his beefsteak over to find a vulnerable point of attack.

"Well," she continued, "I've observed the Sabbath ever since I've been in this 'ere town, an' what I've observed ain't any credit to it. I hope they'll pass a law as'll make every man go to church or to jail, that's what I hope!"

"My dear Mrs. Bilkins," retorted Tom, "this is a free country, and I'd like to see any pack of religious fanatics oblige me to attend church when I don't want to go!"

Mrs. Bilkins put on her gold-rimmed "specs" and stared long and indignantly at the audacious speaker.

"I see how it is," she remarked, at length, "you want to go down to the post-office every Sunday mornin', with the other heathen men-folks, an' open an' read your mail, an' loaf in the drugstores, an' smoke bad cigars an' talk politics! As if that couldn't be done on week days! I'm ashamed o' you, young man!"

"I don't suppose," broke in the doctor, reflectively, "that there's anything wrong in what you have mentioned. And as far as this convention is concerned, they will find it difficult to restrict the personal liberty of people who are not religiously inclined."

"Don't you fool yourself," snapped our landlady, beginning to get angry. "You fellers can buck agin' politics all you wont to, but you'll find it harder to buck agin' religion. There was a feller in our town down east as didn't want the church bells to ring on Sunday mornin' cause it waked him up outer his beauty sleep; an' so he complained agin' 'em as a nuisance, an' the other heathen men in the town backed him up, an' made the a'thorities pass a law as no church bells should be ringed. Well, them church people, as had been as meek and quiet as Moses so long as they could jingle the bells and try to down the noise o' the rival churches, these same folks became roarin' lions o' indignation. They went to that 'ere complainer's house an' fetched him away, an' carried him up inter the church tower, an' tied the bell-rope around his neck.

" 'Now,' says they, 'what have you got to say?'

" 'Jest this,' says he, 'your a set o' rabid fanatics, an' your religion ain't skin deep.'

" 'Then,' says they, 'as we can't ring the church bells, we'll ring your neck. Pull him up, sexton!'

" 'Hol' up,' yells the wictim, 'I ain't werry pertic'lar about them bells. You can ring 'em for all I care. It's better to be kep' awake Sunday mornin' than be killed entirely.'

"So they let him off, an' the church bells in that town hes been ringin' ever sence."

"But these people in South Dakota are not content to ring their bells," said the colonel, "they want to oblige us to attend church whether we want to or not."

"Well, why shouldn't they?" she replied, "it don't hurt none to go to church, an' it's good discipline. It makes us appreciate our blessin's a good deal harder. A pusson as never goes to church can't realize the fun there is in stayin' away, an' somebody's got to support these ministers what is gittin' thicker an' thicker every day, or else they'll be obleeged to work fer a livin', an' religion will be at a standstill. An' that ain't all this conwention orter do. They orter obleege the sexton ter search every woman's pocket fer gum an' candy, and to arrest every man what puts buttons in the conterbushun box.33 Them is needed reforms. I tell you, people has lost all respect fer religion, now'days, an' if they won't be pius o' their own accord, it must be druv inter 'em by the iron hammer o' the Law. A close Sunday observance would mean to you boarders a clean shirt ev'ry Sabbath mornin', a sermon as 'ud teach you that life [is] not an empty dream, but is full o' ups an' downs — more downs nor ups — cold pork an' beans fer dinner, Sunday-school, an' prayer meetin' in the arternoon, more serious thoughts an' achin' backs in the evenin', an' a good night's rest. No politics, no cigars, no turkey dinner, no flirtin' or visitin' with pritty gals, no rest. An' then, if you didn't feel on Monday mornin' that this 'ere is a glorious existence six days in the week, the law could be repealed; but I expect, arter you'd tried it awhile, you'd think as Shakespeare did, or else it were Ella Wheeler Wilcox or Ed. Lowe or Billy Carleton — I don't know which an' I don't care — but this is what he thunk, an' I agree wi' him —

'To appreciate heaven well
It's well fer a man ter hev
Jest fifteen minits o' hell.' "

. . . .

She Prepares a Treat for the Boarders Which Leads to a Strange Comedy of Errors

21 June 1890

Local Finnish immigrant Isaac Hirvaskari, better known as Ike the Finn, had been predicting rain with startling success since the middle of May, and on the seventeenth of June a forecast "soaker" during the night ensured his popularity as a weather prophet. In the midst of this continuing moisture, both editor Baum and landlady Bilkins began to promote South Dakota with a little more enthusiasm. Although a few people still worried whether the moisture had come soon enough, Baum remarked on 7 June that such people "never will be satisfied until they get to heaven." Life in Dakota was good, Baum claimed, with only the opportunity to hear a good concert of classical music missing.[34] Mrs. Bilkins's boarders, in contrast, mourned the lost opportunity to buy beer in the local saloons. Ever since the Supreme Court ruling on interstate commerce, however, original packages had become readily available, and rumors abounded that even beer could be found for a price.[35] As everyone suspected, Mrs. Bilkins had her own liquor supply.

"Yes," said our landlady, as she picked a fly out of the cream jug and fed it to the cat, "this is a great country an' no mistake. There ain't nothin' on earth as we don't have."

"Except beer," quoth the colonel, sotto voce.

"Yes, an' religion!" replied Mrs. Bilkins, catching the remark, "but most things you can count on findin' right here in Dakota. For instance, what do you think is on that dish?"

"I should judge," replied the doctor, as he eyed the dish critically, "that they were fried door-knobs."

"No," said Tom, "they look more like fricasseed over-coat buttons."

"Or broiled butter plates," hazarded the colonel.

"All wrong, gen'lmen," declared our landlady, much gratified, "them's

mushrooms, an' growd in our own door yard! I don't blame you for not knowin'
'em, for they're a skeerce luxury in these here settlements."

"I suppose the rain brought them up," remarked the colonel, taking one
upon his plate.

"Yes, Ike Fin he brung the rain, an' the rain brung the mushrooms. But that
ain't all the rain did. I tell ye, it were a corker an' no mistake. An' the mos'
dredful part of it were its comin' in the night. It seemed a pity to have poor
Harvey Jewett pumpin' water out o' his cellar all night, an' stoppin' every two
minutes to yell 'dam that Fin!' instead of tryin' to dam the water. An' the boys
say the water run inter Al. Ward's milk an' filled the cellar o'the National Bank
so full that it a'most watered the stock. An' Cap. Hauser he'd forgot ter git
his cow in, so he wadded out in the pasture with his pants rolled up ter the
knees, an' the rain comin' down as thick as the subscription papers is on the
merchants; an' Cap. he got hold o' the stake pin an' says he, 'so boss!' an' tried
to pull it up, an' jest then his foot slipped an' he took a bath for the fust time
in years in water that didn't cost a quarter a barrel. But some neighbors dug
the mud out o' his eyes and ears an' saved him the expense o' a funeral. An'
the next mornin' Miss Felch's hired gal she made a raft out o' a barn door an'
poled out to the wood pile to get enough wood to light the fire. Them are tall
yarns fer a drouth struck country, but they're kerrect, an' you can bet on it."[36]

"The farmers must be glad of the rain," remarked Tom, with his mouth full
of mushrooms.

"Yes, but they still croak. The latest story is that the wheat all caught cold
because o' the damp weather, an' has sore throats; an' they say Higginbottom
bought a cord o' pills from Doc. Fowler to try an' cure 'em. But o' course ——
Hey! What's wrong, colonel?"

The boarders looked at the veteran and sprang to their feet in terror. His
eyes rolled upward, his mouth was wide open, his tongue hung out, and his
hands clutched wildly at the air before him!

"Oh Lor!" screamed our landlady, "my poor dear kernul! — what is it?"

The sufferer made an effort and gasped,

"I'm poisoned!"

"Pizened!" shr[ie]ked Mrs. Bilkins, "how?"

The colonel pointed to the mushroom dish.

"Those," said he, "are toadstools!" and relapsed again into contortions.

Tom and the doctor grew visibly pale, while Mrs. Bilkins burst into tears
and cried

"Oh, what shall we do?"

"Brandy!" gasped the colonel.

Our landlady flew out of the room and presently rushed in with a large black bottle which the colonel clutched fiercely.

Tom caught a wink from the corner of the veteran's left eye and immediately came down with convulsions. The doctor looked puzzled for a moment, but as the brandy disappeared between the two sufferers like bargains at a quarter-off sale he too showed symptoms of poisoning and was only able to seize the antidote in time to consume the last drop.

"Tell you what," remarked the colonel, as the boarders walked down the street shortly afterward quietly puffing their cigars, "I've long suspected that Mrs. Bilkins kept a bottle for emergencies, and I thought I'd see if I couldn't get her to treat. Those were mushrooms all right, but it was a clever scheme."

"It was," agreed Tom.

"And it worked beautifully," said the doctor.

At that moment Mrs. Bilkins was eyeing ruefully her empty bottle.

"O' course," she soliloquized, "I knew mighty well that them was toad-stools, but I didn't think they'd poison nobody, an' I wanted to make 'em believe as this was a great country. But there's no fool like a old fool, and I've lost a pint o' Jim Ringrose's pride. No — " she continued, as she picked up the bottle, "I hain't neither! I was so flustered that I guv 'em the vinegar bitters! But it cured 'em jest the same, an' if I don't write a recommend for that 'air medicine, my name ain't Maria Bilkins!"[37]

. . . .

She Announces Her Birthday and Makes an Even Exchange With the Boarders

28 June 1890

Continuing with his theme that Aberdeen offered everything to the prospective settler, Baum reported on 28 June: "The great v[a]riety of fruits and vegetables in Aberdeen would astonish some of the cities of the effete east, which are considerably behind us in the matter of such luxuries. Today our stores are selling watermelons, cherries, strawberries, raspberries, pears, peaches, apples, apricots, grapes, bananas, oranges, . . . and everything usually procurable in the east between the months of June and October." This litany of edibles must have sounded like a good birthday supper to Baum, who used it as an opportunity to explore the age and character of his landlady.

"Today," murmured our landlady, as she rolled out the dough for the fried cakes and cut them out with a teacup and made a little hole in the middle with her brass thimble to save the dough; "today is the university o' my birth."

"What's that?" asked the doctor, looking up dreamily from his paper.

"She means her birthday," explained Tom, who was tying the cat by the tail to the tea-kettle.

"Oh," remarked the colonel, looking uneasy.

"I well remember," continued Mrs. Bilkins, wiping her eye absent-mindedly with the back of her hand, and leaving a white ring of flour around it, "my birthday last year. You all made me such pritty presents!"

Tom and the doctor exchanged glances of alarm and the colonel rattled a few loose coins in his pocket and sighed as he replied,

"Yes, and you gave us a delicious supper in return."

"So I did," replied our landlady, blushing with pleasure and the heat of the cook stove. "I remember it well. There were strawberry short-cake an' a watermillion an' a cherry pie an' lots o' other delicates. Now, gen'lmen, how old do you s'pose I am today?"

"About sixty," replied Tom, with a grin.

"Wrong!" replied Mrs. Bilkins, with a frown, and she threw the dough so viciously into the hot lard that it spattered onto the cat.

That usually mild creature gave an unfeline howl of anguish and sprang from the table, while the empty teakettle being attached to her extremity flew into Mrs. Bilkins' face, the bottom blacking her other eye, while our landlady started back with a scream of dismay and fell into Tom's lap, whence they rolled upon the floor together.

As the cat made for the door she passed under the chair the doctor had tilted back against the wall, and the teakettle striking the legs with full force brought the learned physician down on top of the others, where he became entangled in Mrs. Bilkins' hoops and yelled "fire!" at the top of his voice.

The colonel laid down his paper and came to the rescue. He took the doctor's hands out [of] our landlady's wig and Tom's head out of the flour barrel and stood each upon his feet, while Mrs. Bilkins picked her upper teeth out of the oven and put herself generally to rights.

"This," said the colonel, sternly, to the originator of all the trouble, "comes from playing boyish tricks with cats."

"And also," added Mrs. Bilkins, "from slandering a woman's age!"

"Quite true," replied the culprit, "I knew she was only fifty."

"Fifty!" replied the doctor, scornfully, "she isn't forty yet!"

Our landlady smiled through all her troubles.

"Gentlemen," said the colonel, "I happen to know that you are doing Mrs. Bilkins an injustice. I seldom fail to guess one's age correctly, and I put down her age at just thirty-four."

Our landlady actually beamed upon him.

"You shall have that short-cake, colonel," she whispered, "if berries are 20cts a quart!"

The veteran walked away with a grim smile.

"I have saved a dollar on her present by that speech," he reflected.

"A little while ago," said our landlady to the others, as she again kneaded the dough industriously, "we was talkin' of presents."

"Yes, I remember," replied the doctor, ruefully.

"We took the hint," declared Tom.

"What hint?" said Mrs. Bilkins, innocently, "I was only goin' to say as I must send Doc. Fowler a present, for I hear he's goin' to be married."

"Nonsense!" replied Tom, "he's only going to stand up with the groom."

"Oh, is that all? Well, I guess I'll give him the present, anyway, for it's probably the nearest he'll ever come to bein' married hisself. An' it ain't right for us to forget our friends, for it's these little offerin's that make us realize that it's better to live than to be buried by a eight dollar undertaker."

"Mrs. Bilkins," said the doctor, admiringly, as he lit his cigar and started for town, "you'd make a good enough orator to edit a daily paper. Good-bye — I won't forget you are thirty-two today."

"Perhaps," ruminated our landlady, as left to herself she picked her favorite piece of gum from where it was stuck on the under side of the cake basket, "I might ha' give it to 'em a little too hard. It ain't that I wanted the presents so much, for I'll give 'em a big supper to make up for it; but when a lady gits to be my age a birthday is a important event, an' I don't mean to be tr[e]ated with disrespec' by my own boarders — that ain't my style!"

. . . .

She Celebrates the Fourth and Relates

Her Varied Experiences

5 July 1890

"The wear and tear of a Fourth of July celebration would kill off four-fifths of our population if it lasted a week instead of a day," editor Baum asserted the day after Aberdeen's Independence Day extravaganza. Preparations had gone on for two weeks, with main-street businessmen contributing time and money to multiple committees on parades, speeches, races, and ballgames scheduled for the Glorious Fourth. Baum, who served on the "wagons of character representations" and baby show committees, acted as a judge for both events and as an aide for the races and games, some of which carried $300 and $400 purses. The day itself opened at sunrise with the firing of anvils (setting off gunpowder on them by lighting it) and closed well after dark with firework displays. The "Band of Imported Calithumpians," a group of local men and boys who impersonated other townspeople, proved to be one of the most popular attractions, while two brass bands, one supporting Huron for state capital and the other Pierre, and a large group of Sisseton Dakota Indians added music and native dancing. Attending these many events were five to six thousand people who rode in from the country and surrounding communities on excursion trains.[38]

Like other frontier towns, Aberdeen hoped such festivities would signal its coming of age as a cultural center. Essential to this image was the group of American Indians who had been invited to participate. Baum's sister-in-law Helen Leslie Gage described the scene for her hometown New York state newspaper, the *Syracuse Standard*. "Our Indian is much more of a curiosity on the streets than he would be in Syracuse," she asserted, even though only "one hundred miles west of here is the [Great] Sioux reservation of 25,000 Indians" and "a few miles east" are the Sissetons and the Wahpetons. Gage and other town boosters wished to assure would-be immigrants that Aberdeen had matured to such an extent that hostilities from the Sioux (Dakota/Lakota/Nakota peoples), who had annihilated Custer's cavalry only fourteen years earlier, were no longer a serious threat or, in fact, even a moment's concern. The invited Sissetons came into town, set up their tents, drew their promised rations, and began to advertise their show, which would be held in Baum's own office building, the Excelsior Block, at eight o'clock in the evening. "It was," Gage reported to the *Standard*, "a barbaric scene, and possibly would have been wierd [*sic*] and at times solemn in their native forest or on the wild, unsettled prairie, dressed in their ancient tribal costumes; but in this plastered hall, dimly lighted by two kerosene lamps, . . . it was somewhat ludicrous; and yet . . . impressive as the relic of customs fast giving away to the advance of the pale face, and which in a few years will be but a tradition."39

While Aberdonians thus congratulated themselves on their own progress and anticipated the rapid passing of indigenous customs, "Our Landlady" captured a man-on-the-street view of the same event which was both less propaganda-oriented and more illustrative of the tensions between the two cultures. Through Mrs. Bilkins, Baum reflected the townspeople's attitudes toward the Indians and their imperfect understanding of European customs. The Indian visitors, for example, might not realize that items found on clotheslines or window sills were not theirs for the taking. If they helped themselves to such things, the settlers considered them thieves.40 In another frequent misunderstanding of the period, both Gage and Baum used the common term "squaw" without considering that their Sioux neighbors might find the label demeaning.

"It's lucky for me," said our landlady, as she staggered in from the kitchen with the bread plate, "that the Pilgrim fathers didn't make a declaration o' independence every day, for if we had to celebrate many of 'em, I wouldn't have no time to keep boardin' house."

"Did you participate in the festivities yesterday?" asked the colonel, politely. "Participate?" replied Mrs. Bilkins, "well I should smile! Who didn't? But them injines spiled all o' my enjyment. Jest when the bands were playin' the beautifulest, I'd think o' them custard pies in the back kitchen and wonder if some injine warn't pryin' up the winder an' stealing 'em fer his squaws, an' that brought my heart up inter my throat. An' then when the procession comed along, every gal around me fell in love with the marshal o' the day, 'cause he looked so scrumptuous an' sot so straight in his saddle, an' that made me feel bad, 'cause I knew he were a married man. An' then everybody yelled 'Hooray for Huron!' an' the same folks yelled, 'Hooray for Pierre!' an' I knew that wasn't right, 'cause it would rattle Steve Hawkins an' he wouldn't know which town his inwestments were in. An' considerin' as he bought up the celebration for $2.50 he ought not to be bothered.

"An' then a tall galoot a ridin' of a bicycle run over my left corn, an' 'afore I recovered myself along comed the thumpdoodlums an' nearly scared me outer my wits."

"You did have a bad time," said the doctor, "still, many enjoyed the day."

"Well, the day wern't without its dispensations," observed our landlady reflectively. "The skim-milk ice cream an' the artesian lemonade warn't bad, an' the Aberdeen Guard gals was wuth seein'. An' then to see them fellers climin' greased poles an' runnin' races an' jumpin' up like a set o' fools wasn't such bad fun neither."

"Did you attend the ball game?" asked Tom.

"Oh, yes, — at the Opera House."

"No! No! that was the baby show."

"Well, that were the only bawl game I had any time for, an' o' course the fool judges guv the prizes to the homliest babies an' the prettiest mothers.

"I allus notis as that's the case. But still, with all the drawbacks, I'd a got along fust rate if I hadn't took it inter my head ter see the injine's war dance. I paid my money to a greasy lookin' injun an' walked in an' stood up. At one end o' the hall was a big chief named Cowjumps, an' back o' him were some sleepy-lookin' squaws an' dried-up babys, an' in the circle were the villainist lookin' lot o' red devils as I ever seed, pushin' each other round the ring an' yellin'.

" 'Hi-yah! hip-yah! hi-yah! hip-yah!' an' drummin' on a big kittle an' shakin' some tommyhawks and knives over their heads.

" 'What's up?' says I to the policeman.

" 'Hush!' says he.

" 'What's got 'em riled?' says I.

" 'Nothin',' says he, 'they're dancin'.'

" 'Oh!' says I; 'well if they had a master they'd do it more polite.'

"An' just then I catched sight o' my red bed-spread, as I'd leit out on the line, on one o' the dancin' injins' shoulders. I didn't wait for nothin', but I jest busted inter that ring o' war dancers an' clubbed my umbreller in my fist an' belted him a good whack over the shoulders. He knew what I wanted in a minit and pulled out a watch an' handed me fer a bribe.[41]

" 'Not much!' says I, 'you just gimme that 'air bed-spread!'

"An' he give it up. He said he found it in the band wagon, but I knowed as he was lyin'.

"This little rumpus broke me all up an' I went down to the P.G.'s. — I guess that means pritty gals — an' had some ice cream an' went home.

"I didn't see but one fireworks, an' that was a sky-rocket as comed through the front winder while I was sayin' my prayers. If I could find out who shot it I'd make him pay fer the glass, but as I can't, I'll jest contribute it as my share o' the celebration."

· ·

She Discourses upon Lo[v]e and Politics

12 July 1890

On 6 June the Farmers' Alliance and the Knights of Labor had created a third party, drafting a platform that called for "money at cost, transportation at cost and land for those who use it."[42] This new Independent Party (later called the Populist or People's Party) scheduled its first state convention for 9 July in Huron. During the interval the Republican newspapers of the state editorially pounded the new party. The *Aberdeen Daily News* regularly accused the Independents of "flirting" with the Democrats. When the state equal suffrage organization also called a meeting in Huron, for 8 July, the *News* began to see "dalliances" between Independents and suffragists, as well. At least three of the women who signed the call for the suffrage meeting were wives of Farmers' Alliance officers, and on 11 July the *News* editor concluded that the women's meeting was intended to "bolster up the tottering fortunes of their [now Independent] husbands."[43] The suffragists, who actually met to resolve their own considerable differences, nevertheless used the opportunity to send a delegation to the Independent convention to ask for the party's endorsement of woman suffrage. The new party did pass a pro-suffrage resolution at the last minute, but none of the party's major candidates endorsed it for fear that it would cost them votes.[44]

Editor Baum found most Republican press coverage of the Independents overblown. "The *Pioneer*, although a republican paper, is disposed to judge these men very leniently," he remarked in his 12 July report of the party convention. "They have an undoubted right to form a third or independent party if they choose — independence is our national priv[i]lege." For the time being, he concluded, "the Independent movement is one to be regarded with interest rather than fear." When focusing his landlady's attention on the Independents, Baum picked up the imagery of secret alliances and elopements to poke fun at both the *News* and the party. Except for Cholly (Charles Howard), however, the first names in this column do not seem to relate to individuals involved in politics. Instead, they are common Aberdeen names of the period and may have hinted at various romances-in-progress, allowing local people to read the column on two levels.

"Times is pretty dull nowadays," said our landlady, as she killed a fly buzzing against the window with her slipper, and scared a lot more away from the sugar-bowl; "there don't seem to be nothin' goin' on but politics. I s'pose you've heard about Cholly?"

"No," replied the doctor, "I havn't. What about him?"

"Why he's goin' to run agin' Ben Harrison for the presidency."

"Nonsense!"

"That's what I tell's him. But he says if he can't be president he'll be state senator."

"Why not vice-president?" asked the Colonel, sarcastically.

"Because our Cholly won't have nothin' to do with vice. He'll take all he can get and get all he can, but he draws the line at that. All his friends are workin' for him, especially the G.A.R.'s, an' you'll either see somethin' or else you won't see nothin', you mark my words."

"How about the independents?" asked Tom.

"I'll tell you. The other mornin' I was sound asleep when I heerd a queer noise. It sounded like a turkey mother callin' her chicks to see a worm. At fust I thought it was a gang o' burgulers, but when I got up an' stuck my head outer the winder I see it was some gals cluckin' to some other gals in the house oppersite.

" 'What's up?' thinks I, fer it was only five o'clock, but I didn't see nothin' up but the gals. Well, they kep' cluckin' till they woke up the whole neighborhood, an' then they woke up the gal. Then several young fellers jined 'em an' I saw to onct that there was an elopement goin' on on a big scale. So I threw my shawl over my head an' rushes out, just as they was startin' up the street.

" 'Hold, villin!' says I to one o' 'em, givin' a reglar war whoop, 'unhand that gal!'

" 'Unhand yourself,' says Nat, 'what do you want?'

" 'I want you to restore them gals to their homes. No elopin's goin' on under my nose if I knows it!'

" 'Fiddlesticks!' says Alf. 'We ain't elopin', are we Hat?'

" 'No, are we Lu?' says she.

" 'We're just goin' fer a mornin' walk,' says J.B., lookin' mad.

" 'At five o'clock?' says I, sardineically.

" 'That's the best time,' says Eva, sweetly, 'for the air is fresh an' cool an' it gives us an apetite for breakfus'. We go every mornin' an' walk about two miles an' it's more fun than the measles!'

" 'Here comes Carrie,' says another, 'now let's leave this ole meddler.'

" 'Thanks,' says I, 'if you don't like my company, don't cluck so loud as to raise the hull neigborhood. We ole folks ain't all in love, an' we needs our rest!' an' wi' that I slams inter the house an' watched 'em go up the street, an' I thought they was about as independent as any folks I ever seed. But I wouldn't like to feed 'em if they takes these long walks every mornin', although they do say as folks in love don't eat much."

"Speaking of eating," remarked the colonel, "have you heard that Al. Ward was sun-struck yesterday?'"

"Yes, but I knew that suthin' would strike Al. if he didn't put the quality o' grub up an' the price down. I'm thinking o' advertisin' this 'ere boardin' house in his front winder, but I don't care to ruin Al cause he's got a good heart, so I guess I won't interfere with his trade just yet."

. . . .

She Buys a Cow and the Boarders Help Her Milk it

19 July 1890

Politics continued to preoccupy townspeople as the Republicans met in both city caucuses and the Brown County convention during the week. Serving as secretary for Aberdeen's fourth ward caucus, Baum recorded the election of physician S. Jay Coyne as delegate to the county meeting. In the only disharmony at the city level, members of the third ward objected to the speed with which delegate nominations were rushed through in their district and put up an opposing slate. At the county convention three days later, the antiprohibition and temperance wings of the party squabbled over a wordy resolution on prohibition. Dr. Coyne, who chaired the meeting, objected to the resolution on principle, reminding temperance advocates that the state constitution already prohibited saloons. Rev. Frank A. Burdick then scolded Coyne for speaking on the proposal while acting as chairman.[45] Later, when Burdick cast three votes on a proxy, Coyne demanded to see his credentials, proclaiming that Burdick "has sneaked in at the back door of this convention and insulted your chairman."[46] Burdick successfully met the challenge, but Coyne's stand against the prohibition measure plagued him all week.[47]

Other political stories in the news included Marietta Bones's newest attack on Susan B. Anthony through a letter to the *Minneapolis Tribune*. Baum editorialized that the sooner both women were "muzzled effectively the better for all true friends of the [suffrage] cause." In spite of the hubbub, Mrs. Bilkins turned her attention to domestic issues, but, like editor Baum, she never quite forgot the political backdrop against which she worked.

"Gentlemen," said our landlady, as she met the boarders at the door with her own sweet smile, (copyrighted), "I've bought a new cow!"

"A live one?" asked Tom, with interest.

"A milch cow?" queried the colonel.

"A live milk cow!" responded Mrs. Bilkins, bobbing her head impressively.

"A cow," remarked the doctor, fanning himself gently with his straw hat, "is a delightful animal. She not only ministers to the wants of humanity, but she is mild in disposition, gentle in temperament and recognizes man as her friend and master."

"I suppose," said Tom, "you refer to the female cow."

The docter looked puzzled, but vouchsafed no answer.

"I thought," continued our landlady, "that you might like a little new milk for supper, and so, as we have a little time, you can come out in the back yard and see me milk her."

This delighted the boarders and they repaired to the rear of the house and gazed with awe and respect upon the sleek and gentle bossie.

"What do you call her?" inquired the colonel, putting up his eyeglasses for a close inspection.

"I haven't named her," smiled the landlady.

"Call her Elnora," suggested Tom, "or stop — Clochette — that's better!"

"S[h]e is named Clochette," said the doctor.

"Dear me!" said Mrs. Bilkins, "I haven't any milking-stool!"

"That's bad," responded the colonel, "I suppose it's a necessity."

"Well, in my days," said Mrs. Bilkins, grimly, "folks didn't stand up an' milk."

"I have it!" said Tom, and he rushed into the house and returned with the piano stool.

Mrs. Bilkins eyed it dubiously.

"It ain't quite accordin' ter parliamentary rules, as Doc. Coyne said when he called Elder Burdock a sneak thief, but I guess it'll do."

She took the new, bright ten-quart pail in her hand, and followed by Tom with the piano stool approached the gentle bovine and patted her on the head.

"Cattle," she remarked, "likes to be petted. Jest set the stool handy."

Tom did so, and the cow licked Mrs. Bilkins' hand and swung around upon her hind legs until the stool was out of reach.

"So! Clochette," said the doctor.

Tom replaced the stool, and again Clochette described a circle with her hind legs.

"Try the other side," suggested the colonel.

Tom did so, and the cow moved the opposite way in the same manner.

"The proper way to milk Clochette," said the youth, as he wiped the gathering perspiration from his forehead, "is to get her alongside a board fence."

"But, unfortunately," replied the doctor, "we have no board fence handy."

"This thing," said Mrs. Bilkins, "must be done business like. This here Klokettle, or whatever her name is, is gentle enough, but we are strange to her. Now let me be the general an' you'll see how nice I manage her. Here, Tom, you hold her by the horns."

Tom accepted the nomination with as much alacrity as our Cholly could have shown, and grasped Clochette firmly by the horns.

"Now, Doc, you stand ready with the pianner stool, an' the colonel can stand on the other side o' her an' keep her from swingin' round."

The colonel calmly took his position, while the doctor put the stool in place and Mrs. Bilkins seated herself — the cow meanwhile chewing her cud with a ruminating air.

"This," smiled our landlady, beginning to milk, "is business! — So! Teakettle! — Doc., you hold her tail so's she can't switch it inter my eye every minnit. — There, see how nice the milk is — so white an' —— ."

A slight interruption here occurred. Clochette sided away from the pail; the colonel exerted his strength and pushed her back again. Clochette stepped into the tin pail with such force that she became frightened. At the same moment the doctor unwisely jerked at her tail and Tom pushed her head down.

You can imagine the result. In an instant the scene changed. The piano stool went through the kitchen window with a crash. Mrs. Bilkins' legs might be seen struggling violently from the top of the garbage barrel; the tin pail flitted neatly over the colonel's head and the milk trickled down his neck; the doctor landed in the coal-house and Tom in the neighbor's premises, while Clochette took a vacation and browsed gently in a far-away pasture.

To remove the pail and extricate Mrs. Bilkins from her uncomfortable position was the work of a moment to our gallant colonel. Presently the doctor and Tom joined them, but no one looked toward Clochette.

"Colonel," said Mrs. Bilkins, huskily, "take this nickle an' go over to Cap. Hauser's fer a quart o' milk."

"If you will excuse us," said Tom, lightly, "the doctor and I will go to our room and prepare for supper."

Left to herself for a moment, our landlady tacked her shawl over the broken window and whispered softly to the cat:

"A woman is allus a fool when she asks a man to help her do anything. If I'd a been alone, that Klokettle an' I would a had it out, an' I'd a milked her or broke her neck. But the men-folks spiled it all. They think they can rush a cow like they rush a third ward caucus, but they'll find they can't. A cow is a female, an' she wants her rights, an' after all, I dunno as I blame her so much as I do Doc. fer bein' such a fool as to pull her tail."[48]

. . . .

She Talks About Railroads and Various Minor Matters

26 July 1890

Beginning with a "mass meeting" on 19 July, the citizens of Aberdeen spent the week attempting to secure a branch line of the Northern Pacific Railroad from Oakes, North Dakota, to Aberdeen and from thence to Pierre (residents of the temporary capital, eager to secure a railroad prior to the November elections, were heavily involved in the scheme). To entice railroad officials southwest, Aberdeen proposed to furnish a right of way through the city, twenty-five acres for depot grounds, and certain monetary considerations as well. By Saturday, two hundred fifty Aberdonians had signed bonds guaranteeing the payment of $50,000 to a Saint Paul construction company.[49] "All that is needed," Baum reported, "is for the city council to issue warrants for the construction of a boulevard through the city, which they will do when authorized by a four-fifths vote of the people." The special election was called for 11 August.[50]

Various "minor matters" of the week included the Democratic city caucuses and the county convention, at which, Baum reported, "harmony and despair reigned supreme" as the party picked its "martyrs." The Independent candidate for governor, Henry L. Loucks, spoke at the opera house on Wednesday night, making "a fool of himself before all intelligent men — and a hero of himself to his firmest adherents," Baum averred. Col. Dennis M. Evans, editor of the *Aberdeen Daily News*, departed for the state press association meeting,[51] and C. Boyd Barrett, editor of the *Aberdeen Evening Republican*, joined his wife, who was, the *News* reported on 26 July, "rusticating" at a popular resort on the Minnesota border. The absence of the daily editors gave Mrs. Bilkins an opportunity to reflect on their editorial styles.

"I've had a great deal to worrit me this week," said our landlady, nervously, as she put the saucer of fly-poison on the floor for the cat, and set the saucer of milk on the window sill.

"Politics?" queried the colonel, carelessly.

"Not exactly. I've ben workin' on this 'ere boulevard deal. Ye see if we don't git a full vote, one that's unanimosity, we can't git the railroad, an' so when I heerd as there was some kickers I thought as I'd go out an' tackle 'em. An' a hard fight I've had with 'em. But I've conquered, an' there won't be but one vote agin' that boulevard on election day. There's one feller that has got Bowels by name but not any by natur' that still kicks because it's his constitutional trouble, but nobody minds him anyhow."

"The town ought to be grateful for your labors," said Tom.

"That ain't the p'int. I'm grateful to myself, an' that settles it. What propity I owns, I owns, an' I knows which side o' my bread is buttered. Now, if it hadn't been fer this here boardin' house I could a made a heap o' money this week. First comes a feller an' says the editor of the Daily Nuthin' has gone to Big Stone to get rusty, an' wants me to be the editur wile he's gone.

" 'How much do I git?' says I.

" 'Oh,' says he, 'the reglar editur gits about one lickin' a week, a cussin' about forty times a day, free whiskey from the 'riginal package houses an' boards and finds himself.'

" 'Don't he git no chairmanship of the jimicrat central c'mittee?' says I.

" 'Hardly ever,' says he, quotin' Pinafore.

" 'Then,' says I, 'I don't want the job.'

"Well, he hadn't no more nor gone, when another feller arrives an' says:

" 'Ma'am,' says he, 'Kernel Puffball is gone ter the editorial meetin', an' we'd like yer to edit the Daily Anything.'

" 'I'm afeared I ain't ekal to it,' says I.

" 'Well,' said he, 'all you need is the New York and Chicago papers to steel from, an' the 'cyclopedia an' dicshunary. Four pounds o' conceit a day would make the people think as the editur were still to home, but no brains is necessary.'

" 'Brains,' says I, lookin' as mad as Billy Paulhamus when he misses a caucus, 'is all I can furnish, an' you'll have to excuse me.' So, neither the Daily Nuthin' nor the Daily Anythin' will git edited, an' perhaps the people can read 'em without swearin'."

"A sad state of affairs," remarked the doctor, mildly.

"Yes, most as sad as Al. Ward, when he got through wi' the masons this week. Al. he hankered as much to be a mason as he did fer cushions and stickin' plaster after he got his degree. They say his shins was all black an' his back a sight to behold. But they let him live, an' he's grateful fer that. He says he'd ruther hear Loucks lecture on finance than to do it agin, but, as they never innishiate a feller but once, I guess his misery is over."

"By the way," said the colonel, "I haven't seen our cow lately."

"No," returned our landlady, with a sigh, "I sold her las' week ter a feller as keeps a baby farm. It gives a person a air o' wealth an' respectability ter have a cow in the yard, but Klokettle an' I didn't agree, an' I never tried to milk her but onct."

. . . .

Our Landlady

2 August 1890

Hot, searing winds and stifling temperatures had plagued Brown County and most of South Dakota during the hottest July on record. Crops withered in the field, and as harvest began, farmers reported that yields averaged only eight to ten bushels an acre of second- and third-grade wheat. Tempers frayed as everyone recognized that the hard times were not yet over, and the heat went on unrelieved.[52] For those who wished to forget their troubles and slake their thirst with a bit of beer or whiskey, the original package joints accommodated their needs, even as the local enforcement committee campaigned to close them down. The law regarding such establishments was "very uncertain just now," the Aberdeen police chief admitted to the *Saturday Pioneer*. District Attorney Edward T. Taubman shut down one establishment only to have it reopen in a new location within a few hours, the proprietors having lost just one keg of beer in the process.

The chairman of the prohibition committee, however, suspected that enforcement suffered because District Attorney Taubman lacked commitment to the effort. Consequently, he daily badgered Taubman about his inability to close the most notorious place of all: the premises of Henry Goodwin, who operated out of a shed behind his former liquor store. On a day when the temperature reached 104 degrees in the shade, the determined temperance disciple fronted the district attorney in the post office, demanding to know what Taubman was doing to resolve the Goodwin case. The affair ended in fisticuffs and a flurry of press coverage and editorials. Baum stood up for Taubman, remarking, "We may not agree with his views, but he is frank and square-toed, and a manly sort of fellow altogether, although inclined to be loud-mouthed and aggressive."[53] Heat, prohibition, hard times, and the ever present politics constitute the background against which Mrs. Bilkins and her boarders enjoyed a shipment of Georgia watermelons that Aberdeen grocer A. Harry Olwin had just received.

"Times is dull, is they?" inquired our landlady, as she cut into the watermelon with a business like air, "well, they may be to you, put they're lively enough fer some folks. Rustlers don't know what dull times is, it's only such perfeshional men as you, doc, or such loan agents as the colonel, (as hain't had nothin' to loan in six months) or sich worthless clerks as Tom, who spends his time waitin' fer the customers as don't come, that finds times dull. The farmer what's harvestin' has to rustle after he cuts one stalk o' wheat to reach another 'afore he loses sight of it; the politicians has to rustle to build fences, although why they do that when most of 'em hain't got no lots to put 'em on beats me.54 The temperance men has to rustle so as people won't think that prohibition don't prohibit; the District Attorney has to rustle ter prove he's got it in fer the 'riginal package houses when he hain't; the ministers has to rustle for congregations — them as hain't throwed up religion fer politics55 — the business men have to rustle fer trade — the newspaper men has to rustle fer proof that every other newspaper man is a villian — an' so it goes, plenty to rustle for if you mean business, an' ain't under the soaperiferous influence o' the hot weather."

"Another piece of melon, please," said the doctor, mildly.

Mrs. Bilkins glared at him and cut a thin slice off the small end.

"To eat that would be suicide," he remonstrated.

"It costs just as much a pound as the core," returned our landlady, "and I can't afford to waste it. Some folks wants to make a meal off the delicates o' the season. What'd I furnish that mush an' milk fer if it wrrn't to fill ye up so you wouldn't want to git fat on watermelon? Some folks hain't got no sense, nohow!"

"They're going to have another opera," said Tom, to change the subject, "and I've been asked to sing in the chorus."56

"Well, you can do as you please," returned Mrs. Bilkins, "but I hain't got no patience with them uproars. I'll git all the singin' I want when I'm an angil in heaven — but p'raps you don't expect to git there, so you'd better do yourn on earth."

"I am sorry, my dear Mrs. Bilkins, that you do not seem to be in good spirits today," said the colonel, quietly.

"Not any. No spirits has passed my lips fer a week."

"I mean that your equanimity is disturbed — that you are not in very good temper."

"Oh, I'm riled, am I? Well, I guess you'd be riled if you was me. Why, I went down to Miss Chowder's to have my front bangs curled this mornin' right after breakfast, an' there I sees a crowd o' young fellers waitin' in the settin'-room.

" 'What'r you here for?' says I, 'you fellers hain't got no bangs.'

" 'No,' says one, 'but we's got mustaches!'

"An' I declare the hull lot was there to have their mustaches curled! An' the young ladies took longer to curl one mustash than they do three pair o' bangs, an' so I sot an' sot till dinner was ready, and my bangs hain't curled yet, an' there's a prayer meetin' tonight an' I won't dare face the deakin' nohow."

"That's too bad," replied the colonel, as he glanced at Tom, who blushed and tried to straighten out the curls in his mustache.

"Was Al. Ward there?" enquired the doctor.

"No — Al. curls his'n over a crowbar; but speakin' o' him reminds me of a good joke. Ye see Al. he let the barber — Pabst — git inter him fer a four dollar meal ticket, an' when he found the feller was a goin' ter leave town last Wen'sday he sent Dave and a officer down to the train to stop him, or collect the ducats.

" 'Well,' says Al., when Dave come back, 'where's the money?'

" 'Couldn't get it,' says Dave. 'The feller cried and said as he were a orphan an' we had to let him go.'

" 'Cried, did he?' says Al. 'Why, you chicken-hearted independent, he's got four dollars wuth o' my vittles in his insides! I'll capture him if it costs a million dollars!' an' he buckled his vest tighter an' rushed down to the depot. Well, by-'n-by he come back, kinder slow like. 'Where's the money,' says Dave. 'Why,' says Al., 'he cried an' said as he'd only seven dollars to take him to Californy, an' a feller as'll take a poor kid's last dollar is mean enough to join the demicrats. Tell you what, boys, that feller had a mother once.'

"There was a hushed silence all through the room, an' more'n one man at the lunch counter dropped a tear inter his mush an' milk. An' then Al. sighed an' went off to hunt up Skip. The last time I heard of 'em they was talkin' politics with Goodwin. It's a simple little story but it shows that even pirates may have hearts, an' I advise any feller what's a good cryer to go down to Ward's and board on tick!"

. . . .

She Exposes a Practical Joke and Tells About
the Goose Quill Kiss

9 August 1890

In spite of hard times, or perhaps because of them, Baum announced on 9 August that the subscription list for the *Aberdeen Saturday Pioneer* had reached 2,500 and advertising rates were therefore going up 50 percent. Rehearsals began for operettas to be held during the state fair in September, with Baum taking major roles in both *The Little Tycoon* and *The Sorcerer*. Sharing the billing were Imogene ("Gene") Van Loon and Hiram ("Hi") Pratt, two of Aberdeen's young "unmarrieds." Trade in Aberdeen remained dull, but betting on horse races inexplicably picked up, and the *Aberdeen Daily News* recorded winning times of 2:48 and 2:54 during the week. On 8 August, the paper announced that a crowd had gathered the day before to watch barber John O'Daniel and businessman William H. Paulhamus race their colts in two heats. O'Daniel's won with a best time of 2:58. "It is said," the *News* continued, that "O'Daniel got another big offer for his colt after the race but declined with thanks. John evidently thinks he has got something good." At the fairgrounds to watch this race had been Mrs. Bilkins, who had her own opinions about the barber's colt — and about the courting practices of young Aberdonians.

❧ "Well, I'm all tuckered out," exclaimed our landlady, as she entered the dining room in time to throw her hymn book at the cat, who was quietly eating out of the cream p[i]tcher.

The first result was to frighten the household pet so badly that she jumped from the table to the window sill, (upsetting the fly trap into the stewed prunes in her flight), and alighting upon a strip of sticky fly-paper she uttered a screetch of dismay and sprang into the arms of her mistress, who promptly threw her out of the wi[n]dow — paper and all. The second result was that the colonel was induced to look up from his paper and ask,

"Been to prayer-meeting, ma'am?"

"Well, not exactly," responded our landlady, as she made preparations for tea, "this 'ere is a sort o' religious community, an' thought if I went to a hoss-race without my prayer book, some one would know where I was goin'. This church business covers a multitude of sins."

"Where was the horse-race?" inquired Tom, with sudden interest.

"Oh, out to the Fair grounds. You see, there's a barber here named John, as is got a colt that's no earthly good, an' the boys are havin' lots o' fun with him. He can't trot fer sour apples, that's the fact, but John thinks as he's the best race hoss in Ameriky. Billy Paulhamus pertended he wanted to race with him, an' so they went out to the grounds, an' got John to drive his nag around till it was all tuckered out. Then Billy brought his hoss out an' let the colt beat him two straight heats. It were a burning shame to treat the poor barber so. The jedges and starters they were in the game, an' when the colt made a mile in five minits an' a quarter they tole the poor fellow that his time was 2:58! Five minits is the best that nag will even do. Baldwin, as has been guyin' John fer a long time about his hoss, made him an offer o' six hundred dollars, — when he wouldn't give six cents — for the colt, an' o' course the barber wouldn't take it."

"Are they trying to get the barber to make a bet?" asked the doctor.

"No — they ain't so mean as to work him fer money. It's jest a guy — that's all. Queer ideas folks git nowadays of fun. In my times fun was fun, an' don't you fergit it. Now look at this goose-quill deal. That shows how the kids nowadays is demoralizin'."

"What about the goose quill?" asked the colonel.

"Why, I didn't know anything about it myself until the other night. I was settin' on the back stoop in the dark, thinkin' of religious matters, when I noticed the forms of a couple o' young people comin' round the corner of a neighbor's house.

" 'Now, if you won't tell,' says a gal voice, 'I'll show you how it's done.'

" 'Oh, I won't tell,' says a boy's deep rich bass voice.

" 'This idea o' kissin' through a goose quill,' continued the gal, 'is my own inwention. You get a kiss just the same only it's removed to a respectful distance. Do you feel able to go through the ordeal, Hi?'

" 'You bet I do,' says the feller, 'let's have it!'

"Then I heard a sound like as if some one had pulled his foot out o' some wet mud an' the feller yells,

" 'Why, Gene, you've pulled a piece out o' my cheek!'

" 'Oh, no, that's the beauty o' the thing, you know when you've got kissed. How do you like it?'

" 'Oh, under some circumstances it's all right, but I think I like a meat kiss better.'57

" 'But that's improper,' says the gal. 'The idee of the goose quill is that it makes kissin' proper. All the gals has got 'em now.'

"An' then the young folks went away an' left me to my horrified reflections. I don't approve o' this goose quill arrangement. There's only one proper way to kiss as I knows on, an' when I was a gal the young folks would scorn goose quills. Of course, this 'ere's a free country, but sence that night, whenever I see a young feller with a round red mark on his cheek, I feel kinder sorry for him, because I know that the march o' Civilization and the inwention o' the goose quill kiss has cost him one of the pleasantest and most innocent delights of youth — well — yes — an' ole age, too, fer that matter!"

. . . .

Our Landlady

16 August 1890

Each Saturday, under the heading "Particular Paragraphs: Pleasing Personals of Prominent People," the *Saturday Pioneer* listed the comings and goings of Aberdeen's citizenry. Throughout late July and early August the column filled up with the names of young and old who escaped the heat on picnics, boating expeditions, and camping trips. Those who stayed in town began to prepare for the South Dakota State Fair, just four weeks away. The businessmen of the city, bidding for this event early in the year, had secured the prize after seventy of them signed a bond assuring the state agricultural board that they would provide fairgrounds and buildings. Unfortunately, a June windstorm subsequently damaged the fences and wooden structures on the grounds, and repairs would be costly. At a meeting on 13 August, Charles N. Harris, Aberdeen's representative on the State Board of Agriculture, who had procured the fair for the Hub City, assessed each of the seventy bondsmen a fee of ten dollars to cover repairs. If this levy did not bring the necessary money, the newspapers reported, new assessments would be made.[58] After repairs were estimated at $1,700, Baum asserted that the fair was a matter "of advantage and importance to every citizen of Aberdeen" and suggested that "the most manly course" would be for "each and everyone to contribute toward the loss, even if it is no more than a dollar, and not oblige the public-spirited citizens whose enterprise secured the state fair for our city to foot the unavoidable loss incurred." Mrs. Bilkins, mindful of hard times, sallied forth to see how the assessment fared among the main-street merchants.

"Things is awful dull jest now," remarked our landlady, as she threw her shawl over the broom handle and mopped her face with her apron, "an' the folks as knows when they're well off will either stay to home and loaf or go on their summer vacation. An' that reminds me that there's lots of folks in this town as tells the newspaper men they're going away, an' then don't go, an' they git the repertation o' bein' Summer excursionists without the expense. Jest tell me where the papers hain't told the people Max Bass was agoin' to, for instinct; an' yet Max has staid to hum all the time an' tended to his knittin', which the immigration folks usually does just before election, so's when the new appointment arrives they'll be on hand to receive it."

"A mere matter of business," said the colonel, as he cut into the pumpkin pie.

"So's everything a mere matter o' business. Now, Tom here were on that Fair Grounds bond, and he might 'a gone jest as well on a coffee grounds bond fer all the money he could pay. An' so I tried to help him out by going to our public-spirited citizens today an' tryin' to get some contributions to help out the boys as is got stuck on this bond deal. I went into a drug store an' bought a stick o' gum.

" 'How's times?' says I.

" 'Good!' says he — the proprietor.

"Then I tackled him fer his subscripshun.

" 'Times is to[o] hard,' says he, 'I've just bought a lot in Chicago an' I can't pay no ten dollars on no bond, nohow.[59] If they wants five dollars o' my little savin's, they can have it.'

"I were so disgustid that I left him an' went inter a hardware store an' bought an ounce o' nails.

" 'How's times?' says I.

" 'Good,' says he.

" 'Are you goin' to pay up on that bond?' says I, careless like.

" 'Not much,' says the gentlemanly proprietor, 'it's all right to sign a bond, cause it makes you solid with the people, but when it comes to payin' it, it's another act. The Lord didn't want no fair grounds and so the wind blew 'em down.'

"Well, I left the cuss an' come away, an' made up my mind that I woldn't enquire no further. But I guess there's enough outsiders as'll chip in to make up fer the chumps as won't pay."

"You interest yourself too much in other people's business," said the doctor, quietly, "to be very popular. A good many of your criticisms have leaked out, someway, and if you ever hope to change your name, you will have to be more careful."

"Fiddlesticks!" exclaimed our landlady, "if folks don't like my style they needn't listen to me. I've got to keep busy somehow, an' this 'ere boardin' house don't fully occupy my time. An' you'll find I'm pretty near right, too. As fer gettin' married agin, I'm losin' all hopes. The young folks is all a pairin' off an' leavin' no feller fer me. There's goin' ter be four bran' new weddin's in October, an' as soon as the weather gits cooler I s'pose there'll be a lot more. The goose quill kiss has accomplished its purpose and is going out o' fashion. When a gal goes to a picnic now, she just takes her goose quill along so's her ma won't suspect nothin', but I never see one as was wore out yit. But that ain't none o' my business. If the young folks can't enjoy theirselves, what's the use o' bein' born? Only it makes me sad to think how soon they'll all be marred off, fer then even kissin' won't delay a feller when he starts off to town at midnight fer a bottle o' soothin' syrup. It's the way o' the world, an' I agree with Shookspear when he says:

> 'Go it folks while yer young,
> Fer when ye git old ye can't.' "[60]

. . . .

She gives a Picnic to the Boarders and Writes a Proclamation

23 August 1890

On 10 August the president of the United States signed legislation that granted states full control over all intoxicating liquors within their borders, including those shipped in original packages. The next day Henry Goodwin declared that his original package joint had closed for good. Six days later Mayor Bob Moody authorized the chief of police to warn all proprietors of card rooms that he was about to enforce a long-standing city ordinance that prohibited gaming tables of any type within the city limits.[61] The era of original packages and gambling resorts had ended; the era of home brew, blind pigs, and drugstore saloons was about to begin. On the eve of this development, Baum penned one of his more charming "Our Landlady" columns, poking fun at the sudden strong enforcement sentiment in Aberdeen. Sparkling with a rare good humor, Mrs. Bilkins provided abundant eatables as both the Dakota landscape and the prohibitionists proved parsimonious.

"Now this," observed our landlady, as she sat in the shade of her parasol and an enormous tree fully six feet high, and watched the festive Jim meander sluggishly at her feet like the slowly welling leak in a bucket of dishwater, "this is what I calls rusticatin'. When I invited you boarders to this here picnic, I intended you should enjoy all the delights of natur'. No one sighs fer the seashore when on a stream of this size you can see shore on both sides o' it — excuse me, colonel, ain't you well?"

"He has simply fainted," returned the doctor, gravely, as he fanned the veteran gently with his straw hat. "Perhaps he might be restored if we had a bottle of — "

"Tom, fetch out that bottle of birch beer," interrupted our landlady with an alarmed look.

"I'm afraid that birch beer — "

"Oh, don't you worry. As Narregang says, 'what's in a name?' The Kernel won't kick on the contents."

The colonel didn't. He took a hearty draught and was himself again.

"It strikes me," said Tom, who was endeavoring to find a place to drop his brand-new fish-line, "that the first thing to do at a picnic is to eat."

"A capital suggestion," said the doctor, approvingly. "I suppose, Mrs. Bilkins, that you did not forget the eatables?"

"Not much. Now colonel, look lively, fetch over that big basket — not that one — that's only fer show.

"O' course, we four peoples couldn't eat a barrel o' truck, but I didn't want the neighbors to think I was stingy, an' so I brung all the baskets I had in the house.[62] Here, Tom, jest take the pickles out o' that custard, an' doc, you set them bottles in the water to cool, an' Kurnel, see if you can scrape the butter off'en that cocoanut cake, while I spread the table cloth and pick the boiled eggs out of the sandwiches. — That's the stuff — pitch in, boys! don't be afraid — I won't punch yer tickets fer this 'ere meal — it's my treat. Doc, a little more beer — ahem! birch beer, I mean, — thanks. Now, fellers, ain't this jest glorious?"

No one replied, but each one was so busily occupied that Mrs. Bilkins seemed to consider an answer superfluous.

Finally the meal ended, and the boarders lit their cigars and lay under the shade of the saplings, while Mrs. Bilkins sat on the edge of the bank and drew forth her pencil and note-book.

"What are you writing," asked the colonel, after watching her silently for awhile.

"Oh jest a proclamation."

"A proclamation?"

"Fer Bob Moody. He kinder run short of ideas an' asked me to help him out."

"What's it about?" inquired Tom.

"Well, if you won't tell, I'll read it to ye. But you mustn't give it away, because he hain't signed it yit, an' until he does it ain't public property."

"Oh, we won't say a word."

"Then listen:

" 'Gen'l Orders number 'steen.

" 'Mayor's orfise. To ther sitizens uv this here burgh. As it hez comed to my nolidge that certin bad, wicked people hev bin in the habit ov meetin at houses and playin sech sinful games as progressiv uker and drive whisht, which aint either progressin or drivin the road to desency an public order, I thearfore, bein duely elected by frank hagerty, and the other sitizens of this hear town, do forbid, now an forever and ever, amen, sich unlawfull doins in the fucher. An playin marbels and tag in the public streets, and all uther gamblin except in stocks and morgages is hearby strictly prohibitid. For, havin witnessed the grate success of the Sabbath day, I propoas to have every day Sabbath in this hear town, so as my administrashun wil be appresheated by all free and liberal minded citizens.' "

"That won't do," said Tom, decidedly, "it's carrying the thing too far. He'll think you're guying him."

"No, I think he'll like it. There's two ways to become famous — one's by bein' very bad, an' the other's by bein' very good. Now, it ain't in Bob to be very bad, an' yit he wants to git famous. An' if he'll jest continue his policy by addin' mine to it he'll have the biggest name o' any mayor in South Dikoty, an' the ministers'll have to preach seven days in the week to keep the people okipied. But then — "

A horrible occurrence cut short our landlady's explanation. The bank on which she was sitting caved in suddenly and precipitated her violently into the placid bosom of the Jim. With a shout that was half grief and half joy, the boarders came to her rescue, and fished her, limp and dripping, from the impromptu bath.

"Now," said the colonel, as he assisted her into the wagon, "you know what a cold water administration is."

"Yes," replied our landlady with a shiver, but a twinkle in her eye, as she wrapped the table-cloth about her damp form, "but it didn't need that illustration to show me I didn't like it. But this ain't no time to talk politics. Drive on, doctor, an' if you don't want Goodes to sell a twelve dollar coffin, drive like blazes!"

. . . .

She Attends the Convention and is Disgusted with Politics

30 August 1890

As South Dakotans sweltered in the dog days of summer, the political climate of the state also heated up when suffragists met in state convention in Mitchell on 25–27 August and the Republicans on 27–28 August. "I believe it would not be as bad for the people of South Dakota if they should have a drowth for ten years, as that women should be deprived of suffrage for ten years," Rev. Anna Howard Shaw told assembled suffrage delegates.[63] To take this message to the nearby Republican convention, the suffragists elected eight representatives, but the Republicans — embroiled in an intense battle over congressional nominees — barely noticed them. Hardly noticed as well were the claims and aspirations of the elected Brown County delegation, which included physician S. Jay Coyne, real estate broker Frank A. Brown, and mortgage collector Dan Shields, among others.

As the Republican convention approached, the local delegates had bragged that the prominence of their county in state economics and politics entitled their man, Henry C. Sessions of Columbia, to the nomination for one of two congressional seats.[64] Baum, on the other hand, declared on 23 August that "a man who thinks he can predict the final composition of the [Republican] state ticket is either a Solon or an ass" and suggested that incumbent John Pickler of Faulkton held the secret hearts and best political interests of most Brown County delegates. On 16 August he had speculated that Sessions's name "will be used as a leverage, and in that way may accomplish some good," but "if Brown county secures an office, it will be something else and some other man will get it."

Baum's assessment proved politically astute and much more accurate than that of Brown County conventiongoers. Delegate Dan Shields had loudly predicted victory for Sessions, only to be publicly humiliated when, the day before the convention, Sessions withdrew in favor of Pickler. Baum's landlady concluded that United States Senator Richard F. Pettigrew of Sioux Falls had pulled the strings that resulted in this embarrassment, and, indeed, a letter from Pettigrew to Sessions confirms this judgment. The two politicians had struck a deal to give Brown County a state government office and Sessions a political appointment if he would withdraw from the race. Brown County delegates, however, could not lower their expectations and compromise. "I know that the delegation acted contrary to your judgment," Pettigrew wrote to Sessions, "they made perfect fools of themselves and I think I came very near telling them so. They could have had the position of auditor which is the best office in the state, but I suppose your delegation had so many candidates that they could not agree upon any one."[65]

The county Republican delegation returned shamefacedly from this fiasco, but a local event took the spotlight off their failure. "The demure tranquility of our city was overthrown last Wednesday evening by the news of a genuine sensation," Baum announced on 30 August. Charles Gavin, a twenty-one-year-old hotel clerk at the Sherman House, had eloped with Estel Smith, age seventeen. The young couple had met on the Fourth of July when Gavin, a judge for the ladies' riding event, awarded the prize to Smith. "Naturally," Baum reported, "Miss Smith appreciated this favor, and an acquaintance was formed which rapidly ripened into a more tender feeling." Greeting the romance with dismay, the young woman's parents forbade the two to meet, whereupon Smith fled to the arms of her beau, who took her to the county seat of Columbia and married her. Friends interceded for the young couple with her family, giving the affair a happy ending, and Baum concluded, "The *Pioneer* wishes them well and hopes that on their journey through life they may see the world through the same rosy-hued glasses that now dazzle their eyes." The event caused Mrs. Bilkins to lapse once again into poetry.

"Well, I declare," exclaimed our landlady, as she opened the dining room door in time to catch Tom dancing with the hired girl, while the colonel beat time on the bottom of a tea-tray, and the doctor sat perched upon the side-board whistling the heel and toe; "well I declare if ye ain't worse nor a lot o' delegates!"

The colonel threw the tray under the table with a bang; the hired girl flew into the kitchen and slammed the door behind her, while the doctor slid gracefully from the side-board, and Tom with a red face and an embarrassed look sat down carelessly in the bread-pan full of "sponge," which stood upon a chair.

"Home from Mitchell?" inquired the doctor, in his best off-hand manner.

"No!" snapped our landlady, "I'm there yet." And she proceded to hang up her hat and shawl, after which she opened the kitchen door and informed the girl that "she'd give her half an hour to pack up her duds an' quit these diggin's."

The colonel winked at the doctor, the doctor winked at Tom, and Tom scraped the dough off the seat of his pants with a thoughtful air.

"Did you attend the equal rights convention?" inquired the colonel, pleasantly, when Mrs. Bilkins seemed to have regained her equanimity.

"Equal rights nuthin'!" retorted our landlady, "their meetin' was a second-class affair. You see Doc. Coyne got a fair-haired patient soon after he got there that kep' him busy, so I got his proxy an' swung with the Brown county delegation. Didn't we have a time though? Well I guess! The delegates from all the other counties was tied together with strings, an' ole Pettigrew he had the ends o' all the strings tied to his suspenders. An' Brown county delegates was all tied with one string too, an' every feller he thought he had hold o' the end o' the string. An' a fine circus it was. When anyone axed us what we wanted we yelled 'the yearth!' an' then the band would play 'Never no never no more.'

" 'We've got this thing in our own hands,' says Dan Shields, 'an' we mean to keep it.' An' so they let us keep it.

" 'Let's get on the band wagon,' says I.

" 'That's where we are,' says Frank Brown, but somehow the other fellers didn't come our way, an' the Sessions axle grease clogged our wheels so's the vehicle wouldn't move. It's all right; we got what we deserved, but if Brown county had a' whittled a lot o' men outer a pine block they would a been jest as good."

"The result should teach us to aspire to unity in our own ranks," remarked the colonel, grimly.

"It should teach us to keep outer politics," retorted Mrs. Bilkins. "Brown county weren't needed in that convention. We might o' stayed to hum an' saved our money. When we're such fools as ter buck agin' the powers that be, an' get in the soup, it's time to begin playin' checkers an' leave politics alone. But I hear you've had an elopement while I was gone."

"Yes, a quiet one."

"It's quite romantic. It makes a person think o' Pyramid an' Thisbee. An' so I've writ a stanza on it as follers:

> "When Cholly saw 'Stel
> In love he fell,
> An' swore she was wuth havin'.
> So he took her away
> To Columb-i-a,
> An' now she's Missus Gavin."

. . . .

She returns from her Vacation and Visits the Fair

20 September 1890

Mrs. Bilkins's three-week working vacation "explained" the absence since 30 August of the "Our Landlady" column, reflecting the fact that Baum had been too busy to write the weekly satire. Beginning on 15 August he had launched a monthly financial journal called the *Western Investor* to boost South Dakota among easterners. After months of prodding the business community to rustle for outside investors, Baum had put his own time and money into the effort. The new periodical contained articles "pertinent to finance" as well as serious discussions of South Dakota's investment potential.[66] The newspaperman had also acquired "the sole right," granted by the state agricultural board, to print the program for the 1890 state fair to be held in Aberdeen on 15–19 September. Further, on 6 September local citizens subsidized the printing and distribution of 12,000 copies of the *Aberdeen Saturday Pioneer*'s "grand boom edition . . . devoted to advertising the Fair throughout South Dakota."[67] What little time these extra printing duties left the editor, his theater activities consumed. Baum not only spent weeks rehearsing the roles of Rufus Ready in *The Little Tycoon* and Dr. Daly in *The Sorcerer* but also served as stage manager for the productions, which would net the Episcopal Ladies Guild over $200.[68]

When fair week finally arrived, eight brass bands met the special trains bringing 8,000 to 10,000 visitors daily into the Hub City to view horse races, agricultural displays, balloon ascensions, tightrope acts, and amateur theatricals. Republican, Democrat, and Independent candidates spoke each evening from headquarters in downtown Aberdeen or from temporary quarters at the fairgrounds. Pierre and Huron, chief among the state capital contestants, had raised almost a million dollars between them by selling city and county bonds, and supporters spread the money with a liberal hand, hiring bands and giving out promotional items. Printed ribbons, or "badges," added splotches of color as fairgoers expressed their support for one city or the other. Each side declared that its opponent's badges were seen mostly on women and children — that is, nonvoters — but as enthusiasm grew, Pierre supporters began to sense victory and claimed a 20,000-vote majority.[69]

Wednesday, 17 September — Women's Day — drew the biggest crowds to hear national and local suffragists speak from the grandstand platform. Susan B. Anthony, Henry Blackwell, Reverend Anna Howard Shaw, and Reverend Olympia Brown had reached Aberdeen early in the week. Signing her hotel register "Perfect equality of rights for women is the demand of Susan B. Anthony," the venerable organizer of the South Dakota campaign signaled her steadfast determination despite a grueling summer of travel and speechmaking.[70] Anthony's critics, never far behind her, criticized the seventy-year-old's short speech, but Shaw's charismatic platform performance stilled even the loudest antisuffragists.

Typically, Baum's fair-week column touched on all the important happenings but paid most attention to a tightrope act that the *Aberdeen Evening Republican* termed an "amusing burlesque."[71] In targeting the performer's act, Baum developed the character of Mrs. Bilkins further, using a storytelling device that shows her to be gullible, literal-minded, inexperienced, and somewhat humorless. Mrs. Bilkins's narrative recalls Huck Finn's description of the circus clown in Mark Twain's *Huckleberry Finn* (1884): in both instances, the narrator tells in deadpan manner a story that the reader, who is more knowl-edgeable than either Huck or Mrs. Bilkins, can perceive on two levels.[72] Thus, Baum and his fellow Aberdonians could not only congratulate themselves on the Hub City's cosmopolitan appearance and attitudes during fair week but also feel superior to all the country folk in town for the event.

"Yes," remarked our landlady, as she gathered up the watermelon rinds to make sweet pickles of and the seeds to plant in the spring, "you can bet I'm glad to get home agin. This goin'-a-visitin' ain't what it's cracked up to be. You see I visited my sister in Eurekie, and had to do all the housework and take care of three babies besides, an' so, arter three weeks of hard work I decided to come home an' take a rest."

"Have you attended the fair?" inquired Tom, as he pinned two Wolsey badges together and used them for a necktie.

"You bet! I went Wen'sday, that were women's day, although the women goes most every day so's there'll be some one to wear Pierre badges. The children got away with a good many Pierre badges, too, so Huron needn't think her badges is the only ones there is wored."

"How did you enjoy the races?" asked the colonel lighting a Pierre cigar.

"Fust class. But the most soul inspirin' thing was the tight-rope act. Well sir, would you believe it, that feller actually walked backwards on a tight rope, a good ten foot from the ground! — an' all he had to keep him from fallin' was a long pole that he could touch the ground with if he didn't happen to balance all right. An' then he sot right down on that rope an' staid there until he got his breath. An' then he tried to git up an' couldn't. An' the crowd yelled to encourage him. An' then he wiped his brow on his costume and kissed his hand an' tried it again. An' the crowd yelled so that he finally got up. An' after that he slid down inter a trapeze and hung on by his toes while he picked grass with his teeth. If he'd been a taller man he'd a bumped his head. This feller had more hair-breadth escapes to the square inch than a man would who eat reglar at Ward's. The sight was sickenin' in its awe-inspirin' grandeur. Many of the ladies turned away their heads to avoid seein' him tear up the yearth with his nose, but I was so hoaror-struck that I couldn't take my eyes off'n him. Well, at last he took hold of the ground and let go with his feet, an' the whole crowd heaved a sigh of relief, for they knew then as he was safe.

"Sam Vroom said he wouldn't done it fer ten dollars an' a baby, because it would a disarranged his front hair so. But it was a great fair an' no mistake. Colonel, you're too near the stove, your coat is burnin'."

"No," said the colonel, "it's my cigar. Did you hear Miss Anthony speak?"

"I tried to, but she didn't seem to have much to say 'cause she's said it so many times already. An' the boys kep' yellin' 'has she came?' an' then the crowd would yell 'not yet!' in reply. But some of the Reverend ladies panned out all right. Things was so mixed up that I didn't know when I got home whether I was a woman-suffrage-anti-Pierre-prohibition-jack-pot woman, or a anti-rights-anti-Huron-anti-up-anti-prohibition-anti-boodle-all-wool-an'-a-yard-wide politician; but judgin' from my conglomerated feelin's I guess I was."

"Have you kissed the baby?" inquired the doctor, solicitously.

"Not yet, but unless this round of dissipation comes to a bust pretty soon there won't be nothin' else left to do. Between the fair and the operar, an' Doc. Fowler's weddin' an' Jay Paulhamuses last diamond ring, Aberdeen folks is gettin' pretty near rattled, an' nothin' but a rise in wheat will bring 'em to their sober senses."

After putting the paper to bed on 20 September, Baum left for Chicago to meet his pregnant wife and their three sons, who had been "sojourning during the summer farther east." In Chicago, Baum talked to grain brokers, hoping to bring South Dakotans the news they most wanted to hear. On 4 October he reported that soon wheat prices "will go up like a balloon" even though "the bears have expended nearly every device conceivable to prevent the natural rise in grain" that the shortage might cause. Dakota was not worse off than other states, Baum concluded, "and those who leave here to seek fairer fields will in most cases escape the frying-pan to fall into the fire." This sentiment became Baum's steady refrain over the next few months.

During its editor's absence, the *Aberdeen Saturday Pioneer* of 27 September carried only reprints from other papers and dry snippets of local news. Even the layout lacked the usual pizzazz that Baum's touch gave to the publication. Since the *Pioneer* made no excuses this time for the absence of Mrs. Bilkins's usual contribution, the *Aberdeen Daily News* took a stab at it the next day: " 'Our Landlady' has been sick, very sick, the past week, from an overdose of her own hash. It did not kill her, however, and she may be expected on the hurricane deck as usual in a few days." Mrs. Bilkins and the newspaper's usual sparkle returned with Baum the following week.

. . . .

She Discusses Timely Topics and Criticises

some Aberdeen People

4 October 1890

"If there is one thing more than another which seems to be constitutional with the American people," Baum editorialized on 4 October, "it is to cry 'hard times.' If a merchant is not making all the money he could wish he groans 'hard times.' . . . We wish we dared state how many people have expressed to us this fall a wish to 'leave this cursed country.' " Those who did move on to the next boomtown were "a mat[t]er of indifference to the steady and hard-working part of the community who are 'here to stay,' " the editor concluded. With the *Western Investor*, Baum had demonstrated his commitment to the future of Aberdeen and South Dakota. Were the rest of the citizens willing to invest the same dedication and effort? Specifically, Baum pleaded with them to help themselves by means of irrigation, something he had been promoting since May. The failure of the 1890 wheat crop and the stagnant market prices following the scanty harvest had finally persuaded the leaders of Aberdeen to embrace the idea and hold a convention to study the issue. Frank Hagerty and other bankers announced that they would lend money to "good farmers" who wished to irrigate, and the convention asked the county to finance well-drilling.[73]

"Two years will find the Jim River Valley under thorough irrigation," wrote an enthusiastic Baum after the convention, "and producing crops which will be the wonder and admiration of the world, and the means of enriching every farmer in its area" (Baum would expand on this prophecy in two January columns). To ensure this future, he proposed that the county buy the machinery and let the farmers themselves supply the labor. Asking his readers to comment on the suggestion, he cautioned: "Only remember that there is no time to be lost, and that if you intend to reside in South Dakota Y O U are morally and through personal interest obligated to take part in this discussion. Let us lay our plans for a battle which will effectually annihilate the demon, Drouth." Mrs. Bilkins, however, expressed the author's skepticism about the willingness of Aberdonians to do anything but complain.

"The people of Aberdeen," said our landlady, as she set the pumpkin pie on the sideboard and placed a piece of poison fly paper over it to protect it, "are different from most any people I ever seed. This 'ere is a western community, but the people are lots more effeeter here than they are in the yeast. When a man looses a penny through a hole in his pocket he goes an' gits it sowed up so's it won't happen agin. When a boy looses anything through a hole in his pocket, he sets down and cries. Now Aberdeen folks is jest like that boy."

"Mrs. Bilkins," remarked the doctor, laying down his paper and wiping his spectacles complacently, "you are speaking in parables and I, for one, do not comprehend the tenor of your remarks."

"I don't care whether my remarks is tenor or bass," snapped our landlady, as she wiped the butter knife on her apron and placed it on the dish; "what I says is gospel truth, and you'll find it out! Why, here we are in the very flower garden o' the yearth. Here we are in a country where the sile is richer and deeper than in any other part of Ameriky; where the poor eastern farmers have found peace and plenty, where the bankrupt eastern merchant has found a good trade and a good livin'; where clerks has blossomed into store-keepers and penny-ante men into bankers, an' convicks inter lawyers, an' salvation army dodgers inter ministers, an' roustabouts inter real estate and loan agents. An' they all fell inter soft snaps an' thought as they was great men in disguise, an' they'd never let their neighbors know the truth about the matter. Everything they had they owed to good crops an' when the crops went back on 'em they was a pitiful sight. They howl, an' they kick, an' they scream; an' say they'll quit the blasted country an' the Lord forgive 'em for ever comin' here — forgittin' all the time that if they hadn't come they'd probably starved to death 'afore now!"

"I think, Mrs. Bilkins," broke in the colonel, "that your remarks are too general. There may be some such as you mention but I am sure you recognize the fact that there are still many good and true men in Aberdeen," and he twisted his moustache and looked at her appealingly from out his eagle eye.

Our landlady was not proof against the handsome colonel's fascinations. She drew the back of her hand politely across her nose, smoothed her back hair dreamily, and stirred up the omelet with the stove hook and a coyly unconscious air as she replied:

"No, I know there is good men here — but they ain't very plenty, and what there is ain't got the pluck to take the hard times by the neck an' choke 'em off as they'd orter. They set down an' groan an' say they wish Aberdeen had some men to boom things the way Sioux Falls is doin' an' all the time fergetin' that they is the men to do it an' that they c a n do it if they wanter, an' that even today Aberdeen is capable of havin' a bigger boom than any other city in the state if her people would only let capital fights an' foreign investments alone, and use the means of prosperity that are layin' idle at their hands. If only every man would say 'I will do suthin' ' instead o' sayin' 'why don't somebody else do suthin'?' times would change mighty quick."

"You speak with deep feeling, ma'am," said Tom, fishing a collar button out of his sauce and putting it carefully in his vest pocket; "Do you know, Mrs. Bilkins, that the best hold you have upon your boarders is ministering to their curiosity? One never knows what he will discover next! It's like a lottery."

"Life is a lottery," sighed our landlady, as she fastened one end of her bangs which had become loose and dropped down; "an' it's a wonder they don't pass a law agin' living for that reason. A good many folks come to Aberdeen an' invested, and now howls because there's come a little backset and they'd like to git out. Why, even Frank Hagerty says to me the other day, 'I've just come from West Surperior,' says he, 'an' it makes me tired to think as I must stay in Aberdeen, an' can't git where the rustle is.'

" 'Frank,' says I, 'it's just like a feller gittin' married; he may git a good woman but a homely one, an' when he sees han'somer women he may hanker arter 'em, an' think his ole woman is no good. But it ain't no use; you're tied an' you must make the best of it, an' ten chances to one you'll get more solid comfort out o' that ole woman than you would if you had one o' them lively beauties that wear out quick. The honeymoon of Aberdeen's boom prosperity has wore off but she's good an' solid yit, an' there's lots o' solid prosperity and comfort to be got outer her. Be true to her — don't hanker arter the flesh-pots o' Tennessee an' Huron an' West Superior, an' you'll make more solid money outer your first love than you could outer a hundred towns that goes up like a rocket and comes down like a stick!' "

"Did he see the force of your argument?" asked the colonel, curiously.

"He did. 'It were a temporary weakness, Mrs. Bilkins,' says he, 'an' you can put me down to stick harder nor any fly paper in Ameriky.' An' he'll do it. But he's only one of 'em. If Aberdeen folks would all go to work to make the most outer their town, an' shut their eyes to the outside world, it wouldn't be long before we would be the most prosperous community in the northwest. I ain't talkin' to hear myself talk. I may keep a boardin'-house, but I knows my business an' a good many other folkses business, too!"

. . . .

Taken in the early 1890s, this photograph of L. Frank Baum
shows the columnist as he looked when he lived in Aberdeen.
C.C. Packard, photographer, Kalamazoo, Michigan.
Courtesy of L. Frank Baum Collection, Alexander Mitchell Library

Maud Gage, daughter of feminist Matilda Joslyn Gage, married L. Frank Baum in 1882. Courtesy of L. Frank Baum Collection, Alexander Mitchell Library

Taken at the meeting of the International Council of Women in Washington DC, 1888, this group portrait includes persons important to the 1890 South Dakota suffrage campaign. Seated second from right is Matilda Joslyn Gage, Baum's mother-in-law, who founded the Woman's National Liberal Union. Seated second from left is Susan B. Anthony, who managed the 1890 South Dakota effort. Seated third from right is Elizabeth Cady Stanton. Courtesy of Dacotah Prairie Museum

The cover of the 1941 South Dakota Writers' Project edition of Baum's columns depicted the hefty landlady and her passion for the colonel. André Boratko, director of the South Dakota Art Project, chose to illustrate the 29 March 1890 column in this cover drawing.

*On Aberdeen's Main Street in winter, a group of businessmen
shoveled a path to the post office and Salisbury's book and cigar store.
Courtesy of Dacotah Prairie Museum*

*On the first of May 1890, liquor stores were no longer legal in South Dakota.
As stock shown here suggests, however, the liquor trade was lucrative in Aberdeen
before prohibition. Courtesy of Dacotah Prairie Museum*

L. Frank Baum experienced firsthand the trials of photographing a baby, but his four-month-old son, Harry Neal Baum, appears tranquil in this J. Q. Miller photograph dated 1 May 1890. Courtesy of Brenda Baum Turner and Michael Patrick Hearn

With military-style uniforms and decorated lances (background), the Aberdeen Guards drilled for fellow Hub Citians. Captain Frances ("Fannie") Hauser is standing far left in the back row of this 1890 J. Q. Miller photograph. Courtesy of Matilda J. Gage Estate—John J. Ackley, administrator, Sally Roesch Wagner, biographer

The Aberdeen Guards may have been the prototype for the girl armies that appear in Baum's Marvelous Land of Oz. *Here, as illustrated by John R. Neill, General Jinjur leads her Army of Revolt.*

The boy followed after them, carrying several baskets and wraps and packages which various members of the Army of Revolt had placed in his care. It was not long before they came to the green granite walls of the City and halted before the gateway.

90

Gen. Jinjur's Army of Revolt

The Guardian of the Gate at once came out and looked at them curiously, as if a circus had come to town. He carried a bunch of keys swung round his neck by a golden chain; his hands were thrust carelessly into his pockets, and he seemed to have no idea at all that the City was threatened by rebels. Speaking pleasantly to the girls, he said:

"Good morning, my dears! What can I do for you?"

"Surrender instantly!" answered General Jinjur, standing before him and frowning as terribly as her pretty face would allow her to.

"Surrender!" echoed the man, astounded. "Why, it's impossible. It's against the law! I never heard of such a thing in my life."

91

In the summer of 1890 Brown County State's Attorney Edward T. Taubman had his hands full trying to please prohibitionists and shut down blind pigs. Baum called him "frank and square-toed" but "inclined to be loud-mouthed and aggressive." From George W. Kingsbury, History of Dakota Territory

Campaigning for location of the state capital reached a crescendo during the 1890 South Dakota State Fair in Aberdeen. Huron and Pierre each hired a band to promote its cause, but Pierre supporters sensed victory and claimed a 20,000-vote lead. Courtesy of Codington County Historical Society, Inc., Watertown SD

Women's reading clubs met weekly during the fall of 1890, leading Baum to poke fun at their motives in his 15 November column. Courtesy of Dakotah Prairie Museum

Henry L. Loucks, president of the South Dakota Farmers' Alliance, was the Independent Party's candidate for governor in 1890. Courtesy of South Dakota State Historical Society–State Archives

William F. ("Buffalo Bill") Cody had enjoyed good rapport with Sitting Bull during the 1885 Wild West Show circuit. The two are shown here in Montreal. Courtesy of South Dakota State Historical Society–State Archives

Charles A. Howard, a young National Guardsman and city alderman in 1890, would later become a state senator. From George W. Kingsbury, History of Dakota Territory

William E. Kidd, a radical Populist, had taken over the Aberdeen Evening Republican *when he was sued for criminal libel in the winter of 1891.*
Courtesy of South Dakota State Historical Society—State Archives

By 1902, Baum had achieved prosperity as the author of two best-selling children's books. Courtesy of L. Frank Baum Collection, Alexander Mitchell Library

Jewett Brothers deliverymen distributed wholesale groceries and drugs to the small towns of northeastern South Dakota and southeastern North Dakota. Courtesy of Dakotah Prairie Museum

She Discourses on the "Hard Times Club,"

and tells a Story

11 October 1890

Beard, Gage, and Beard, general store, announced on 13 September that they would begin selling merchandise for cash only, reducing prices as low as possible to retain customers. The "cash system" soon became a sign of the times as numerous grocers and clothiers declared their unwillingness to grant credit. All over town the hard times were making themselves felt. The "young bloods" of Aberdeen, those who had not left for "the flesh-pots o' Tennessee" or elsewhere, faced the social season of 1890–91 with little cash in their pockets. A few of them lacked winter overcoats as well, for an unscrupulous furrier had recently absconded with garments stored for the summer in his care.[74] Whether the young men who gathered in the stores, offices, and boardinghouses of Aberdeen had "thunk up" the Hard Times Club for their own amusement or Baum created it for this column, Mrs. Bilkins's description carried political subcurrents that ridiculed the arguments and motives of Independents, especially gubernatorial candidate Henry Loucks. More overtly, the club structure with its position of an "Outer Guard" resembled that of the popular fraternal lodges of the era, and its schedule anticipated the church "sociables" that began the same week with a Presbyterian-sponsored bonnet social.

"One of the nonsensicalist things I've heard of," said our landlady, as she skimmed the milk carefully and poured the blue fluid into the cream jug, "is that 'air Hard Times Club. It may be a funny thing to talk about, but what'll it amount to?"

"I haven't heard of it," replied the doctor, as he picked a spoiled fly out of his coffee.

"Why, the young fellers is realizin' that if they go inter serciety this winter they can't pay their board bills, an' if they pay their board bills they can't monkey much with serciety. An' so they thunk up a scheme to revolutionize serciety itself and still keep the future voters with 'em, an' they calls this ijea the Hard Times Club."

"Who belongs to it?" asked the colonel, as he broke a piece from his toast with several powerful blows of the carving knife handle, and soaked it in his coffee.

"Oh, lots of 'em. There's Wendell, an' Winsor, an' Waterman, an' Milligan, an' Sam Vroom, an' Skip, an' Corwin, an' lots more. They wanted Al. Ward fer president but Al. he said times were too hard. You see, he knew he'd have ter set 'em up if he accepted an' so they made him Outer Guard instead, where his expenses will be light. Doc Fowler wanted ter join, but they told him there was a limit to everything, an' no man what smoked ten cent cigars could enter their sacred precincts. Married men can't belong. As ex-Governor Loucks wrote 'em when he declined to run fer treasurer o' the club, says he: 'they must lie in the beds theys made fer themselves an' if they hain't got any beds they must lie anyway." That may sound like a Loucks argument, but the club adopted it unanimous!"

"What is their plan of operation?" asked Tom, looking lovingly at his one nickel.

"Why, they're goin' to give a series of parties. The gals will furnish the music theirselves, and the club will meet at each other's houses — that is, those that's got houses. The refreshments is limited to crackers an' cheese an' spring water, and the gentlemen is allowed to dance in their stocking feet, so no shoe leather will be wore out unnecessary.

"The gals will furnish the refreshments an' also one small boy to be paid by the gals' fathers, to carry the club overcoat from one member to another on the nights o' the parties. In this way all can wear the overcoat by turns an' avoid beatin' the clothing stores outer more'n one garment."

"I'd like to join that club," declared Tom.

"And I," said the colonel.

"And I," said the doctor.

"It's got eighty-four members now," said Mrs. Bilkins, "an' the number's increasin' every day. August Witte were innishiated yesterday. No one can jine that don't want more'n he's got the money to pay for.

"The club's goin' to boycot all the banks and collectors and has passed a resolution to ignore the conterbution boxes in all the churches. Oh, it's a fine idee, an'll help the boys out amazin'.

"I hear the city's goin' to economize too. When the uncommon council wanted to discharge Street-comish Lewis our Cholly got up an' said they might jest as well discharge the mayor. 'Why don't you?' said one o' the fathers. 'Well,' says Cholly, 'I move we discharge Mayor Moody.' There was a bust of applause at this, but one o' the uncommon upset the deal by sayin', 'I move an amendment that we discharge the mayor an' all the common council, an' let Cholly run the city!' That made everybody laugh an' peace was restored. But it wasn't a bad idee an' if the amendment had carried I don't know but what we'd been just as well off anyhow!"

She Confides to the Boarders a Deal to Advance
the Cause of Equal Suffrage

18 October 1890

With only three weeks remaining before the election, campaign organizers accelerated activities. As secretary of the Aberdeen Equal Suffrage Association (ESA), Baum received a circular from state headquarters outlining the election work. "In every voting precinct," the communication read, "appoint a committee to make a house to house canvass" and "appoint a number [of women] to look after refreshments." Serve lunch at the polls, if only coffee and sandwiches, and sing suffrage songs to make it "a general jubilee," the state ESA urged.[75] Baum apparently appointed Mrs. Bilkins to the committee on refreshments, even though she harbored a certain skepticism about the plan's effectiveness. Organizers intended the food and music to sway Independent, Republican, and Democratic voters alike to the cause of woman suffrage, but in Mrs. Bilkins's case it worked the opposite way, swinging her allegiance at least temporarily to the Independents, who had promised her a short-term deal that she could not refuse.

As Baum knew, the Populist movement had put some severe strains on the state suffrage campaign. Before Susan B. Anthony agreed to come to South Dakota in April to lend financial support and national speakers to the fight for a constitutional amendment, Henry Loucks and Alonzo Wardall of the South Dakota Farmers' Alliance promised her that their organization would support woman suffrage within the Republican party, making "of themselves a balance of power to compel the Republicans to put a woman suffrage plank in their platform."[76] Reasonably assured that a major party would support the issue, Anthony came west in hope of victory. In June, however, Loucks and Wardall led the third-party movement, and the woman suffrage plank became one of the first casualties of party politics. The Independents ignored the issue "for the avowed object of winning the votes of the anti-prohibition & anti-woman suffrage" immigrants. "Hence," Anthony concluded, "their influence while seemingly friendly — will be virtually against us."[77]

When the Republican press charged in June that the suffragists were "dallying" with the Independent party to bolster the new Populist movement, Anthony wrote to Alice Pickler, "We must not allow ourselves to *even seem* to be playing into [the Independents'] hands."[78] Avoiding the association proved to be difficult, however, especially after the Republicans also reneged on putting a woman suffrage plank in their party platform at the end of August. Throughout September both Republican and Independent leaders distanced themselves from the issue. Many local Independents, however, remained willing to support the cause in a public forum.[79] In Brown County the Independents took an aggressive pro-suffrage stance, clearly hoping to use the issue to their own advantage. On 9 October the Independent nominee for attorney general declared his support for women's rights and asserted that "any candidate who would not define his position on this subject, was a political coward."[80] William E. Kidd, a member of the Brown County Independent Committee, invited a suffragist speaker to the upcoming Independent barbecue. The party's candidate for county treasurer, Norwegian-born merchant John A. Fylpaa (pronounced "fill pa"), declared his support as well.[81]

Anthony and other national speakers counseled suffrage workers to create their own speaking platforms and avoid associating with third-party politics. They foresaw that the dominant but threatened Republicans would lose sympathy for the cause and join the Democrats in voting against the amendment. Nevertheless, local workers frequently took the easiest course, speaking from the offered Independent platforms and claiming that they reached more men by doing so.[82] Baum's "Landlady" column implied that suffrage workers had little to gain from making deals with Independents — who were supposedly already committed to the cause — and the negative effect on Republicans could already be seen. "Once give women the right to vote," a Brown County Republican wrote to the *News*, "and seven-eights of them would knife the republican party. . . . They would be found in every third party move that might be inaugurated. . . . Indeed, they belong to the Loucks party now. Let them go to him for recognition."[83] Baum's landlady must have been just the sort of turncoat these fearful Republicans dreaded.

"Sometimes," said our landlady as she deftly stopped a hole in the coffee pot with a small piece of the dishrag, "I think the world is all goin' wrong, an' then, when I gits all discouraged, suthin' comes up to set it right agin. It's pritty evenly balanced, to tell the truth, an' them as philosophizes can see the good in human natur'."

"When you moralize," said Tom, finishing a sad inspection of his laundry list, "I know there is something in the wind. What is it, Mrs. Bilkins?"

"Well," she answered, "it's rayther a private matter, an' I agreed not ter let it git out."

"But," protested the colonel, getting excited at the prospect that something was being withheld from his knowledge, "we are all members of one family, my dear Mrs. Bilkins, and it is only right that we should know anything that concerns you."

"Won't you tell?" she asked hesitatingly.

"Never!" declared the doctor, and the others looked as solemn and virtuous as possible and shook their heads.

"Well then," began our landlady, "I've bin a good deal bothered to know how to boom Ekal Suffridge at the polls. The C'mittee wants us to set up the refreshments, but the grocers is onto the deal and has all adopted the cash sistem to avoid donatin' anything to the good cause. When you set out to refresh a lot o' voters you've got a big job on hand. They'll drink more coffee an' eat more san'wiches nor Pharaoh's army, an' they'll wipe their mouths on the tablecloth an' go off an' vote agin' ekal suffridge an' then come back an' eat agin. It's this thing that got me kinder discuridged like. If we only had the means to give each voter a free dose o' fizik, as John Firey is promisin' to do fer any one as votes fer him, we might git along. They wouldn't hang around like they does at the refreshment tables, but would vote quick and run. But fizik ain't in our line an' so I got discuridged. But yesterday a little feller with archery legs an' a convalessin' mustash comes an' knocks at the door an' says, 'Slacker rick em stan flor a' crummin.'

" 'Nix cum a rouse,' says I.[84]

" 'Oxcuse me,' says he, 'I thought you was a Norske woman.'

" 'No,' says I, 'I'm a Yankee.'

" 'Well,' says he, 'is this the charmin' Miss' Bilkinses dear baardin' house?'

" 'No sir,' says I, 'this 'ere is the cheapest boardin' house, countin' by receets, in the Unitid States of Americky. But who air you, sir?'

" 'Feel-yer-paw,' says he.

" 'No,' says I, with kinder virtuous indignity, 'I won't feel yer paw til I knows who ye air.'

" 'That's my name,' says he, with a sort o' sad an' reproachful smile.

" 'Oh,' says I, struck all of a heap, 'you're the injipendent what wants ter be county treasurer.'

" 'Them's my sentiments, mom,' says he.

" 'Next year,' says I, 'I'll talk to yer, but this year I can't vote.'

" 'But you're on the ekal suffridge c'mittee,' says he, 'an' I thought perhaps we could make a deal. Ye see I'm chock full o' deals. I ain't the sort o' stuff what gives up when I knows I'm beat. If there's anything in deals I mean to worry Frank Raymond into an early grave 'afore election.'

"Well, here was my chance. Here was the means to feed the hungry voters on election day. 'What's yer deal?' says I.

" 'Well,' says he, 'it's jest this. Nearly every blamed injipendent is a ekal suffragist, but all the ekal suffridgists ain't injipendents by a blamed sight.

Now if you people will git all the suffragists to vote fer me I'll agree to git all the injipendents to vote for ekal suffridge, an' more'n that, I'll pay fer all the refreshibles when I git hold er the county money.'

" 'Will you?' says I, joyfully.

" 'You bet I will,' says he, 'an' I'll send ye down from my store in Frederick six cans o' mackerel fer sandwiches an' a gallon o' molasses to sweeten the coffee free of charge.'

"Well, I was that flumbusterkated that I fell on his neck an' he fell on the table an' the table fell on the cat. But we signed the agreement in black an' white an' the cause is safe. What do you think o' that deal?"

"Ahem!" said the colonel, "it seems a good one for Fylpaa, but what will you get out of it?"

"What?" replied our landlady in amazement, "why, vittles — that's what we'll git; an' it seems ter me that you've lived long enough at this here boardin' house ter appreciate what vittles is."

"Yes," returned the colonel, slowly, "I think I have."

. . . .

She Relates some Exciting Ancedotes and Attends the Independent Barbecue

25 October 1890

Three weddings, a fire, and an Independent barbecue kept the Hub City humming during the week. Two couples tied the knot on Tuesday evening, but *the* social event took place on Wednesday when Baum's friend George B. Kimberly wed Eva Finch at Saint Mark's Episcopal Church in front of the most "fashionable [and] representative audience" ever gathered there. The engraved invitations set the ceremony for seven o'clock in the evening, "but long before that hour the church was filled with ladies and gentlemen in full dress who eagerly awaited the arrival of the wedding party," Baum reported. The Reverend Doctor R. J. Keeling, Episcopal rector, "performed the ceremony in an impressive manner." The occasion apparently went off without a hitch, but Mrs. Bilkins titillated her boarders with the story behind the story.

On Tuesday morning a "slight blaze" at the Carril M. Coe residence brought out the fire department. A defective gasoline stove had ignited the fire, but Mrs. Coe grabbed the garden hose and extinguished the flames before the firemen arrived. The *Aberdeen Daily News* reported that the loss was "in the neighborhood of $150."[85] Mrs. Bilkins's report of the same event, suggesting how the damage might have come about, initiated Baum's criticism of the fire department. Although most jabs appeared in his editorials rather than his saritical humor columns, the critical comments would ultimately lead a local pundit, who signed himself Truthful Zeke, to suggest that the department hire Mrs. Bilkins. " 'Baum's landlady' could be secured at a reasonable salary" to keep the fire alarms from waking townspeople, Zeke wrote, "and the Lord knows she is quiet enough."[86]

Friday, a cold but sunny day, brought a large crowd to the fairgrounds for a much ballyhooed Independent rally and barbecue. Organizers had promised "good music, eloquent speeches, roast ox and hot coffee" at an "old-fashioned rally of the common people."[87] From the grandstand, various Independent orators addressed the crowd throughout the day. "Instead of the calm and intelligent discussion of political principles," the *News* complained, "the harangues were tirades of abuse. . . . This constant sour-milk-and-wind diet seems to produce a sort of cholic [*sic*] which is apparent at every turn."[88] Mrs. Bilkins also found the diet a little too rarefied for her taste.

"I can't understand," said our landlady, as she began clearing off the table just in time to prevent the colonel from helping himself to a third piece of pie, "why there's such a rush to git married jest when the cool weather comes on. This marryin' goes in streaks, I've noticed. It's like a drove o' cattle; they hesitate a long time about crossin' the road, but when one gits over the others go with a rush. But there's one o' the wictims that come pretty nigh losin' his gal this week."

"How was that?" asked Tom.

"Why he thought he'd jest take a little nap 'afore the ceremony to gain strength, an' so he laid down an' went ter sleep. An' the folks got all ready an' went ter church, an' the bride an' her folks waited an' waited and behold the bridegroom didn't cometh. An' his best man got skeert and rushed up ter his room an' found him in bed.

" 'George,' says he, 'fer God's sake git up!'

" 'Bankrupt stock,' says George, beginin' to wake up, 'sell 'em fer half price.'

" 'Great Heavings, man! air you mad?' yells his best man, pullin' him onter the floor.

" 'S'matter,' says George, rubbin' his eyes, 'fire?'

" 'No, no!'

" 'Murder?'

" 'No! wuss, you loonatix, wuss! It's a weddin'!'

"An' then the happy bridesgroom remembered and jumped inter his swaller-tail quicker'n Harvey Jewett could foreclose on a grocery store. But when they got to the church the minister was missin'. An' so the best man rushed up ter his room and found him asleep too.

" 'Arise, Revenue Doc.,' says he, 'put on your togs an' walk, or you'll miss your fee!' An' the Revenue Doc. leaped with one jump inter his clothes, an' rushed to the church, and skinned up the middle ile, an' jest missed a harrowin' death be fallin' through the register, an' then he did lightnin' change act an' come forth serene in his pontifical robes an' did the job up to the everlastin' satisfaction o' the contractin' parties. An' the audience never knew how near they missed seein' the show. The only great mistake he made was to make the groom say as he'd "obay" the bride, but as wee'l join [we'er goin'?] ter have ekal suffridge, that ain't a bad innovation."

"Some queer things happen in life," said the doctor, "and many exciting incidents never come to the knowledge of the public."

"That's true," quoth our landlady, "now I don't usually run to a fire, but I did galivant up ter that one at Coe's the other mornin', and I wouldn't a' missed it fer a farm. The wall got afire back of the gasoline stove, an' the smoke went 'atween the ceilin' boards and oozed out 'atween the shingles on the roof. Miss Coe she put the fire out in a jiffy, and when the trouble was all over up galloped the chief o' the fire department followed by the hose cart an' the whole town. The smoke was still a pourin' gently through the shingles, as it hadn't had time ter escape, an' it set 'em all crazy.

" 'Hitch onter that 'air hydrant!' yelled the chief, an' the men yelled an' cussed an' tumbled over each other, an' fit an' cussed agin an' hitched on. By that time the crowd had jumped onter the little roof and begun to tear off the shingles an' the roof-boards with pickaxes an' they played the hose onter the smoke till it didn't have the heart to show itself any more. An' the bystadders bossed the job an' hooted an' told the firemen their business an' the excitement run high, I tell ye. It was nigh noon 'afore the excitment calmed down an' I got a chance to go in an' see that the fire had damaged the buildin' about $5 wuth and the firemen about $145 wuth. That's the way with fires, but they're a heap sight more excitein' than a injipendent barbecue on a cold day."

"Oh, you attended it, did you?" asked the colonel.

"Yes. I don't often miss a free feed — an' at heart you can bet I'm a injipendent fust, last an' in between. But the grub was disappointin'. It didn't have no salt on it, an' the first piece I got was burnt to a crisp. 'Gimme some a little rarer,' says I ter my friend, Feelyerpaw. He did, but it were so rare that it hadn't really got baked through, an' so I quit eatin' an' went around advisin' the wimmen an' children an' a few men I found not to eat nothin' or they'd die o' dyspepsia 'afore election day. An' I made up my mind then an' there that the next time I went ter a barbecue I'd stay to home and eat pancakes, an' I'll come out ahead!"

. . . .

She Gets Her Dander up and Goes Back on Politics

1 November 1890

As the election of 4 November 1890 loomed ever closer, editor Baum counseled his readers not to join the "independent rebellion," urging them to think hard before abandoning the Republican Party. "What reason is there," he queried on 1 November, "for supposing that the amateur politicians should be able to direct the wheels of the government more beneficially than the experienced engineers whose skill has brought prosperity, progression and reform to the land?" Study the Republican Party's record, he suggested, "from the day when our country was saved by the strong right arm of republicanism to the present, when we stand the most prosperous among the world's nations." Part of the G O P's thirty-year record included the recent passage of the Silver Purchase Act and the McKinley Tariff. The Independents were not happy with either measure, but Baum had been supporting both. "Shall we abandon the policy of protection," he asked, "after all it has done for us, to enter upon a policy which we have tested many times to our immediate, unfailing and tremendous loss? Shall we again rob ourselves of the rewards which have so richly come from the restoration of silver?"[89] In his last preelection editorial he exhorted readers to confirm their belief in these issues, to vote for Republican candidates and woman suffrage.

Throughout the campaign Baum had generally confined his political discussions to the issues, but his fellow editors were less restrained. From the beginning the *Aberdeen Daily News* roundly abused the Independent candidates, and in the last weeks the Independent press stepped up personal attacks on its opponents as well. The mudslinging led the *News* to hope that "sensible men are not governed by passion and prejudice" and to urge its readers to "guard against any startling stories which may be circulated in the interest of any party" during the last week of the campaign.[90] Meanwhile, Pierre and Huron boosters continued to throw money and promises around in support of their towns. The South Dakota Supreme Court knocked down Pierre's attempt to establish polling places in unorganized counties, but dirty tricks and shady deals seemed to multiply as the election neared. When she recollected herself, the Independent Mrs. Bilkins saw the issues a little differently from the Republican Baum, of course, but it was the conduct of the campaign that captured her attention, for right in the middle of it all were the Aberdeen "boys."

"Yesterday night," said our landlady, as she set the table carefully, and arranged a knife, fork and spoon beside each boarder's plate, "were Allhalloween an' there were quite a select party held ter celebrate the event."

"Did you go?" asked Tom, eying the table hungrily.

"You bet I did, an' I'm glad of it, although I feel almost as rocky as the fellers did as went ter Columbia We'nsday night. All the boys was with our party, an' the fust thing we done was to bob fer apples. As apples is high priced this year everybody laid 'emselves out to git suthin'. Tommy Camburn he bobbed fer an appel marked 'apintment,' but it had so much Moody grease on it that he couldn't get hold. Johnnie Drake he bobbed fer another 'appintment' appel, an' cried because he said Jumper had hoodooed it. Jump he bobbed fer an appel marked 'popularity,' but it were too smooth fer his teeth. Hank Williams were after a boodle appel an Johnnie Firey fit him so hard they didn't either of 'em git it. Billy Kidd grabbed a appel marked 'injipendents truths,' an' found it rotton inside, an' Frank Brown's 'speckilation' appel were as holler as a drum. Slosser wanted the biggest appel they was there, an' he got his fangs on it, too, but when he opened it, it were full o' wind and gaul an' he didn't seem ter enjoy it much. Elder McBride got his eye on the 'Pierre' appel an' worked like a nailer for it, but when he got it he found it stuffed with bogus checks and mortgaged lots, an' the dominie looked kinder sad arter that.

"Then the boys tried goin' down cellar backerds with a candle an' a lookin' glass. Johnnie Firey nearly fainted when he saw Hank Williams dressed as Fate lookin' over his shoulder, an' Judge Crofoot smiled kinder meloncolic at the reflection o' Johnnie Adams in his lookin'-glass. August Witte got skeert at seein' Bob Moody smile outer the glass at him, an' Cholly Howard saw a picter where all the common council was on their knees beggin' ter him fer help. All Dan Shields saw was a big dollar an' a packidge of Cholly Harris' stickers an' he groaned in speerit because he couldn't git the dollar.

"Finally I got disgusted with the hull thing an' when Jim Ringrose suggested that it would be more fun to go out and ring door bells, I come home feelin' as mad as a wet hen."

"It seems to me that that is your natural condition. The world don't agree with you."

"It may be I'm soured," snapped our landlady in answer to the impertinent remark of the colonel's, "but I think it's most enough to sour anybody, the way this political champaign is a goin'. Take the capital fight, for instance. There's more dirty work done by the real estate robbers o' Pierre and Huron in one day than there is by the biggest pack o' thieves in the country in a hull year. I hain't got nothin' agin' the towns, mind ye, it's the people as is runnin' them as is disgustin' everybody that is anybody. If I had a right to vote next Tuesday I'd jest vote fer Bath fer the capital an' keep my self respec'. But the wimmin don't vote yet, er things would be different."

"I'm sorry," said the doctor, in his mild voice, "that you see fit to criticise people who are only endeavoring to turn an honest penny. But the capital fight is only a small part of the campaign. Now, in politics — "

"It's worse!" she yelled, slamming down the potatoes so fiercely that the dish separated gracefully into several portions, "it's enuff sight worse. The republicans is chokin' the pore injipendents, an' the demicrats is boostin' up the farmers an' laughin' in their sleeve at the muddle things is in. It ain't their picnic. This 'ere fight is 'atween the injipendents and the republicans, an' if the grand ole party didn't have that ole war reckerd ter back 'em they'd come outer the little end o' the horn, too."

"I am aware," said the colonel, sarcastically, "that you favor the independents, but don't forget that in the hour of the nations' peril — "

"Fiddlesticks!" cried Mrs. Bilkins, glaring at her opponent, while she brought her clenched fist down plump into the butter dish, "that fight's been fit thirty year ago! W'ats that got ter do with that 'air McKinley an' that Silver bill an' such nonsense? The injipendents is in the right, only I don't like their kind o' mud-slingin' any more'n I do the republicans. It's a shame fer them to write sech mean things about Johnnie Adams an' Frank Raymond an' Jump' an' Hank Williams, as has never done no harm to a livin' critter, an' only works for the interests o' their feller men. But it's just as bad on the other side. Slosser's paper is so dirty nowadays that you kin hardly read it, an' the republicans calls my pore friend, Feelyerpaw, a villin an' pritty near proves it, too! They've found out all the wicked things as Loucks an' Scattergood an' the other fellers has done when they wasn't thinkin' an' told folks all about it, without considerin' their feelin's, an' even nice, innercent Tom Campburn is gittin' so he tells stories. Now then, let me ask ye, if there should happen, by any chance to be an honest man left in South Dikoty, what's he goin' ter vote fer?"

"The grand old party!" exclaimed the colonel.

"Independence and the Farmers' rights!" declared the doctor.

"Democracy," said Tom, "first, last and — "

"Nothin' o' the sort," interrupted our landlady, "if he's really honest, he'll jest vote fer ekal suffridge, Bath fer capital, an' — "

"Well?"

"An' put the rest o' the tickets inter the fire."

. . . .

She has her Last Say concerning Politics, and Criticises a Society Event

8 November 1890

On election evening national returns came in quickly, showing the Democrats making startling gains in Congress, but local news trickled in. "Even the county committee," Baum reported as late as Saturday, "is not much wiser as we go to press." Amendment issues, capital location, and local measures had caused voters to split their tickets, complicating the sorting, counting, and judging of the election. Even so, a few outcomes were painfully obvious.

Suffering a massive defeat was the woman suffrage amendment. "The defeat of Equal Suffrage," Baum wrote, "will stand as a lasting reproach to the state of South Dakota." The *News* declared that Democrats had opposed it for fear the wives and daughters of Republicans would vote against them; the Republicans had feared the votes of Independent women; and others "regarded it as an experiment of too doubtful utility to be engrafted on the constitution."[91] Woman suffrage organizers reasoned that with three political parties, three amendments, and capital boosters to distract voters, no one had even paid enough attention to understand the proper way to vote.

Ballots could be misleading in an era when each party printed its own, without the involvement of state or county officials.[92] Instructions to voters were printed in the newspapers but did not necessarily appear on the ballots themselves. Further, the stark language of the amendment question was itself obscure: "Shall the word 'male' be stricken from Section one of Article seven, of the constitution? Yes. No." The proper instructions told voters to vote yes by erasing or scratching out the "no" and to vote no by crossing off the "yes." This procedure would leave the word "yes" or "no" on the ballot for counters to tabulate.[93] Unfortunately, large numbers of people misunderstood, believing that a scratched "yes" was a vote in support of the amendment. Baum noted that in many cases the pro-suffrage workers themselves had misled voters into scratching the wrong word.[94] Typically, the columnist could also see the funny side of this issue, for it worked both ways, and some men who meant to vote against the amendment inadvertently voted for it.

By 8 November the meager returns also showed that the results of the general election were much closer than expected. Although the state Republican ticket had pulled through, the county candidates appeared to be neck and neck with the Independents in most races. (Ultimately, the two state senators and eight representatives would all be Independents, and only five of the ten county officers would be Republicans.) In addition, Pierre was leading Huron by a good margin. The Republicans had underestimated the Independents, Baum admitted, but his opinion of their politics remained unchanged. "Judged from an unbiased standpoint," he remarked, "they are seeking to rectify some evils which have never existed, and to counterbalance others which are existent with those no less to be condemned and avoided."

Though not embracing their program, he nevertheless praised their conduct. Independent voters had come to the polls with ballots already marked, refusing to talk to Republican or Democratic ward heelers and poll workers whose "one and two dollar bills which had been provided for various regulation needs were not required," Baum remarked. Not all voters had been so circumspect, a point the columnist made without subtlety in a rough drawing, labeled "Ye Honest Voter," that accompanied the "Our Landlady" column. In this crude illustration a tophatted voter held one hand behind his back while another slipped money into it. "Nothing can be more disgusting to the honor and intelligence of our country," Baum concluded editorially, "than the corruption which of late years has lingered like a deadly stench around the polling places."

Mrs. Bilkins agreed, swearing off politics but failing to leave her critical attitude behind as she took up society topics. At the "phantom party" that Harvey Jewett and his wife hosted on 6 November, the guests had been handed a sheet, pillow case, and mask and escorted to dressing rooms. When they emerged, "all were so thoroughly disguised," the *News* reported, "that husband could scarcely recognize wife or wife husband. Many of the young people were completely at sea and talked in tenderest tones to some 'old married person' who led them on for a time with keen relish."[95] Though the landlady professed to be scandalized by such goings on, editor Baum, who attended with his wife and forty other people, pronounced the phantom party a "decided success."

❦ "Anything new?" inquired our landlady, as she dumped the buckwheat cakes upo[n] the table and salted the butter well so that the boarders would not eat of it too freely.

"Yes," replied the doctor, briskly, "Mrs. Oleson has presented her husband — "

"I mean about election," explained Mrs. Bilkins, straining the coffee through a piece of flour sack.

"No," replied the colonel, who had just come in, "no one can tell anything about the result of the election."

"Well," replied our landlady, "as far as that goes there's several results as I knows of, myself, although the county c'mitte may be in blissful ignoramus. Ye see I was 'pinted to go ter the polls and hold the voters in line fer ekal suffridge an' 'injipendence.' So I goes over to our ward an' sets to work. I had 'em all put a cross on the 'yes,' so's the counters would know as they was votin' fer ekal suffridge, an' when Elder McBride come in he wouldn't do it nohow, 'cause, he said, women had sufferin' enough. So he put a cross on the 'no' an' chucked it in the box. Pritty soon Frank Brown, that knows everything about politics, come in an' says we was all wrong an' that the elder had voted fer ekal suffridge. An' the elder was so skeert he dasen't go home till midnight, an' then he wished he hadn't gone home at all. I'm sorry I made such a mistake. Cap. Hauser he begun to explain to me how it was early in the mornin', but the polls closed before he got through, so it didn't do [n]o good. I think I seed more scandalous things done on 'lection day than ever Ed. Lowe dreamed of in all his philology, as Shookspear says. A man would walk in and loaf around a little while, an' then some Pierre feller would take him inter a corner an' talk ter him a minit, an' the man would put his hand behind him and then put it in his pocket an' walk up ter the polls an' vote while the other feller watched him like a cat does a mouse. Oh, I tell you, this is a great country, and jest about as free as a dictionary is that you git by buyin' forty dollars wuth o' goods at a store. Instid o' havin' one king, we've got hundreds, an' they run the government for what money there is in it, an' the people fer what money they can git out of 'em. I think the reason they calls these politicians 'rings' is because there ain't anything square about 'em. But there, I've had enough of politics to last me a life-time, an' if you boarders don't give the sujec' a rest you can find some other boardin' house."

"I'm sure," exclaimed the colonel, "that I've not said a word."

"No, you republicans don't say much jest now."

Tom smiled sweetly and our landlady caught him at it.[96]

"Oh, you injipendents is as lively as Narregang at a 'fantom party,' but when you've been in politics a year or so you'll be as corrupt as a pail o' sour kraut. It takes politics to knock the honesty out of a person."

"Yes," remarked the doctor, dreamily, "you've had some experience yourself and you ought to know."

Mrs. Bilkins looked at him rather sharply, but said nothing. She simply poured a half-frozen fly out of the milk pitcher into his second cup of coffee, and handed it to him with a sigh.

"That 'Phantom Party' seems to have been a great success," said Tom, to change the drift of conversation.

"P'raps it were," retorted our landlady, "but it don't seem ter me to be proper fer gals and fellers ter galivant around in their night-dresses an' sheets an' sich things. There's a place fer everything an' the place fer sheets is on the beds; fer night gownds also. It must a been a funny thing. They say George Kimberly made frantic love ter another man's wife, thinkin' it were his own, an' the married wimmen never got so many chances to dance at a party in their lives because the fellers didn't know who they were. Quincy Braden couldn't understand why everybody was onter his disguise until he took his sheet off an' found 'Braden' marked on it in big letters in indellible ink. Narre, he found a fantom as jest suited him an' danced all the evenin' with her, an' he told me in confidence he really thought he was falin' in love with her. His feelin's was like mixed pickles when she unmasked an' he found it were his wife all the time. This here maskeradin' may be all right, but as fer me, I'd ruther go to a temperance oyster supper or a experience meetin' any time."[97]

. . . .

She Organizes a Reading Club in the Most Approved Style of the Art

15 November 1890

With the return of cold weather, news of women's reading clubs had prolifer-ated in all the newspapers. Groups such as the Wednesday Reading Club and the Pleasant Hour Reading Club reported that they had sponsored "elaborate" luncheons, suppers, and dinners for their members. In October the Ladies' Reading Circle hosted its annual supper for the husbands, at which, the *Pioneer* observed, the gentlemen "eyed each other askance to see what was the proper thing to be done." What seldom seemed to be done was any reading. Since 1 November the only mention of authors or literature had come from a newly formed club which told Baum that *Ben Hur* "will probably be the next work taken up."[98] The editor and publisher of the *Pioneer* had a vested interest in seeing that Aberdonians took their reading more seriously. He announced on 15 November that he had "perfected arrangements with Harper & Brothers, of New York, whereby we can supply their popular periodicals in connec-tion with the *Aberdeen Saturday Pioneer*." With a four-dollar subscription to

Harper's Magazine, one could receive a free 1891 subscription to the *Pioneer*. Hastily rethinking last week's condemnation of society doings, Mrs. Bilkins now aped the activities of the "sassiety" matrons of Aberdeen.

"I never thought," declared our landlady, as she sharpened the carver on one of the doctor's old boots, preparatory to an attack on the beefsteak, "that I should ever be drawed into the gaudy whirl o' sassiety."

"You mean the giddy whirl," remarked Tom.

"Perhaps, young man, you knows what I means better than I do myself, but I doubt it. If I'm to be a sassiety woming I'll be a out an' outer, and don't you fergit it, nuther!"

"That's right, Mrs. Bilkins," said the colonel, soothingly, "but may I ask what branch of society you are at present shining in?"

"Why, cert, Kurnel, o' course you may," replied our landlady, beaming again. "Ye see, the thing as is the cheese just now is them 'air readin' clubs, an' so Miss Smithers an' I, we made up our minds we'd have one, too. You ain't anybody in Aberdeen if you ain't joined a readin' club. So we called a meetin' of all the prominent boardin' house keepers 'xcept Jim Ringrose, an' talked it over. When the meetin' were assembled I did like Jump allus does, and made myself Chairman. When I'd stated the objec' o' the meetin' Miss Johnsing got up an' said as readin' were a art she never buckled to, an' she thought she was too old to learn now.

" 'Tain't ne'ssary to read,' says I; 'I never heerd that they did that at the readin' clubs.'

" 'What do they do, then?' says Miss Johnsing.

" 'Why, *eat*, you fool!' says I, slightly losin' my temper at so much ignorance in the nineteenth centenary.

" 'Then,' says Miss Johnsing, 'I'm your huckleberry.'

"At that Miss Smithers slapped her face, an' quiet was restored.

" 'O' course,' says I, 'we've got to have a name. There's the West Hill Readin' Club, an' the We'n'sdy Readin' Club, an' The Pleasant Hour Readin' Club an' the Bildin' an' Loan Readin' Club, an' we've got to be jest as high toned as any of 'em.'

" 'An' don't any o' them 'air clubs do no readin'?' asked Mirandy Jenkins. Miss Smithers raised the back o' her hand to her, but I stopped the row with a look an' answered perlitely:

" 'No, you ijut, they don't. Some has luncheons an' some grand dinners an' some refreshments — but they all eat. An' once a year they invites their husbunds to a feast.'

"'That lets me out,' says Miss Jones — the one as is crossed-eyed, 'I ain't got no husband, an' I never will have, so there!'

"Well, I saw the thing would bust up in a fight yet if I didn't interfere, so I says, soothin'ly, 'my dear, you can invite Doc. Fowler. We'll make a by-law to that effec'.'

"'Doc. he's allus been mad about these wimmin's parties, an' once threatened to git up a "afternoon beer" fur the men, but prohibition throttled the skeme. Now we'll put Doc. on our list an' one more misguided man will be saved by a woman's smile — Miss Joneses smile!'

"Miss Jones was so tickled she larfed, an' quiet was restored.

"'I perpose,' said Miss Smithers, 'that we call this here club the Bilkins Readin' Club.'

"Everybody hoorayed, but I knew Miss Smithers did it so she could borrow my clothes line of a Monday, so I thunk twice 'afore I accepted the honor. But a woman likes fame as well as a man, so I smiled sweetly an' said: 'Thanks, I accept with reciprocity. An' I move that Miss Smithers has the fust meetin' at her house.'

"Everybody yelled approval excep' Miss Smithers, an' I knew by the way her back humped that she saw I'd got even with her."

"So the reading club is an accomplished fact," remarked the doctor, with an amused air.

"Yes, and you can bet you collar it's a daisy an' a reg'lar sassiety deal. Miss Smithers has so much pride that she'll do it up brown, an' I think the thing'll be a success. We're going to announce that we're reading Ella Wheeler Wilcox'es works, but o' course everybody'll know that's jest a perlite lie, an' that we don't read nuthin'. I hear the West Hill Club wants to cunsolidate with us, but the Bilkins Club must sink or swim on its own merrits, an' as long as I'm the chairman, you can gamble your socks it'll swim!"

The satire in this column resonated within the community, resurfacing in mid-February 1891 when the Wednesday Reading Club held its annual feast for husbands and friends. The group spent the evening writing poetry, an example of which appeared in the *News* on 21 February. Dedicated to the club, it began:

You think that you are awful smart

And every Wednesday read,

But when the truth is really told,

You only go to feed.

You talk about your neighbor,

And gossip all the while —

Then tell your suffering family

You've been reading up Carlyle.

Three weeks later, on 7 March, the *News* published a friendly report of the Wednesday Reading Club and counseled the women to take "no heed" of the "despiteful things" people said, such as the comment that "they meet not to read but to feed and to wag their tongues to the hurt of others." Baum's criticism appeared to have stung a little.

. . . .

She gives the Boarders a Thanksgiving Dinner and Discusses her Blessings

29 November 1890

Thanksgiving Day 1890 dawned on new troubles in South Dakota. The Lakota, or western Sioux, were dancing the Ghost Dance and congregating in large groups. The Hub City unit of the National Guard was on alert, and the people of Aberdeen were anxious. "According to the popular rumor the Indians were expected to drop in upon us any day the last week," Baum observed on 29 November, "but as our scalps are still in a healthy condition it is needless for us to remark that we are yet alive and undisturbed." The fall weather had been remarkably mild, allowing people to save on heating costs, but potatoes, which the "poorer people live on . . . almost entirely" when cheap, were selling for one dollar a bushel, the short crop having driven the cost seventy cents over the usual price.

Earlier in the month the president had designated Thursday, 27 November, as a day of national thanksgiving, but the community was finding the counting of its blessings more difficult each day. Calling the holiday "the hollowest and most insincere of all the mockeries which usage has accustomed us to," the editor aired his own growing disheartenment at conditions in Dakota as he contemplated the American custom of preparing "a better dinner than we can afford, and overload[ing] our stomachs to an alarming degree." Only "one man out of a hundred," he concluded, "and one woman out of fifty goes to church and hears the minister tell how much they have to be thankful for, and a very few sound their own hearts and decide that the blessings which they have at[t]ained are very meagre, and are owing fully as much to their own unaided exertions as to the grace of God."99 Mrs. Bilkins counted blessings enthusiastically, but the boarders, like Baum, had to stretch to do so.

"There's an old sayin'," remarked our landlady, impressively, as she plunged the fork into the turkey and waved the carving knife gracefully in the air to point her remarks, "that sufficient to the day is the evil of tomorrer; therefore, eat, drink and be gay, fer tomorrer we go back to hash agin."

"That is a noble bird," declared the colonel, eying the turkey in a friendly manner, "and worthy to be the emblem of a Thanksgiving feast."

"Yes," replied our landlady, "an' it cost nine cents a pound. We've got this much to be thankful for, anyhow, that turkeys is cheap — an' very fillin', too."

"I suppose," remarked the doctor, reflectively, "that we have many other things to give thanks for, if we could only remember them."

"To be sure," returned our landlady. "We can give thanks that the Injins haven't tommyhawked us yet, an' that the county seat is where it can set fer keeps, an' that the weather keeps mild so's the coal will last longer, an' that the capital fight is over at last, an' that the injipendents is skeert to find 'emselves in power at last, an' that every merchant is sellin' goods cheaper than anyone else, an' that Harvey Jewett is still outer the poor house, an' that boardin' houses has all got good credit at the grocers yit, an' that there's so many tea-parties that folks can economize on grub at home, an' that the mayor ain't struck fer higher wager because he works so hard for the good o' the city, an' that the newspapers are able to run, whether folks pays their subscription or not, an' that opera companies is scarce at $2 apiece, an' that turnips is cheap if pertaters is dear, an' a good many other things. More turkey, doc?"

"Well, a little," he replied, taking a shoe-button that had been concealed in the dressing out of his mouth, "but the blessings you enumerate are the blessings of a community. Now do you think that individually we have anything to be thankful for?"

"In course I do! If we hadn't we'd a moved inter some community a leetle better off ter eat our thanksgiving dinner. Now, fer my part, I'm thankful that I got a week's board outer Tom, here, yesterday."

"And well you may be," replied that young man, helping himself to the last of the gravy, notwithstanding he discerned a hairpin in the bottom of the bowl; "and the doctor can be thankful for all the patients he'll get tomorrow because they will overeat today."

The doctor brightened up.

"To be sure," he exclaimed, "I had forgotten that."

"What," said Tom, "have I got to be thankful for?"

"That you ain't a bigger fool than you air," retorted Mrs. Bilkins, as she brought in the mince pie; "for any feller that'll deny his blessin's a day like this ain't fit to be outer a loonatix asylum."

"I suppose that you are right," replied the youth, "for misfortune is only comparative after all, and no one is so badly off that he mightn't be worse. It's hard to be called a fool, but I remember that I did pay you the board and so I won't resent it."

"That's right; we'll leave resentment to Loucks an' the minister that didn't get invited out to dinner today — if there is any. But say, Kernel, you seem to be kind o' thoughtful, — what have you to be thankful for?" "I was thinking," replied the veteran; as he took a tooth out of the mince pie and laid it on the side of his plate, "that I ought to be thankful because when I bought my last suit of clothes I got two pair of pants instead of one — otherwise I should have to parade the streets this winter in my natural-wool underware."

"There!" cried our landlady, triumphantly, "ye see we've all got suthin' to be thankful for if we only stop to think it out. I make no doubt but people in the effet yeast thinks us Dakota sufferers won't give no thanks today, but that's where they're off their belt. This thanksgivin' is a glorious instertution, an' I for one am glad as I live in a state where there's still suthin' to be thankful for, an' turkeys is cheaper nor beefsteak!"

. . . .

Our Landlady

6 December 1890

The first hints that trouble was brewing among South Dakota's American Indian population had appeared in early November when reports indicated that Kicking Horse, a Lakota disciple of the Ghost Dance movement, had converted the legendary Hunkpapa Sioux leader Sitting Bull to the new religion.[100] In Aberdeen, the election and reports of destitution among farmers in outlying areas of Brown County kept attention focused elsewhere until the middle of the month. A full-scale "Indian scare" broke on the town's consciousness on 18 November when the *Aberdeen Daily News* headlined that "bellicose" Indians from Standing Rock reservation appeared ready to descend on Fort Abraham Lincoln near Mandan, North Dakota. Sandwiched midway between the Sisseton-Wahpeton reserve about sixty miles to the east and the Standing Rock and Cheyenne River reserves about ninety miles to the west, Aberdeen and its citizens suddenly became aware of their vulnerability should the Indians, who had been living quietly since the turbulent events of 1876–77, decide to go to war again.

The governor put Aberdeen's Company F of the National Guard on alert, and news poured in that roving bands of Lakotas were moving off the reservations and that settlers were abandoning farms to congregate in larger settlements. The text of a sermon by Short Bull, another Lakota leader of the Ghost Dance movement, appeared on the front page of the *Aberdeen Daily News*, describing the coming millennium when the Messiah would eliminate the white race from the earth. Aberdonians struggled to assess their danger and sort fact from fiction — and fright.[101] The Mandan scare soon proved to be exactly that, and by 22 November the *News*, which bulletined the latest Associated Press dispatches and other telegraphic messages on Main Street, ventured to employ humor to calm people. The Aberdeen Guards under Captain Fanny Hauser were reported to be readying for war, while Charlie Howard and other young men of Company F were said to be fleeing to the East. "Editor Baum," the *News* reported, "says the people of Brown county can whip the Sioux with cordwood. The editor is noted for being contrary and the young bloods refuse to have their high hopes thus dashed to pieces. They say they will die before they will fight with such undignified weapons."[102]

A week later, however, Baum had actually counted the guns in town — only fifty rifles, some of them unusable — and the unease intensified at the news that Major General Nelson A. Miles, commander of the Military Division of the Missouri, was mobilizing troops. "Alarmist Miles," as the *News* called him, characterized the situation as "serious" and rehearsed the grievances of the Lakotas, who had just ceded a large portion of the Great Sioux Reserve to the United States. The promises made them for that cession had not yet been kept; Congress had cut ration appropriations for the third year in a row; and the crop failure of 1890 had combined to make the Lakota a desperate people who would, Miles said, "prefer to die fighting rather than starve peaceably."[103] Among the Lakotas themselves, the new Ghost Dance religion promised the return of the old lifeways, and Sitting Bull and other adherents stressed that the dance was "a religious dance, so we are going to dance until spring."[104]

Judging Sitting Bull to be an unstable element who was likely to join the larger group of dancers congregating on the Pine Ridge Indian Reservation in the South Dakota Badlands, General Miles sent William F. ("Buffalo Bill") Cody to the Standing Rock reservation on 28 November to "secure the person" of the old medicine man. The agent of the reserve considered the one-person attempt ill-advised and stalled Cody long enough to telegraph to Washington D C for a presidential override of Miles's order. Buffalo Bill left empty-handed, and the dancing at Standing Rock continued.[105]

The situation seemed to be sufficiently under control for Baum to editorialize on 29 November that the scare had passed but had been unfortunate for

South Dakota. "After two years of successive crop failures," he wrote, "comes the Indian scare, and the consequence is we are getting a very bad name. Hundreds of settlers have felt that this was the last straw and have gone to other states." The crop failures could not be helped, he opined, "but the Indian scare was a great injustice, and when we realize that it was all the work of sensational newspaper articles, we are tempted to wish that the press was not so free, and could have some wholesome strictures laid upon it." The *News* agreed, saying the next day that the alarm was ridiculous because "the red men themselves were very much disturbed over the reports that the white settlers were alarmed." They feared for their own women and children, "knowing that if the whites were thoroughly aroused they would annihilate every tribe." The affair was "a case of mutual scare," the *News* editor concluded.

Mutual or not, the alarm continued, as Lakotas from the Rosebud reserve in south-central South Dakota began to move west toward the Badlands, slaughtering and herding government cattle as they went. Individual communities bombarded the governor's office with requests for arms and ammunition, and the senators from North Dakota, South Dakota, and Nebraska asked Congress for a joint resolution authorizing the secretary of war to issue munitions to the states.[106] During the debate an Indiana senator argued that additional rations for the Sioux would make more sense, recalling General Miles's statement that the Lakota were starving. Senator Gilbert A. Pierce of Bismarck, North Dakota, paraphrased in the *News* of 4 December, countered that he "had sometimes wondered that the white people in that region did not themselves go on the war path, because they were hungry." On 6 December Baum reported that the governor had sent Aberdeen one hundred Springfield rifles and five thousand rounds of ammunition "to inspire confidence until the Indian troubles are over." Calm did seem to be returning, as the newspapers focused on formation of state, county, and city relief organizations and prepared to war against privation during the coming winter. The landlady's attention remained focused on the Indians, however. Even though she had heard all the news, she thought it best to investigate on her own.

🌿 "Well, here I am again," cried our landlady, as she threw open the door and walked in upon the startled boarders, "an' you can bet I'm glad to get back, fer I'm nearly starved to death."

"Glad to see you, ma'am," said the colonel, "sit down and have some dinner. The hired girl don't feed us quite as well as you did, but we've managed to get along."

"Oh, I see!" exclaimed Mrs. Bilkins, eying the spread upon the table critically.

"Fried chicken, 'scalloped oysters, sweet pertaters, an' — Great Scott! I'll bet that girl ain't got two cents left in that ten dollar coupon book I give her jest 'afore I went away!"

"Probably not," returned the doctor, "as I had to order the dinner today on my own responsibility. But here you are, fresh from the reservations and you haven't told us anything about the Indians yet."

"That's so," exclaimed our landlady, "but this reckless prodigalness clean druv the Injins outer my head. Oh, yes, I've been to the reservation all right enough — bearded the lion in his whiskers so to speak, an' I'm alive yit to tell the tale."

"Tell us all about it," urged Tom, as he drew his chair to the stove and lit a cigar.

"I will. Ye see, arter the president wouldn't let Buffalo Bill run this campaign ter suit hisself an' General Miles, I made up my mind I'd take the thing inter my own hands and find out what the red demons intended to do, or not to do, as Ham expresses it. Fer this skare is like the bile on a man's tenderloins, it assumes tremenjous proportions without amountin' to anything, an' is more of a nuisance that it is a bother. So I tuk the President's Message, and the Life o' Buffalo Bill an' the Cranmer Contest Case an' put 'em in my reticule along with some crackers an' cheese an' my knittin' an' started fer the seat o' war. I thought if I struck anything rich I'd telegraph it to the New York papers an' make my expenses an' a reckerd as a female correspondint. Well, I struck the reservation about noon. I hired a boy to drive me half way, but he took to his heels an' so I druv on alone. Pritty soon I come to the camp an' found it deserted and the bones o' some of the government cattle strewed about the ground. But the fire was still smolderin' an' so I pushed on rapidly, as they say in the novels. Arter awhile I caught sight of a large body of Injins jest ahead o' me. 'Hol' up!' I yelled, but they turned and saw me, an' givin' a whoop o' terrer they run fer their lives. But my nag was a good one, an' arter I'd begun to read the President's Message to him he run so fast that he caught up with the Injins in no time an' they threw 'emselves on their knees an' begged fer mercy.

" 'Here you, "Hole-in-the-Face," ' says I, fiercely, 'what do mean by runnin' away? Come up here an' explain yerself!'

"Now, Hole-in-the-Face is one o' the bravest Sioux outside o' Sioux Falls, an' he come up kinder sad an' says: 'Don't hurt us, Miss' Bilkins, an' we'll never do it agin.'

" 'Why should I hurt you?' says I.

" 'Why,' says he, 'the scouts is all bringin' in word that the whites is all risin' agin' the Injins an' so I was kinder afraid when I saw your complexion.'

" 'Hole-in-the-Face,' says I, sternly, 'do I look as if I'd hurt a pore Injin?'

" 'No,' says he, 'but Candidate-afraid-of-his-Pocketbook was in the camp this mornin' an' said the rumors o' the whites risin' that we'd heard was all true. He said that the whites was all starvin' in Dakota, an' the government wouldn't give 'em any rations, an' so they was comin' to rob us Injins of what we had. I tell you the Injins is pritty badly skeert an' they're leavin' their homes an' bandin' together fer mutual pertection.'

" 'What about them oxes what I saw the remains of at the camp?' says I.

" 'Oh,' says he, 'if we hadn't killed 'em the whites would, an' self-preservation is the fust law of a good politician.'

" 'But about that ghost-dance,' says I suspicious like.

" 'Why,' says he, 'we live in a free country. We Injins can vote an' you wimmen can't, an' don't you fergit that.[107] Religion is free as water an' much more plenty. If there's any fault found with our runnin' our religion to suit ourselves we'll jest join the independents, an' then I guess you'll be sorry you spoke.'

" 'Hole-in-the-Face,' says I, 'is this a square deal?'

" 'It is,' says he; 'jest look at it yourself. Here we Injins has been drawin' rations from the government an' layin' by our savin's till we've got in pritty fair shape, an' just when we least expect it, here comes a risin' of the starved whites, an' they're liable to swoop down on us at any minute an' rob us o' all we possess.'

" 'No,' says I, 'they're afraid o' your swoopin' down on them.'

"He laughed sourkastically. 'What have they got as we want?' says he; 'Nothin'! But the Injuns has got lots that the government has guv 'em that the whites would like to have for themselves. No, Miss Bilkins, you can't fool me like that! But my braves is gettin' anxious to remove their property out o' harm's way, so good day to ye, as the legislater said to Gid. Moody.'

"I saw it were no good arguin' with him, so I druv sadly back. Wherever I went the Injuns was fleein' in one direction and the settlers in another. I've telegraphed the truth to all the papers, but they ansered an' said:

" 'We ain't lookin' fer truth — can get all we want fer a cent a line, but a good lie is wuth a dollar a word to us any minnit.'

" 'You're a set o' rascals!' I telegraphed back.

" 'If it was a news item,' they answered, 'we'd give ye a cent a line fer that assertion, but it ain't, so shet up!'

"Well, I shet, an' come home, a sadder but a hungrier woman. This gittin' at the truth ain't what it's cracked up to be, an' the next time I mix up in the Injin troubles I'll let somebody else do the mixin' an' devote my time to economizin' on coupon books."

Although Baum did not again focus his landlady's attention on the "Injin troubles," they were far from over. Tension and fear increased after 15 December, when Sitting Bull died in an arrest attempt that Miles, now completely in control, had ordered, and Big Foot's band slipped away from the military on the Cheyenne River reservation.[108] The situation no longer lent itself to humor, and Baum's fear for himself, his family, and his livelihood in Aberdeen made him uncompromising in his opinions about how to resolve the problem. On 20 December the editor mourned Sitting Bull's death, recalling the "proud spirit of the original owners of these vast prairies" and rehearsing the "selfishness, falsehood and treachery" that had marked the white man's dealings with the Indians. With Sitting Bull gone, however, "the nobility of the Redskin is extinguished," he declared, and "the best safety of the frontier settlers will be secured by the total annihilation of the few remaining Indians." When news of the army's bungled encounter at Wounded Knee on 29 December reached Aberdeen, Baum condemned the incompetence that had resulted in so many casualties, but he did not relent. The scare and uncertainty had shown him and all of the settlers that had the Indians decided to annihilate the whites themselves, rather than wait for the Messiah to do so, many lives would have been lost before the army arrived.[109] "Our only safety," he wrote on 3 January 1891, "depends upon the total extermination of the Indians. Having wronged them for centuries we had better, in order to protect our civilization, follow it up by one more wrong and wipe these untamed and untamable creatures from the face of the earth." Baum's reaction reflected the concerns of the time and place.[110] He never expressed this view again throughout his long writing career.

. . . .

She Enjoys a pleasant chat with the Boarders

20 December 1890

Although Aberdonians remained apprehensive about the military situation, holiday promotions and festive events began to occupy their attention, as well. Baum did not write an "Our Landlady" column for his 13 December issue, remarking that his news space was somewhat curtailed "owing to a rush of holiday advertisements." Business was "booming in holiday goods," he reported, "and the merchants are correspondingly happy. There is still some money left in this country, and those who have it do not intend to forfeit their Christmas celebration." Mindful that not everyone prospered, the editor also observed that the Ladies Benevolent Society had scheduled a charity ball and the Presbyterian church planned a "Grand National Holiday Kirmess" for 23 and 16 December respectively. At the kirmess, an elaborate event designed to raise money for charitable causes, a program of music and tableaux featured Baum as Father Time. Throughout the month the weather continued mild in Dakota, though the East labored under two feet of snow and recurring blizzards. In political circles the upcoming election of a United States senator during the legislative session in Pierre generated new speculation among Aberdeen hopefuls. To accommodate the extra news and Christmas rush, Baum expanded his issue of 20 December to twelve pages, running a number of full-page advertisements from local merchants. The landlady, who must have studied these extra ads — which Baum labeled "good reading" — had found a "bargain" or two.[111]

🌸 "This coffee," remarked our landlady, as she poured out the colonel's cup and adding the skim milk stirred it vigorously with her own spoon, — for she liked the colonel; "this coffee is the Crushed Politician brand, an' I bought it yisterday of a agent fer a quarter with a diamond necklace set in tin throwed in."

"It tastes of crushed politician," said Tom, moodily.

"Named after the republican county committee, probably," added the doctor, sipping it warily.

"The necklace were worth a quarter any day," declared our landlady, "an' the agent said if the coffee weren't good he'd refund the money. Now, Kurnel, tell me the solid artesian truth, is that 'air coffee any good?"

"Well," replied the colonel, sadly, for he knew that a woman is ever sensitive about her coffee, "I believe that I'd get my money back — that is, if you ever expect to see him again — which you probably don't."

"No," sighed Mrs. Bilkins, "I'm allus gittin' fooled. It's jest like the time I went to the Curmess, wich some feller said would a been a dog-gone mess if the cur had been left off; but I heered Tom say as there was goin' to be a quart 'et an' a quint 'et an' I wanted to go an' help eat 'em. But the lunch was pritty high fer the kind an' there weren't a quart of it altogether, much less a quint. But there! I ain't got nothin' to say agin' the show, fer these church doin's is gen'ally wuth the money an' goes to a good cause, — that is, the receipts nearly allus pay the expenses. When they don't, them that's worked the hardest has to put up the rest o' the shuks, an' imagine they'll find their reward in Heving, where church sociables are at a bigger discount than Crismus presents in a barber shop. Now I've got to work all my spare time to turn my lavender silk fer the Charity Ball, fer I wouldn't miss it fer a farm. You'd have to go with me, Kurnel, fer it ain't proper fer a lady to go alone, an' you can borry George Cadwell's swaller-tail, that he ain't wore sence the prize fight. I hope Narre. will be there so's I can jest grab him around the neck an' swing him in a good old-fashioned waltz, fer Narre. is a great dancer an' loves to spin."

"It's almost too warm for a dance," said the colonel, with a troubled face.

"Well, it is rather summery. I got a letter from my brother in Oshkosh the other day, an' he says in it, says he, 'here you've ben slavin' fer six year in Dakoty an' what have you got?'

"An' I ansered an' says: 'we've got the beautifullest weather in Ameriky,' says I.

" 'Then,' he writ back, 'send me two barrels an' a hogshead, for it's so rainy an' nasty here that I ain't gone to the bank fer three days, an' my money drawers is runnin' over!' That's jest like my brother, he allus liked a joke. But speakin' o' jokes, a feller walked inter Salsberry's yisterday an' says, 'hev you got a dairy fer sale?' 'No,' says Skip, with a grin, 'but Mr. Leavitt hes got one he'd like to dispose of.' O' course the feller meant a writin' cullender, but Skip is nothin' if he ain't funny. He's goin' down to Pierre this week to see if they won't make him United States Senator. I'd ruther see Kernel Evans there, myself, but the town can't hardly spare him. Well, Christmas is comin' mighty quick now, an' everybody'll be jest as happy as if we was all Senators. The only thing that worries me is that all the stores is sellin' for less nor cost an' I expect we'll have all the merchants on the town after New Years. But I s'pose it can't be helped unless everyone insists on payin' 'em a fair profit, an' it ain't in human natur' to do that."

. . . .

She Fills the Colonel's Stocking and Talks
of the Charity Ball

27 December 1890

> Christmas time had come and gone, Baum observed in the 27 December issue of the *Pioneer*, and in spite of hard times, men all over the city were "proud possessors of daintily worked slippers," pen wipers, neckties, and "various plush gimcracks" that would be added to "collections amassed in years gone by." Although a simple gift would have sufficed to show affection, "Americans

never do anything by halves," Baum remarked, and would "willingly put themselves to serious inconveniences to be able to give their loved ones a present worthy of the high esteem they bear them." Mrs. Bilkins, who esteemed the colonel no less than other smitten women of Aberdeen valued their beaux, had taken to heart, like the good American she was, the notion that "it is more blessed to give than to receive."

Fellow Aberdonians of all walks of life had done the same, making the Charity Ball sponsored by the Ladies Benevolent Society of Aberdeen on 23 December the social event of the season. In March 1890 Baum's sister-in-law Helen Leslie Gage had spearheaded the organization of the society to help about twenty families make it through the end of the previous winter. The group had reorganized in November to aid the increasing numbers of destitute persons in Brown County, where suffering had become acute. The county commissioners were supporting as high as sixty-two people in some townships. In one month they had allocated more than $1,000 for coal for the poor, almost $700 for groceries, and close to $100 to transport people back to families in the East. To support this effort, the Ladies Benevolent Society collected clothing and food and sponsored the Christmas Charity Ball as a fund-raiser. Charging a dollar per person, the women sold over three hundred tickets, netting $200 after expenses were paid. "It is doubtful if this large sum . . . could have been secured in the same length of time by any other plan," the *News* remarked.[112] Attendees at the animated affair appeared to be "wholly oblivious to the fact they were, by their presence, rendering assistance to the suffering poor," Baum reported on 27 December. He also noted, as his landlady did, that some of the dancers "might have use for that dollar before Ceres smiles again upon our land."

"I say, Kernel," shouted our landlady, at the head of the head of the front stairs, "if ye want to see wat's in your sock an' eat the pancakes while their smokin' jest rustle a little an' come down to breakfus'!"

"What's that?" demanded Tom, as he came down stairs, "has the Colonel been hanging up his stocking?"

"Nothing of the kind," growled the veteran, making his appearance, "don't let Mrs. Bilkins make a fool of you."

They entered the dining-room, and there, sure enough, was a military looking stocking hung by the mantel and bulging out in a suspicious way.

"Ahem!" remarked the Colonel, turning red, "where did that sock come from?"

"Well," replied our landlady, reluctantly, as she looked fondly upon the

Colonel's manly form, "it might 'a come outer the mendin', but the presincts is from Santa Claus sure!"

"Open it," said the doct[o]r, entering the room.

"Open it," laughed Tom, "and we'll see what the Saint has sent you."

The Colonel looked from one to the other with a puzzled air.

"If this is a brutal joke," he suggested, "someone will die, but if it is a kind remembrance of Mrs. Bilkins, why I'm bound to accept it gratefully."

Our landlady smiled and blushed, and blew her nose on her apron with an embar[r]assed air.

"You know, Kernel," she murmured, "that you allus was my favrite; not as you pays your board so mighty reglar as you might, but you allus treats me as a gentleman should treat his landlady, an' I flatters myself I know a good man when I sees him."

The Colonel bowed mechanically.

"Examine it, do!" urged Tom, refer[r]ing to the stocking, "for we're getting hungry."

The Colonel unpinned the neatly-mended sock and took out a small parcel which he opened with a trembling hand.

It contained a yellowish looking cigar which he laid upon the table and Tom pocketed promptly.

The next production was a gaily-decorated blotter, bearing the inscription

"If you love me
As I love you,
No nife shall cut
Our love in to."

Tom laughed, the doctor coughed and the Colonel wiped the perspiration from his brow and made another dive at the sock.

"This," said he, "must be meant for a pen-wiper."

"Nothing of the kind!" protested Tom, indignantly, "it's a lock of hair, and it looks awfully like Mrs. Bilkins'."

The colonel darted a fierce glance at him and dropped the memento into the coal hod. Our landlady stopped giggling and looked solemnly out of the window.

"Boys," said the colonel desperately, "let's postpone the rest till new years."

"By no means," replied the doctor, "I am very interested and you know 'hope deferred maketh the heart sick.' "

"An' there's no good doctor in the neighborhood to cure it," murmured our landlady.

"Go on," said Tom, "I think the next is a doll."

"No," said the colonel, examining the article musingly, "it's a picture of Ed. Lowe."

"What on earth makes his pockets bulge out so?" inquired the doctor.

"I suppose," replied the colonel, "that he was still secretary of the county committee when that was taken."

"That 'air," broke in our landlady, "was all a mistake, I — that is — Santa Claus, must 'a got hold o' the wrong pictur in the dark."

"Then he should certainly apologize," said the colonel. "What's this?"

"That," replied our landlady, with interest, "is a great thing. You can use it fer a watch key, a can-opener, a manicure set, a bread toaster, a watch charm or a corkscrew. I bought it at 33⅓ per cent off, an' — "

"*You* bought it!" shouted the colonel. "Now let me ask you, madam, by what right you inflict blotters and cigars and watch charms and locks of hair upon an inoffensive man? Have I ever done anything to warrant — "

But our landlady had flown to the kitchen, and when she came back with red eyes and a plate of steaming cakes a quarter of an hour afterwards, the donations of Santa Claus had disappeared and the doctor was reading the paper and Tom teasing the cat and the colonel looking out of the window with an air as if wholly unconscious of the late unpleasantness. For they all liked Mrs. Bilkins, and a truce had been patched up with the colonel — at least until after breakfast was over.

"How did you like the Charity Ball?" inquired the doctor, as our landlady poured out the coffee.

"Well, it were considerable high jinks," she replied, as the sunshine of her smile broke through her clouded face (copyrighted), "but I didn't stay long because it were so mixed an' Cholly Howard jumped on my toe so hard that I could not dance another step. But Miss. Joneses hired gal she said she never had so much fun in her life, and there was all the high toned an' the low toned jest mixed up like a hasty puddin' fer sweet Charity's sake, an' the sassiety made a heap o' money, too, altho' some cranky ones said the orchestra got half the receipts an' Hazeltine half an' the poor the other half. I seed a good many there that I know ain't paid their board bills fer weeks, but as long as it were for charity they're excusable for blowing in a dollar that way."

. . . .

She Visits the Great Downditch Farm and tells the
Boarders of its Wonders

3 January 1891

On 16 December 1890 the *Aberdeen Daily News* had printed "The Wonderful Updyke Farm," in which two traveling salesmen discussed the chance visit of one of them to a farm located "in Brown county north of Aberdeen, between the Great Northern railroad and the Northwestern." In this piece of speculative promotional fiction, an artesian well supplied the power to a dynamo that allowed the Updyke family to cook, churn, wash, light their buildings, iron, plow, harrow, seed, and harvest electrically. In addition, the garden could be lighted at night, extending the growing season. On 30 December, in response to numerous questions, the *News* published "The Updyke Farm Revisited" in which the salesman again exclaimed over the irrigated farm, where the "dynamo attached to the artesian well is allowed to run all the time like the water, and therefore electricity is always on tap." During this visit he had sampled strawberries from Updyke's "winter garden," which featured an electric current that kept it free from pests. An electric incubator turned 5,000 turkey eggs each day, its capacity restricted only by the farmer's inability to secure more eggs locally. The editor added, somewhat vaguely, that "it is proposed to form a miniature of the farm in all details and exhibit it at the World's Columbian Exposition, at Chicago." The potential benefits he listed pricked the interest of fellow Aberdonian Sairy Ann Bilkins.

"Gentlemen," said our landlady as she entered the room at which the boarders were at supper, and threw her hat on the side-board and hung her shawl over the doctor's head; "this kind o' life ain't worth the livin', an' if ever I were sick o' this 'air boardin' house I am this minute!"

"What's wrong?" inquired the colonel, wonderingly, "I thought you had been on a visit to the Updyke farm, and to have you come home in such a humor as this is astonishing."

"Updyke!" cried our landlady, with an unmistakable sneer; "I hain't been near that wretchid hole; but I've been to a much more wonderful place."

"Indeed," quoth Tom, "here — sit right down in this chair and let me feed you 'scalloped oysters while you tell us all about it."

"All right, but don't interupt me, for every word I'm goin' to say is gospel truth. Well, you know I sot out fer the Updyke farm. I got the best directions I could, an' travelled over the prairie till I most thought I'd lost my way. Bimeby I come to a feller ridin' swiftly along in a waggin. I rubbed my eyes in amazement fer a minit, 'cause there was no hoss or beast o' any kind hitched to it. Then I yells out, 'hullup.' He did, comin' to a period right by me."

"A period?"

"Well, a full stop. I asked him how in blazes he made his waggin go by itself.

" ' 'Lectricity,' says he; 'ye see, the machinery is stored under the seat. All I have to do when I want to go is press a button, an' she rushes.'

" 'How do you guide it?' says I.

" 'By this little wheel — like steerin' a ship. It beats bicycles 'cause you can carry a load an' it ain't no exertion.'

" 'Who inwented it?' says I.

" 'Downditch,' says he.

" 'Well,' says I, 'can ye tell me where the Updyke farm is?'

" 'Updyke,' says he, thinkitively, 'why, he used to work for Downditch, but his farm's a good ways off — on the other side of Aberdeen.'

" 'Dear me,' says I, 'then I've walked all this ways fer nothin'. I wanted to see all the wonders he does with 'lectricity an' a artesian well.'

" 'Humph!' says he, 'why don't you go on to Downditch's? Beats Updyke's all holler. Jest take that trail ter the right an' it'll fetch ye there. So long!'

"He teched his button an' the waggin whirled away, an' I thought my best plan was to foller his advice, so I took the path ter the right, an' bimeby I come to a lot o' buildin's all clustered together an' painted pure white. The biggest one, all wings an' angles an' coverin' about a acre o' ground, I tuk to be the house, so I meandered up to the front door, an' seein' a electric button, I pushed it. Instanter the door flew open an' I started to step inside, but my feet went out from under me an' I went kerflop inter a big arm chair, which was on rollers an' started to once to move down the hall with me in it. A door opened as we come to it, an' as we passed through some little steel arms jumped down an' ontied an' tuk off my bunnit and jerked off my shawl, an' away we glided to another door. This opened automatic'ly, too, an' we entered a small room as I took to be a study. In it was a thoughtful lookin' man, who looked up an' bowed pleasantly as my chair stopped alongside o' his'n.

" 'How do, Mrs. Bilkins,' says he.

" 'Howdy,' says I, 'but how did ye know my name?'

" 'It was writ inside yer shawl,' says he, 'an' the machine as took it off read it an' telephoned it to me.'

"I looked at him in wonder. He smiled an' touched a button on his vest.

Instantly a handkercher flew out of his pocket, wiped his nose an' went back agin, all of its own accord.

" 'May I ask your name?' says I.

"He touched another button on his vest an' a card flopped out of his buzzum which read: 'Aesop Downditch, Scientist, Born at Ipswich, 1821, graduated at Redfield College; fer ferther particulars, see autobiography, price $1. Fer sale here.'

" 'You must be my guest until termorrer, Mrs. Bilkins,' says he, 'let me interduce ye to my wife an' dorter.' He teched a button on the table an' instantly two doors opened on opposite sides o' the room an' his wife an' darter rolled in on chairs an' smiled an' bowed. Mr. Downditch interduced me an' soon we was all buzzum friends.

" 'It's time fer dinner, papa,' says Clarabel, his dorter.

"Mr. Downditch touched a button on his vest an' his watch flew outer a pocket an' opened in front o' him.

" 'So it is,' says he, 'how tempus does fugit.'

"He an' his wife an' darter then all teched a little button that was on the outside o' the arm o' their chairs, an' a wash rag o' satin came out an' washed an' dried their faces quickly an' gently. I did the same an' I must say such an' inwention removes all the terrors o' wash day.

" 'How is this did?' says I.

" 'All 'lectricity,' says he, smilin'. 'The power to run the motor is furnished by our artesian well, an' by a little inwention I have arranged so that all the little household an' personal duties are performed by 'lectrical apparatus, an' it saves us no end o' trouble.' He teched another button on the table as he spoke an' at once the table sank through the floor an' another rose in its place, all set fer dinner an' kivered by the most luxuriousest meal you ever heard of. There was nineteen courses an' eatables of every description, from peaches an' cream to fried manna with nectar sauce. I tell you, fellers, such board is wuth a hundred dollars a week. We eat an' drunk all we could — that is, I did, an' when we was through the table disappeared through the floor agin.

" 'Who washes the dishes?' says I.

" 'We employ the same agent that prepares the food an' sets the table — 'lectricity;' says Missus Downditch. 'But it's time fer the theatre; would you like to attend it, Mrs. Bilkins, 'afore you retire for the night?'

" 'You bet!' says I, 'I want to take in the whole aggregation 'afore I leaves. It'll make the folks in Aberdeen sick when I tells 'em about it.'

"Mr. Downditch touched a button on his vest an' shrugged his shoulders by 'lectricity.

" 'It ain't any more'n any on 'em can have,' says he, 'if they puts down artesian wells and utilizes the water properly. I bid you good evenin', Mrs. Bilkins.'

"As the chairs of us three ladies moved away I saw Mr. Downditch press a vest button an' open his mouth, an' the next instant a lighted cigar was in his mouth an' he was puffin' away contentedly. I tell you I wished I could bring that vest home to you boarders! It would surprise you. But I s'pose Downditch couldn't spare it. Well, the room we was wheeled to was furnished jest like a Oproar House. 'It's a model o' the Madison Square theatre,' says Mrs. Downditch. A big phonograph played the overture, an' then the characters o' the play come out an' acted. They was all dummies with phonographs inside of 'em, an' the power was furnished by the artesian well.[113] It was a good show though, an' after it was over I bid the ladies good-night.

" 'When you git to your room,' says Missus Downditch, 'tech that 'air button on the side o' your chair.'

"Then the chair started an' wheeled me through the halls till it finally entered a good sized room. The only piece o' furniture in it were the bed, but that was a corker. The head of it was as high as the ceilin' an' was sunk inter the wall, an' jest above the pillers was a row o' buttons. It had a lace cover an' looked so soft I wished I didn't have to undress 'afore I got inter it. But I remembered what Missus Downditch had said, so I pressed the button on the chair. Instantly a number o' steel arms shot out an' undressed me in a jiffy, an' flung a embroidered night gownd over my head an' there I was! Before I had recovered from my surprise the blame thing lifted me up an' shot me inter bed, the bed clothes turnin' down jest before I landed. The bed was nice an' warm, bein' heated by 'lectricity. As my head touched the pillow it set off a music box that played 'Hard Times come agin no more,'[114] until I was fast asleep. I woke up in the mornin' feelin' as happy as an editor who's got a new subscriber, an' lay thinkin' what a glorious thing artesian wells is. As I did so my eye caught the row o' buttons on the head-board. I teched one an' a large box-like lookin' thing swooped out in front o' me, with a rubber tube hangin' to it which plumped inter my mouth. The box had several buttons labelled coffee, tea, chocolate, rum-punch, water, an' so forth. In spite o' me I winked at the one as said rum-punch, an' it was so delicately adjusted that it set the thing off, an' I tell you it was a drink worthy o' Taubman. I teched the next button an' my face was washed in a jiffy. The next one brushed my hair an' done it up; the next one shot me outer bed plump inter the chair. By techin' the same button I did last night I was dressed and then the chair moved away toward the breakfast room.

"Mr. Downditch greeted me with a smile an' asked me if I had rested well. I told him I had, an' then I sot to work on the best breakfast I ever tackled. Mr. Downditch then excused himself as he had some business to 'tend to, and he bid me good by with a smile an' left.

" 'What a nice man your husband is,' says I to Misus Downditch. 'He's allus smilin'.'

" 'Oh, yes,' says she, 'he smiles by 'lectricity.'[115]

"Well, after that I kept my thoughts to myself, fer fear the 'lectricity should get hold o' them.[116] I come away soon after breakfast an' after a long journey here I am! Now, gentlemen, don't look at me so queer. I ain't crazy by a long shot. I've jest told you the plain facts. An' now let me ask you, do you think, after all that luxury, that I'll be content to settle down an' wash dishes agin? Never! This 'ere establishment is a goin' to have a artesian well with electricity attachments, if it takes every dollar I've got in Hagerty's to sink it!"

. . . .

She Tells the Boarders How to Make a fortune

10 January 1891

Settlers who "think they have nothing left to stay for" are leaving, but "they are missing it," wrote Edward Bach in Baum's *Western Investor*. Dakota, he and others now admitted, suffered from cycles of dry and wet, but 1890 had ended the drought. The heavy moisture received early in the summer, though too late to effect change that year, signaled that a moisture cycle had commenced, and by the time it ended, artesian-well irrigation would be in place to combat the next season of drought. As a result, investors were cautiously optimistic. "I would say," Bach continued, "to those who hold mortgages on [Dakota farm] lands: 'Do not sacrifice on them. Hang on. You will find that they are worth every dollar in them, and every dollar of interest.' " No better investment could be found, because people who had become discouraged were willing to sell quarter-sections at low prices. People who stay and invest, he predicted, "will find themselves well off in time," whereas those who return to the East "will have to compete for work in that already over crowded labor market."[117] Taking Bach's advice, Mrs. Bilkins invested her boardinghouse earnings and boomed South Dakota with enthusiasm, although her arguments, like those of many Dakota boosters, were getting a little ragged.

🌸 "The fools," said our landlady, as she mashed the potatoes vigorously, "ain't all dead yet."

"No," said Tom, with a half sigh. "I realize that every day that I linger in Aberdeen when I should be in some better country."

"Fiddlesticks!" ejaculated Mrs. Bilkins fiercely, "that's just what I was a talkin' about. To think of the idjuts leavin' Aberdeen just at the time when her troubles is about over, nearly makes me sick."

"Why should one stay?" demanded Tom; "with the same amount of energy it requires to earn a crust here, I could get a full loaf anywhere else. Why should I stay? Do I owe anything to Aberdeen?"

"Prap's not," replied our landlady, putting the dinner upon the table, and sharpening the carver upon her instep, "but you owe suthin' to yourself, certain. There's ben hard times here, that goes without tellin' but the hard times is about over. We are as sure o' gittin' a crop next year as we are o' livin' til the time comes. It might a ben better to hav' gone away two year ago, when the troubles begun, but to go now, when they's about over, is rank foolishness. Before you can hardly git settled in some other locality, you'll be startled by the news o' the crops in South Dakoty, by reports o' the thousands flockin' in to the most fertile country on the yearth, of the artesian wells goin' down until the ground is like a peppar box, of the rapid rise in real estate until in no other country will land bring so high a price as in the basin o' the Jim river. Tom, jest lem'me tell you a secret.

"All the money that I earnt in the last ten year in Aberdeen I've been a puttin' inter land. The other day I got a quarter section near Bath fer a hundred dollars — wuth five thousand any day, an' yisterday I took a feller's mortgage an' his land an' giv' him enough to get out o' the country with, — an' all it'll cost me is the interest on the mortgage! I'm a holdin' that quarter fer eight thousan' dollers, an' I'll git that fer it inside o' two year. I wasn't very rich when I hed a few hundred dollers laid by from keepin' boardin' house, but today, when I think that I've turned nearly every hundred inter a quarter section o' land, I tell ye it makes me feel like a second Jay Gould. 'Afore a year is out there'll be a big cry fer land in the Jim River valley, an' by holdin' to it a little while longer my fortune is made. Gentlemen, there's goin' ter be the biggest excitement in these parts the west has ever knowd. If ye leave here, you'll want to git back as quick as the Lord'll let you, an' if you stay, — why you've got the biggest chance to make money you ever had or ever will have. I ain't much of a prophet, usually, but I'll stake my reputation that before one year is past Aberdeen will be so busy and boomin' she won't know herself, an' the dull times will be forgot an' never brought to mind. Write that in yer hat an' don' fergit I said it. More steak, Kernel?"

· ·

Choice Selections from Her Rambling Remarks

17 January 1891

Twenty-two years after leaving Aberdeen, Baum still remembered his hand-to-mouth existence there. "I used to go out and rustle up my own ads and set 'em up," he reminisced, "and when the tramp printer would desert me I would take a fling at the type case, and then I would go out and deliver the papers to my advertisers on a Saturday afternoon so I could collect enough money for a ham sandwich and a cup of coffee."[118] In January 1891, however, the pages of the *Aberdeen Saturday Pioneer* did not discuss the editor's financial difficulties. He continued to promote South Dakota and try new advertising schemes, even though events in the community pointed to almost universal difficulties involving collections. Some businesses, like Thompson's grocery and Hagerty's bank, went bankrupt when they could not collect on accounts owed. Notices of chattel mortgage sales filled the newspapers. For a laborer named George Miller, the situation reached a climax when a seemingly well-to-do Aberdeen resident either would not or could not pay for water pipes that Miller had laid. Desperate, Miller began to dig up the pipes, continuing even after the mayor ordered him to quit. When given a choice between a five-dollar fine and a nine-day jail term, Miller took the time.[119] As Mrs. Bilkins's poem "The Collector" suggests, Baum could sympathize both with the hapless collector and with the person unable to pay. Within two weeks he would announce that the price of the *Pioneer* was "ten cents per month, payable in advance to the carrier."

Although the three vignettes in this column may seem unrelated, Aberdeen's business community undoubtedly perceived a connection. The town had lost a five-year-old cracker-making business to Sioux Falls only two weeks before learning that the larger city had also captured the 1891 state fair. William E. Kidd had recently announced that the *Aberdeen Evening Republican* could no longer continue and he would publish a weekly only. The Independent editor blamed the failure of his daily on "lack of patronage" by Republican businessmen, which had its roots not only in the hard times but in the recent disappointment they had suffered at the polls. Kidd's caustic editorial style also contributed to his financial woes, for the publisher had been arrested for criminal libel on 15 January.[120]

"There's a horrible tale of suffering come to light," said the doctor at the breakfast table the other morning.

"What is it?" inquired our landlady, always interested in relieving the distressed.

"Why, the police found a poor collector lying on a marble doorstep in Aberdeen almost frozen and starved to death, and a prominent citizen, who is building an addition to his house to accommodate his bills, took him in and cared for him and took up a collection to send him to Pierre."[121]

"Yes, I heerd tell o' that," said our landlady, "an' I've writ a little pome on the teching incident. It reads like this:

THE COLLECTOR

"He enters the room with a pensive air an' takes of [f] his hat an' slicks his hair, an' places his little bill right where t'will meet his wictim's stony stare. An' the wictim he says, 'I guess that's square, an' quite kerrect, but I declare, I hain't a penny o' cash to spare. Jest call agin — ta, ta! — ah there!' An' the collector goes out in the winter air, an' under his breath he swears a swear. An' says, if the lord will let him git there he'll hie to a country where a crop failure's rare.

"An' fer my part," concluded our landlady, "I'm willin' to see him go."

———————

"Sioux Falls is gittin' everything," said our landlady the other day. "She's got the State Fair now, an' you bet she'll keep it."

"Aberdeen usually gets something," remarked the Colonel in an aggravated voice.

"So she does," agreed our landlady. "Sence we got a Commercial Club Aberdeen usually gits left! It ain't so comfortin' a reflection as a mirror in a barroom, but it's the condensed essence o' truth jest the same!"

———————

"If I was Billy Kidd," said our landlady, as she mixed the pancakes, "I'd change my name."

"To what?" queried Tom.

"Well, at fust I thought he could change it to Cap. Kidd because he roved, ye know, an' Billy he might do likewise. But as that would suggest freebootin' to the people, perhaps that wouldn't be healthy for him. Then there's Billy Goat — that's a commoner name nor Billy Kidd, an' would be a sort o' scapegoat from the late onpleasantness."

"You're rather hard on the poor fellow," said Tom.

"No," she replied, "I'm very fond o' him, but he's too old to be a Kidd any longer an' I think Billy Goat'll jest suit him."

The disconnected sections of this column probably reflect both the manner in which Baum wrote the weekly "Our Landlady" and the stress under which he was working. Of his writing techniques, Baum would later remark, "The odd characters are a sort of inspiration, liable to strike me any time, but the plot and plan of adventures takes considerable time to develop." In crafting a novel, Baum would jot down character sketches and incidents — much like the three vignettes in this column — on stray pieces of paper until he had enough to form a book, "stringing the incidents into consecutive order, elaborating the characters, etc."[122] In mid-January 1891, economic stress was taking its toll on Baum's ability to concentrate sufficiently to "string" unrelated incidents into Mrs. Bilkins's usual mealtime diatribe. The column did not appear at all in his 24 January edition. Rather than write columns, Baum sought frantically to deal with new competition from the *Aberdeen Daily News.*

In boom times the *News* could afford to let Baum's newspaper capture a share of the local news market and most of the social and literary audience. By January 1891, however, dull trade, a change in the governing party in Brown County, and financial reverses suffered in the Hagerty bank failure drove the *News* into active competition for Baum's readers. The Updyke farm columns in December had signaled the change, as had the *News* staff's greater attention to women's reading clubs and other social groups. The official announcement came on 31 January, when the *News* declared its intention to become an afternoon rather than a morning paper, to suspend publication on Sunday rather than its usual Monday, and to expand to seven columns rather than six in order to "make room for more literary and local matter of permanent interest."

Baum did what he could to control the damage. On the same day he announced that the *Pioneer* would become a Sunday paper (printed Saturday evening, delivered Sunday morning) of "the highest literary and news character." He would expand from eight to twelve pages and increase his reviews of national journals and books. In addition to Bill Nye's syndicated column, he began to offer more boiler plate of state and foreign news, literary features, humor, household hints, and odds and ends. Time would tell whether it would be enough.

. . . .

She Reads a Chapter in "Looking Backward" to the
Astonished and Interested Boarders

31 January 1891

Beginning his report of the week's society events on 24 January, Baum remarked, "These social hours are worth much more than their cost in the forgetfulness they afford of the bleak and uninviting prospects which stare us in the face during the day's scarcely requited labors." Only the weather remained fair, allowing youngsters to spend the warm evenings playing marbles under the city's electric lamps.[123] Baum and other town boosters continued to report that the drought had broken or, at any rate, that "two years will find the Jim River Valley under thorough irrigation and producing crops which will be the wonder and admiration of the world."[124] The bleakness of the present, however, led Baum to escape into the future. To do so, he borrowed the technique that Edward Bellamy had used in his popular utopian novel *Looking Backward, 2000–1887*. In Bellamy's 1888 fantasy, a young man falls asleep amid the poverty, unemployment, disease, and political corruption of America in 1887 and wakes up in the year 2000. From that vantage point, he looks back at the changes that have taken place to create a world of material abundance, technological advancement, and social harmony.[125]

Moving forward only five years, Baum's landlady left poverty, drought, and dull trade behind and speculated on the coming prosperity of Aberdeen. Local satire rather than utopian social commentary was Baum's aim, for the underlying society projected in his column had changed little. All the same, the columnist sent messages to his Aberdeen readers. First, the people and organizations projected to become prosperous in the Brown County of 1895 were those whose ingenuity, business practices, and stability Baum judged suitable for hard times. In many cases he proved an excellent prophet (Alonzo Ward and the Building and Loan Association, for example, did prosper in the Aberdeen of the future), but more important, he articulated for his readers a concept they would use to console themselves in years to come. As friends and comrades left, as severe business methods came into practice, as hopes withered, people across the Great Plains came to see the era of drought and depression as a test of character. The hard times drove out the weak-willed, "no 'count people," leaving the capable and strong to inherit the future.[126] And what a comfortable, technologically advanced future it was to be, according to Mrs. Bilkins.

As always, Baum's imagined inventions have an originality all their own, as does the "stranger's directory phonograph," or "phone'," which becomes interactive with Mrs. Bilkins. The device would reappear later in Baum's

1913 novel, *The Patchwork Girl of Oz*, in which the impudent phonograph goes by the name Victor Columbia Edison, whose primary function is to play music badly. The landlady's more practical "phone'" was based, as was her "automatick stenogripher," on the recent arrival in Aberdeen of a "'full blooded' phonograph" from which recorded shorthand notes could be transcribed "by anyone who can treaddle [*sic*] the machine and write English language." The owner of this new device received daily visitations from Hub City residents who found "great pleasure in examining and testing the wonderful machine."[127] Baum had obviously stopped by.

🌸 "This 'ere," said our landlady, as she sat by the fire mending the colonel's socks, "is a world o' change. Nuthin' stands still except the dude when he's a gittin' his pictur' took or his moustash waxed, an' one age succeeds another with lightnin' like rapidity."

"It is only," said Tom, solemnly, "when I feel in my pockets, that I realize there is no change."

"Everything progresses an' evolutes an' merges an' bubbles an' emanates an' convalutes inter suthin' else. Everything changes — ' "

"Except the weather," put in the doctor.

"I never realized," continued our landlady, ignoring her interruptions, "how liable we was ter change till this mornin'. Ye see, when I was younger I used to be kinder somnambulary — "

"What?"

"Walked in my sleep, ye know. Well, I thought I'd got all over that until this mornin'. Ye see, I went ter bed kinder worried an' onsettled last night, an' I must a had 'em agin — the somnambularys, I mean, — 'cause when I woke up this mornin' I found I'd writ a long letter to my brother Jake in my sleep."

"Very curious," remarked the colonel.

"Yes, but the most curiousest thing of all was that I'd writ as if it was 1895, which ain't fer five year to come."

"Ah, I see — looking backwards."

"I should think it were lookin' a good ways ahead. But that letter had a good many strange things in it an' I've kinder wondered if the prophet's robe didn't kind'er fall on me in my sleep an' lead me to write that 'air epistal. Fer it's nearer to a prophecy than anything else."

"Read us the letter," suggested the colonel, "it may cheer us up a bit to know how things will be five years from now."

"Yes — do!" entreated the doctor.

"Werry good," said Mrs. Bilkins, with a pleased air as she drew a carefully folded document from her bosom. "I'll fire it off, but don't you interrupt me, fer I ain't responsible fer all I say in my sleep. The letter begins this way: —

"DEAR JERRY: — Havin' jest arrived here in the great metropilis o' Aberdeen, which is in the Garden of Eden, — formerly state of South Dakoty, I wind up my automatick stenogripher to dictate to you a few lines 'afore the gong rings. The air ship on which I arove were uncomfortably crowded, havin' on board a lot o' passengers from Weisbeer, that new continent lately diskivered by Jim Ringrose at the North Pole. The ship were in charge o' Capt. Sam Vroom and were two hours late, as usual. Immejutly on my arrival I went to the Creamery Hotel, which Al. Ward has jest opened at ten dollars a day. I got a room on the sixteenth floor as were quite conwenient. Seein' a stranger's directory phonograph in the room I touched it off an' listened to the followin' while I smoothed my hair: 'Aberdeen, Garden o' Eden, the center o' the wonderful irrigated valley o' the Jim. The most fertile an' productive land in the world surrounds this busy metropolis an' pours its treasures into the city's marts, from whence they are airshipped to all parts of the world an' also to Pierre. Aberdeen owes its wonderful growth to irrigation an' the Buildin' an' Loan Association, an' is the largest city but one on the western continent. Its principal exports is wheat, corn, pertaters, loose gold, diamond dust an' bond coupons. Hank Williams also sometimes exports a groan. Climate, salubrious. Inhabitants sober an' friendly, popilation unknown.'

" 'How's that,' says I.

" 'Begun countin' it two year ago an' ain't finished yit,' says the phonograph.

" 'Who's Mayor,' says I.

" 'Jim Davis, you fool,' says the phonograph.

" 'Why d'ye say fool?' says I.

" 'Because yer so ignorant o' our great men. I s'pose ye don't know Congressmen Ed. Mutz an' Skip Salisbury; ner that Frank Beard is Senator; ner that Cranmer an' Kennedy is fightin' fer district attorneyship, while Taub. looks smilin'ly on; ner that the postmaster's got so busy he's had ter drop politics, ner nothin' else. Go 'long!'

" 'Ye're a impident phone',' says I, 'an' I'll report ye.' But I went along. After dinner I went out on the big piazzer an' sot down.

" 'Baum's Hourly Newspaper!' yells a feller rushin' up with a book as thick as yer head.

" 'Why, Georgie Slosser,' says I, 'is this you?'

" 'You bet,' says he, 'I'm just coinin' money. Got the control o' the sales on this piazzer. Buy a copy? Best paper in Aberdeen.'

" 'Allus was,' says I, 'yes, I'll take one.'

"Well, I sot an' read all the news an' noticed that Aberdeen had changed since the great depression of '91. Here was an advertisement o' Narregang's Bank of Eden, with a capital o' ten millions an' a surplus of twenty. I noticed that Waterman's Aberdeen Band had jest giv' a successful performance at the court o' King Stanley, o' Africa. Here was Scott's Drug Store offerin' to sell patent faith cure at ten cents a bottle an' Scott's Lymph cure for sour stomachs at a dollar a can. Also that he was goin' to close out an' move to Chicago. Here it told how Luke an' Merten had given a picnic to seven hundred employees, includin' all but the help in their woolen mills an' shoe factories at Bath, which couldn't be spared. Also a report o' the row the police had tryin' to keep the crowds away from Beard an' Gage's big department store on last market day. There was a pictur' of McWilliam's new white marble block on the second page, which showed up finely. Taken altogether, things seemed to be rushin' in Aberdeen.

"Jest then my attention were arrested by a shout, and a chariot dashed by drawed by ten milk-white steeds.

" 'Who's that?' says I to a bystander.

" 'Him?' says he, 'why that's President Crose o' the Alliance, the biggest man in Eden, an' the richest.'

" 'Thanks,' says I, 'I might a knowed it. But tell me, was that Ed. Lowe that I seed drivin' the electric car that just passed?'

" 'Probably. It's a belt line, an' he allus likes to be in the ring. Good day, ma'am, if you want any other information just consult a phone'.'

"But I sot an' watched the stream o' people glide by an' thought o' the poor, misguided folks what left Aberdeen a few years ago, just because a crop failed. If they could a seen ahead they couldn't been driven away with Kuehnle's Injun clubs. But p'raps it were best. The no 'count people was got red of an' only the solid ones left, such as is the rich folks o' Aberdeen in 1895. But, dear Jake, I must draw this 'ere letter to a close. I'll write more about these wonderful things termorrer.   Yourn sisterly, SARY ANN BILKINS[128]

"But," added our landlady, as she folded the sheet with a sigh, " 'afore I could write more, I waked up, an' it were too late. Somehow it don't seem like a dream to me, but more like a vision that may come to pass in proper time."

. . . .

She Discusses New Inventions with the Boarders

8 February 1891

"While the world jogs on in its accustomed ruts," Baum asserted on 8 February, "experiments are in progress which will eventually revolutionize all transportation, and many things besides." "The *Pioneer* man" claimed that he was "always intent upon examining each marvel of this age of invention," and the concept of an airship had particularly caught his fancy in recent weeks. W. W. Pennington, an Illinois inventor and "personal acquaintance of Capt. [C. R.] Hall" of Aberdeen, had scheduled a trial of his airship from Mount Carmel, Illinois, to Chicago via Saint Louis in mid-November.[129] After much postponement, the flight took place at the end of January 1891. Of course, the editor noted on 8 February, hitches had developed — the machine did not go as fast, as high, or as far as predicted — but these were mere details that would be worked out. In Baum's view the airship had proved "so successful that the most skeptical cannot longer disbelieve in the ultimate practicability of the invention." As the reader already knows, neither Baum nor Mrs. Bilkins harbored much skepticism when it came to the marvels of the age, and the landlady's confident predictions are almost three decades premature.

Adding a somber note to the futuristic speculation in this final "Our Landlady" column were the crop failures and poverty in Dakota. The fact that farmers and county officials had recently renewed their search for seed and feed gave special urgency to Baum's projections about the airship's future usefulness. Although Brown County commissioners distributed coal, food, and other supplies to the needy, those who applied for such public aid found it difficult, as the landlady pointed out, to keep their positions "in bong tong serciety." Among the downwardly mobile of Aberdeen was editor Baum himself, who was finding it impossible to collect money, pay bills, and face his straitened financial circumstances with equanimity. The landlady's final words dovetailed with Baum's own experience and provide an apt index to his state of mind — the light tone cannot quite mask the underlying bitterness. Nevertheless, despite adversity, Sairy Ann Bilkins remained a Dakota rustler to the end. Baum's readers would have expected nothing less.

"I read in the papers," said our landlady, as she finished sewing a button on the doctor's overcoat and bit off the thread, as a woman will, "that the great air ship is goin' ter be a success, after all."

"Yes," said the colonel, by way of reply, "it looks as though they will be able to make it work after they've rectified a few mistakes."

"Of course," said Mrs. Bilkins, "the thing wouldn't be perfect the first time — it ain't in natur'. The cost of sewin' a yard of cloth on the first machine Howe inwented were six dollars. But he made it work in the end, an' I'll bet a cookie to a rat trap that this 'ere flyin' machine'll do the same."

"If it does," said Tom, "the railroads will be ruined."

"An' serve 'em right," exclaimed our landlady, taking her gum from the inside band of the colonel's Sunday hat; "they've beat the people long enough an' tyranized over 'em with a rod o' iron, an' I, fer one, will be glad to see 'em shut up shop. A air-ship can call for ye at your own residence, whenever ye hoist a signal flag. People will own their private ships, too, an' go where they pleases an' if anyone wants ter quit Dakoty then why they can step inter their airships an' float around till they come to a place as is got a crop. There's other things that private airships is good for. You can go on a picnic any time you like an' take the whole family. The hired man can use it to go arter the cow with, an' it'll save him the labor o' leadin' her home by hitchin' her to the ship an' skimmin' along the surface o' the ground. At election time they can make the pollin' places air ships, an' when the ballot closes the ships can rise ter a moderate distance where the candidates can watch 'em, an' the votes be counted without any chance o' futher contests. Stanley won't be anywheres. If a feller wants to explore Africa he can do it with neatness and despatch in his air-ship. If he wants ter go ter the North Pole he can do so — pervided he don't freeze. A trip to Europe will be as cheap as livin' to home, fer all you need is a stock o' pervisions. I tell you there ain't no end to an air-ship's usefulness, an' I'm glad to see 'em a success."

"There are a good many novel inventions lately," remarked the doctor, in a ruminating way.

"Yes," acquiesced our landlady, "an' Aberdeen ain't far behind other cities, either. Al. Ward has jest inwented a way to work over frowy butter an' make it gilt-edged creamery, an' he'll make a fortune out o' it. Wendell has inwented a way to set in a chair an' go to sleep with his feet on a red-hot stove without even burnin' the shoe leather — but he won't make a cent on that. A bank cashear down to Ipswich has inwented a way o' lettin' his bank bust an' makin' folks think that he's only closin' out an' will pay 'em back their deposits next new years. The News has inwented a way o' makin' both ends meet, to their own surprise an' the grief o' their army o' readers. Mayor Moody has inwented a way o' makin' himself solid with the people at the expense o' the chief o' perlice. The blind pigs has inwented a way o' siccin' the prohibitionists onter the druggists an' escapin' themselves — oh, there's no end of inwentions, only they don't find a way o' makin' a dime buy a dollar's wuth, ner to give us a crop next year if there ain't no seed in the ground. There's an' irrigation business it will pay the geniuses to work at. They might also find a way to pay yer bills when you can't collect a cent to do it with; how to set through a sermon with a calm face when you know you've got ter put a nickel in the conterbushun box; also how to get help from the county commissioners an' keep your posish in bong tong serciety. But these things'll all be found out as the country progresses."

In spite of their humor and confident pronouncements about the future, Baum's final "Our Landlady" columns revealed the author's painful struggles with financial difficulties and the need to make a decision about leaving Aberdeen. The 10 January 1891 column sketched clearly the arguments for staying in or leaving Dakota, as if Baum were debating the issue with himself. Mrs. Bilkins's line of reasoning urged the editor to trust in the future of Dakota. "Before you can hardly git settled in some other locality," she predicted, "you'll be startled by the news o' the crops in South Dakoty." Tom argued the opposing view: "With the same amount of energy it requires to earn a crust here, I could get a full loaf anywhere else. Why should I stay? Do I owe anything to Aberdeen?" The landlady's response, that he owed something to himself, was the crux of the argument. Baum had to decide whether he and his family would be better off if they left or stayed.

He was not forced to grapple seriously with the question until after the disappointing November 1890 election, when the defeat of both the suffrage issue and the local Republican slate shattered any hopes for political patronage for his newspaper or printing shop. During the summer, business had been brisk, with "the hooks full of job copy and 'advs.'" that kept the presses humming.[1] When trade fell off in August, Baum noted that "most of us are so thoroughly established here that we cannot pull out without serious loss."[2] A few days later he launched his monthly promotional publication, the *Western Investor*. Using its pages to solicit eastern investors and capital, the editor displayed his commitment to Aberdeen and his disgust with the Hub City commercial club.[3] While he was beginning this optimistic venture, however, harsh summer winds and a rainless July and August again destroyed the wheat crop. The extent of the catastrophe did not become immediately evident, and even though times were hard, Baum's job printing department seems to have done a brisk business; he published extra editions during the state fair, for example, as well as the official fair program.[4] Although Mrs. Bilkins's enumeration of blessings at Thanksgiving was somewhat bleak, she could still be thankful "that the newspapers are able to run, whether folks pays their subscription or not" (29 November 1890).

All the same, the final calamities that would end Baum's chances in Aberdeen had already reached the horizon. The Indian scare and the extravagant way it was reported throughout the United States annihilated any remaining hopes of continued eastern investment and settlement in South Dakota in the near future. Even so, Aberdeen-based investors might have hunkered down and weathered the drought and the short-term effects of the bad publicity had the Hagerty bank failure not robbed many of their remaining capital.[5] On 17 January 1891, Mrs. Bilkins's poem about collectors captured the new reality in South Dakota as Brown County homesteaders and businessmen began to lose their enterprises to mortgage companies. The weeding-out process thus begun would leave Brown County with three thousand fewer residents by 1895.[6]

As people began to leave and money became ever scarcer, Baum's subscriptions, which had totaled 3,500 at one time, dwindled to 1,400. He told an eastern advertiser that it was "only by the hardest efforts that he prevented the whole lot from going to hell." That advertiser found Baum's frankness appealing and continued to purchase space in the *Pioneer*, but others did not.[7] As job printing also became scarce following the election, his job printer moved on, and Baum himself set type, laid out advertisements, and collected his meager income. To lure subscribers, he offered various premiums and sold magazine subscriptions from his newspaper offices until late January 1891, when competition forced new measures. The *Aberdeen Daily News*, which had suffered the loss not only of public patronage but also of capital through the Hagerty bank failure, began to compete for the *Aberdeen Saturday Pioneer*'s shrinking pool of readers by expanding its own local coverage.[8] Baum's struggle over the decision to leave Dakota was nearing its end.

The editor's efforts to establish the *Pioneer* as a twelve-page Sunday literary paper indicated that he still considered Aberdeen a good place to live. The presence of Maud Baum's family made it especially attractive. And, as Mrs. Bilkins noted on 10 January 1891, "It might a ben better to hav' gone away two year ago, when the troubles begun, but to go now, when they's about over, is rank foolishness." Baum had invested time and money in Aberdeen and felt "thoroughly identified with the city's institutions and enterprises."[9] Finding "the shoulder to shoulder way in which we all stood together to boost our little town" an asset, Baum remained confident that the town's future as a metropolis was merely delayed.[10] The 3 and 31 January 1891 columns overtly stated their author's belief that the technological advances of the late nineteenth century would transform life in the area, ensuring prosperity for those who stayed. Along with Mrs. Bilkins, most Aberdonians were convinced that the town needed only "irrigation an' the Buildin' an' Loan Association" (that is, capital investment) to blossom into "the largest city but one on the western continent" (31 January 1891).

Such dreams made good newspaper copy, but financial reality and other circumstances dictated that Aberdeen's future would be less pretentious. The continuing drought and the need to solicit seed wheat and feed for Dakota farmers had damaged the state's short-term investment future and credit rating just as the nation as a whole was sinking into the financial depression of the early 1890s. In the years to come, small-scale irrigation, crop diversification, and good management would gradually ease the state's financial problems, but industry and capital investment came slowly to Dakota. Aberdeen's crisscrossing railroads kept its economy alive, allowing it to survive and become South Dakota's second largest city by 1910.[11] Long before that modest future could be realized, however, ill health, family responsibilities, and creditors finally forced Baum to choose a different destiny.

Writing from California in 1917, Baum remarked offhandedly to his niece in Aberdeen that "in that god-blasted country you live in, one's sporting blood needs to be 100% pure."[12] Throughout his life a weak heart had thinned Baum's sporting blood, and in the early months of 1891 other physical problems further sapped his strength, hastening his decision to leave South Dakota. The final impetus seems to have been the response that followed his 14 February editorial urging economy in the school system and condemning the school superintendent's high salary and poor performance. Three days later the high school students wrote the *Aberdeen Daily News*, roasting Baum and asking citizens to "refuse patronage to a public nuisance [the *Pioneer*] that is constantly engaged in making scurrilous attacks upon its superiors."[13] Baum responded that as a Dakota editor, "with the skin of a rhinoceros and a soul like the Kohinoor," he did not mind "a gentle 'roasting,' " but this attack had been both "scandalous" and, for an editor who prided himself on his evenhandedness, totally unexpected.[14] Whether or not the request for a boycott had any effect on the paper is unknown, but it took its toll on Baum's health. He spent the next two weeks in bed.

The removal of a ranula from under Baum's tongue in early March revived him, but the editor now put his efforts into searching for a job. With three young sons and a pregnant wife, he had to earn more money than his weekly newspaper could any longer supply. During its last months of existence the *Aberdeen Saturday Pioneer* lost its sparkle, for its editor was either sick in bed or job hunting in Minneapolis and Chicago. Some evidence suggests that Baum's mother-in-law, who was living with them at the time, managed the newspaper during March while the publisher searched for other employment.[15] In any event, on 24 March the Baums' fourth son and last child entered the world, intensifying his father's search for greater security.

In April 1891 the *Aberdeen Daily News* reported that Baum's health had been "very poor for several months and for this and other reasons he . . . concluded to accept a position on one of the leading dailies in Chicago [the *Chicago Evening Post*], where, if the work is somewhat arduous it is all along one line and is devoid to a large extent of worry and anxiety."[16] This quotation, coming as it does from a fellow Aberdeen editor, allows the reader to sense the stress and strain that Baum's Dakota enterprise had placed upon him. His myriad tasks — writing and issuing a weekly newspaper and monthly investment publication, overseeing advertising and job printing departments, selling magazines to supplement his income, and trying to please Aberdeen readers as political parties splintered and belts tightened — provided little peace of mind and even less money. On 4 April Baum returned "the plant and good will" of the *Aberdeen Saturday Pioneer* to John Drake, who sold the equipment and disbanded the paper.[17] After he became famous, Baum would be able to find humor in this financial necessity, telling people that he published the *Pioneer* "until the sheriff wanted it worse than I did."[18]

Meanwhile, however, Baum's next years in Chicago were equally hard. He worked briefly in a poor-paying newspaper job and then as a traveling salesman before he found a career in trade journalism and writing children's books.[19] After his highly successful 1900 novel *The Wonderful Wizard of Oz* went on to become an even more successful Broadway extravaganza in 1902, a Hub City contemporary remarked, "If there had been more children and more pennies in [Aberdeen], the author of *Father Goose* and the *Wizard of Oz* might still be selling balls and bats and baubles and gewgaws to Young America."[20] Baum himself noted long afterward that "as the years pass, and we look back on something which, at the time, seemed unbelievedly discouraging and unfair, we come to realize that, after all, God was at all times on our side. The eventual outcome was, we discover, by far the best solution for us and what then we thought should have been to our best advantage, would in reality have been quite detrimental."[21] Baum moved on to better fortune, and gradually his South Dakota failure became "hallowed by time" as he recognized the value of this "phase of life" on the western frontier.[22]

For all its hardships, the Aberdeen phase of his life afforded the author a rich store of experiences for use in his literary works. The Dakota prairie and its wildlife — prairie dogs, buffalo, gophers, crows, and grasshoppers — provided settings and characters for shorter fiction such as his "Animal Fairy

Tales," which were published in the *Delineator* in 1905, and the Twinkle Tales, a series of small books for young children that appeared in 1906.[23] His fourteen months as a newspaper editor also gave the author an unparalleled opportunity to examine, talk about, critique, and satirize the concepts and issues of the 1890s. The rich stew of ideas that critics claim underlies the story line of *The Wonderful Wizard of Oz* and his other Oz books (for example, the regionalism of America, the radical politics of the Great Plains, Theosophy, technological progress, monetary reform, women's rights, utopianism) originally bubbled throughout the pages of the *Pioneer*, receiving satirical treatment in the "Our Landlady" columns or serious explication on the editorial page.[24] From these beginnings Baum went on to craft his fairyland of Oz, leaving the misery of Dakota behind. Also left behind for us to rediscover over a hundred years later was Baum's frontier legacy: that preeminent Dakota rustler, Sairy Ann Bilkins.

*

NOTES

ABBREVIATIONS

AAN	*Aberdeen American-News*
A&BC	*Aberdeen and Brown County, S.D., Illustrated*
ACD	*Aberdeen City Directory, 1889–1890*
ADN	*Aberdeen Daily News*
AER	*Aberdeen Evening Republican*
ASP	*Aberdeen Saturday Pioneer*
AWN	*Aberdeen Weekly News*
AWR	*Aberdeen Weekly Republican*
BCD	*Brown County Directory, 1887–8*
GSB	T. Clarkson Gage Scrapbook
SDESA	South Dakota Equal Suffrage Association
SDSHS	South Dakota State Historical Society

INTRODUCTION

1. Koupal, "From the Land of Oz," p. 47.

2. Hearn, "L. Frank Baum: Amateur Printer," pp. 11–18, and "L. Frank Baum: Chicken Fancier," p. 24; Gage, "L. Frank Baum before He Came to Aberdeen," pp. 1–3; Martin Gardner, "The Royal Historian of Oz," in Gardner and Nye, *The Wizard of Oz and Who He Was*, pp. 20–21; Robert S. Baum, "The Autobiography of Robert Stanton Baum, Part I," p. 17; Greene and Martin, *The Oz Scrapbook*, pp. 4–5; Ford and Martin, *The Musical Fantasies of L. Frank Baum*, pp. 7–10; Koupal, "Wonderful Wizard of the West," p. 204.

3. Baum and MacFall, *To Please a Child*, pp. 1–7, 10, 42–46, 76–78; L. Frank Baum to T. Clarkson Gage, 30 July 1888, Baum Collection; ADN 4 and 29 April 1891. For information about Baum's life in Chicago and his later life and work, see Baum and MacFall, *To Please a Child*.

4. Greene and Martin, *Oz Scrapbook*, pp. 4–5; Baum to T. Clarkson Gage, 8 June 1888, Baum Collection.

5. Baum to Gage, 30 July 1888.

6. Cleworth, "Brown County Agricultural History," pp. 32–33, 39–40; BCD pp. 19–20; South Dakota Commissioner of Labor Statistics and Census, *Census Report of South Dakota for 1895*, p. 16; South Dakota Department of History, *Second Census of the State of South Dakota*, pp. 22, 36; Robinson, *History of South Dakota*, 1:842; Lauterbach, *First There Was the Prairie*, p. 32; Humphrey, *Following the Prairie Frontier*, p. 98. A good example of Aberdeen boosterism appears in ADN 30 October 1889, where the

editor declares that the city "has justly earned the distinction of being the 'Railway Hub' of the Dakotas."

7. *BCD* p. 20.

8. Carpenter, Diary, 18 June 1888; Baum to Gage, 8 June 1888; Gage, "The Dakota Days of L. Frank Baum," pp. 5–8.

9. Baum to Gage, 30 July 1888.

10. Baum to Gage, 30 July 1888. Many of Baum's biographers suggest that his first love was the theater. In Aberdeen, Baum took various roles and served as stage manager for many performances in 1890. His plans for forming a stock company and managing an opera house did not work out, however, for the town already had both an opera house (albeit a poor one) and a manager.

11. *ADN* 2 October 1888.

12. *ADN* 12 October 1888.

13. *ADN* 15 May, 9 and 27 June, 18 and 21 August, 11 and 26 October 1889. During the summer Baum also traveled to Edgeley in northern Dakota and McPherson County in central Dakota to write about German-Russian settlers "for Harpers' publications" (*ADN* 10 July 1889). An excerpt of his report appeared in *ADN* 24 July 1889.

14. *ADN* 2 November 1889.

15. *ADN* 12 November 1889.

16. *Webster Reporter and Farmer* 5 December 1889.

17. Baum to Gage, 30 July 1888; *AAN* 21 May 1961; Chattel Mortgage between Maud G. Baum and Henry M. Marple, 28 December 1889, Baum Collection; *ADN* 19 October 1888.

18. *ADN* 21 October 1888.

19. Cleworth, "Brown County Agricultural History," pp. 54–55, 58–65; Torrey, *Early Days in Dakota,* pp. 76–77. Baum's career as a Dakota businessman is explored further in Gage, "Dakota Days of L. Frank Baum," pp. 5–8.

20. *ADN* 1 January 1890.

21. *AWR* 23 January 1890; Bill of Sale between Maud G. Baum and Helen L. Gage, 18 January 1890, Baum Collection.

22. Helen L. Gage, "L. Frank Baum: An Inside Introduction," p. 269.

23. *ADN* 19 April 1890; Gage, "Dakota Days of L. Frank Baum," p. 8.

24. *ACD*; *A&BC*; Lyon, "Significance of Newspapers on the American Frontier," pp. 9, 12. A recent book, Cloud, *Business of Newspapers on the Western Frontier,* offers new insights on western journalism as a financial venture.

25. *Aberdeen: A Middle Border City*, pp. 49–52, 66–68; *AER* 18 March 1890; *ADN* 19 and 26 January 1890. The fortunes, names, and numbers of newspapers in Aberdeen changed with startling rapidity, making an accurate accounting difficult. In mid-May 1890, for example, the *Dakota Knights of Labor* made its appearance with one of Baum's former job printing employees as major investor and print foreman. In August

two diehard Democrats started the weekly *State Democrat*, to be "published in the interests of the straight democratic party" (*ASP* 16 August 1890), because the formerly Democratic *Republican* was becoming Populist in sentiment. Sometime in 1890, new political allegiances moved the *Ruralist* to Huron. See *ADN* 11 May 1890; *ASP* 24 May 1890; and *Dakota Ruralist* 10 January 1891.

26. Baum's newspaper as a whole and its contributions to his later books are explored in Koupal, "Wonderful Wizard of the West," pp. 203–15.

27. Humphrey, *Following the Prairie Frontier*, p. 81.

28. "[August C.] Witte Reviews Development of City since 1881" (clipping from Aberdeen newspaper), 31 January 1929, GSB.

29. Algeo, "The Names of Oz," pp. 130–46, discusses Baum's creation of names in the Oz books and his regular use of characterizing and punning names.

30. Baum and MacFall, *To Please a Child*, p. 65; Moore, *Wonderful Wizard, Marvelous Land*, p. 52.

31. Holmes, *Autocrat of the Breakfast-Table*, p. 80. The reader is tempted to wonder if the doctor in Baum's landlady columns is meant to suggest Holmes himself; Baum replicates the autocrat's softheartedness toward the landlady in his doctor's treatment of Mrs. Bilkins (see her assessment of the doctor in the 12 April 1890 column).

32. *Baum Bugle* 28 (autumn 1984): 13; *Syracuse Standard*, 1 March–30 August 1884. In addition to the similar-sounding titles and the term "Our Landlady," the Syracuse series contains puns, sight dialogue, and commentary on social events that recall Baum's Aberdeen columns. However, even such well-developed offerings as that of 10 May 1884, "The Landlady Sees Fraud," do not suggest Baum's outrageous humor and inventiveness; instead, they seem labored and overly long.

33. Whitcher, *The Widow Bedott Papers*, p. v; *Dictionary of American Biography*, s.v. "Shillaber, Benjamin Penhallow" and "Whitcher, Frances Miriam Berry"; B. P. Shillaber, "Oracular Pearls," in Shillaber, *Partingtonian Patchwork*, pp. 151–74. One can argue that the model is far older, going back to Benjamin Franklin's Silence Dogood, a widow whose opinions appeared in the *New-England Courant* in 1722; See *Benjamin Franklin, Writings*, pp. 5–42.

34. Interestingly, Whitcher signed her Widow Bedott sketches with "Frank," and Baum's first three "Our Landlady" columns are signed "Pete." For more on Whitcher, see Morris, *Women's Humor in the Age of Gentility*.

35. "57th Performance Tuesday, April 27th, 1880 . . . Neil Burgess in Petroleum V. Nasby's (D. R. Locke's) dramatization of the celebrated Bedott papers, entitled Widow Bedott," *Haverly's Theatre Programme* 27 April 1880, Williams/Watson Theatre Collection; *Dictionary of American Biography*, s.v. "Whitcher, Frances Miriam Berry"; Burgess, *The Widow and the Elder*; Curry, Introduction to Marietta Holley, *Samantha Rastles the Woman Question*, p. 17 n.4; Bijou Opera House, advertisement for *Vim*, 17 April 1883, and Novelty Theatre, advertisement for *Vim*,

21 April [1884], Williams/Watson Theatre Collection; Burgess, *Neil Burgess' New Play, entitled Vim.*

36. Robinson, "A Century of Liquor Legislation in Dakota," pp. 288–89; *ASP* 3 May 1890; Koupal, "From the Land of Oz," p. 48.

37. Koupal, "From the Land of Oz," p. 50.

38. *ASP* 25 January, 1, 8, and 22 March, and 3 May 1890; Reed, *The Woman Suffrage Movement in South Dakota*, pp. 17–18; Norlin, "The Suffrage Movement and South Dakota Churches," pp. 310, 332–33; Wittmayer, "The 1889–1890 Woman Suffrage Campaign," pp. 208–10.

39. *ASP* 15 February, 19 April, and 3 May 1890.

40. *AER* 14 and 19 May 1890.

41. *ASP* 19 April 1890. Baum's view of women is readily visible in his fourteen Oz books, where he creates a utopia in which the important rulers are women. For further discussion of Baum's feminine utopia, see Moore, *Wonderful Wizard, Marvelous Land*, pp. 130–50; Vogel, "The Amazonia of Oz," pp. 4–8; and Luehrs, "L. Frank Baum and the Land of Oz," pp. 55–57.

42. *ASP* 15 March 1890. For further discussion of Baum's opinion of western women, see Koupal, "Wonderful Wizard of the West," pp. 208–12.

43. Cleworth, "Brown County Agricultural History," pp. 45, 50; Tryon, "Agriculture and Politics in South Dakota," p. 284; *ADN* 7 June 1890; Koupal, "From the Land of Oz," p. 52. A recent assessment of the Farmers' Alliance and the grievances that led to the formation of a third party can be found in Remele, "God Helps Those Who Help Themselves," pp. 22–33.

44. *ASP* 1 February 1890.

45. Littlefield, "The Wizard of Oz: Parable on Populism," pp. 47–58, first suggested that the *Wizard of Oz* was an allegorical *critique* of Populism, which would be in keeping with the political philosophy Baum revealed in the *Aberdeen Saturday Pioneer*. Recently, however, commentators seem to be using Littlefield's ideas to suggest that Baum himself was a Populist who supported the movement. See, e.g., Dregni, "The Politics of Oz," pp. 32–33; or Genovese, "Tin Men and Witches Feud over Populism." In contrast, Leach, "Clown from Syracuse," p. 11, on the basis of further research dismisses the Littlefield reading, claiming that Baum never even mentioned the Populists in his newspaper (Leach apparently did not realize that the Independents were the "Populists" of 1890). Of the many who have discussed Baum's politics, only Erisman, "L. Frank Baum and the Progressive Dilemma," p. 617 n.3, identified Baum's "lifelong Republicanism."

46. *Dakota Ruralist* 10 January 1891; *ADN* 11 May 1890; Sannes, "Union Makes Strength," p. 37; Quinion, "James H. Kyle," pp. 311–12; Remele, "God Helps Those Who Help Themselves," p. 24 n.7.

47. *ASP* 8 November 1890.

48. Wittmayer, "The 1889–1890 Woman Suffrage Campaign," pp. 214, 217, 219.

49. *ASP* 1 February 1890.

50. *ASP* 25 January 1890.

51. Algeo, "Oz and Kansas," pp. 135–39. Baum's interest in Theosophy and Spiritualism is beginning to receive more attention from critics. See, e.g., Leach, "Clown from Syracuse," pp. 5–9.

52. *ASP* 18 October 1890.

53. *ADN* 30 December 1890.

54. Wagenknecht, *Utopia Americana*, p. 148.

55. *ASP* 18 October 1890 and 24 January 1891.

56. Matilda Jewell Gage, "To the readers of *The Baum Bugle*," p. 16.

57. *AER* 18 March 1890.

58. *ADN* 17 February 1891.

59. *ASP* 21 and 28 February and 7 March 1891.

60. *ADN* 23 December 1890 and 1 January 1891.

61. *ASP* 27 December 1890. Unlike the affair over the superintendent, this exchange was amicable, and as Truthful Zeke pointed out, Baum misconstrued his playful comments in order to use "the opportunity to advertise his paper (its price recommends it) and his late stock in trade, the dime novel" (*ADN* 31 December 1890). Baum's exchanges over Spiritualism and especially the expanding Hagerty bank failure, however, became exceedingly bitter. See *ASP* 17, 24, and 31 January 1891; *ADN* 27 January 1891.

62. *ASP* 28 February, 7 and 21 March 1891. Baum had a tumor removed from under his tongue in early March.

63. On the flyleaf of this bound file of the *Pioneer*, Maud Gage Baum wrote that she presented it to the Alexander Mitchell Library in September 1926. It was probably Baum's personal file copy. The 22 November 1890 issue is missing, and the South Dakota Writers' Project records indicate that it was already missing when project workers used the file in 1939. See WPA Writers' Project Collection, box 18, folder 4.

64. M. Lisle Reese, former South Dakota Writers' Project director, to the author, 8 May 1992.

65. Reese to author, 8 May 1992; Maud G. Baum, Affidavit, 15 August 1940, WPA Writers' Project Collection, box 18, folder 10.

"OUR LANDLADY"

1. Carpenter, Diary, 24 January 1890.

2. The first three "Our Landlady" columns carried this by-line. Baum signed some of his early satirical features with fictitious names — for example, a satire on church socials couched in a letter-to-the-editor format carried the signature "Dugout" from "Dugout Township, S.D." (*ASP* 22 February 1890) — but soon discontinued the practice. The by-line PETE on at least one satirical piece in the *Aberdeen Daily News* suggests that

Baum had contributed commentary to that paper before taking over the *Pioneer*; see "A New Catechism," *ADN* 12 September 1889.

3. Spaeth, *Read 'Em and Weep*, p. 152.

4. *First Presbyterian Church*, n.p.

5. *ADN* 8 March 1890; Pulliam, *Harriman*, pp. 16–17.

6. In September the *North Dakota Republican* would write that Barrett "is in Aberdeen yet, while many of his old time enemies are scattered over the country, and [one] is on the Pacific Coast. Blood will tell" (quoted in *AER* 15 September 1890).

7. Since the middle of February the Aberdeen press had been boasting that fresh strawberries led the bills of fare at local hotels, illustrating that despite "reported drouth and great distress," South Dakotans were enjoying "the latest delicacies of the season" (*ADN* 18 February 1890). On 8 March, Baum noted that grocers Thompson and Kearney had shipped in a large supply of Kentucky berries, which "our poverty-stricken citizens soon bought up, . . . nor haggled at the price, which was astonishingly reasonable." Although such promotional sentiments pervaded most comments on imported fruit, editor Baum could be depended upon to tell the other side of the story before long. On 17 May he explored the nature of shipped-in delicacies in an eight-stanza poem titled "Fresh Strawberries":

> Along came the farmer the very next day,
> And picked both the ripe and the green.
> And sent them away on the big railway
> To the rich folks in Aberdeen.
>
> They travelled for many a long, weary day,
> 'Til covered with dust and looking quite gray
> And jostled 'til many were forced to decay
> And others were shrivelled and dried on the way.
>
> They came at last to a grocer's stall
> And the grocer gaily shook them up,
> Put the dead at the bottom — the living on top,
> And a card labelled "Fresh" he placed over all!

8. *ASP* 1 March 1890. "Outsiders," Baum noted years later, when Aberdeen finally got a new theater, "judge the enterprise of any city by its newspapers and theatres — if they are good the town is alive" (Baum to Mr. McKeever, 28 May 1913, in *Aberdeen Daily American*, 15 June 1913).

9. *ASP* 1 February, 1, 8, and 15 March 1890; *ADN* 25 January, 21 and 23 February, 2, 4, 5, 11, 14, and 15 March 1890.

10. "Whiskey Was Merchandise Stock in 1880," c. 1922, Vertical Files, s.v. "History"; *ASP* 15 and 22 March 1890; *ADN* 23 October 1889, 8 January, 4, 18, and 21 March 1890. The text of the law, from which the quotations are taken, appeared in *ASP* 15 March 1890.

11. A good example of Baum's sympathy for farmers occurred in his poem "Nance Adkins" (*ASP* 1 March 1890). In twenty sentimental stanzas he recounted the story of a proud and impoverished farmer who told his wife,

> To be sure, I might ha' mortgaged
> All we have to buy us feed
> 'Til there comes another harvest
> *If we only had the seed.*

> Yes — I know — I might a' had it.
> But the false pride held me back:
> I *could'nt* make the "application"
> An' *beg* — not fer a single sack!

In the happy denouement the wife secretly made the application, and the farmer accepted aid from her. Baum signed the poem Louis F. Baum, a name he had used on the stage and in the city directory. In Aberdeen, he used either L. F. or Louis F. Baum, rather than the more familiar L. Frank Baum that appears on his books.

12. The doctor's attitude toward the doughnut recalls a family story recounted in Baum and MacFall, *To Please a Child*, pp. 50–51. Called "the affair of the Bismarks," the anecdote records a battle of wills between the newly married L. Frank Baum and his wife, Maud, that involved his buying a dozen jelly-filled doughnuts (Bismarks) for breakfast without consulting her about her meal plans. After Baum failed to eat all the pastries, Maud continued to serve him the stale offerings each morning, retrieving them from the garbage and other disposal sites. The biographers concluded that Maud got her point across, teaching Baum that "in her way" she "was as stout a battler for 'women's rights' as her mother had ever been."

13. Baum was playing on the common name for poisoning agents or nostrums designed to eradicate bodily ills. For example, during August and September 1890 the *Aberdeen Evening Republican* carried advertisements for the following potions: "Rough on Rats," "Rough on Worms," "Rough on Toothache," "Rough on Dirt Soap," "Rough on Corns," and "Rough on Itch."

14. *ADN* 7, 8, 9, 10, 11, and 13 April 1890; *ASP* 12 April 1890; D. S. White (president of South Dakota Board of Pharmacy) to Arthur C. Mellette, 17 March 1890, Mellette Papers, box 4.

15. *ADN* 13 April 1890.

16. *ASP* 12 April 1890; also see Baum's editorial of 15 March 1890.

17. Baum explored this concept in his second Oz novel, *Marvelous Land of Oz*, in which General Jinjur's army of girls took over Oz and put men in charge of the households. In one scene the men were "sweeping and dusting and washing dishes, while the women sat around in groups, gossiping and laughing." Doing the housework and taking care of children was, one aproned male complained, "wearing out the strength of every man in the Emerald City." When asked how the women had previously

managed the work so easily, the man sighed, "Perhaps the women are made of cast-iron" (pp. 170–71). After liberation, both men and women happily returned to their traditional tasks.

18. The *Baum Bugle* 29 (autumn 1985): 19 reproduced this column and the accompanying picture of Harry Neal Baum dated 1 May 1890, suggesting that the column *anticipated* the photographing of the four-month-old. I suspect that the column recounted the actual event and that either the photograph is a retake (a frequent necessity) or it was dated on the day printed rather than the day taken.

19. Here, either the typesetter or Baum got confused. This name should be "Tom," Baum's fictional boarder, rather than "Taub," the Aberdeen attorney who is mentioned later in the column. In Baum's sprawling hand writing, Tom and Taub would have looked quite similar.

20. *ASP* 3 and 10 May 1890; *ADN* 29 April 1890.

21. *ADN* 9, 11, 24, and 30 April 1890; quotations are from 24 April.

22. *ASP* 3 May 1890. Baum announced the contest on 19 April.

23. The *Aberdeen Evening Republican* dubbed the state seed wheat commissioners who went east with Governor Mellette in March to solicit money "a flock of frosted spring robins" who brought back $50,000 "pecked and wormed from the unwilling east." While the *Aberdeen Daily News* crowed over the commission's success, the *Republican* contended that the "paltry" amount would cost the state "at least $500,000 in reputation" and that the spring robins "should put their heads under their wings, poor things" (28 March 1890). The *News*, meanwhile, congratulated Edward Bach, a local commissioner, as the "boss 'spring robin' " who, outside of Mellette himself, had been "the most successful in securing friends for seed and feed" (4 April 1890).

24. This passage foreshadowed a key element in the *Wizard of Oz*. Recounting the building of his capital city, the Wizard says: "Then I thought, as the country was so green and beautiful, I would call it the Emerald City, and to make the name fit better I put green spectacles on all the people, so that everything they saw was green" (Baum, *New Wizard of Oz*, p. 187). The Emerald City was no greener than "any other city," but the people, like the farmer's horses, were duped into thinking otherwise. See also Hearn's notes in *The Annotated Wizard of Oz*, p. 268.

25. Mrs. Bilkins took her inspiration from the Bible: "All flesh is grass, and all the goodliness thereof is as the flower of the field: The grass withereth, the flower fadeth: because the spirit of the Lord bloweth upon it" (Isaiah 40:6–7).

26. For example, on 6 June 1890 alderman Charles Howard joined the Ancient Arabic Order of Nobles of the Mystic Shrine at Sioux Falls. As a candidate, he was "taken across the burning sands of the desert and through the howling wilderness upon patient camels and finally landed safely in El Riad temple there to rest after an arduous and exciting journey" (*ADN* 8 June 1890). This image brings to mind the various journeys that Dorothy and others take to reach Oz and the Emerald City. Four

impenetrable deserts (the Deadly Desert, the Impassable Desert, the Shifting Sands, and the Great Sandy Waste) separate Oz from the rest of the world. Whether the author had the ritualistic journeys taken in fraternal societies or the journey to Oz in mind, Baum's dying words were reported to have been "Now we can cross the Shifting Sands" (quoted in Baum and MacFall, *To Please a Child*, p. 275).

27. Carnes, *Secret Ritual*, pp. 8–9; *ASP* 10 and 17 May 1890; *AER* 21 April 1890; United Workmen of South Dakota, *Constitution, General Laws and Rules of Order*, [p. 1].

28. Sannes, "Knowledge Is Power," pp. 407–8, 414–15; Garlock, "Structural Analysis of the Knights of Labor," pp. 1, 4–8, 402; *ADN* 11 May 1890; *ASP* 24 May 1890; Carnes, *Secret Ritual*, pp. 9, 32–33. Carnes also suggests (pp. 146–50) that the secret ritualistic aspects of the lodges helped to resolve questions about masculinity.

29. *AER* 6 May 1890; *ADN* 6 and 8 May 1890; *ASP* 10 May 1890.

30. Carnes, *Secret Ritual*, p. 34, says that many early ritual activities "perched precariously at the edge of humor" and that many first-time initiates "expected the ceremony to be funny." When asked to describe initiations, fraternal members "commonly chose humorous prevarications. . . . The most common jokes had it that candidates were forced to ride a goat or were stretched upon a gridiron and tortured." The humor in this "Our Landlady" sketch certainly fell into this pattern, as did a later mention of the initiation rights of the Masons in Baum's 26 July column.

31. *ADN* 12 April 1890.

32. Baum, *Marvelous Land of Oz*, pp. 83–95, 247.

33. The same issue of the *Pioneer* carried this squib: "Mr. Fraud, (in church, as his suspender button comes off.) 'Thank God! The box is coming this way, and I forgot to bring any change this morning. It will make a little more work for Marie but that don't matter.' "

34. *ADN* 16 May 1890; *ASP* 17, 24, and 31 May, and 7 June 1890. Noting on 31 May that Edward Strauss, the court musician of Vienna, was performing in Boston, Baum remarked, "We have nearly every advantage here in Dakota with which our eastern brothers are blessed, but for the first time in years we experience a thrill of envy that we shall be unable to hear the great Strauss orchestra."

35. *ASP* 28 June 1890.

36. Some variation of these "tall yarns" did happen during the 3½-inch cloudburst on the night of 17 June. The cellars of the Jewett Brothers enterprise, for example, and that of several other concerns flooded when the city's rudimentary sewer systems failed to contain the downpour (*ADN* 18 June 1890).

37. Which it "ain't," as the reader knows; the landlady's first name was Sairy. Baum may have forgotten, or his typesetter may have misread the name, or Mrs. Bilkins may have been making a statement of some kind. The editors of the 1941 edition of the columns solved the problem by eliminating Maria from their copy. See South Dakota Writers' Project, *L. Frank Baum's "Our Landlady,"* p. 33. Perhaps

Baum's Aberdeen readers pointed out his error; at any rate, he did not make this mistake again.

38. *Official Program of the Grand Celebration of July 4th, 1890*, copy in GSB pp. 148–49; *ASP* 28 June and 5 July 1890; *ADN* 21 June, 3, 4, and 5 July 1890.

39. Helen L. Gage, "Like the Pale Face." Gage's different account for the local audience (*ASP* on 12 July 1890) contains more details and less boosterism. For more on the place of American Indians in such festivities, see Miller, "The Old-Fashioned Fourth of July," pp. 118–39; and Hamer, *New Towns in the New World*, pp. 211–15.

40. The commonness of this misunderstanding is explored in Hamer, *New Towns in the New World*, pp. 217–18. For a different point of view, see White, "Indian Visits," pp. 102–4.

41. Both the *News* and the *Pioneer* reported on 5 July that insurance agent Albert F. Milligan had been "relieved" of a "fine gold watch" on the Fourth of July.

42. *AER* 1 July 1890.

43. Susan B. Anthony took these accusations quite seriously, writing to Alice Pickler that she and her husband must help her to "save the E.S.A. from the charges that are hurled at us — that we are *coquetting* with the Independent party" (Anthony to Pickler, 23 June 1890, SDESA Papers). The damage was already done, however. As many suffrage supporters feared, the perceived alliance between the two groups did much to alienate Republican voters. See Anthony to Mrs. L. E. Wimans, SDSHS.

44. *ADN* 24 and 26 June, 12 and 24 July 1890; Wittmayer, "The 1889–1890 Woman Suffrage Campaign," p. 217. Both the Farmers' Alliance and the Knights of Labor had endorsed suffrage earlier, but the cause was an early casualty of political party posturing.

45. *ADN* 13 and 16 July 1890.

46. *AER* 15 July 1890.

47. Coyne finally wrote a letter defending his position (*ADN* 18 July 1890), in which he noted that those Republicans who believed in licensing liquor rather than prohibiting it had, once the prohibition law was in place, "accepted prohibition and yielded their preference" as good party members should. They had made no attempt to repudiate the constitution of the state or the principles of the party, Coyne pointed out, and "there was no more necessity for the resolutions [on prohibition] than there would be for an honest man to proclaim his integrity before his character had been assailed."

48. The last three paragraphs of this column were eliminated from the 1941 edition. In some ways, the omission improved the broad comedy of the sketch, but it destroyed the political message.

49. *ADN* 18, 20, 22, and 24 July 1890.

50. The bond passed with a 90 percent majority, and on 23 August Baum announced the formation of the Duluth, Pierre & Black Hills Railway to be operated by the Northern Pacific. Grading began at once, but this project, like many development schemes of

the era, became a casualty of the 1890s recession and never materialized (*ASP* 16 and 23 August 1890; *ADN* 12, 17, and 22 August 1890).

51. Although "momentarily sore at heart," Baum did not attend this meeting because "in this office the dull season has failed to penetrate, and the busy hum of presses which reaches our ear and the hooks full of job copy and 'advs.' before us, render us disposed to be content with things existent" (*ASP* 26 July 1890).

52. South Dakota Weather Service, Tabular Summaries, February–September 1890; *AER* 1 August 1890; *ASP* 9 August 1890.

53. *ADN* 12, 24, 25, 27, 30, and 31 July and 1 August 1890. All quotations are from *ASP* 2 August 1890.

54. The Republican state convention would be held at the end of the month, and the press noted that many politically prominent South Dakotans were passing through Aberdeen to solicit votes in Brown County, "a greater area than the state of Rhode Island" (*ADN* 2 August 1890). For example, the Honorable D. W. Diggs of Milbank, campaigning for the state treasurer nomination, had been to both Mitchell and Aberdeen "looking after his fences" (*ADN* 29 July 1890).

55. Two famous Aberdeen divines had been spending more time on political than church issues. The Reverend James H. Kyle, a Congregational minister, had given a rousing Fourth of July oration from the balcony of the Sherman House, condemning big business, criticizing unrestricted foreign immigration, and supporting universal suffrage, education, and prohibition. In his audience were the assembled delegates to the Brown County Independent convention who, next day, nominated him to run for the state senate ("The Speech That Made Him Famous," *Sioux City [Iowa] Journal* 19 February 1891; Webb, "'Just Principles Never Die': Brown County Populists, 1890–1900," p. 367). The other politically active clergyman was Father Robert W. Haire, a Roman Catholic priest who had just become president of the newly formed Dakota Knights of Labor publishing company. Father Haire's political activism in labor, suffrage, and prohibition circles led his bishop to suspend him from priestly duties in late May 1890 (*ADN* 11, 16, 20, and 25 May 1890). Although he did not share their political viewpoints (except in support of woman suffrage), Baum knew both men: he had been at social gatherings with Kyle and would serve with Haire as fellow delegate to the district equal suffrage convention in August. See *ASP* 5 April 1890; *ADN* 10 August 1890.

56. The Ladies Guild of Saint Mark's Episcopal Church had announced that it would sponsor two operettas during the state fair in September. Baum would play Mr. Daly in *The Sorcerer* and Rufus in *The Little Tycoon*. See *ASP* 9 and 16 August 1890.

57. This early use of "meat" to distinguish a real kiss is interesting. In his Oz books, Baum used "meat" as an adjective to differentiate between characters of flesh and blood (such as the Wizard, the Munchkins, the Cowardly Lion) and those that were alive but not organic (the Tin Woodman, the Patchwork Girl).

58. *ADN* 18 January, 12, 13, 14, and 15 August 1890.

59. Baum is referring to druggist Horace F. Scott. See the glossary.

60. Baum had expressed many of these sentiments on 10 May 1890 in "The Editor's Musings" column, concluding, "To get all the meat from the nut of life is the essence of wisdom. To earn contentment is the noblest ambition. The miser is never contented, no matter whether his hoard be a dollar or a million. Therefore, 'eat, drink and be merry — *for tomorrow you die!*'"

61. *ADN* 10, 12, and 17 August 1890.

62. Baum was also poking fun at the habits of Aberdeen picnickers who packed enormous amounts of food. On 9 August he described a typical excursion: "On last Wednesday afternoon a jolly party of young folks loaded the White Wings bus with a precious cargo of eatables and drinkables" and "drove out to Oleson's grove to bivouac. The hammocks were swung amongst the huge trees, the watermelons and beverages carefully iced, and the overworked and tired fugitives prepared to enjoy themselves. . . . With eating and drinking and song and laughter, the hours sped fleetly away, and by the light of the rising moon they drove back to town thoroughly delighted with their trip."

63. Quoted in *ASP* 30 August 1890.

64. See esp. *ADN* 15, 22, and 29 August 1890.

65. Pettigrew to Sessions, 29 September 1890; see also Pettigrew to A. C. Mellette, 11 August 1890, Mellette Papers, box 4. On 2 September the *Aberdeen Daily News* attempted to explain the Brown County delegation's failure to return with an office as a matter of principle rather than dissension in their own ranks.

66. Baum announced on 19 July 1890 that he intended to launch a new journal. On 16 August he reported that the *Western Investor* "was issued from this office the 15th, and is a very neat and readable affair." Claiming a circulation of 20,000, he explained that the journal would "properly represent the interests of the Northwest throughout the east." No copies of this publication are known to exist, but a description in the *Aberdeen Daily News* (26 August 1890) tells us what it looked like: "It is a neat four column quarto, well printed and arranged and contains matter pertinent to finance and western investments." Reducing the circulation to only 19,000, Baum's rival hoped that "his courage may be rewarded with abundant shekels." Subscriptions cost fifty cents a year, and Baum boasted on 29 November that it was "considered the best paper on finance in the west." The flavor of the *Western Investor* can be deduced from an article reprinted in the 15 November *Aberdeen Saturday Pioneer*: "South Dakota's Future," written by Edward Bach, frankly acknowledged that the state appeared to be prey to cycles of drought and gave an honest assessment of problems and future possibilities. It concluded that the time was ripe for a new, modest resurgence in land values as the dry cycle receded and urged easterners to invest while prices were low. Another excerpt, published in the *Aberdeen Daily News* on 4 September, boosted the Dakota Building and Loan Association. The *Western Investor* seems to have thrived through October

and November (Baum hired Camilla Jewell to work in its offices on 18 October) but vanished without a trace within the next few months.

67. *ASP* 30 August 1890. Baum's strong support of the 1889 Territorial Fair, along with his Republican partisanship, may have earned him these opportunities in 1890. The previous year he had used the back of his Baum's Bazaar business envelopes to advertise the fair, touting Aberdeen as "The Ry. Hub" of Dakota in an elaborate engraving (Baum to Bud Jones, 23 May 1889, Baum Letters). The Bazaar owner had also rented display space at the fairgrounds to promote his business (*ADN* 7 and 26 September 1889). In keeping with his earlier efforts, Baum's 1890 boom edition of the *Aberdeen Saturday Pioneer* featured photoengravings of the fairgrounds as well as articles on local businesses and businessmen.

68. *ASP* 6 and 13 September 1890; *AER* 25 September 1890; *ADN* 5 September 1890.

69. *ASP* 20 August 1890; *ADN* 16, 17, 18, and 19 September 1890; Schuler, "In Pursuit of Permanence," pp. 35–36; *AER* 23 September 1890.

70. Quoted in *ADN* 17 September 1890.

71. *AER* 18 September 1890.

72. Twain, *Adventures of Huckleberry Finn*, pp. xvii–xix, 124–26.

73. *ADN* 6 September 1890. The convention took place on 30 September.

74. *AER* 13 September 1890; *ADN* 12 September 1890.

75. Circular, Nettie C. Hall, State Supt. Election Work, to Women of South Dakota, 15 September 1890, SDESA Papers.

76. Anthony to Mrs. L. E. Wimans.

77. Anthony to Alice Pickler, 14 June 1890, SDESA Papers.

78. Anthony to Alice Pickler, 23 June 1890, SDESA Papers. See *ADN* 24 June 1890 for an example of the charges.

79. R. F. Pettigrew to Philena Everett Johnson, 25 July 1890; Will F. Bailey to Ada C. Bowles, 12 August 1890; Olympia Brown to Susan B. Anthony, 3 September 1890; Irene G. Adams to Dear Friend, 16 October 1890, all in SDESA Papers.

80. *AER* 10 October 1890.

81. William Kidd to [Will F. Bailey, secretary of state ESA], 13 October 1890, SDESA Papers; *ASP* 18 October 1890.

82. Ellen A. Nichols to Will F. Bailey, 2 September 1890; Emma S. DeVoe to Bailey, 3 October 1890; and Seslina S. Thorp [?] to Mrs. Wardall, 10 October 1890, all in SDESA Papers.

83. *ADN* 25 September 1890.

84. The "little feller" is addressing Mrs. Bilkins in Scandinavian-sounding gibberish. Responding with a German phrase that is as unpolished as her English, she tells him "Don't come around here." I am indebted to Melvin Wall of Pierre, South Dakota, and to Don Sneen of Augustana College in Sioux Falls, South Dakota, for their help in evaluating Baum's "Norwegian."

85. *ADN* 24 October 1890.

86. *ADN* 23 December 1890.

87. *AER* 9 October 1890.

88. *ADN* 25 October 1890.

89. *ASP* 4 October 1890.

90. *ADN* 28 October and 1 November 1890.

91. *ADN* 7 November 1890.

92. Circular, Emma Smith DeVoe to "Lovers of Freedom in South Dakota," 22 November 1890, SDESA Papers. DeVoe claimed that some ballots were printed with only the word "no" appearing after the amendment, saving the voter the trouble of crossing off anything.

93. *ADN* 28 October 1890; Republican Ticket, 1890, Republican Circulars.

94. Indeed, Baum himself contributed to the confusion, garbling the instructions in his preelection issue. "All electors," his sample ballot read, "desiring to vote in favor of any of the foregoing amendments must erase the word 'YES' after each amendment so opposed" (*ASP* 1 November 1890). After the election, Matilda Joslyn Gage reported that a prominent county suffragist from Westport had helped voters "fix" nearly two hundred ballots against suffrage before discovering her error and then could hardly believe her mistake even after it was pointed out. Her misadventure may have been the prototype for Mrs. Bilkins's faux pas. See Gage to Lillie Devereaux Blake, 15 November 1890.

95. *ADN* 8 November 1890.

96. In the 1 November column just before the election, Tom had shown himself to be a Democrat. Baum is probably suggesting that collusion among Democrats and Independents cost Republicans the election. Other Republican editors had been hinting at this relationship from the beginning, accusing Democrats of dallying with Independents despite protestations of party loyalty.

97. An "experience" meeting was one at which participants "testified," or related their religious experiences.

98. *ASP* 18 October and 15 November 1890.

99. *ASP* 15 November 1890.

100. *ASP* 1 November 1890. Other sources identified the disciple as Kicking Bear.

101. *ADN* 18, 19, 21, 22, 23, 25, and 29 November 1890; *ASP* 29 November 1890.

102. *ADN* 22 November 1890. This quotation may refer to something Baum had written in the missing 22 November issue of the *Aberdeen Saturday Pioneer*.

103. Quoted in *ADN* 3 December 1890.

104. Little Wound, quoted in *ADN* 23 November 1890. See also Utley, *Lance and the Shield*, pp. 292, 311.

105. Utley, *Lance and the Shield*, pp. 293–94. See also Steele, "Buffalo Bill's Bluff."

106. *ADN* 29 and 30 November, 2, 3, and 4 December 1890.

107. Baum was alluding to the recent election in which the woman suffrage amendment had been defeated, as was an amendment that would have denied suffrage to all American Indian males who were supported by the government. "Red men of all conditions can vote," the *News* grumbled after the election, "while women a thousand times more competent, are denied the right" (*ADN* 19 November 1890). Most people believed that the "peculiar wording" of the Indian suffrage amendment had worked in the Indians' favor in the same way that the confusing instructions for the woman suffrage amendment had worked against the women.

108. *ADN* 16, 17, 19, 25, and 27 December 1890; *ASP* 20 December 1890.

109. The *Aberdeen Daily News*, for example, stated this concept clearly on 29 December 1890.

110. Although Baum used greater hyperbole than others, his opinion was not unique, nor did it bring a reprimand from townspeople or fellow editors. The *Aberdeen Daily News* (27 December 1890) editorialized that the governor should arm the citizens and send the army home: "Put it in the hands of practical men, and the Indians who were not 'good' would be few and far between without much ado, or waste of time." See also *ADN* 23 December 1890.

111. "The Editor's Musings" column of 8 Feburary 1890, in which Baum discussed "mercantile fabrications" and lies in pricing merchandise, makes a good companion piece for this column.

112. *ASP* 15 March, 6, 20, and 27 December 1890; *ADN* 11 November, 6, 10, 12, 14, 19, 24, and 25 December 1890. The quotation is from 25 December.

113. In 1890 Baum clearly foresaw that technology would make entertainment available to those far removed from theatrical centers such as New York. As his technical knowledge increased, his ideas of theatrical reproduction became more sophisticated. In a futuristic essay written in 1896, not only did phonographs still reproduce the human voice (Sarah Bernhardt's), but in addition a "reflecting kinetoscope" projected the figures. See Baum, "Yesterday at the Exposition," p. 34.

114. "Hard Times, Come Again No More" was the title of a popular song, a "rather doleful ditty," that the country's general prosperity had caused to be forgotten (*ADN* 21 October 1888). Baum's use suggested that it was back in vogue in Aberdeen, at least.

115. The 1941 edition of "Our Landlady" columns ended this one here, possibly because the editors thought this sentence a better punch line, little realizing the irony in the reference to Hagerty's bank failure.

116. This remark, humorous though it is, hinted at Baum's fears concerning the future use of electricity. He explored the concept more fully in a 1901 science fiction novel in which the Demon of Electricity presented a young boy with an Automatic Record of Events that captured any occurrence, anywhere, for recall on a televisionlike device. After using it unwisely, the young hero returned it to the demon, asking, "What

right have you to capture vibrations that radiate from private and secret actions and discover them to others who have no business to know them?" (Baum, *The Master Key*, p. 236). At the turn of the century such devices seemed just around the corner, and in 1896 Baum had predicted that "thought-transference" from "solitude rooms" would replace the telegraph ("Yesterday at the Exposition").

117. Bach, "South Dakota's Future," *Western Investor*, reprinted in *ASP* 15 November 1890. Baum also used many of the same arguments in the 25 October *Pioneer*.

118. Quoted in "Old-Style Fairyland Too Remote, Says 'Oz' Man" clipping, c. 31 March 1913, Baum Scrapbook.

119. *ADN* 28 October 1890, 2, 3, and 23 January 1891; *ASP* 18 October 1890.

120. *ADN* 4 and 16 January 1890.

121. Baum may have had Frank Hagerty in mind here, as either the prominent citizen or the collector. He noted on 24 January 1891 that the Hagerty bank failure was total but that Hagerty's hopes were "not amongst those which lie crushed beneath the ruins"; instead, he had gone to Pierre, "lobbying and wire-pulling, full of political ambitions and schemes, and plans for money getting."

122. Baum to S. C. Britton, 15 January 1912, quoted in Greene, "The Writing of Two L. Frank Baum Fantasies," p. 14.

123. *ADN* 28 January 1891.

124. *ASP* 4 October 1890.

125. Koupal, "From the Land of Oz," p. 56.

126. Shortridge, *The Middle West*, p. 18; Nelson, *After the West Was Won*, pp. 153–54; Koupal, "From the Land of Oz," p. 57.

127. *ADN* 24 October 1890.

128. Baum usually spelled the landlady's first same "Sairy."

129. *ASP* 9 August and 25 October 1890.

EPILOGUE

1. *ASP* 26 July 1890.

2. *ASP* 2 August 1890.

3. Baum published the first issue of the new journal on 15 August 1890, claiming a circulation of 20,000. An article from the *Western Investor* (reprinted in *ASP* 15 November 1890) told local readers, "Those who stay [in South Dakota] will find themselves well off in time, having a home and competency for their old age, while in going east they will have to compete for work in that already over crowded labor market."

4. *ASP* 30 August, 6 September 1890.

5. *ASP* 29 November 1890, 24 and 31 January 1891; Watson, "Last Indian War"; Huntzicker, "The 'Sioux Outbreak' in the Illustrated Press."

6. Kidd, "Address of William E. Kidd, People's Party Convention"; Cleworth, "Brown County Agricultural History," p. 40.

7. "Quaint Verse Brings Fame," clipping from a Syracuse NY newspaper, 11 November 1899, Baum Clipping Files. Baum frequently retold this story of the eastern subscriber who succumbs to the honest approach. The 1899 version is the earliest I have found, but the tale appears elsewhere in various guises and is fictionalized in *Aunt Jane's Nieces on Vacation* (pp. 99–100), which he published under the pseudonym of Edith Van Dyne. In writing this book for young girls, Baum called on many of his Dakota newspaper experiences.

8. *ASP* 15 and 29 November, 6 December 1890, and 31 January 1891; "Old-Style Fairyland Too Remote, Says 'Oz' Man," Baum Scrapbook; *ADN* 31 December 1890, 31 January 1891.

9. *ADN* 4 April 1891.

10. Baum to J. H. McKeever, 15 June 1909, Baum Letters.

11. Cleworth, "Brown County Agricultural History," pp. 112–57; *Brown County History*, pp. 299–314.

12. Baum to "Dear Old Til" [Matilda Jewell Gage], 2 August 1917, Baum Collection.

13. *ADN* 17 February 1891. Baum's critical editorials on the Hagerty bank failure (24 and 31 January 1891) and a sarcastic and atypically bitter piece about Senator Gideon Moody (17 January 1891) may have contributed to this strong reaction.

14. *ASP* 21 February 1891.

15. *ASP* 28 February, 7, 14, and 21 March 1891. Matilda Joslyn Gage had arrived in Aberdeen in October 1890. Beginning with the 28 February issue the editorials no longer contain much evidence of Baum's writing style or, after 7 March, any commitment to local events. The last two extant issues, 14 and 21 March, carry columns signed by Matilda Joslyn Gage.

16. *ADN* 4 April 1891.

17. *ADN* 4 April 1891; *Aberdeen: A Middle Border City*, p. 50.

18. Quoted in interview with Maud Gage Baum, *Syracuse Herald–Syracuse Sunday American*, 30 July 1939.

19. Baum to "My darling Mother," 16 January 1894, Arents Collection, New York Public Library, copy in Baum Papers; Baum and MacFall, *To Please a Child*, pp. 76–82.

20. Torrey, "So. Dakota Is Proud of L. Frank Baum." This essay, revised after Baum's death, appears in Torrey's *Early Days in Dakota*, pp. 75–79.

21. L. Frank Baum to "My dear son" [Frank J. Baum], 2 September 1918, Baum Papers.

22. Quoted in Torrey, "So. Dakota Is Proud of L. Frank Baum." See also Baum to McKeever, 15 June 1909. Baum always professed an affection for Aberdeen, claiming it as one of his homes, along with Syracuse, Chicago, Lake Macatawa (Michigan), and Hollywood.

23. The nine short stories from the *Delineator* are collected in Baum, *Animal Fairy*

Tales, and the Twinkle Tales — under the pseudonym Laura Bancroft — in *Twinkle and Chubbins*.

24. In particular, see "The Editor's Musings" column, which appeared weekly from January to May and throughout December 1890. For a critical discussion of the Oz books, see Attebery, *The Fantasy Tradition in American Literature*, pp. 83–108.

Aberdeen Guards: During 1890 this patriotic drill team became a standard participant in the town's entertainments. Formed in April as an auxiliary of the Grand Army of the Republic, it consisted of daughters of Civil War veterans who had fought for the North. Baum called the twelve young women a "female band of Lancers" because they drilled with lances festooned with red pennants (*ASP*, 31 May 1890). Under command of troop captain Frances ("Fannie") Hauser, they gave their first exhibition on 28 May, but their most ambitious performance took place on the Fourth of July, when "every movement was carried out with automatic precision," Baum wrote, "and the Guards looked as sweet and demure as Raphael's cherubs, instead of being simply every-day girls when their soldier-like clothes are doffed." The occasion also featured a tableau in which the guards "looked patriotic enough to sacrifice their gum, if necessary, for the good of their country" (*ASP* 5 July 1890).

Adams, Johnny: John E. Adams, born in 1857 in Patterson, New Jersey, had been city editor of a Meadville, Pennsylvania, paper until he studied law and moved to the frontier. Settling in Columbia, Dakota Territory, in the early 1880s, he became mayor in 1887, the same year that the town lost the Brown County seat to Aberdeen. After his term Adams relocated to the new county seat, setting up offices in the Northwestern National Bank building. In 1890 he ran for county judge as a Republican against Democrat Louis Crofoot, and Baum noted that the two were "having a neat little strife all to themselves" with no Independent candidate in the running. Regretting that one good man would have to "take a back seat," the editor correctly predicted that it would not be Adams (*ASP* 25 October 1890). A contemporary biography remarked that Adams was "justly regarded as a typical representative of progressive western manhood" (*A&BC*). In 1900 he would be mayor of Aberdeen.

Alley: Elias H. Alley, who came to Aberdeen from Minneapolis in 1881 to open a feed and flour store, became Aberdeen's first mayor. In 1890 he was a Brown County commissioner and the man in charge of the county's emergency seed wheat and feed distribution program. He also negotiated with Minneapolis money men to finance county warrants and arranged to buy seed grain from local elevator companies.

Anthony, Susan B.: In November 1889 the president of the South Dakota Farmers' Alliance, Henry L. Loucks, invited national suffragist leader Susan B. Anthony to Aberdeen to address the group's convention. Loucks promised Anthony that the alliance would support suffrage during the upcoming 1890 campaign by forcing the Republican Party to add a suffrage amendment to its state platform. Early in 1890, after the two national suffrage organizations merged into the National-American Woman Suffrage Association, Anthony became vice-president at large amid much controversy. On her seventieth birthday (15 February 1890) Baum responded to her critics. "In her lifetime," he wrote, "she has done much good for her cause, . . . and if it is true that she has striven to amass a fortune through her labors, she has never been ungenerous or penurious when the cause of woman suffrage demanded monetary expenditure." He added that critics such as Marietta Bones had "greatly maligned" her, but at the same time he found the birthday adulation she was receiving overdone: Anthony was "no more than an earnest, hard-working woman" who "could never attain to the eminence of many women connected with woman suffrage who are dead and gone, and many as well who are alive and respected today" (*ASP* 15 February 1890). Baum presumably had both his mother-in-law, Matilda Joslyn Gage, and Elizabeth Cady Stanton in mind. When Anthony came to South Dakota in April to take over the state's campaign for suffrage, the controversy followed her. In addition, Loucks and the Farmers' Alliance, rather than supporting the movement from within the Republican stronghold, had formed a third party that failed to include suffrage in its platform, fearing it would cost votes. As the election approached, the seventy-year-old campaigner began to suffer from the rigors of the stump in a sparsely settled and politically hostile frontier state. The strain showed itself in her poor performance on the platform, most notably at the state fair on Women's Day, as Baum's 20 September column indicated. *See also* Bones, Mary Etter; Pickeler, Mrs. Alice

Auditor. See How, Major

Bach: Edward Bach, manager of the C. N. Nelson Lumber Company and trustee of the Aberdeen National Bank, was one of the most dedicated members of the state seed wheat commission, serving as northern South Dakota superintendent for distribution. On 4 April 1890 the *Aberdeen Daily News* proclaimed him "the boss 'spring robin' of the new season" because, excluding Governor Arthur Mellette, he had been "the most successful in securing friends for seed and feed." An able speaker and writer, Bach frequently spoke on financial issues and contributed "South Dakota's Future" to Baum's *Western Investor*. In January 1891, at the request of fellow believers like Baum, Bach also lectured in support of Spiritualism.

Bagley's elevator: Bagley and Cargill was one of four elevator companies in Aberdeen that accepted county warrants for seed in March 1890. Dighton McGlachlin, the company's Dakota superintendent, arranged for the construction of all Bagley and Cargill elevators in the state.

Baldwin: The would-be purchaser of barber John O'Daniel's horse in the 9 August column was a fellow Main Street merchant, either Royal J. Baldwin, a restaurant owner and former saloonkeeper, or Winfield Baldwin, a confectioner.

Bared, Fred.: Baum transposed the letters in this name, for he meant Fred C. Beard (pronounced "baird"), the brother of Henry C. and Frank Beard. Even though Fred had large real estate holdings in Aberdeen, in February 1890 he joined the group of Aberdonians who traveled to Tennessee. By late March he and Major Luke A. Burke had opened a real estate office in Knoxville, from which they planned to participate in the booms of the "New South." "I may drift back to Aberdeen in time," Baum quoted Beard on 22 March, "but I shall stay as long as there is enough Tennessee gold in my pockets to hold me there."

Barnes, Ira: An early Dakota pioneer, Ira Barnes homesteaded near Parker in 1872. In 1883 he moved to Aberdeen, where he managed the Barnes and Persons Lumber Company. More important, he was president of the Northwestern National Bank, which offered to take city warrants at par after a Republican administration won the city election of 15 April 1890. After the election Barnes became president of the school board. Baum's gentle touch with satire showed when he portrayed the businessman as "kinder outer politics." A local directory called Barnes "a representative citizen [who was] always active in business, social, political and other matters" (*A&BC*).

Barrett, B. S. (Buzz-saw), Majah or Major: C. Boyd Barrett, a Confederate veteran of thirty-eight battles, contributed greatly to the flair and character of Aberdeen in the 1890s. Barrett was a fastidious dresser with courtly manners — except when he lost his temper, which was often; then the major was formidable. Coming to Aberdeen in 1884, he had bought the *Aberdeen Evening Republican* and transformed it into the first Democratic paper in the northeastern section of South Dakota. From April 1888 to April 1890 the Democrats dominated the Aberdeen city council, controlling appointive positions and the city payroll, and Barrett's job-printing shop held the contract for city printing — a perk for which the other editors regularly abused him. Baum, as a Republican and a Yankee, did not bring out the best in Major Barrett, and the two editors held a running feud in their papers. It came to a head on 15 March 1890, when Baum referred to the city administration as "the boodle firm of Howe [auditor], Stearns [mayor] & Barrett." The major retaliated with a vicious editorial accusing Baum of embezzling funds from the 1889 city baseball team (for which Baum had served as secretary), among other things, and concluding that he would not fill his columns "with any more replies to [Baum's] slush, but [would] leave Mr. Baum and his journal to drop back into the obscurity from which we have for the moment lifted him" (*AER* 18 March 1890). Baum replied that "Minor Barrett is one of those malicious curs who slink in a corner and howl while honest men walk by." Having once had a dog named Major, he said, he objected to "calling this parody on humanity by the same appellation" (*ASP* 22 March 1890). True to his word, Barrett did not respond to Baum's comments, but Baum continued to lambast his rival, and the major cut the *Pioneer* editor off his mailing list. Barrett lost the city printing to the *Aberdeen Daily News* with the election of a Republican administration in April 1890. That fall both political and financial difficulties led him to lease the *Republican* — stipulating only that it should continue to support Pierre for state capital — to Populist William E. Kidd while he took time off to visit Virginia. Barrett's personal adherence to Democratic politics had its reward in 1894, when he became receiver of the Aberdeen land office.

Bass, Max: Born in Bohemia and educated in Vienna, Max Bass emigrated at the age of twenty-four, settling in New York. Moving west with the American frontier, he became deputy commissioner of immigration for Dakota Territory in 1886. Four years later he was in Aberdeen, serving as deputy for South Dakota Commissioner of Immigration Frank Hagerty. Later that year Bass accepted a position with the immigration department of the Great Northern Railroad and, in spite of bad publicity surrounding the drought and declining economy of the 1890s, convinced thousands of German farmers to choose Dakota. In recognition, North Dakota named one of its new towns Maxbass in his honor. Prior to the 16 August 1890 "Our Landlady" column, announcements of Bass's trips on behalf of immigration had showed up in the personal columns of Aberdeen newspapers. On 8 August he traveled to Big Stone Lake with his wife, two days later to Saint Paul, and on 16 August to Webster, South Dakota — or so he claimed.

Bath: The next town east of Aberdeen on the Chicago, Milwaukee & St. Paul Railroad, Bath had a three-story hotel, a livery barn, three general stores, and Mrs. Bilkins's vote for state capital. Mrs. Bilkins may have been on to something, for it was at Bath that six women claimed the right to vote in the election for county school superintendent, a right that the constitution already granted them. "Their ballots were received by the courteous judges, placed in a box by themselves and forwarded to Columbia" (*ASP* 8 November 1890).

Beard, Frank: Frank Beard was the third partner in the Beard, Gage and Beard general store, of which Baum's brother-in-law, T. Clarkson Gage, was second and Henry C. Beard was first. All three men were from Fayetteville, New York, and had come to Aberdeen as founding fathers in 1881. The Beards were also large landholders in the area. Frank Beard had been involved in the statehood movement and had acted as Brown County delegate to the 1887 state constitutional convention, held in Aberdeen. He was a successful businessman but would not, as Baum predicted in his 31 January 1891 column, become a member of any legislative body.

Beard an' Gage's: Beard, Gage and Beard (which the local children dubbed "Birdcage and Bird") handled "everything in dry goods and general notions." It was the oldest general merchandise store in Aberdeen, had "the best carpet and tapestry rooms west of the larger cities" (A&BC), and also handled groceries, as Baum's column of 22 March 1890 makes clear. Further, the partnership of Henry C. Beard, T. Clarkson Gage, and Frank Beard platted the West Hill addition to Aberdeen in 1883, constructed an artesian well and irrigation plant in the 1890s, and involved itself in other community enterprises. In January 1891 the firm pronounced itself happy with its sales for the past year, but to survive the "close time of Winter" it inaugurated giveaway drawings as a new form of advertising, promising "something for nothing" (ASP 24 January 1891) — a scheme that proved popular with customers.

Becker, Clarence: Clarence L. Becker, real estate man and ticket broker, boarded at the Becker House, one of Aberdeen's many family-run hotels. Although he ran for justice of the peace in the Republican caucuses on 10 April 1890, other members of the Becker family were prominently involved in the "People's caucuses." Baum made it clear that he thought Clarence had made the better choice.

Big Stone: Located about one hundred miles straight east of Aberdeen, Big Stone Lake resulted from a widening in the Minnesota River, which ran along the South Dakota–Minnesota border for thirty-six miles. The scenic bluffs and dells surrounding the lake attracted Aberdonians to "rusticate" near its cool shores through the hot summer months of July and August. Townspeople took the train to the Aberdeen "colony" of privately owned cabins on the Minnesota side or, on the South Dakota side, to Simpson Park, established by seven Methodist Episcopal church elders in 1889 in order to maintain a morally safe summer resort and to promote religious and educational interests. Aberdonians Ralph L. Brown and William Fielder were two of the seven, and, not incidentally, the buying and selling of real estate at the park constituted the founders' third purpose.

Blind pigs: Illegal drinking establishments became known as "blind pigs" when a Massachusetts liquor dealer, dodging his state's 1838 law banning the sale of liquor, sold customers the right to look at his blind pig and then gave the gawkers a "free" drink. Law enforcement officials attacked Aberdeen's versions of the blind pig throughout the fall of 1890, but in February 1891 public attention turned toward pharmacists. Originally, Aberdeen's nine druggists had banded together to defy the law's provision that allowed them to sell liquor for "medicinal, mechanical, sacramental and scientific purposes" provided they applied for a permit, decrying the process as demeaning. As trade became dull and the nine drugstore owners dwindled to six, however, the pact broke down. The first permit was issued in November. Baum's 8 February 1891 column indicated that he, at least, clearly recognized that the state prohibition law pushed the responsibility for liquor regulation onto the shoulders of druggists and directed temperance scrutiny toward them, as well. The *Aberdeen Daily News* of 31 January 1891, for example, accused the legalized druggists of being only slightly more responsible than illegal establishments because, although they did not tolerate loafers or "trap the young and unwary with music and side issues," they sold plenty of liquor all the same. Coming to their defense, Baum averred that with only six drugstores in the city, "prohibitionists will find the blind pigs a better field to work in" (*ASP*, 8 February 1891).

Bly, Nellie: When Elizabeth Cochrane of Cochran Mills, Pennsylvania, went to work at age twenty for the *Pittsburgh Dispatch*, her editor suggested the pen name Nellie Bly, from a Stephen Foster song. Bly became an undercover reporter, exposing the factory conditions in which women and children worked, among other things. Her reputation led her to a job with the *New York World*, which sponsored her 1889–90 trip around the world. In 1895 as the drought continued to affect the West, Bly would travel to Nebraska and South Dakota, sending back to the readers of the *World* first-person accounts of the continuing effect of the drought (see Nostwich, "Nellie Bly's Account"). The same year, she would marry millionaire Robert L. Seaman and leave the newspaper field.

Bones, Mary Etter: Marietta M. Bones, who lived in Webster, South Dakota, about fifty miles east of Aberdeen, had been vice-president for South Dakota of the National Woman Suffrage Association. Along with Matilda Joslyn Gage (Baum's mother-in-law), Bones dissented over the merger of the two national suffrage associations — the American and the National — that took place in February 1890. Susan B. Anthony, who pushed the merger through, notified Bones early in the year that her association with the new National-American Woman Suffrage Association would terminate on 17 February 1890. Anthony's peremptory letter was both unfair and tactless, and Bones displayed her bitterness publicly. She accused Anthony of embezzling money that had been donated for the South Dakota suffrage campaign, and the affair polarized the ranks of state suffragists, destroying their effectiveness. Worse, the press frequently belittled the women's disagreements and their cause. Even Baum, though he usually treated the two women fairly and always took woman suffrage seriously, made sport of the public feud. On 29 March, for example, he reported, "Susan B.'s right ear has been burning, and she knows someone has been talking ill about her. She says she feels it in her Bones." When the 1890 suffrage amendment failed at the polls in November, Bones blamed Anthony. "Under different management," she asserted, "there is no doubt the amendment would have been endorsed by the people" (quoted in *ASP* 8 November 1890). Within eight years, Marietta Bones's bitterness would lead her to renounce the cause of woman suffrage and become an able spokesman for the opposition (see Bones, "A Duty, Not a Privilege").

Bowels: Baum's pun (26 July 1890) may revolve around the name of George Bolles, the city treasurer. A Michigan native, Bolles served either as treasurer or auditor of Aberdeen for over thirty years. Advertisements for his real estate and insurance business carried the line "Collections made and Taxes paid" (*ACD* p. 3). His fiscal conservatism may have led him to protest the measures his fellow citizens were willing to take to secure a railroad in the summer of 1890.

Braden, Quincy: John Quincy Adams Braden was appointed register of the Aberdeen land office in January 1890. Coming to the Hub City from Minnesota in 1883, he had established a law practice and real estate business. A masonic grand master, a National Guard captain, and a painstaking official, Braden was a popular member of the Aberdeen community.

Brockway, Cholly: Charles L. Brockway clerked at the Coe and Howard Abstract Company, one of twenty-three real estate and loan companies that flourished in Aberdeen during its first decade. His duties for the company frequently took him to Columbia, the county seat, but like other young "exiles" who boarded there during the week, Brockway usually made it back to Aberdeen for the church socials held during the winter of 1890. Far from economizing, Brockway had, Baum observed, "bid as freely and liberally as the others" when the Young Ladies Guild put its members up for auction as a fund-raising gimmick on 21 January (*ASP* 25 January 1890).

Brown, Frank: Frank A. Brown came to Dakota Territory in 1882 after studying law at the University of Illinois. He had lived in Watertown, Clark, and Huron, teaching school and operating a newspaper, before locating in Aberdeen in 1887. There, he joined his brother Ralph L., and the two became law partners, real estate agents, bankers, and land speculators. After Ralph opened a branch office of Brown Brothers in the southern states in 1890, Frank stayed in South Dakota to become commissioner of immigration for Brown County and secretary of the State Land Company (an organization Aberdeen businessmen had started in order to speculate in Huron property while booming that town for state capital). Both brothers supported the prohibition movement, but Ralph was the more ardent advocate. As the *Aberdeen Daily News* reported on 6 March 1890, "Now, Frank is fully as good a fellow as Ralph, but he is not quite so religious. In fact, Frank sometimes — well, he is not quite so religious as Ralph." In August 1890, Frank A. Brown served as a Brown County delegate to the Republican state convention in Mitchell.

Brown, Ralph: Ralph L. Brown came to Aberdeen in 1882 and opened the law, loan, and real estate office that would become Brown Brothers in 1887, when his brother Frank joined him. A charter member of the Methodist Episcopal Church of Aberdeen, Ralph Brown championed temperance; in 1889 he personally visited every South Dakota county east of the Missouri River to stump for the constitutional prohibition clause. In 1890, as opportunities began both literally and figuratively to dry up in South Dakota, Brown led the movement to invest in such southern states as Alabama, Georgia, and Tennessee. "The development of the mountainous portion of the south is marvelous," he said. "Mining industries and manufactories have been built up, northern capital has been freely invested and everything bears the mark of progress and prosperity" (quoted in *ADN* 19 January 1890). The *Aberdeen Evening Republican* accused him on 10 February 1890 of abandoning South Dakota before the deleterious effects of prohibition on the business community could be felt, but Brown actually opened his first southern office in Harriman, Tennessee, a temperance town. By 1892 he was managing the Brown Brothers' southern branch out of Ashland, Kentucky. He would return to Aberdeen in 1899.

Buffalo Bill: On 21 November 1890 an *Aberdeen Daily News* correspondent found Wild West showman William F. ("Buffalo Bill") Cody ensconced in Major General Nelson A. Miles's headquarters in Chicago. Miles was out, but Cody informed the press that the general had just received word by telegram that troops had skirmished with the Lakotas between Rushville, Nebraska, and the Pine Ridge Agency in South Dakota. "If let alone by the government," Cody said, General Miles would "settle the trouble expeditiously" (quoted in *ADN* 21 November 1890). After all, he had Buffalo Bill to help him. Though better known in 1890 for dime novel exploits and public spectacles, the showman had been chief of scouts for Lieutenant General Philip H. Sheridan from 1868 to 1872. He had also enjoyed good rapport with Sitting Bull during the 1885 circuit, when the Hunkpapa chief traveled with his Wild West troup. His reputation with the military still intact, Cody apparently convinced Miles that he could persuade Sitting Bull to submit peaceably. Arriving at Fort Yates on the morning of 28 November with the title of "colonel," the showman flashed orders signed by Miles that authorized him to arrest Sitting Bull. The agent and officers in charge, who had been working with Sitting Bull for weeks, deemed the scheme foolhardy, especially as Cody had arrived slightly drunk. They conspired to keep him that way until presidential counterorders could come through. Cody next surfaced on the Pine Ridge reserve in early January as a staff member of the governor of Nebraska, claiming the right to fight Indians "by virtue of his Colonel's commission." Baum concluded that "this doughty warrior (in novels)" coveted "some free advertising to enable him to start another show" (*ASP* 10 January 1891).

Bugle: Since neither the suffragists nor Alice Pickler nor Major Burke published a paper in 1890, the "Bugle" in Baum's 8 March column is a fictional construct meant solely to tweak the sensibilities of C. Boyd Barrett. The *Aberdeen Daily News* had referred to Barrett's Democratic paper on 1 February 1890 as "the hand organ which is freely lubricated with soap from the city treasury," and Baum's doctor alluded to this comment when he said of the fictional Bugle,

"Well, even a hand-organ is better than no organ at all." As the sins of Barrett and the *Republican* constitute the underlying theme of this column, Baum was suggesting that men such as Major Luke A. Burke, a fellow Democrat, were disgusted enough with Barrett and his editorial diatribes to start a competing newspaper. Baum's suggestion, though premature, proved insightful: that fall two fellow party members established the rival *State Democrat* when Barrett, who disagreed with the Democratic nominations for the general election, refused to publish the ticket in his newspaper.

Buildin' an' Loan Association. See Dakota Bildin' and Loan assassination

Burdock, Elder: Reverend Frank A. Burdick, a staunch prohibitionist and secretary of the South Dakota State Senate in 1890, earned Baum's sly comment regarding his name and age (17 May 1890) when he took on an Episcopal bishop, William H. Hare. Burdick criticized Hare for signing an antiprohibition letter to the state legislature with the title "Missionary Bishop of South Dakota." Such a signature, Burdick suggested, implied that Hare was speaking for the whole religious body of South Dakota, whereas in fact he had "no more authority than any private citizen." Bishop Hare found this criticism amusing, since Burdick signed his protest with an even longer and more official-looking title of his own: "Presiding Elder of Aberdeen District Methodist Episcopal Church" (*ASP* 8 March 1890). Elder Burdick contributed heavily to the convoluted resolution on prohibition that upset the Republican county convention — and Doc Coyne — in July.

Burke, Major: Luke A. Burke, born in Virginia, had attained the rank of brevet major during the Civil War. In 1881 he moved to Dakota Territory, where President Grover Cleveland rewarded his loyalty to Democratic politics in the mid-1880s by appointing him receiver of the United States Land Office in Aberdeen. In January 1890, under a Republican administration, Burke could be found in McCaull, Webster and Company's Aberdeen land office, "warming his feet on the radiator and transacting any land business that [might] come his way" (*ADN* 25 January 1890). Unfortunately, not much came his way, and he soon joined Fred C. Beard, another land speculator, in a venture in the South until a reelected President Cleveland again favored him, appointing him to the Internal Revenue Service.

Butler's Signal Service: A man of many talents and skills, Walter P. Butler had been a college instructor, lawyer, historian, and draftsman before he came to Aberdeen in 1881 at age twenty-three. There, he started a lumber business and a brickyard, drew maps to advertise Dakota Territory, and, as city engineer, put in Aberdeen's first sewer system. From 1887 to mid-April 1890 he partnered A. H. Olwin in the Red Front Grocery Store. In January 1890 Butler also became a volunteer weatherman for the United States Signal Service, causing Baum to observe that he "seems a man of many vocations," who "does them all well" (*ASP* 25 January

1890). As soon as his barometers, thermometers, and other equipment arrived from the War Department, Butler began to fly weather flags from the top of the Red Front, signaling weather conditions for the next twenty-four hours. Previously, the only weather stations in Dakota had been at Huron and Bismarck.

Cadwell, George: George L. Cadwell Jr., an 1882 Minnesota emigrant to Dakota, served as cashier of the First National Bank and secretary-treasurer of the Aberdeen Savings Bank. Because he also commanded Aberdeen's Company F of the South Dakota National Guard during the 1890–91 Indian scare, the young first lieutenant received a lot of good-natured teasing from newspapermen whenever community tension seemed to need release. Baum's 20 December column may contain an example of such ribbing in its reference to a much-ballyhooed boxing match that took place on 11 December for "the heavy weight championship of South Dakota" and a purse of one hundred dollars. The hefty two-dollar admission charge had a great many Aberdonians professing to be uninterested, but the *Aberdeen Daily News* reporter spotted "a sprinkling of bankers, lawyers and business men" in the crowd (*ADN* 12 December 1890). Mrs. Bilkins's sharp eyes picked Cadwell out of the throng, it seems. While poking fun at the young banker's extravagances, Baum may also have been pointing out that Cadwell's military duties kept him too busy for socializing during the renewed panic that followed Sitting Bull's death on 15 December.

Camburn, Tommy; Campburn, Tom: A popular farmer from the Putney area of Brown County, Thomas E. Camburn served on the State Board of Agriculture and had been marshal of the 1890 state fair in Aberdeen. Fresh from this triumph, he was chosen as assistant secretary of the county Republican central committee, a position that put him in charge of $3,000 in campaign funds and enhanced his ability to make political appointments or to be appointed if the Republicans won that fall. By mid-October, "genial Tom Campburn" had taken charge of the Republican committee rooms, which were "pretty lively nowadays," Baum reported (*ASP* 11 October 1890). As the political mud began to fly just before election, Camburn backed up his candidates even though, as Mrs. Bilkins suggested, some Republican claims may have contained more fiction than fact.

Carleton, Billy: On 7 June 1890, Mrs. Bilkins is remembering the poem "Gone with a Handsomer Man" by Will Carleton, a Michigan journalist who wrote newspaper poetry, gave public readings, and published nine volumes of collected works, including *Farm Ballads* (1873) and *City Legends* (1889). Russel Nye (*Unembarrassed Muse*, p. 116) commented that Carleton "specialized in exactly the right blend of sentimentality, rustic humor, and dialect." On 6 July 1890 the *Aberdeen Daily News* reported that Carleton commanded $250 to $350 per poem.

Cavanaugh, Jack: Garret J. ("Jack") Cavanaugh was the retiring chief of police who "went out when the republican administration came in." As police chief, he had made "a handsome picture in his suit of blue and with well waxed mustachios" (*ADN* 28 March 1891).

Cholly. See Howard, Cholly

Chowder's, Miss: While Miss Chowder and her shop are obviously fictional constructs, they attest to the fashion consciousness of Aberdeen men and women. Even though the city directories of 1887–88 and 1889–90 do not list hairdressers for women, various barbers, "hair bleacheries," and discreet in-home beauty parlors did exist to help Aberdonians follow the dictates of fashion. On 19 July an *Aberdeen Saturday Pioneer* advertisement announced: "Life is too Short to worry about your hair this hot weather. Bangs cut and curled for 25c at 263 Ninth avenue." Apparently, as Baum's column of 2 August suggested, both men and women took advantage of this service. Baum's humorous view of fashion-conscious Americans would later lead him (in "Queer Visitors") to send the Scarecrow, Tin Woodman, and other Oz characters to see "Mme. Qui-Sym, Beauty Specialist," whose business sign claimed, "Homely Folks Made Radiantly Beautiful While You Wait."

Coe, Miss: Mrs. Carril M. Coe "showed great presence of mind and but for her the interior of the [Coe] residence would have been greatly damaged" by fire, the *Aberdeen Daily News* reported on 24 October 1890. "She grabbed the hose, turned on the water and entered the burning building, mastering the flames before she ceased her efforts." While this self-sufficient woman was saving her home, her husband, Carril, was putting in his day as an abstractor with the Coe and Howard Abstract Company.

Columbia: Located seventeen miles northeast of Aberdeen, Columbia was officially formed in November 1879, roughly a year before Brown County itself was organized and eighteen months before Aberdeen came into existence. The town was the original county seat and at first grew rapidly. In the mid-1880s, however, it lost the opportunity to become a transportation hub when the railroads crisscrossed instead at Aberdeen, which had been platted in January 1881. When it also lost the county seat to Aberdeen in 1887, Columbia began to decline. It successfully challenged the loss in the territorial supreme court, and the offices were returned in November 1889, but a year later, when the new state constitution permitted yet another vote on the issue, Aberdeen won a decisive and final victory. Baum's columns reflect the rivalry between the two towns and the fact that from the 1889 supreme court decision to the November 1890 general election, county officials and those who had court cases or other concerns in the county seat but resided in Aberdeen were commuting to Columbia to take care of county business. On Wednesday, 29 October 1890, Sam Vroom, Hank Williams, Charles Brockway, and other members of the "Court House Crowd" hosted a reception and ball in Columbia that drew over forty people from Aberdeen. Those who drove carriages, the *Aberdeen Daily News* reported on 30 October, "did not return until the new day was dawning and will not be in a hurry to make their appearance down town this morning."

Commercial Club: The city businessmen had dubbed their commercial group the Aberdeen Club when they founded it in 1888, but the newspapers referred to it simply as "The Club." Baum's remarks on the organization were always scathing, beginning with his consternation when The Club called the March 1890 seed wheat convention in Huron rather than Aberdeen, not even promoting the hometown to that extent. "Won't somebody please sharpen a long stick and stir them up a little," Baum lamented. "We'd like to hear them roar once (for Aberdeen) and see what it would sound like" (*ASP* 1 March 1890). He complained about their expensive quarters, which they had financed for $5,000 in 1889 rather than building a much needed new opera house for the community. Club dues were a prohibitive fifty dollars a year, ensuring that only Aberdeen's social and commercial elite could belong. In September 1890, as hard times reached main street, a drastic lowering of dues enabled the group to welcome forty new members. Opining that it would now "come nearer being the voice of the people," the *Aberdeen Evening Republican* hoped that at least it would no longer "be the voice of a few sleek silk stocking gentry" (*AER* 10 September 1890). In the winter of 1890–91 The Club initiated a sheep-raising scheme to diversify Brown County's economy, but as Aberdeen continued to lose businesses and people, Baum and his landlady remained skeptical that it had truly changed. In a 3 January 1891 editorial, after the five-year-old Lillibridge's Cracker House had removed to Sioux Falls, Baum accused the group of socializing rather than rustling on Aberdeen's behalf. The landlady obviously agreed.

Common council. See Uncommon council

Corwin: Milton T. Corwin, a bachelor, kept books at the Keystone Mortgage Company of Aberdeen.

Cowjumps: In a 12 July 1890 article for the *Aberdeen Saturday Pioneer*, Helen Leslie Gage identified one of the Sisseton Indian chiefs who performed on the Fourth of July as "Pe-te-cap-e," which she translated as Cow Killer. This chief, she wrote, "fanned himself with a bunch of turkey feathers as languidly as a Broadway exquisite." When the dancing began, however, Cow Killer and the other men would "work themselves into a frenzy, jumping about like an Iowa twister, first on one toe, then on the other" — suggesting the original model for Baum's "Cowjumps" of 5 July.

Coyne, Doc.: S. Jay Coyne, surgeon for the Chicago, Milwaukee & St. Paul Railroad, had an Aberdeen partnership with fellow physician Louis F. Diefendorf. In July 1890 Aberdeen's fourth ward sent Coyne as delegate to the county Republican convention, where he became presiding officer and, as the *Aberdeen*

Daily News remarked on 16 July, "properly insist[ed] on proper credentials."
After Coyne objected to the resolution on prohibition, however — he preferred
licensing and taxing liquor to prohibiting it — the *News* editorially slapped at
antiprohibitionists in the party. The doctor defended himself in a long letter
to the *News*, although Baum remarked that Coyne's objection to the resolution
"was but a manly and straightforward statement of his personal idea on this
subject, and really requires no public explanation" (*ASP* 19 July 1890). Like other
antiprohibition men, Coyne also objected to woman suffrage. Before the state
Republican convention in August, editor Barrett reported that delegate Coyne
"intends to record his vote against woman suffrage and prohibition if these
questions are brought before the convention. The Dr. is a straight republican
with all the isms left out" (*AER* 26 August 1890). Baum's readers must have been
highly amused at the thought of the decidedly unproper and uncredentialed
Mrs. Bilkins using the good doctor's proxy to vote for woman suffrage and other
radical notions. *See also* Diefendorf, Doc

Cranmer: Simeon H. Cranmer's contemporaries observed that he "sacrificed his
means and spent his time liberally" on social causes (*A&BC*). A Nebraska lawyer
and teacher, Cranmer homesteaded in Edmunds County, Dakota Territory, in
1884, moving to Aberdeen in 1889 to become president of the Union Banking
Company. He and his wife, Emma A. Cranmer, supported prohibition and
women's rights; Simeon served as president of the Aberdeen Equal Suffrage
Association when Baum was secretary. In January 1890 the Cranmers started an
industrial school for working girls, giving free instruction in reading, writing,
arithmetic, and literature to fifty women who had "no previous advantages of
education" (*ASP* 12 April 1990). Simeon Cranmer's dedication to social reform,
as well as his friendship with William E. Kidd and Father Robert Haire, led
him to join the Independent party and run for Brown County state's attorney
against Republican Samuel A. Kennedy. Prohibition advocates critical of the
retiring Edward Taubman thus hoped to elect one of their own to take charge of
closing down original-package joints and blind pigs. The official election count
showed Cranmer to be twenty-three votes short after the county canvassing
board disqualified the ballots of "an Independent township" on a technicality; if
counted, the returns from Greenfield Township would have given Cranmer (and
other Independents in close races) the victory. Cranmer immediately "served
notice of contest on Mr. Kennedy, states attorney elect" (*ADN* 15 November
1890) — inexplicably hiring Taubman as his lawyer — and the court overturned
the "official" results in December. The "Cranmer Contest Case" would not
be resolved that simply, however. The county commissioners failed to approve
Cranmer's bonds, and Cranmer and his lawyer fell out when the Independents
accused the commissioners of conspiring to keep Taubman in the post. On

31 January 1891 Baum speculated in "Our Landlady" that the issue would remain unresolved five years later. Another court case and a citizens' board finally put Cranmer to work, but the new district attorney found he did not like Taubman's job after all and served only one term. As he attempted to enforce the state's prohibition law, the Independent was "surprised to find himself condemned by BIG INTERESTS," his daughter later confided (Greenman, *Higher Than the Sky*, p. 37). The battle-weary Taubman would not have been surprised at all.

Creamery Hotel: In his speculation that Alonzo Ward would open a hotel, Baum missed the mark by two years. The three-story Ward Hotel would not open until 1897, but Ward's creamery business began on 27 January 1891, when he and C. L. Parkhurst organized the Aberdeen Creamery Company to buy butter from area farmers for cash. If things went well, they intended to open a general creamery business, purchasing "milk and cream in liberal quantities" and installing machinery to produce five hundred pounds of butter a day (*ADN* 27 January 1891). Baum admired Ward's entrepreneurial skills, and he may have been privy to his future plans. The businessman appeared in more "Our Landlady" columns (twelve) than any other Aberdonian. *See also* Ward, Al.; Ward's

Crofoot, Judge: Louis W. Crofoot, Democratic lawyer and territorial judge of the Seventh Judicial District in 1888–89, had come to Dakota Territory from Pontiac, Michigan, in 1882. A contemporary publication labeled him "a standing example of the much-doubted fact that honorable men can be good lawyers" (*Historical and Descriptive Review*, p. 55). Although Crofoot and Baum served together as judges for an oratorical contest for young women sponsored by the Congregational church in July 1890, the two men found themselves on opposite sides that fall when Crofoot accepted the Democratic nomination for county judge. Baum lamented that only one good man could win the election and accurately foresaw that Crofoot's Republican opponent, John E. Adams, would emerge the victor. In October, in a move that Baum wholeheartedly approved, Crofoot became secretary of the newly incorporated Dakota Irrigation Company, working with other Brown County professional men to sink experimental wells and interest the federal government in supporting irrigation.

Crose, President: George G. Crose was president of the Dakota Farmers' Alliance Company, one of many offshoots of the Dakota Territorial Farmers' Alliance (others included the Alliance Publishing Company and the Alliance Aid Association). The Alliance Company, which retained its ties to the parent Farmers' Alliance organizations of both North and South Dakota, bought farm machinery and equipment at cost and, after expenses, sold them to alliance members "at from ten to fifty per cent less than they can buy elsewhere" (*ASP* 21 June 1890). The company started an insurance business as well. Noting that "the concern is in excellent financial condition," Baum reported that company stockholders had reelected George Crose as president on 13 January 1891 (*ASP* 17 January 1891). Simultaneously, Crose, a Republican-elected alderman of Aberdeen's first ward, was being considered as a compromise candidate for United States senator to break the voting deadlock between Republicans and Independents in the South Dakota senate. Such a compromise would, Baum opined, "be welcomed by all the more liberal men of all parties" (*ASP* 3 January 1891). As he projected the future of Aberdeen, however, Baum (correctly) did not place Crose in politics. The allianceman's well-known and respected "executive ability" (*ASP* 12 April 1890) and the fact that he had an artesian well on his Hyde County farm led Baum to speculate that he would be the wealthiest Aberdonian of 1895.

Curmess: Modeled on an outdoor festival traditional in the Low Countries, the Grand National Holiday Kirmess (variously spelled Kermis, Kermess, or Kirmes) of 16 December 1890 offered the women of the Presbyterian church a chance to combine bazaars, music, and tableaux in an evening of entertainment for the benefit of the poor. Five booths decorated for five "national" holidays — New Year's Day, Washington's Birthday, Decoration Day, the Fourth of July, and Christmas — dotted the floor of the Aberdeen Opera House. Dressed as characters such as George and Martha Washington or Santa and Mrs. Claus, five couples sold food and crafts appropriate to each holiday. On stage, a quartet and quintet sang between such tableaux as "The New Year and the Old," in which Baum played Father Time. As "Our Landlady" suggested on 20 December, elaborate entertainments of this type sometimes cost more money to put on than they brought in, with organizers and participants picking up the difference. Baum's newspaper had earlier explored this reality in a clever letter signed "Dugout," from "Dugout Township, S.D." According to the "rural correspondent," the "young ladies' sisiety of the 'Benevolent Bountiful Benefactress,' has been quite successful. . . . [Its] thirteen members . . . have succeeded in raising $27.50 at an actual cost to their parents of only six dollars a member. Verily charity suffereth long and is kind" (*ASP* 22 February 1890).

Daily Anythin': In his July 1890 spoof of the two daily newspapers, Baum referred to the *Aberdeen Daily News* as the Daily Anything. Founded in 1886, the *News* began as an afternoon paper "with but two sides printed at home" (*ADN* 27 July 1890). In 1887 its owners incorporated as the Daily News Company, purchased the Associated Press franchise, and began publishing the paper as a morning edition. By 1890 the plant employed over forty people, with Colonel Dennis M. Evans as editor. The financial depression of 1890–91 and the failure of the rival *Aberdeen Evening Republican* led the *News* to return to afternoon publication, a more economical arrangement because of train and employee time schedules. Announcing this and other changes on 31 January 1891, the newspaper claimed that management and editorial staff would "be in no wise changed," but the

Hagerty bank failure soon forced out business manager George Schlosser and other stockholders. The company changed hands many times over the years, yet the paper itself outlasted all its competition, surviving as part of the present-day *Aberdeen American-News*. As a true Dakota booster, Baum congratulated the *News* on its 1891 decision "to economize," and even though its new emphasis on literary items and local news competed directly for his own audience, he gallantly remarked that the changes gave evidence "of considerable enterprise and prosperity" in the city's only daily (*ASP* 8 February 1890). His landlady's 8 February assessment contained more bite.

Daily Nothin': In 1890 the *Aberdeen Evening Republican*, which had been Aberdeen's first newspaper, operated as the city's afternoon daily. Edited by C. Boyd Barrett, the *Republican* espoused Democratic politics, but it did not survive the political turmoil of 1890 with either politics or editor intact. Barrett, who had grown disgusted with local Democrats, left the business about the time the new *State Democrat* began in October 1890. He leased the *Republican* to his assistant editor, William E. Kidd, who continued it as a Populist newspaper. Early in 1891 economic circumstances forced Kidd to discontinue the daily edition and publish only a weekly, which he eventually renamed the *Star*.

Dakota Bildin' and Loan assassination: Organized in 1888, the Building and Loan Association of Dakota was "the conception and production of western men." It boasted that its "plan" was "mutual" and therefore "absolutely solid and safe." The assets of the association went from $1,722 in December 1888 to $558,240 in July 1890 to $710,000 in January 1891. Borrowers got "their money at cost and loans [were] made only to stockholders" (*A&BC*). "When we think of the unassuming, modest little concern that started in Aberdeen only two years ago," Baum wrote on 31 January 1891, " . . . we can only conclude that the Building and Loan Association was founded on the right principles, and has had the right kind of men at its helm." This statewide organization was an outgrowth of the Aberdeen Building and Loan Association, of which T. Clarkson Gage, Baum's brother-in-law, was vice-president. Before going statewide, it had facilitated the building of about two hundred Aberdeen houses.

Dave: Dave (2 August 1890) is probably David Jones, a long-time employee at Al Ward's establishment. As times got harder in Aberdeen in the fall of 1890, Jones, like the barber Pabst, considered moving on and went to Minneapolis to look for a position. He returned to Ward's within a few days "with the declaration that South Dakota [was] good enough for him yet awhile" (*ADN* 18 December 1890).

Davis, Jim: Aberdeen was home to two men named Jim Davis: James H. Davis, secretary of the Aberdeen Abstract Company, and James P. Davis, who engaged in his own real estate business. Neither man was likely to be overworked in a time of drought and sluggish land sales (8 March 1890), but by 1895, according to

Baum's projections (31 January 1891), rising land values could again push such men to local prominence.

Dennis, L. C.: Leander C. Dennis belonged to the legal firm of Dennis, Hute and Luse, which specialized in debt collection and whose "zeal in pushing this branch of business is as great a terror to the debtor as it is a source of satisfaction to the creditor" (*ADN* 24 February 1888). On 8 March 1890, Mrs. Bilkins may have hoped Dennis could help her collect on the political promises she had received. A politician himself, Dennis represented Brown County in the state senate during 1890, winning election as a Republican.

Diefendorf, Doc: Louis F. Diefendorf was a pioneer Aberdeen physician and surgeon, possibly the first doctor to locate in town, making him a respected and venerable member of the community. A serious physician, he was a charter member of the Dakota Medical Society. Antiprohibitionist S. Jay Coyne was his associate. Although nothing suggests that Diefendorf or Coyne had this problem, frontier doctors were notorious for their affinity to alcohol; in one form or another, alcohol was a major component in the medical remedies of the time.

Dill; Dill-ole-man: Charles H. Dill worked as a traveling agent and deliveryman for Jewett Brothers, wholesale grocers. A bachelor who roomed at Ward's, Dill attended the many social happenings of 1890. On 15 February, Baum reported that he had been partnered by "an aching void" at the most recent Young Ladies Guild dance.

District Attorney. See Taub; Taubman

Downditch, Aesop: This fictitious character (3 January 1891) is a takeoff on the equally fictitious Farmer Updyke created by the *Aberdeen Daily News.* Interestingly, Baum made his character a local product, born in Ipswich, South Dakota, and educated at Redfield College, a school south of Aberdeen. Even in his fantasy columns, Baum consistently supported the hometown product. This ingenious inventor is not an eastern industrialist but a western "rustler" who enjoys all the comforts of gracious living on the Dakota prairie.

Drake, Jedge: Like Baum, John H. Drake came from the Syracuse area of New York state. He moved to Dakota Territory in the 1870s, settling first in Watertown, where he was elected judge of Codington County. Relocating to Aberdeen in 1881, Drake started the *Dakota Pioneer*, issuing its first number on 5 August. As editor, Drake was "ready for a 'scrap' at all times with anybody" and was therefore "a typical Dakota hustler" in the eyes of his friends back east (*Syracuse Standard,* 2 August 1887). In the late 1880s Drake tried to sell his newspaper several times, but none of the buyers could make a go of it. When Baum took over and renamed the paper in January 1890, the *Aberdeen Evening Republican* accused him of "trying to resusitate the dead duck of the masculine gender under a new name" (28 January 1890). Like the previous owners, Baum eventually failed, and the paper reverted to Drake once more. The judge finally broke up the plant, selling the equipment piece by piece, when President Benjamin Harrison appointed him United States consul to Kiel, Germany, in 1892. Before that time, South Dakota's Governor Arthur C. Mellette had appointed him to the seed wheat commission that controlled relief funds and grain in the spring of 1890. On 15 March 1890, however, Mrs. Bilkins implied that his interest in political appointments outweighed his dedication to that cause. His hope of preferment had not abated by 1 November, but his aspirations were still premature. After his time in Germany, Drake returned to Syracuse in 1894 rather than risk the depressed economy of Aberdeen.

Eurekie: Eureka, South Dakota, a town about fifty miles northwest of Aberdeen, had been platted in 1887 by the Chicago, Milwaukee & Saint Paul Railroad. The following year, immigrants from nearby states as well as from Russia and Germany occupied the surrounding farmland. In 1892, when good weather returned to the region, Eureka became a national wheat market, shipping three to four million bushels of grain from the local depot.

Evans, Kernel: Colonel Dennis M. Evans, editor of the *Aberdeen Daily News*, filled three to four columns each day with discussions of political happenings from a partisan Republican stance. From June to November 1890 he ceaselessly pounded the Independents and their candidates, bordering on libel in his attacks. Baum chided him for his zeal against the new party and accused him of "the bold but reckless practise of robbing the dictionary of some of its most murderous words and the encyclopedia of some of its most heart-rending ideas" (*ASP* 5 July 1890). After Evans accused Baum of being "a noodle-pated scribbler" and informed his readers that Pierre was Latin for Peter, Baum called on the ghost of Romulus to "inform the gallant colonel that he is not so successful a polyglot as he is a polywog" (*ASP* 12 July 1890). In December 1890, Evans's politics led him to pen more painfully erudite essays in support of Republican candidates for United States senator.

Fair man, the: R. A. McWilliams, a Canadian native, operated the Fair, a "large, bustling mart, where almost anything 'under the sun' is exhibited and offered for sale at fabulously low prices." He had opened the store in September 1889 with a stock worth $8,000. Three years later, in the heart of the depression, his stock was worth five times that amount, and he employed thirteen people. He accomplished this economic miracle through adherence to "strict principles of underbuying and underselling for cash" (*A&BC*). Prior to Baum's column of 19 April 1890, these principles propelled the grocers of Aberdeen into a pricing war that the newspapers dubbed "a tea party." After McWilliams announced that he would sell forty-cent tea for twenty-five cents, rival grocers Thompson and Kearney ran advertisements that disparaged the quality of McWilliams's tea and claimed that he lied about his percentage of profit. Calling the partners the one-hundred percenters, the Fair man responded: "While the aristocratic hundered [*sic*] percenters wail . . . and growl about the crops, the weather and the mud, we care never a continental for time, place or circumstanc[e]" (*ADN* 20 April 1890). McWilliams claimed that he maintained his low prices by buying his own goods in person at eastern factories, where he paid cash in exchange for good discounts. The Fair man's business practices presented a strong contrast to those that had driven Baum from retail trade in the winter of 1889. Baum, having less than $2,000 of capital to invest, had both bought and sold on credit. In January 1891, even as the newspaperman teetered on the brink of another reversal in fortune, his landlady foresaw continued success for McWilliams (31 January 1891).

Feel-yer-paw; Feelyerpaw. See Fylpaa

Felch, Miss: The personal columns of the *Aberdeen Saturday Pioneer* mention both a Miss Felch and a Mrs. H. H. Felch, the latter of whom kept a boardinghouse before starting a dressmaking business. A "hired gal" referred to in Baum's column is usually fictional, but the one mentioned on 21 June could be real. Most of the other flood stories in that column are based on actual happenings during and after the cloudburst of 17 June 1890, when 3½ inches of rain fell after dark and flooded the city's sewers.

Fielder, Bill: Reverend William Fielder, a presiding elder of the Methodist Episcopal church, served as president of the South Dakota Enforcement League, the group that had drafted the 1890 prohibition bill. Throughout the debate on the bill, Baum criticized Fielder for the niggling details contained in the proposed legislation. On 15 February he noted that the Reverend Fielder "thinks of adding a clause to his bill prohibiting inhabitants of South Dakota from raising chickens. He says he [don't] want any cock-tails in the state." Baum continued his ridicule after the bill passed, remarking on 29 March, "Children brought up on a bottle are invariably addicted to liquor, and Mr. Fielder regrets now that he did not insert a clause in the Prohibition bill forbidding it." Fielder also served on the executive committee of the state Equal Suffrage Association.

Fin, Ike: Isaac Hirvaskari, a native of Siikajoki, Finland, immigrated to Michigan before homesteading in 1883 near the Finnish settlement of Savo in Brown County. Throughout May and June 1890 he gained fame for using an onion to predict the weather with a high rate of success. When a cloudburst he had forecast arrived as scheduled on 17 June, he was invited to join the Fourth of July parade in Aberdeen as the "famous Finn weather prophet." Decked out in top hat and striped trousers, Hirvaskari reportedly enjoyed his moment of fame. Relieved Aberdonians needed someone to thank for what they saw as a lifting of the drought, and Baum remarked that "he is Dakota's great man today," equating his success at forecasting with an ability to bring the rain itself (*ASP* 28 June 1890). Similarly, the *Aberdeen Daily News* noted on 5 July that the "Finn Seer Held His Hand" on the Fourth, ensuring sunny weather.

Firey, John: In the 1890 election, "that old reliable democratic war horse" John H. Firey ran for state senator against Republican Hank Williams and Independent James Kyle (*AER* 22 July 1890). A registered pharmacist, Firey had left his native Illinois in 1882 and started the first drugstore in the year-old settlement of Aberdeen. The young man's support for Democrat Grover Cleveland earned him the local postmaster's job in 1885. Meanwhile, his drugstore grew to be the largest in town, putting a dose of tonic for all voters within his capability. Free "vittles" or other refreshments appear to have been the universal path to a voter's heart. Reporting on 18 October that Mrs. John H. Firey had recently hosted the Ladies' Reading Circle's annual husbands' evening, Baum confided that some of the men present had overeaten, "but when they recollected that John was still running for office their consciences were eased." In spite of such inducements, Independent Kyle won the election, an outcome that Baum seemed to hint at in his column of 1 November.

Fisher, Chollie: Charles A. Fisher, an early Aberdeen postmaster, began a real estate, insurance, and loan business with Charles C. Fletcher in 1887. Baum hinted at Fisher's political aspirations in his 8 March column, and indeed, after the April 1890 election, the Republican mayor did appoint Fisher to the post of city auditor.

Fletch; Fletchie: Charles C. Fletcher was one of the new members initiated along with L. Frank Baum into the Ancient Order of United Workmen in May 1890. A real estate agent, Fletcher had prospered during the good crop years of 1886–88. Always elegantly dressed and gallant, the former Iowan had a reputation as a lady's man, which may be why Baum likened him (10 May 1890) to Byron's hero Mazeppa, who got in trouble over a woman.

Fowler, Doc.: De Witt Clinton Fowler received his medical degree in 1863 and became a surgeon with the Nineteenth New York Cavalry during the Civil War. He came to Aberdeen in 1882 as part of the larger group of settlers from the Syracuse area of New York who had followed T. Clarkson Gage and the Beards to the Dakotas. Pursuing his medical career on the frontier, Fowler became superintendent of the State Board of Health. By all accounts, this dedicated physician was firmly wedded to his profession, making house calls no matter what the weather or circumstances. Baum called him "that princely entertainer, courtly gentleman, accomplished musician, distinguished scholar and able practitioner." Although he served as best man at the wedding of Frank Beard and May Burke in late June 1890 and apparently participated in some September nuptials as well, Fowler himself never married. The doctor enjoyed financial comfort, living in "superb parlors, drawing rooms, apartments and kitchens" in which he feted his friends (*ASP* 22 February 1890).

Frederick: A Brown County town about twenty-five miles north of Aberdeen, Frederick was near the North Dakota border. The Chicago, Milwaukee & Saint Paul Railroad, which platted the town in 1881, had brought in large numbers of Norwegian and Finnish immigrants to settle the surrounding farmlands. In fact, the town took its name from the railroad's Finnish immigration agent, Kustaa Frederick Bergstadius. In the summer of 1890 woman suffragists found the area's Scandinavian settlers to be strongly in support of their work, mustering 115 people to listen to speakers and 63 to join the local Equal Suffrage Association. Throughout the next two or three decades the area would continue to back liberal causes, forming a strong pocket of support for the Socialist Party.

Fylpaa: John A. Fylpaa, a native of Norway, came to Frederick, South Dakota, in 1882 and started a modest general store. When his brother Thomas joined him in 1884, they opened a larger "Dry Goods, Groceries, Glassware and Clothing" business that served the community for many years (*BCD*). Although Baum referred to him as "the forlorn hope of the Independents," Fylpaa's nomination for Brown County treasurer had surprised the Republicans, who considered the successful merchant a tough candidate to beat. On 18 October, Baum noted that the Independents were concentrating their efforts for success on Fylpaa, "whatever his claims for suffrage are based upon." Although Baum found Fylpaa's support of suffrage suspiciously convenient (18 October 1890) and his political rhetoric half-baked (25 October 1890), the merchant was well known throughout the county and, despite smear campaigns (1 November 1890), won not only in 1890 but also in 1896 and 1898. "His reputation for honesty has become a proverb — 'as honest as John Fylpaa' — being a common expression up north," the Populist press bragged in the *Aberdeen Star* (29 October 1896).

G.A.R.'s: The Dakota Department of the Grand Army of the Republic (GAR), organized in 1883, reflected the fact that large numbers of Civil War veterans had settled in Dakota Territory. On 12 January 1884 thirty-three GAR members chartered Aberdeen's Robert Anderson Post No. 19, which by 1890 had more than a hundred members. The post also boasted an active Women's Relief Corps auxiliary and a young women's precision drill troop, the Aberdeen Guards. Baum's column of 12 July 1890 suggests the attention the veterans' group paid to young South Dakota National Guardsmen such as Charles Howard.

Gavin, Cholly and 'Stel: The thwarted romance of twenty-one-year-old hotel clerk Charles Gavin and seventeen-year-old student Estel Smith provided Aberdeen residents with all the drama and none of the tragedy of classic myth and theater: it ended happily in the young couple's marriage and reconciliation with the wife's parents.

Gene: Imogene ("Genie" or "Gene") Van Loon — a stenographer at Hagerty & Company, Bankers — frequently sang roles in Aberdeen's amateur theatricals, appearing, for example, as Aline in *The Sorcerer*. In his critique of her performance, Baum remarked that Van Loon had a "sweet and refined face," a "modest demeanor," and a "rare judgment" (*ASP* 20 September 1890). Such a talented and popular young woman would surely be involved in the romantic goings-on of Baum's 9 August 1890 column.

George. See Kimberly, George

Ghost-dance: According to a syndicated article in the *Aberdeen Saturday Pioneer*, Kicking Horse, a Miniconjou Lakota from the Cheyenne River reserve (usually identified as Kicking Bear), had visited Wovoka, the Paiute prophet of the pan-Indian Ghost Dance movement. Returning to share the story with Sitting Bull and other Lakotas, Kicking Horse reported that God had told the prophet that "he himself would wipe out the white race from the face of the earth. God told him the earth was getting full of holes, and many places were rotten. He would gradually send a wave of earth, twenty feet or more, over the country. It would move slowly, and the Indians must keep dancing so as to keep on top, and so when the wave had passed all the whites would be burried [*sic*] underneath, and the Indians would be on top." The Lakota dead would come back to life; the buffalo would return; and things would be "as they were hundreds of years ago" (*ASP* 1 November 1890). Sitting Bull and other adherents, notably Little Wound, stressed that the movement was religious and that Lakotas should have the same ability as whites to pursue religious freedom. Unfortunately, the warlike rhetoric of some preachers, the "bullet-proof" shirts worn by dancers, and the underlying promise of white annihilation convinced the military that if the movement was not already a call to war, it soon would be.

Gilmore, Teek: The residence of Theodore A. ("Teek") Gilmor on Seventh Avenue was the location of the second 1890 social of the Young Ladies Guild of Saint Mark's Episcopal Church. Gilmor, a clerk at Beard, Gage and Beard's general store, served as the affable host of the 28 January 1890 progressive euchre party that ended with an oyster supper. In 1892 this New York state native would own his own grocery store.

Goodes: Called "the prince of furnishers," John T. Goodes ran the J. T. Goodes Furniture Company. Typical of the time period, he also advertised his services as undertaker and embalmer, promising "no business of importance entrusted to subordinates" (*ACD* p. 3). In his spare time Goodes managed the Aberdeen Opera House, and his wife directed the operettas that the Ladies Guild of Saint Mark's Episcopal Church offered during the state fair in September. In August 1890 Baum was attending rehearsals under her supervision for the role of Rufus in *The Little Tycoon*.

Goodwin: Henry Goodwin ran a wholesale liquor dealership until state prohibition made the activity illegal on 1 May 1890. With the advent of the original-package loophole, Goodwin continued to "do business in a rough shed in the rear of his former place." Some of his customers broke into an abandoned building nearby, using it as a drinking and gambling "resort" (*ADN* 24 July 1890). The uncertain interpretation of prohibition laws prevented District Attorney Taubman from closing Goodwin's shop until 10 August, when federal legislation put original packages under state jurisdiction. The next day Goodwin declared "that he had closed his place with the intention of keeping it closed" (*ADN* 12 August 1890). Although the Republican newspapers and local enforcement league made the Democrat Goodwin sound like an unsavory character, in fact he held a different political stance on prohibition and was attempting to save his business. In May 1890 he estimated that prohibition would not only cost him $20,000 but force him to leave the state to pursue his livelihood.

Gould, Jay: In his 8 February 1890 column Baum may have been playing with the similarity between the names of railroad magnate Jason ("Jay") Gould and Aberdeen resident James J. Gould, who was a shipping clerk for Edmund H. Roche, wholesale liquor dealer. James J. Gould, a young bachelor staying at one of the town's many boardinghouses, was a likely participant in the various church socials. By the time of the 10 January 1891 "Our Landlady" column, however, liquor dealer Roche and his employee had left Aberdeen, and Baum was clearly referring to the enterpreneurial skills of financier Jay Gould, who had begun his career by buying up small railroads.

Guilded Clique: This 22 February 1890 pun refers to the women's groups of Saint Mark's Episcopal Church, the Ladies Guild and the Young Ladies Guild (the latter was renamed the Guild of Saint Agnes in April). The younger organization sponsored the innovative 1890 socials that began with the auction at Samuel Jumper's house on 21 January. Maud Gage Baum belonged to the group of older women, the Ladies Guild, which had been established to raise funds to meet the church debt.

Hagerty, Frank: Frank H. Hagerty's story was Aberdeen's favorite rags-to-riches tale. Born in Pennsylvania, he had come to Jamestown, Dakota Territory, in 1881 with only $18.50 in his pocket. Instead of money he had "first class natural ability, energy, pluck, shrewdness, and these, supplemented by honesty and a spotless integrity, soon did for him what a large sum of money of itself could not have done," the *Aberdeen Daily News* proclaimed on 24 February 1888. In Aberdeen's first year the young entrepreneur persuaded Jamestown bankers to furnish money for a two-thirds interest in a large tract of land near the new boomtown. Hagerty made over $75,000 in less than eighteen months when the property was annexed to Aberdeen in 1882 as the Hagerty and Lloyd's addition. This profit served as capital for the banking business he started that same year, and he invested heavily in other Aberdeen businesses, including the *Aberdeen Daily News*, an electric company, a telephone company, and a brickworks. The newspapers published his story far and wide as an example of the opportunities in Dakota. "Ponder over it, young men of the east," one 1882 example implored, "you who are plodding along in the office and workshops of the crowded east, note the possibilities of the future for you in the golden northwest, and immediately pack your 'gripsacks,' pocket your little savings, and take Horace Greeley's favorite advice, and 'go west'" (GSB p. 116). In 1889 Hagerty became territorial and then state commissioner of immigration under Governor Arthur C. Mellette. A firm supporter of Mellette and prohibition, Hagerty commanded a leading position in city and state politics. In 1890, as vice-president of the Aberdeen Club, he called the March seed wheat convention and attended it as a delegate from Brown County. In the summer and early fall he invested heavily (and with much publicity) in irrigation ventures, sinking his hopes and his banking capital in Aberdeen rather than speculating on land in Harriman or West Superior. Although Baum's columns implied that Hagerty was a bit tight with his money, the banker actually had a well-merited reputation for good deeds and had donated land for several early churches and schools. In editorials right after the closing of Hagerty's Aberdeen bank in October 1890, Baum observed that Hagerty's generosity and kind heart had gotten him into trouble and predicted that the enterprise would soon reopen. In mid-January, however, Baum suggested that Hagerty's reputation for charity had led his stockholders to back him in risky ventures. They had, after all, allowed the already overextended banker to risk capital in manufacturing and testing well-drilling rigs in the summer of 1890. Baum's comments did not sit well with Aberdonians who overlooked the popular Hagerty's wrongs as "errors in judgement." One of the banker's apologists remarked that since Baum had recently failed in business himself, his remarks reached "the acme of meanness" (quoted in *ADN* 27 January 1891). In Baum's opinion and that of his many empty-handed depositors, however, the banker's most recent error in judgment had knocked "him from his popular pedestal and [taken] all the heroism out of him." Hagerty had apparently turned over personal property to one of his politically connected depositors (probably outgoing county treasurer Hank Williams) instead of giving it to his creditors "in equal portion" (*ASP* 31 January 1891). Within a few months he lost most of his businesses. When Mellette passed him over for reappointment as commissioner of immigration, Hagerty went west once more, to the boom areas of Washington state, to seek new opportunities.

Hagerty's: F. H. Hagerty & Company, Bankers, one of the area's largest local financial institutions, owned banks in Aberdeen, Claremont, Frederick, Verdon, Warner, and Webster. Senior partner Frank Hagerty epitomized the Dakota booster and had institutionalized his enthusiasm, becoming the state's commissioner of immigration. Ironically, however, the landlady was not likely to sink any wells with her funds, for as Baum undoubtedly suspected when he wrote the 3 January 1891 column, Hagerty's banks in Aberdeen and Claremont had failed along with the crops of 1890.

Ham: Mrs. Bilkins is treating Shakespeare's Hamlet like an old friend (6 December 1890), recalling his soliloquy that begins, "To be, or not to be, that is the question."

Hank. See Williams, Hank

Harriman: The eastern financiers who founded Harriman, Tennessee, were attempting to create a model industrial city, with temperance as its underpinning, although few if any Aberdonians knew about the prohibition stance of the enterprise. Harriman had much to recommend it. Located amid rich mineral resources, good water sources, and lush agricultural lands, the town promised to be the gateway to the Cumberland Plateau in the Tennessee mountains. The East Tennessee Land Company, with Clinton B. Fisk as director, planned to develop railroads and mining and manufacturing enterprises to ensure Harriman's growth. Fisk, a Union general, had been temperance candidate for president in 1888. Walter Harriman, another Union general and a member of the company's board of directors, provided the town's name. Terms for the purchase of lots were generous — one-third down, payable in cash or East Tennessee Land Company Stock, and the balance payable in one to two years. Baum's 1 March column makes it clear that most of Aberdeen saw Harriman as an investment possibility, not a temperance experiment. In fact, the *Aberdeen Evening Republican* charged that Ralph Brown had gone south to avoid the consequences of prohibition, which the editor viewed as crippling to the Aberdeen economy (*AER* 10 February 1890). The same editor reported with glee on 5 May that Harriman was "as dead as a mackerel on the sea shore." In fact, although the excitement had apparently abated by 8 March 1890, the town's future did not grow dim until the Panic of 1893. By 1900 the founding company had gone bankrupt, but Harriman itself survived, even though it never achieved the promise of its birth.

Harris, C. N.; Cholly: Charles N. Harris arrived in Aberdeen in 1882 from Wisconsin. As a lawyer, he spent his early years "driving the fastest team he could hire to reach the land office at Watertown first in his client's behalf" (Allen, "Memories," 12 November 1939). Harris also farmed, raising Black Angus cattle, hogs, and short grains, which led to his appointment to the State Board of Agriculture. In January 1890 he took Aberdeen's bid to hold the 1890 state fair before the board, having polled members earlier for their acceptance. Baum's 8 March column referrs to Harris's experience before that body: he did "control his own vote" but had some trouble collecting on other board members' promises. In the end he got the fair for Aberdeen, but the town had to put up a larger cash bid than backers had anticipated. That fall the Democrats nominated Harris to run for state representative from Brown County. *See also* Jimicrat central committee

Harrison, Ben: Benjamin Harrison, a Republican, served as twenty-third president of the United States from 1889 to 1893. He defeated Grover Cleveland in 1888, and Cleveland defeated him in 1892.

Hauser, Cap.: John Harrison Hauser was a Civil War veteran who had served as captain with the Forty-ninth Wisconsin Regiment. He came to Aberdeen in May 1882, opening a law and land office through which he helped to survey much of the land between Aberdeen and the Missouri River. Filing on a Brown County preemption claim, Captain Hauser and his family settled into the life of Aberdeen, where he became a staunch Republican Party supporter and tireless community worker. He served three terms as city attorney and in 1898 would become county probate judge. In March 1890, as many Aberdonians were speculating on property in the American South, Hauser had probably put money into tea-growing properties with his brother, I. L. Hauser, who lived in Bareilly, India. The cow that Captain Hauser kept on his city property was a luxury that Mrs. Bilkins attempted to emulate in mid-July. Hauser's entire family was involved in the Grand Army of the Republic and its auxiliaries. His wife, Louise P. Hauser, served as an officer in the Women's Relief Corp, and his oldest daughter, Frances, captained the Aberdeen Guards. "Fannie" Hauser had graduated with the second high school class to matriculate in Aberdeen. In 1890 she worked in a judge's office before accepting a position in the Aberdeen public schools that fall. The views of neither "Captain Hauser" — father or daughter — are on record concerning suffrage, but Louise served as treasurer of the local suffrage organization for which Baum acted as secretary. As the columnist's 8 November sketch suggests, John Hauser undoubtedly spent election day 1890 as a poll tender.

Hawkins, Steve: Stephen Hawkins, Aberdeen real estate and loan agent, served as president of the State Land Company, which incorporated in May 1890 to invest in Huron town lots in the hope that the permanent state capital would be located there that fall. Although he attended the state and county Democratic conventions as a delegate, Hawkins's politics appear to have been neutral enough for C. Boyd Barrett to refer to him as "Nondescript Hawkins" (*AER* 22 April 1890). His support of Huron for capital certainly flew in the face of the local Democrats' support of Pierre, suggesting that he may have been attempting to play both sides of the fence.

Hazeltine: Three days after Baum's 27 December column, the Ladies Benevolent Society publicly thanked Ira S. Haseltine, the proprietor of the Hotel Kennard, for "the liberal, gentlemanly, and courteous treatment received at his hands"

during the arrangements for the Charity Ball of 23 December (*ADN* 30 December 1890). Whether or not the hotelkeeper donated the ballroom of his four-story hostelry for the event, the women had received many donations from city businessmen and professed to be more than happy with their final net profit of $200.

Hi. See Pratt, Hiram

Hick inbotham; Higginbottom: James E. Hickenbotham had come to Brown County in 1880, testing the soil "until he found a spot where it was flat, black and deep" (*Early History*, p. 107). In 1881 he brought his family to his farmland about six miles southeast of Aberdeen. Hickenbotham's ability as a farmer became legendary, giving credence to boosters' claims that "Dakota soil well tilled will produce anything" (*ADN* 28 August 1888). He planted ten acres of ash and box elder trees and nursed them and his farmstead through the years of drought, a feat to which Mrs. Bilkins gives a new twist in the column of 21 June. In July 1890 he joined many of his fellow Brown County agriculturalists in supporting the Independent party.

Hoit: James W. Hoit, the son of Colonel James B. Hoit of Minnesota, had come to Brown County in 1880. Working on the railroad and in northern Dakota harvest fields during the summers, the young Hoit and his brother Fred took homesteads and tree claims in the Aberdeen area, building their holdings into a bonanza farm by 1888. James then decided to handle his own grain and feed, entering the market as a grain buyer. At some point the elder Hoit also moved to Aberdeen, and in 1890 he served on the governor's seed wheat commission. In his 3 May column Baum alluded to both James W., as a buyer who docked farmers for impurities in their grain, and his father James B., as one of those who — with the governor — had arranged for the seed and feed distribution.

Hole-in-the-Face: This fictional character's name (6 December 1890) hints at such famous Indian personalities as the Ojibway chief Hole-in-the-Day and the Hunkpapa Sioux warrior Rain-in-the-Face. The latter had a reputation for bravery and sometimes claimed to be the person who had killed George and Tom Custer at the Battle of the Little Bighorn in 1876. The newspapers had recently characterized him as an ex-warrior who was "quietly sleeping" in his tipi on the Standing Rock reserve, suggesting that even if interested in the new Ghost Dance religion, he was not likely to go to war (*ADN* 20 November 1890).

How, Major: Major F. Howe, a lawyer who engaged in the real estate business, was city auditor until the 15 April 1890 municipal election. Throughout February and March the Republican newspapers lambasted him and the rest of the Democratic administration for the high cost of city government. On 4 April the *Aberdeen Weekly News* remarked, "It is an old adage that rats desert a sinking ship. Auditor Howe is advertising his premises, furniture, etc., for sale and announces his purpose of going to England." After the Democrats lost the election, Baum reported on 3 May that Howe had indeed sold his property and was leaving for England, "where, 'tis said, he is interested in a chancery suit. We hope it is not as endless as the one Dickens writes of [in *Bleak House*] and that the late auditor will come in for a slice of the fortune."

Howard, Cholly: Known as "the kid politician," twenty-five-year-old Charles Allen Howard became alderman of Aberdeen's fourth ward in the April 1890 election, thereby earning a seat on the Common Council of Aberdeen. Born in Frontier, New York, in 1865, Howard emigrated in 1883 to Columbia, Dakota Territory, where he took a job as clerk in the office of the Brown County register of deeds. In 1886 he preceded the county seat to Aberdeen, engaging in the real estate business in the Coe and Howard Abstract Company before forming his own partnership. The following year he joined the National Guard, an affiliation that endeared him to the local veterans' post of the Grand Army of the Republic. Howard's political aspirations and youthful brassiness made him editorial fair game, and on 10 May 1890 Baum announced that the new alderman "with his usual lack of bashfulness has already made an effort to capture the council. . . . He evidently considers that when he gets up and 'shoos,' the pack will huddle together and move off in the direction he shoos 'em. . . . As we don't believe Charlie can be snubbed without a strong effort on the part of his collegues [*sic*], we may expect to hear his voice prominent in the meetings." C. Boyd Barrett remarked that the young man had climbed to his position on the necks of traditional, and more worthy, Republicans: "Charley, the kid, is no Jonah. He is more like the whale, and a good one, too, for he appears to have swallowed not only Jonah but all the rest of the council" (*AER* 7 May 1890). As secretary of the Republican fourth ward caucus held on 12 July 1890, Baum was privy to Howard's political intentions that summer; however, the young man would have to wait five years before earning his seat in the state senate. Like Baum, Howard would become a Theosophist, in 1898. Unlike Baum, Howard would remain in Aberdeen, becoming a prominent citizen.

Howe: Given Baum's interest in the inventions of the industrial age, it comes as no surprise that his landlady knew of the trials and tribulations of American inventor Elias Howe, who had taken five years (1840–45) to perfect the sewing machine and thereby revolutionize the garment industry.

Huron: Located about ninety miles south and a little east of Aberdeen, Huron had challenged Pierre for the permanent location of the state capital, and many Aberdeen businessmen — Baum included — supported Huron because of its easy railroad access from Aberdeen. Situated in the population center of eastern South Dakota, Huron seemed to have numerous advantages over Pierre, which perched on the edge of the unsettled western area. Baum summed up the arguments in a poem entitled "Huron for Capital," in which he queried how anyone, "unless his brain is cracked," could vote for "any town side-tracked" (*ASP* 5 July 1890). In late April 1890 Aberdeen businessmen organized the State Land Company to invest in Huron real estate and promote their town's interests in the capital location. After the drain of South Dakota investment capital to the southern states a month earlier, Baum found this new development especially encouraging. "For too long," he wrote on 3 May 1890, "have our people been stagnating, and the most valuable real estate of our country lies idly in the hands of a few people who do not realize its wonderful value in the years to come." Capital promotion activities reached a peak in September at the state fair in Aberdeen — where both Pierre and Huron boosters spent liberally to woo voters — and continued throughout October. Huron supporters had raised almost $300,000 through questionable bonding measures to aid their city's bid for capital location. As the economic climate worsened in the fall, however, the landlady, at least, began to consider Huron a "foreign investment" and something Aberdeen businessmen could no longer afford to subsidize.

Independents; injipendents: After the 1890 state legislature and Congress failed to pass measures put forth by farmers against monopolies and trusts and in support of monetary reform, the South Dakota Farmers' Alliance and the Knights of Labor created the Independent party on 6 June 1890. Drawing many of their members from the Republican rank and file, the Independents held their first state convention a month later, nominating a slate of candidates for state office that featured Farmers' Alliance president Henry L. Loucks at its top. The party campaigned on the slogan "Money at cost, transportation at cost and land for those who use it" (*AER* 1 July 1890). Within two years, the party had joined third-party movements in other states to form the national People's Party. From the 1890 election through 1900 the Populists enjoyed remarkable success in South Dakota, fusing with the Democrats to elect a United States senator in 1891 and a governor and United States congressman in 1896. When the People's Party failed to endorse women's rights at both the state and national level for fear of losing votes, however, many women became disgusted with Populist politicians, as Susan B. Anthony did in 1890. "I left the party," wrote Helen M. Reynolds of the National-American Woman Suffrage Association in 1898, "because so many of [the Populists] refused to endorse suffrage. . . . Every man who refused is a hypocrite and cannot be trusted to stand by any of the other principles of the platform since he upholds class legislation of the most unjust kind" (Breeden Papers). Many South Dakota Independents such as Kidd and Fylpaa individually and publicly — if ineffectually — endorsed suffrage, but after the 1890 election Baum judged the Independents to be idealists who lacked "the experience and ability to reconstruct the debased politics of this country" (*ASP* 8 November

1890). He may have been right, for those in power in South Dakota proved unable to push through most of their reforms. Nevertheless, their ideas had lasting merit, many concepts being implemented years after the Populist Party no longer existed.

Ipswich: Ipswich, South Dakota, was founded in October 1883 when the Chicago, Milwaukee & St. Paul Railway Company extended its line twenty-six miles straight west from Aberdeen. In 1821, of course, neither Ipswich nor South Dakota existed, but such details did not bother Baum, for Aesop Downditch himself did not exist outside the column of 3 January 1891 and the author's imagination. The Ipswich bank cashier in the 8 February 1891 column is probably a veiled reference to Frank Hagerty, who had branch banks in many of the surrounding towns, although apparently not in Ipswich.

Jenkins, Georgie: George W. Jenkins, a lawyer from Davenport, Iowa, had been one of the 1881 pioneers of Aberdeen, where he had immediately acquired property and "entered into the law and land business with characteristic Western energy" (*A&BC*). As Mrs. Bilkins indicated (15 February 1890), he and his partner, Albert W. Campbell, had offices in the Northwestern National Bank building. Baum's 17 May column suggested that Jenkins, who had won a seat on the school board in April, shared his own concern about the superintendent's high salary. A respected professional man, Jenkins would become Brown County state's attorney in 1892.

Jenkins, Mirandy: Unlike the other female characters in the 15 November 1890 column, the fictional Mirandy Jenkins has a first name. Although she is probably an extension of Baum's earlier Miss Jenkyns, that name too closely resembled the name of the real Mrs. George W. Jenkins, who had just that week hosted the Pleasant Hour Reading Club in her home.

Jenkyns, Miss: This dressmaker, along with the other women featured in the 8 February 1890 column, is fictional. The name does not appear in any of the city or county business directories of the period, all of which have dressmaker listings. In fact, most of Mrs. Bilkins's female friends are fictional creations. In using working-class characters to poke fun at the affectations of the upper class, Baum usually avoided personalized references. *See also* Jones; Joneses, Miss

Jewell, Gena or *Jena:* Gena S. Jewell, a young bachelor from New York state, shared rooms with another transplanted Yankee, George Kimberly, and clerked at the post office before taking a position at the Building and Loan Association of Dakota. He was the brother of Sophie Jewell Gage, the wife of Baum's brother-in-law, T. Clarkson Gage. In the 1880s the Jewell family had homesteaded near Amherst, South Dakota, about thirty miles northeast of Aberdeen in Marshall County. As Baum's 5 April column noted, Gena Jewell continued to maintain a farm there. On 29 March 1890 Baum had announced that Jewell would superintend the spring planting but return to Aberdeen around the first of July. "Wonder if there is any special attraction here," Baum queried, "to induce him to abandon cowhide boot and cowboy chapeau for the loneliness of a city life?" Mrs. Bilkins may have let the secret out on 15 February 1890, for apparently his lady love's initials were L. J.

Jewett, Harvey: Harvey C. Jewett and his brother Charles A. came from Ohio to Aberdeen in 1883 to start a retail grocery store called the Red Front. An active Mason, Harvey participated in the organization of Aberdeen's first Masonic lodge at the grocery store that same year. As the Red Front prospered, the brothers launched a far more profitable wholesale grocery and drug business, the first in Dakota Territory. Jewett Brothers representatives such as Charles H. Dill traveled throughout the area, selling and delivering goods to small-town grocers and druggists. For a community on the edge of the frontier, the Jewetts had an impressive business that could well afford to contribute to worthy causes. In March 1887, for instance, the brothers "received thirty carloads of goods in twenty days, including 1,300 barrels of salt and three hundred barrels of oil." In May and June 1888 the concern took delivery of "three carloads of oranges from California, two carloads of lemons from New York, and a carload of tea" (*Brown County History*, p. 290). Within a few years two more brothers came west, and in May 1890 Jewett Brothers opened its first branch business in Sioux Falls, South Dakota, to facilitate distribution of goods in Iowa and Minnesota. Not surprisingly, Harvey became vice-president of the Aberdeen Club on 10 March 1890. (Baum's 10 May column made reference to Aberdeen's new chief of police, the unrelated and relatively unknown John Jewett.) In June the Jewett Brothers' grocery stock sustained considerable damage when the cellars flooded after a cloudburst dropped 3½ inches of rain. In October, as other businesses went bankrupt or relocated, rumors circulated that the company had been offered incentives to move to West Superior, Wisconsin. On 19 October, Harvey Jewett granted an interview to the *Aberdeen Daily News* to allay fears. "Our collections have never been better," he told the reporter, "while our business shows an increase over last year's." Admitting that its business methods were more conservative and harsher than usual, Jewett nevertheless affirmed that the wholesale company had put its money into Aberdeen "with firm confidence in the ultimate prosperity of the country." He echoed Baum's own counsel, noting that South Dakota is on "the eve of the greatest development, . . . and it would be extremely poor business policy to lay down at this time" (*ADN* 19 October 1890). Long after Baum had left, Jewett and his descendants remained successful in Aberdeen.

Jim. See Jim river valley

Jimicrat central c'mittee: Innkeeper James Ringrose's leadership position in the local

Democratic Party led Baum to call it the "Jimicrat party." When the Democrats held city caucuses during the week before the 26 July 1890 "Our Landlady" column appeared, the fourth ward failed to draw a crowd at the appointed place. Those present had then "started in quest of some of the heavier weights of the party, finally bringing up in the parlor of the Sherman house," Ringrose's establishment (*ADN* 20 July 1890). There they elected Ringrose delegate to the county convention that would select the new central committee. Neither Ringrose nor C. Boyd Barrett, a delegate from Aberdeen's second ward, secured a position on this body or on the party slate. Smarting from his personal disappointments, Barrett objected strenuously to the nomination of Charles N. Harris for state representative, refusing to print the county ticket in his Democratic newspaper. The Republican *Aberdeen Daily News* reminded readers that Harris had knocked Barrett unconscious in a fist-fight in front of the Sherman House a few years earlier. The event had "endeared Mr. Harris to the county democracy, but has not made him particularly solid with the Virginia majah." Nevertheless, the *News* concluded, Barrett "has been 'sustained' so often . . . that he will doubtless get this dose down with nothing more than a very wry face" (*ADN* 22 July 1890).

Jim river valley: Familiarly known as the Jim, the James River is the main watercourse of eastern South Dakota. Flowing from north to south through rolling prairie, the river's broad valley offered shade trees and firewood to early plains dwellers. Residents of Columbia lived on the banks of the Jim; Aberdeen residents traveled about ten miles east to reach its shores for picnics or boating parties. By August 1890 the dry weather had begun to tell "on the noble Jim river," the *Aberdeen Evening Republican* reported (28 July 1890), causing it to "dwindle" to a dry bed below Aberdeen. In January 1891 even promoters realized that residents of the much-boosted James River Valley would have to rely on artesian-well irrigation to keep farmlands green during dry years.

Jinkens, George. See Jenkins, Georgie

John: John O'Daniel owned a barbershop on Aberdeen's Main Street. When he and businessman William H. Paulhamus raced their colts on 7 August 1890, Mrs. Bilkins records (9 August 1890) that O'Daniel's won with the best time of 2:58.

Johnsing, Miss: In creating this fictional persona, Baum had doubtless noticed that a large number of Aberdeen's domestic servants bore the surname Johnson. Anna, Annie, Charlotte, Julia, Louisa, and Maggie Johnson all worked in the homes or boardinghouses of Aberdeen.

Jones; Joneses, Miss: The Aberdeen city directory lists twelve Joneses in Aberdeen in 1890, two of them women: Maggie Jones was a domestic in the Charles Wright home, and Mary Jones was a widow who boarded with one of the other Jones families. Numerous Jones daughters probably also existed but were not listed. In his 8 March column Baum may have had a real "Miss Jones" in mind, but he often used the name generically. On 12 April, for example, he wrote, "many a Jones of Jonesville has made his town a thriving community and a familiar name to the world because Jones lived there." The men mentioned in the March column are real, suggesting that Miss Jones is also, but Baum often employed more caution in naming women, and a number of the female characters throughout the columns are either fictional or carefully disguised — especially when they are "friends" of Mrs. Bilkins's or involved in romantic misadventures. The cross-eyed Miss Jones of the 15 November column, for example, is definitely a product of Baum's imagination.

Jump; Jumper: Samuel H. Jumper, the founding father of Aberdeen, had handled the original townsite for the Milwaukee Road, which platted the town in January 1881, and became the first white man to sleep on the site. Displaying typical western entrepreneurship, Jumper immediately set up a mercantile in a tent with fellow pioneer C. A. Bliss. A native of Maine, Jumper had moved first to Minneapolis and then to Aberdeen in search of the better opportunities he soon found in the West. In 1882 he sold his mercantile interests and launched his own banking business, the Farmers and Merchants' Bank (later the First National Bank). In 1886 he organized the first electric light company in town, using a dynamo run by the pressure from an artesian well. In 1888 he became president and founding father of the Building and Loan Association of Dakota and, a year later, brigadier general of the Dakota National Guard. A Civil War veteran of the Maine Infantry, he used the honorary title of colonel. In 1892 a local promotional publication claimed that Jumper was "one of the best known men in the West" (*A&BC*). The fact that so prominent and prosperous a person was among those looking at opportunities in Tennessee in 1890 is a good measure of how depressed the business climate had become in South Dakota. Although he bought three lots in Harriman, however, Jumper stayed put through the hard times, becoming mayor of Aberdeen in 1894. During the election of 1890 he served as chairman of the Brown County Republican Central Committee, a position that brought some unwanted attention from the Independent press.

Keely motor: John W. Keely, a Philadelphian, claimed to have discovered the power of music and invented a sound-wave motor. His methods and many failures "combined to engender distrust and even arouse ridicule." All the same, his mysterious apparatus worked well enough to convince the *Pittsburgh Bulletin* in May 1890 that "a single muscial note can, through Keely's discovery, cause a brass cup full of nails to float in water" (reprinted in *ADN* 10 May 1890).

Kennedy: Samuel A. Kennedy, lawyer and farmer, received the nomination for district attorney "by acclamation" at the 1890 Brown County Republican convention (*ADN* 16 July 1890). As he was already both a member of the South Dakota House of Representatives and a Brown County commissioner, the Democrats charged that he was "pretty well loaded" (*AER* 16 July 1890). Official election results awarded him the victory over his Independent opponent, Simeon Cranmer, by twenty-three votes, but Cranmer contested the election, and a judge determined in his favor in mid-January. Kennedy, meanwhile, had been issued an election certificate and had assumed the job on 5 January. When Cranmer attempted to take office, the Board of County Commissioners, apparently preferring their old comrade, failed to approve Cranmer's bonds. Cranmer charged the board and his own lawyer, Edward Taubman, with conspiring to keep him out of office. Baum's little joke (31 January 1891) that the issue would still be unresolved in 1895 was a sly comment on the case but not particularly prophetic, for Cranmer did ultimately take office in 1891. Kennedy practiced law privately for two years before winning a term in the South Dakota Senate in 1892.

Kid; Kidd, Billy: William E. Kidd, nicknamed "Billy the Kid," came from Michigan to Dakota Territory in 1881, homesteading at Rondell on the southern edge of Brown County. As the drought and depression set in, financial circumstances brought him to Aberdeen in a vain effort to keep his farm (which he would lose to a mortgage company by 1894). In December 1889 he took a job as local reporter at the *Aberdeen Evening Republican*. C. Boyd Barrett boasted that his new employee had twelve years of experience in Democratic journalism in Michigan, but the *Daily News* was less complimentary: "In the malaria beds and cat tail swamps that skirt the Jim river in the vicinity of Rondell there sprung up a journalistic mushroom called 'Billy the Kid' which has been transplanted in the Virginia bogs at the Reprint office, where grow those bright and evening blooming flowers 'our,' 'we,' 'scoop' and 'rustler'" (*ADN* 18 January 1890). If Barrett was a fulminating Democrat, Kidd soon outstripped him, becoming a vociferous supporter of radical causes. He took over the *Republican* in the fall of 1890, changed its Democratic emphasis to Populist, and informed fellow editors that the paper's "opinions will be sufficiently outspoken to penetrate the dullest understanding." Putting the Populist ticket at the head of the editorial column, his first edition instructed voters to "turn the rascals out" (*AER* 7 October 1890). From the beginning of the movement, Kidd served on the Brown County Independent Central Committee, and he ultimately headed the state Populist Party committee. A contemporary remembered him as "a radical of radicals, slow and somewhat reticent in his talk, but a brilliant writer, [who] sure could spread hot stuff on his front page. He was not thought so well of around town, but those who knew him, liked him and had a great deal of respect for him" (Allen, "Memories," 16 November 1939). Baum referred to him on 11 October 1890 as a "mild, harmless, and unassuming man" but changed his mind as the election approached and Kidd's rhetoric blistered the thin skin of local Republicans.

Crowing that the Independent editor had "come to a bad end" when Kidd was arrested for criminal libel in January 1891, Baum added that the libel suit would make Kidd's fortune if he were to go on stage, but "as it is it will probably only make him trouble" (*ASP* 17 January 1891). Baum guessed that much correctly, for the following month Kidd faced a second libel charge, this one brought by Edward Taubman. Launched with such fireworks, Kidd's political career eventually led him to the state legislature (1897–98), where he shepherded the initiative and referendum bill through the legislative process. His obituary summed up his reputation: "He advocated a system of social justice so severe that he often made enemies among the beneficiaries of commercialism. But no political enemy ever doubted his sincerity or his honesty" (*Dakota Ruralist*, 1 May 1902).

Kile, Fred: Fred C. Kile began his journalistic career as local editor at the Daily News Company, but in 1889 he moved to Warner, the next stop south on the Chicago, Milwaukee & St. Paul Railroad, and took over the *Warner Sun*. Shortly before Baum wrote his 15 February 1890 column, a number of young Warner men came up to Aberdeen for a night on the town, during which one of them landed in jail for carousing. When Herbert L. Sill, city editor of the *Aberdeen Daily News*, reported the whole sordid incident, Fred Kile objected in the pages of the *Warner Sun*, making a "roar" about Sill's "freshness." The Aberdeen press in turn chided Kile. "The misguided youth who runs the [*Warner Sun*]," said the *News* on 31 January 1890, "must learn that when his chums come to Aberdeen, get drunk and are placed in jail, the *News* will give the news and no resident of Warner is slurred thereby." C. Boyd Barrett of the *Evening Republican*, however, sent Kile a letter urging him to "Give Sill h — . I'll stand by you" (quoted in *ADN* 4 February 1890).

Kimberly, George: George B. Kimberly's society wedding to Eva Finch on 22 October 1890 brought out Aberdeen's finest. A member of the group of people who had immigrated from the Syracuse and Fayetteville areas of New York state over a nine-year period, Kimberly had arrived in Aberdeen only a few weeks after Baum in the fall of 1888. For a time he had boarded with the Baums and worked at Baum's Bazaar, but in 1890 he shared rooms with Gena Jewell and worked at various hardware stores, where he designed store windows or spent time "on the road." At year's end he married Eva Finch and settled into a position at the Fair.

King Stanley. See Stanley, King, o' Africa

Komishner of emigrants. See Hagerty, Frank

Kuehnle's Injun clubs: In January 1891 a German-born cigar manufacturer named Martin Kuehnle had "a novel and exceedingly attractive show window" on Aberdeen's Main Street. A "big Indian sentinel (on wheels)" welcomed customers outside the store, and a window display of American Indian weapons and a miniature buckskin tipi drew the curious inside (*ADN* 18 January 1890). Claiming that a scout and an Indian policeman had sold him the "war clubs trimmed with feathers and hair," Kuehnle advertised that they had been "picked up on the battle ground of Wounded Knee" (*ADN* 9 January 1891). Such merchandizing showmanship would have appealed to Baum, as would the business acumen Kuehnle showed in naming his locally produced cigars. His five-centers bore names like "Rough and Ready" and "Good Stock," but his ten-centers were called "Dakota O.K." and "Aberdeen Club."

Lacey's: Seth C. Lacey's graduate degree from the University of Michigan allowed him and his son Clarence to specialize in "physicians's prescriptions" in addition to patent medicines. Their drugstore featured a large soda fountain, which added "to the attractive appearance of the store as well as to the wealth of the firm" (GSB pp. 104–5).

Leavitt, Mr.: Mrs. Bilkins's 20 December joke revolves around the fact that Horace W. Leavitt owned the Friesland Dairy in Aberdeen, but Skip Salisbury, bookstore owner, had been advertising 1891 diaries. Leavitt sold his dairy in January and moved to West Superior to start another.

Lewis, Street Comiss'ner; Street-comish: On 14 May 1890 the newly elected city government hired Thomas E. Lewis, an Aberdeen carpenter, as street commissioner at a salary of fifty dollars a month. The day before Baum's 17 May column, Lewis placed this advertisement in the *Aberdeen Daily News:* "Notice is hereby given to all persons having rubbish on their premises to remove the same without delay." At the end of September the city council, in a cost-cutting measure, voted to dispense with Lewis's services. Although Mrs. Bilkins's gossip (11 October 1890) suggested that Charles ("our Cholly") Howard had objected to the dismissal, the official council minutes showed that Howard voted for discharge with the majority.

Loucks: Henry Langford Loucks, born in Ottawa, Canada, in 1846, homesteaded in Deuel County in southern Dakota Territory in 1883 and within three years had become president of the territorial Farmers' Alliance. He began 1890 as a Republican and president of the South Dakota Farmers' Alliance but emerged from the Independent convention in July as the new party's candidate for governor. His third-party candidacy and radical rhetoric soon rattled the Republicans. "Instead of 5,000,000 black slaves," he proclaimed in June, "we have 8,000,000 black and 50,000,000 white slaves to free; slavery more humiliating in that having the power to free ourselves we have not used it" (quoted in *ADN* 17 June 1890). He called for monetary reform, the regulation of railroads, and the processing of agricultural products within the regions in which they originated. On 23 July he spoke on the national banking system and the subtreasury plan at the Aberdeen Opera House. The next day the *News* called the candidate a man of "o'ertowering egotism." Baum found him "earnest, brave and enthusiastic" with "a sort of magnetism about him which attracts his farmer friends," but he accused the Independent of loading his remarks "with misstatements, with wilfully or ignorantly preverted [sic] statistics, with misleading and absurd arguments, well knowing that his enemies are too indifferent to arise in a public meeting and dispute him, and that his friends are not well enough posted to know that he is deceiving them" (ASP 26 July 1890). Throughout September and October the Republican press continually charged Loucks with demagoguery, among other things, and questioned his status as a United States citizen. As Baum predicted, Loucks lost the election that fall, but his monetary arguments and third-party activity had just begun. In December he addressed the National Farmers' Alliance and Industrial Union (the Southern Alliance) in Ocala, Florida, admonishing delegates for having "followed the plough with eyes wide open and the political bosses with eyes tight shut" (quoted in Chamberlin, *Farmers' Alliance*, p. 35). In 1891 he became president of the Southern Alliance, and in 1892 he served as permanent chairman of the People's Party convention in Omaha, Nebraska. A year later he began writing a series of monetary reform treatises, starting with *Government Ownership of Railroads and Telegraph* (1893). Not until 1898 did Loucks return to the Republican fold, with the avowed purpose of pushing through the South Dakota initiative and referendum bill from within the old party ranks.

Lowe, Ed.: Edward W. Lowe, Aberdeen lawyer and real estate agent, was deputy county treasurer and secretary of the county Republican committee. He could have been an amateur poet as well, but the 7 June 1890 column more likely refers to Edward Clarke Lowe, an English cleric, who had published *Young Englishman's First Poetry Book*. Baum may have alluded to the cleric again in his 8 November column but probably not exclusively, for the local man had recently proved quite learned about the ins and outs of elections. As the Republicans attempted to assess their defeat, they frequently asked themselves, "What did it?" Poor crops, hard times, ring rule, and so on were answers proffered in the *Aberdeen Daily News*, but Ed Lowe hit the nail on the head: "It was votes, gentlemen, votes!" (quoted in *ADN* 7 November 1890). Lowe's secretaryship of the Republican county central committee, which boasted a $3,000 campaign fund, was at issue in the 27 December column, and his continued participation in the inner circle of Brown County Republican politics received comment on 31 January 1891. Here Baum proved to be a poor prophet, however, for less than a week later Lowe announced that he would be moving his family to Chicago, leaving Aberdeen and its political rings behind.

Luke an' Merten: William F. Luke and Gustav E. Merten billed their Economy Store as a "dry goods emporium." Established in 1889, it quickly grew to serve a large trade area for hundreds of miles around Aberdeen: "The Economy reaches out into jobbing circles, and its wholesale business has reached no small proportions" (*A&BC*). In January 1891 Luke told the *Aberdeen Daily News* that the store's 1890 receipts had been at least $6,000 more than those of 1889. "Times are close," the owner reported, "but the Economy Store gets there just the same and is not a whit disturbed about the future" (*ADN* 3 January 1891). Taking such confidence at face value, Baum projected (31 January 1891) Luke and Merten's success five years in the future.

McBride, Elder; Rev.: Joseph M. McBride, an Episcopal minister in Dakota Territory since 1876, had been rector of Maud Baum's church, Saint Mark's Episcopal, from 1886 to May 1889, when he became "the Episcopal missionary for South Dakota" (*ASP* 1 March 1890). The Baum and McBride families were active in many church social functions, especially the elaborate operettas put on in the spring and summer of 1890. The two men also shared the church hierarchy's disapproval of the new prohibition legislation but had differing views on other issues. Having once been pastor of an Episcopal church in Pierre, McBride supported that city over Huron, Baum's choice for state capital. The minister also followed Bishop William H. Hare's lead in disapproving of suffrage for women. Just after the November 1890 election the *Aberdeen Daily News* gossiped that "a certain Aberdeen divine" who was opposed to woman suffrage had "made a slight mistake and cast a ballot for the proposition" (*ADN* 5 November 1890). Mrs. Bilkins revealed the clergyman's identity, also recalling that McBride's wife had publicly expressed her views on the issue. "The influence of the wife," Mrs. McBride had declared in March, "is, in my opinion, greater without the ballot." She thought that unmarried women should probably be allowed to vote, however, and concluded, "It seems to me that an easy way to settle the matter would be to submit the question to the women of South Dakota to decide for themselves" (*ADN* 27 March 1890).

McCormick: Two McCormicks lived in Aberdeen at this time, both named John. One gave his occupation as teamster; the other was probably retired but dabbling in one of the many banking or real estate and loan businesses. "McCormick's note" (3 May 1890), however, probably refers to a loan agreement on agricultural equipment manufactured by the Cyrus Hall McCormick company. In this scenario, Miller would be a clerk for one of the eleven agricultural implement dealers located in Aberdeen. In a 28 June article about a local dealer's new steel binder, Baum remarked, "This superior and perfect machine bears the magic name of 'McCormick.'"

McDonald, Miss: Maggie and Bessie McDonald from Oshkosh, Wisconsin, were Aberdeen's premier milliners. Affable and genial, the sisters carried a stock "embracing all of the latest styles in pattern hats, bonnets, frames, plumes, tips, ribbons, laces, velvets, jets, flowers, etc." (GSB pp. 104–5). Each year, Bessie McDonald went east "to procure additional Spring novelties" (*ASP* 15 March 1890) to meet the needs of customers like Mrs. Bilkins. In a lengthy report on Aberdeen's show windows in May, Baum reported that the McDonald sisters displayed "against a background of heavy lace curtains . . . all the latest ideas of Dame Fashion in head gear. . . . and even the male mind, naturally obtuse upon such matters, is forced to marvel at the beauty of the display" (*ASP* 17 May 1890).

McGinty, Dan: The hero of the famous vaudeville song "Down Went McGinty" (written by Joseph Flynn), Dan McGinty represents the "sturdy tradition that all Irishmen are both naive and pugnacious" (Spaeth, *Read 'Em and Weep*, pp. 151–52). The song became a part of the popular culture of the 1890s, with references to it appearing frequently in the newspapers. For instance, on 24 January 1890 the *Sioux Falls Daily Argus-Leader*, under the headline "Nearly Joined M'Ginty," reported that Nellie Bly had "a Miraculous Escape from Going to the Bottom of a Ravine." On 27 January the follow-up story noted that Bly had made it home all right, but "up to noon today McGinty had not been heard from." Baum himself, after mining the song to produce Mrs. Bilkins's feckless boarder, also subjected his 1 February 1890 readers to several puns on the name before penning his own verse: "Then oh for a lodge in some sweet spot / By wildest confines blest, / Where aimless wit can be forgot / Ane McGinty gets a rest!"

McGlachlin, Dight.: Dighton ("Mack") McGlachlin, superintendent of the Bagley and Cargill Elevator Company, attended the 3 March 1890 seed wheat convention in Huron as a Brown County delegate. Born in New York, McGlachlin had emigrated to Iowa as a boy. In 1885, he came to Aberdeen and supervised the construction and operation of the Bagley and Cargill elevators throughout Dakota. Because he "attended to the distribution of about a million dollars each year which was paid out for grain" (GSB p. 30), McGlachlin was in an excellent position to know how much seed and feed South Dakota elevators contained in the spring of 1890. As an elevator man, he also graded grain and docked farmers a set fee per bushel for impurities. A respected member of the Aberdeen business community, he would become mayor in 1896.

Mack. See McGlachlin, Dight.

McKinley: In the fall of 1890 the Independents and many others strongly objected to the McKinley Tariff — sponsored by Republican Congressman William McKinley of Ohio — which raised the duty on some products to an all-time high. Baum, however, endorsed the new law. Believing "in protection as a principle," he asserted that the tariff "can scarcely fail to prove beneficial to the entire county" (*ASP* 15 February and 24 May 1890). In August he observed that although the English protested the "protective feature of our tariff," we have "been able to exist despite their disapprobation" in the past and would do so again (*ASP*

23 August 1890). After the election, even though various Republican defeats —
including McKinley's — were being attributed to the unpopularity of the tariff,
Baum still contended that the law had been framed "in the [interests] of no one
class or industry," appeared "to be just to the majority," and would "eventually
prove advantageous to the country, when it has been thoroughly tested" (*ASP*
8 November 1890). In 1896, when McKinley was running for president on a
platform that promised high tariffs and adherence to the gold standard, Baum
penned a poem in support: "The magic word 'Protection' / Will banish all
dejection / And free the workingman from every care; / . . . [When] McKinley's
in the chair!" (*Chicago Times-Herald* 12 July 1896).

McWilliam's. See Fair man, the

Majah. See Barrett, B. S. (Buzz-saw), Majah or Major

Marple, Harry: Henry M. Marple came to Aberdeen in 1883 and, with Frank Hagerty,
created the banking firm of Hagerty and Marple. In the summer of 1888 Marple
"retired for the purpose of organizing a third national bank" (*ADN* 15 January
1890), but one private and two national banks were already in operation in
Aberdeen. Hence, Marple's new venture, the Northwestern National Bank,
would go out of business in 1892, a victim of the worsening economic climate.
A difference of opinion among board members had led Marple to resign as
president in early 1890, however, with Ira Barnes replacing him. Marple left
Aberdeen in the fall but in the meantime enjoyed the city's many social events,
securing a progessive euchre partner at the 28 January 1890 social. In 1889 he
had been manager, while L. Frank Baum was secretary, of the Aberdeen Baseball
Association. Marple had also been Baum's banker, foreclosing on Baum's Bazaar
at the beginning of 1890.

Masons: The Free and Accepted Masons (26 July 1890), the oldest fraternal group in
the world, supported eleven lodges in Aberdeen in the 1890s, their membership being "the most representative group of the city's citizens" (GSB p. 200).
Masons participated in secret rituals through the various degrees of either the
Scottish Rite or the York Rite, both of which required numerous initiations and
conferrings of rites. *See also* Jewett, Harvey

Mazeppy: The story of Ivan Stepanovich Mazeppa, c. 1640–1709, has been popularized
in Byron's long poem *Mazeppa*. Originally a page in the Polish court, Byron's
hero dallied with his ruler's wife. As punishment, he was bound "with many a
thong" to the back of a wild horse. The horse was let loose to run wild, and
its unwilling passenger watched as "the skies spun like a mighty wheel." The
Cossacks rescued the young Mazeppa, and he eventually became their ruler.

Mellette: Indiana native Arthur Calvin Mellette served as the last governor of Dakota
Territory and the first governor of South Dakota. A lawyer, Civil War veteran,
and author, Mellette came to Dakota in 1878 as register of the Springfield land

office. Two years later he moved to Watertown, where he met John Drake. President Benjamin Harrison, a fellow Indianan, appointed him governor of the territory in 1889, and in October of that year South Dakota voters elected him to a one-year term as governor and named Pierre temporary capital. In November 1890 Mellette won a second, two-year term but only after a difficult year. In January and February, as drought and privation began to take their toll in the state, the governor had visited homesteaders by horse and buggy and had then gone from town to town to solicit funds and seed for relief of the destitute. He also went to Minneapolis–Saint Paul and Chicago on what his enemies called a "begging expedition." In a political year, opponents accused him of appropriating the donated money for his own use and of wrecking the credit of the state. "The trouble actually at the basis of such accusations," an observer noted later, "was that 'boomers' could sell little or no land and the state was injured for business speculation for a period of years" (Cleworth, "Twenty Years," p. 62). Others lauded his efforts. Editor Baum, who enthusiastically supported the governor's bid for reelection, pointed out that Mellette had personally contributed some $2,000 to the cause. "South Dakota," Baum prophesied, "will revere the memory of their first Governor when his maligners are long forgotten" (*ASP* 26 April 1890).

Miles, General: Major General Nelson A. Miles commanded the Military Division of the Missouri, with headquarters in Chicago. A veteran of the Civil War and Indian wars, Miles hoped to bring a diplomatic solution to the volatile situation in South Dakota in 1890. Nevertheless, the general could be "an imperious potentate with his subordinates," and his private arrangements with Buffalo Bill left the commanding officer at Fort Yates in a difficult position (Utley, *The Lance and the Shield*, p. 293). When the Seventh Cavalry attempted to disarm Big Foot's band of Miniconjou Sioux at Wounded Knee Creek on 29 December and took heavy casualties themselves before chasing down and killing Lakota men, women, and children, Baum blamed General Miles for being "weak and vacillating." The result, he said, was "a terrible loss of blood to our soldiers, and a battle which, at its best, is a disgrace to the war department" (*ASP* 3 January 1891). Historians, however, credit Miles with saving the situation on the Pine Ridge reservation, in the aftermath of this catastrophe, by calming tensions and preventing a full-scale war.

Miller: In 1890 as now, Miller was a common name. At least ten people with that surname lived in Aberdeen while Baum did, and the author could have been referring (3 May 1890) to any one of them. *See also* McCormick

Milligan: Albert F. Milligan, general agent of the Saint Paul Fire and Marine Insurance Company, was "popular in society and among acquaintances" (*ADN* 25 January 1891). In January 1891 the depressed business climate of Aberdeen drove him to emigrate temporarily to Texas, but he returned later to become a successful Aberdeen businessman.

Mitchell: Situated about 150 miles south of Aberdeen, Mitchell greeted passengers on the Chicago, Milwaukee & Saint Paul Railroad's east-west route. Named after Alexander Mitchell, president of the railroad, the town had a population of 2,217 in 1890, when both the Republicans and the suffragists held state conventions there in August (30 August 1890).

"Mollie an' the baby": According to an early Aberdeen bandsman, "For Molly and Baby" (3 May 1890) was a popular song of the 1890s that featured a "rapid-fire" drum beat (Allen, "Memories," 12 November 1939). The South Dakota Equal Suffrage Association also attested to its popularity by adapting the tune for its suffrage song "Women and the Ballot," which it published in *South Dakota Equal Suffrage Song Book* in 1890.

Moody, Bob, Mayor: Emigrating from Milwaukee, Wisconsin, in 1882 at age twenty-one, Robert Moody began his career as a humble bookkeeper for the Brown County Bank, which was later reorganized as the Aberdeen National Bank. Working his way up to cashier, he was elected president early in 1890. Baum called him "a remarkable example of western enterprise and energy" (*ASP* 12 April 1890), and his fellow townspeople apparently agreed, electing him mayor at age twenty-nine. In May 1890 his city appointments caused some consternation around town, especially his nomination of Knights of Labor assemblyman John Jewett as chief of police. In political dealing before the election the Republicans had promised the Knights the office of city assessor; afterward, the Republican bankers apparently found this promise unacceptable, and the office of chief of police, the highest paying of the city slots, was offered instead. This appointment also met with resistance, but Alderman Charles Howard pushed it through. C. Boyd Barrett noted that the council had been "handicapped" in its efforts to appoint Jewett "by the fact that there are not enough offices to fill half the promises . . . made before election" (*AER* 6 May 1890). Baum consistently supported the mayor, though regretting that "Mayor Moody seems more inclined to listen to counsel than to stand on his own footing" (*ASP* 10 May 1890), a trait for which he criticized him again in his 23 August "Our Landlady" column.

Moody, Gid.: In the first session of the South Dakota legislature, the Republican-dominated senate elected Republicans Richard Pettigrew and Gideon C. Moody — a former justice of the territorial supreme court and then lawyer for Homestake Mining Company — as the state's first United States senators. Moody, who had drawn the short term that would set up the staggered senate terms for the new state, expected no trouble in getting reelected a year later. The Independent victory in the 1890 election, however, meant that in 1891 Republicans in the state senate would have only a one-person majority over the combined Independents and Democrats. Reflected in Baum's 6 December 1890 column is the speculation, already rife by then, that the legislature would pass over Moody to choose an Independent, which it ultimately did, electing Aberdonian James Kyle. Not an enthusiastic Moody supporter, Baum oozed sarcasm in January 1891: "If he has not set the Potomac on fire, it is because he does not carry matches — not that he isn't able" (*ASP* 17 January 1891).

Mutz, Ed.: W. Edward Mutz clerked at the Red Front Grocery Company and regularly attended the Young Ladies Guild socials. He "secured a prize" at the auction and dance that kicked off the guild's 1890 socials and, the following week, purchased a partner on a string at the progressive euchre party at Gilmor's. In the leaner times of January 1891, he remained cautiously optimistic about Aberdeen's business climate, telling a reporter that Red Front sales in the past year had been gratifying. "Our business has been safe and conservative," he said, "and we are well satisfied with the results" (quoted in *ADN* 3 January 1891). This comment must have sounded like a politician's response to Baum, who promoted Mutz from lowly clerk to congressman in his Aberdeen of 1895.

Narre; Narregang; Narregang's: Spencer W. Narregang, the prosperous farmer and businessman who appears regularly in Baum's columns, was in fact Baum's landlord, being part owner of the brick Excelsior Block where the *Aberdeen Saturday Pioneer* was published. Narregang represented the successful and committed Dakota pioneer. He had homesteaded near Westport, Dakota Territory, in 1882 and moved eight miles south to Aberdeen a year later. Retaining his land, he increased it to three thousand acres. In addition, he owned and operated a mortgage and loan company, a jewelry store, and the Aberdeen Pharmacy. "While not a practical druggist," the *Aberdeen Daily News* reported, Narregang "says he is able to distinguish a quart of spirits frumenti from a box of Ayer's pills." Captain C. R. Hall, a pharmacist, managed the store's prescription department, making "a strong team as Capt. Hall is a fine salesman and Narregang is a royal entertainer" (*ADN* 21 January 1890). In May 1890, Narregang, who had built the Excelsior Block in 1887, took over a suite of "new, luxurious offices," becoming Baum's neighbor and probably his supplier of cigars as well (*ASP* 3 May 1890). With some glee, Baum announced in July that Narregang had imported a huge supply of cigars from Key West, Forida, and was selling them for five cents apiece as a loss leader. These cigars were actually factory rejects, or what the industry called "cripples," but as Narregang said, "What's in a name?" On 6 November both Mr. and Mrs. L. Frank Baum and Mr. and Mrs. Spencer W. Narregang attended the "phantom party" hosted by the Jewetts. Throughout the drought years Narregang stayed in South Dakota, experimenting with crops and trying to attract sugar beet and flax factories to the Aberdeen area. He and Louis Crofoot established the Dakota Irrigation Company in October

1890, sinking wells on their farms and renting rigs to other farmers. When Narregang announced in January 1891 that he had been corresponding with the American Fibre Association about a flax-processing plant that might soon locate in Aberdeen, the *News* responded, "It is refreshing in these days of business depression and political inflation to run across a citizen whose energies have suffered no relaxation and whose best endeavors are being exerted to build up and re-construct, even if tangible results are not as yet at hand" (*ADN* 23 January 1891). Baum agreed, speculating in his 31 January 1891 column that Narregang would be among the prominent Aberdonians of 1895. Though Narregang did remain in Aberdeen, prosperity would prove more elusive. "I spent $50,000 in the development of Irrigation and Sugar Beets," he said years later, "but nothing ever came from it but Experience" (quoted in Cleworth, "Twenty Years," p. 100).

News. See Daily Anythin'

Nolan, Tom: Born in Illinois in 1858, Thomas J. Nolan came to Aberdeen in the winter of 1881. In 1890 he represented the J. I. Case Threshing Machine Company, selling separators and engines throughout the northeast corner of South Dakota.

Oleson, Mrs.: The doctor's patient of 8 November 1890 was probably fictional, but the name recognized the fact that Scandinavians had settled heavily in Brown County. The 1889–90 city directory listed one Oleson (probably a single man), twenty-two Olsens, and six Olsons.

Olwin, Harry: Grocery owner Anthony Harry Olwin, an Ohio native, bought the Red Front Grocery Company from the Jewett Brothers in 1887. He and partner Walter P. Butler also started a modest wholesale distributorship in fancy groceries — coffee, olives, and pickles, among other things. On 1 March 1890 Olwin inaugurated a "Cash System" that allowed him to reduce costs so that cash exceeded credit sales, he reported to Baum in April. Baum's column tweaked the grocer for overpricing and overreacting to the prohibition law, but his methods apparently worked. Olwin remained a successful Aberdeen businessman throughout the depression and long after the more prodigal Baum had left two failed enterprises behind.

Oshkosh: Like many Aberdonians, Mrs. Bilkins seemed to have a brother or cousin in each new boomtown that beckoned settlers and money from Aberdeen. West Superior and Oshkosh, Wisconsin, were the latest to entice the drought-weary inhabitants of Dakota away from their old allegiances. *See also* West Superior

P.G.s: The Presbyterian Gleaners, or P.G.s as the press called them, sold homemade ice cream to onlookers at Aberdeen's Independence Day activities. This young ladies' society of the Presbyterian church rented an old store building where, Baum reported, "daintily attired maidens served the delicious compound with sweet smiles and kisses and cake thrown in, to the tired and famished who dropped in upon them" (*ASP* 5 July 1890).

Pabst: On 1 August 1890 the *Aberdeen Daily News* announced, "Gus Pabst, the barber, has left the city." On 2 August Baum's landlady gave the details.

Paulhamus, Billy: William H. Paulhamus, a Pennsylvania native, served as vice-president of Hagerty & Company, Bankers. Like senior partner Frank Hagerty, Paulhamus had come west as a young man, getting a job as office boy in the bank and working his way up to cashier and junior partner. Baum commented on his prosperity and his interest in politics on several occasions, beginning with the 15 February 1890 column. In early April 1890 Paulhamus toured the South to assess its investment potential but returned to boost Aberdeen instead. For him and other Aberdonians, horse racing and practical jokes (9 August 1890) provided welcome distractions in the slow business climate of 1890. After announcement of the Hagerty bank closing in October 1890, Paulhamus moved on to take a position as cashier in a Sumner, Washington, bank.

Paulhamus, Jay: On 16 September 1890, Jay A. Paulhamus, secretary and treasurer of the Keystone Mortgage Company, returned from an extended business trip to the Pacific Coast in the company, the newspapers reported, of Miss Robie Hagerty. Mrs. Bilkins's allusions to the businessman's "last diamond ring" (20 September) may refer to an engagement in progress.

Peepo: A young bachelor, Fred Peepo worked at the Red Front Grocery and frequented the numerous social events in the winter of 1890. Baum reported on 1 February that "Mrs. F. B. Hoit and F. W. Peepo received the booby prizes without a blush" at the 28 January progressive euchre party.

Pettigrew: In 1890 Republican Richard F. Pettigrew of Sioux Falls, South Dakota, held the reigns of power in the state Republican Party — and the Aberdeen journalists chafed at his control. Baum referred to him as "the Sioux Falls Dictator" (*ASP* 22 February 1890), and Barrett called him "Boss Pettigrew, now known as the [Pennsylvania Senator Matthew S.] Quay of South Dakota" (*AER* 29 August 1890). Emigrating from Wisconsin in 1870 at age twenty-two, Pettigrew had established a real estate and law office at Sioux Falls before serving three terms in the territorial legislature. In 1880 he became territorial delegate to Congress, and in 1889 he won one of South Dakota's two new United States Senate seats. As the election of 1890 approached, Pettigrew was maneuvering to replace one of the state's two Republican congressmen — either John Pickler or Oscar Gifford — with his own man, John Gamble. In his first sally against the incumbents, Pettigrew eliminated outside contenders such as Aberdeen's Henry C. Sessions, whom he promised a position as either state bank examiner or railroad commissioner in exchange for early withdrawal from the race. He sweetened the pot with a promise of appointment for one of Sessions's friends, as well. To keep Brown County Republicans satisfied, the senator offered them the position of state auditor, but Sessions proved unable to control his disappointed delegation. Pettigrew's ploy worked: though Pickler proved too strong for such methods to sway his supporters, Gifford did not. Next, Pettigrew turned his attention to defeating the Independents that fall, recommending that Republicans consider the issue of free silver. In 1896 Senator Pettigrew became one of the organizers of the Silver Republican Party.

Pickeler, Mrs. Alice: From 1880 to 1910, Alice Alt Pickler, the wife of United States Congressman John A. Pickler, was the most prominent supporter of woman suffrage in South Dakota, a fact acknowledged in Baum's 8 March 1890 column. College educated in Iowa, Alice Pickler had moved with her husband to Faulkton, Dakota Territory, in 1879. In 1885 she became superintendent of the Franchise Department of the South Dakota Women's Christian Temperance Union, and early in 1890 she and her husband approached the National Woman Suffrage Association in Washington, D.C., seeking financial assistance for the 1890 South Dakota suffrage campaign. Their effort, and that of others, resulted in the creation of the Dakota Fund under the auspices of the new National-American Suffrage Association. Susan B. Anthony chaired the fund, and it was this pool of money, solicited from donors throughout the United States, that Marietta Bones accused Anthony of embezzling. Throughout the bitter South Dakota campaign, Pickler remained an Anthony supporter (and perhaps a Bilkins supporter, as well). She addressed the August 1890 South Dakota Republican convention, but it did little good, since of all the candidates only her husband endorsed suffrage. In 1900 she would become president of the state suffrage organization.

Pierre: Located almost exactly in the center of South Dakota, Pierre was selected as the temporary capital of the new state in a fall 1889 election. In 1890 the town represented both the seat of state government and the principal contender for permanent capital. Perched on the banks of the Missouri River about 150 miles southwest of Aberdeen, Pierre was an isolated place that Baum generously called "the metropolis of the Missouri," even though he declared it "perfect lunacy for us to locate our capital" there (*ASP* 21 June 1890). The voters decided in favor of that central location in the November 1890 general election. The $462,000 the city raised by selling city, school district, and county bonds that would take years to pay off did much to persuade voters that "peerless Pierre" deserved the prize. Through various means, from bribes of evil-smelling cigars during fair week to outright vote buying at the polls, Pierre boosters succeeded in purchasing the election, Baum implied. "The demoralizing influence of the capital canvass," the *News* concluded, "will leave its influence in politics for a long time to come" (*ADN* 8 November 1890). Baum went further, predicting that South Dakota "will repent in sack-cloth and ashes the deed that is now being so joyously celebrated" (*ASP* 8 November 1890).

Pinafore: Mrs. Bilkins is apparently familiar (26 July 1890) with the Gilbert and Sullivan operetta *H.M.S. Pinafore* and its choral dialogue: "What, never?" "No, never!" "What, *never*?" "Hardly ever!"

Pratt, Hiram: Hiram A. Pratt, a clerk at the First National Bank, sang baritone in a "Tragical Cantanta" given on 24 April 1890 under the auspices of the Guild of Saint Agnes (previously the Young Ladies Guild) of Saint Mark's Episcopal Church. Titled "The Insect and the Bird," the operetta consisted of solo and choral performances (Baum sang tenor), including this refrain: "The Grasshopper sat on a sweet potato vine, / And the big turkey gobbler he came up behind / And he gobbled him down off the sweet-potato vine" (*ASP* 26 April 1890). Pratt's occupation and voice seemed to bring out Baum's love of puns, for he noted that "the only bass thing about Hiram Pratt is his voice, but it only renders his other qualities trebly excellent" (*ASP* 8 February 1890). In his 9 August column Baum paired Pratt ("Hi") with Imogene ("Gene" or "Genie") Van Loon, a frequent soloist in Saint Mark's amateur operettas.

Puffball, Kernel. See Evans, Kernel

Pyramid an' Thisbee: In the 30 August 1890 column, Mrs. Bilkins refers to the Babylonian legend — retold in Ovid's *Metamorphoses* and spoofed in Shakespeare's *A Midsummer Night's Dream* — of Pyramus and Thisbe, whose parents opposed their courtship. Like Cholly and 'Stel, they communicated secretly and finally agreed to elope. The classical story, however, ended in tragic double deaths, whereas in the Aberdeen romance the young woman's friends restored communication between parents and daughter.

Randall, Ed.: Edward Randall supervised the Dakota Newspaper Union, a branch of the Northwestern Newspaper Union of Saint Paul, Minnesota. The guage (obsolete for gauge) pins mentioned in the column of 15 February 1890 would have been small but essential parts of the six new printing machines Randall purchased in January to form a complete stereotyping outfit. Randall, who was also treasurer of the Aberdeen Press Club, ran a business "second to none west of Chicago" and "equipped for turning out any work in the ready print line" (*ADN* 1 February 1890).

Raymond, Frank: On 18 October 1890, Frank W. Raymond was the Republican candidate for Brown County treasurer and John A. Fylpaa's major opponent. A Civil War veteran from Illinois, Raymond had been mayor of a Colorado boomtown before taking a position with the Saint Croix Lumber Company in Aberdeen in 1884. Baum considered him "eminently worthy the suffrage of our people," valuing his "keen intelligence and strong common-sense" as "qualities not to be despised" (*ASP* 9 August 1890). According to the Republican *Aberdeen Daily News*, the Independent *Aberdeen Appeal* had approached Raymond in late October with a derogatory story that it offered to suppress for "a money consideration." Raymond had refused to pay the fifteen dollars, the *News* claimed, and the *Appeal* had published its denunciation. Raymond swore an affidavit to the truth of his claim, as did John Adams, Samuel Jumper, and Thomas Camburn, who had also been approached (*ADN* 30 October 1890). Who was slinging mud at whom is a little unclear, but on 1 November Mrs. Bilkins found both groups guilty.

Redfield College: The Midland Association of Congregational Churches established this institution in 1887 to provide a Christian college for central Dakota and to further "the cause of liberal education in this new West" (*Redfield College*, p. 17). Located in Redfield, a town roughly forty miles straight south of Aberdeen, the four-year college charged ten dollars tuition in its classical, philosophical, or scientific departments, putting its education within the grasp of settlers.

Reprint, the: Baum first referred to his unfriendly rival newspaper, C. Boyd Barrett's *Aberdeen Evening Republican*, as "the Dessicated [*sic*] Reprint" on 29 March 1890. The nickname had originated, however, in the *Aberdeen Daily News*, which implied that the *Republican* used its shears "too freely" (*AER* 17 January 1890). Baum condemned the practice of borrowing items from other newspapers in an 8 March 1890 editorial on editors who "have made the press a stepping stone to their political schemes and lin[ed] their pockets with the proceeds of final proof and legal notices. These people never dip their pens in ink even to give credit for the clippings which fill their 'papers.'"

Revenue Doc.: By thus miscalling the Reverend Doctor R. J. Keeling in his 25 October column, Baum took a sly dig at the organized church. The previous week in his "Editor's Musings" he had been more openly contemptuous, stating that two-thirds of the American population no longer belonged to churches. "While everything else has progressed," he wrote, "the Church alone has been trying to stand still." He accused ministers of being complacent as long as their salaries were forthcoming. "Policy and fashion," not faith, attracted members, he declared, for a religious affiliation is necessary "if I wish to sell my wares, if I wish to attract clients, if I wish to obtain subscribers to my latest financial scheme," because "there is a popular and fallacious belief that a church goer is a good citizen." If a woman "wishes to shine in society," she also must go to church. "Through the Church," Baum concluded, "you can obtain more prestige on earth tha[n] you can in heaven" (*ASP* 18 October 1890). Such sentiments gave more bite to Mrs. Bilkins's malapropism concerning the Revenue Doc. than it might otherwise have had. Keeling, who had been a pastor of Trinity Church in Washington, D.C., and of prestigious congregations in Pennsylvania before traveling west to take charge of Saint Mark's, headed one of the most fashionable congregations in Aberdeen. In December he and Baum would exchange polite but testy letters and editorials on Spiritualism in Baum's "Editor's Musings" column.

Reverend ladies: The 20 September column offhandedly notices the rousing performances of both the Reverend Olympia Brown and the Reverend Anna Howard Shaw, who spoke on Women's Day at the 1890 state fair. Brown, president of the Wisconsin suffrage organization, had a reputation for wit and intelligence, and her speech had been "forcible and earnest," the *Aberdeen Daily News* reported. The paper reserved its greatest praise for Shaw's performance, calling it "a gem in its way — brilliant, argumentative, forcible and exceedingly entertaining." A male audience member reportedly declared that Shaw "could carry this state single handed and alone for woman suffrage if she could find opportunity to address all voters." The Massachusetts clergywoman's "magnificent voice and presence" had definitely impressed the *News*, which generally exhibited a veiled hostility toward suffrage (*ADN* 18 September 1890).

Rhines votin' machine: One of the bills introduced in the 1890 South Dakota legislative session proposed the adoption of the "improved Australian ballot system, employing the Rhines vote recorder and counter. This method of voting, though novel, possesses many important advantages, [e.g.] . . . the doing away with the cumbrous ballot of the pure Australian system, and the celerity and certainty of the counting of the votes by this new 'all American' method" (*ADN* 12 February 1890). The "Rhines improved ballot box" was an early incarnation of the modern voting machine.

Ringrose, Jim: James Ringrose, an Irish Catholic, owned the Sherman House, the most famous of the early Aberdeen hotels and "the social and business capitol of the new town" (*Aberdeen*, p. 60). Possessing an enormous energy, Ringrose became the mainstay of the local Democratic Party and spent his time and attention on the Sherman House bar, while his four sisters ran the restaurant and hotel. After prohibition began in May 1890 the hotelkeeper continued to sell liquor in original packages, and Baum's landlady referred to a bottle of brandy as a "pint o' Jim Ringrose's pride" on 21 June. Not depending on the bar and hotel business alone, however, Ringrose owned a two-thousand-acre farm just outside of town, where he raised grain and horses. As a result, the Sherman House also headquartered the Brown County Agricultural Society, and the affable Irishman served as the society's president in 1887. His contemporaries bestowed the honorary title of "general" on him, and later generations recalled him as a near legendary figure whose geniality was famous all over Dakota Territory. It was Ringrose's larger-than-life presence in the Democratic Party and the social life of Aberdeen that led Baum to call the local Democrats "jimicrats." Not surprisingly, Baum suggested in his 31 January 1891 predictions that the enterprising Ringrose would continue to discover new ways to circumvent the local prohibition laws, even if it meant ferrying willing Aberdonians to an arctic cap made of white beer (Weisbeer) — certainly the largest blind pig of all time.

Roache's: On 22 March 1890, with prohibition approaching, Baum referred to the recent close-out sales at the establishments of Edmund H. Roche, a wholesale liquor dealer, and John G. Roche, a saloonkeeper. In late February 1890, as lawmakers struggled with prohibition measures, both Roches had announced their intention to close their soon-to-be-illegal businesses by the first of April and leave the Aberdeen area. Edmund Roche, after setting up subordinate James J. Gould as a supplier of thirsty Minnesotans, moved his business to Chicago. John Roche moved to the Pacific Coast.

Salisbury, Skip; Salsberry's: Seneca M. ("Skip") Salisbury and brother Elmer E. were partners in the Salisbury Book Store, which began in 1883 as a newsstand in the post office. As the post office moved to larger quarters, so did the Salisbury business, selling newspapers, cigars, stationery, and sporting goods. In the 1890 social season, the previously unassuming Skip Salisbury made quite a splash. "Skip Enters 'Sassiety,'" the *Aberdeen Daily News* announced on 23 January 1890. "He is one of the pioneers of Aberdeen and has always frowned upon society, but seems now resolved to join the mashers, Ward and Vroom, and shine as a social star." At the first Young Ladies Guild auction social, "after the price passed $2," Skip "withdrew from the contest and waited for the next chance." Baum reported that Salisbury was more successful at later events, securing a place at the progressive euchre tables and purchasing one of the high-priced dinner partners at the Gleaners' weight social. In the fall of 1890, in spite of hard times, the "inimitable Skip" again prepared to join in the new, if more modest, social season. As Christmas approached, he advertised "diaries for 1891" in city newspapers. The businessman appears to have been indifferent to politics, refusing to accept Republican nominations for office, which may be the joke in Baum's speculations concerning his political future. Interestingly enough, the Republicans would finally press him into running for county treasurer in 1898, but like Frank Raymond before him, he would lose to John Fylpaa.

Scattergood: John W. Scattergood of New Hope Township, who had been in Dakota since the early 1880s, had accepted the Brown County Independent nomination for state representative. Labeling him "one of our best farmers [who] may be depended on to raise a crop if anyone can," the *Aberdeen Evening Republican* of 19 September 1890 applauded his candidacy. By October, however, strange rumors were circulating: the *Aberdeen Daily News* reported that he had used the alias Harry Burke when he entered the county "a little over a year ago," and "if the name was changed without adequate cause, such a fickle person would hardly be the right man to send to the legislature" (*ADN* 9 October 1890). Scattergood admitted using the name Burke but denied intending any harm. Unappeased, the *News* asserted on 12 October that a year's residence in the county was "short enough time for a square man to become a legislator but it will hardly do for one that's shady." County voters elected him despite the aspersions cast on his character.

Scott; Scott's: When Horace F. Scott, one of nine druggists in Aberdeen, painted his Main Street storefront, Baum reported that he "smiles behind his glistening window panes with a satisfied air" (*ASP* 1 February 1890). His satisfaction must have been fleeting, however, for in the early 1890s Aberdeen could not support nine pharmacists. As he threatened in Baum's 22 March column, Scott began to explore other opportunities, and Baum alluded to the outcome of the search in his 16 August column without mentioning the druggist's name. Scott had just invested in rental property in Chicago, trading a South Dakota farm as partial payment for a lot and two-story brick building on Cottage Grove Avenue. On 25 July the proud owner boasted to Baum that his new property paid 10 percent in rents. Two weeks later the columnist covertly implied that Scott's successful "foreign investments" would enable him to pay the ten-dollar levy for repairing the state fairgrounds. Baum took another dig at Scott's Chicago aspirations in his 31 January 1891 column; more directly, he noted that like most of the other druggists in town, Scott had finally applied for the hated liquor permit prescribed by the state prohibition law. His permit had temporarily been denied "on account of insufficiency of notice" (*ADN* 10 January 1891), but before long, he would be able to sell both homegrown remedies and patent medicines. In two sentences, Baum artfully captured Scott's ambivalence about his future in Aberdeen, but the druggist would not wait five years to make up his mind; he would be gone by 1892.

Senate: Run by Almer G. Cone and Patrick H. Tracy, the Senate was one of Aberdeen's many saloons, each of which had "its quota of tin-horn hangers-on" (*ADN* 30 March 1890). Mrs. Bilkins's cousin Jim represented the men who enjoyed the milieu of these bars, which frequently featured illegal gambling opportunities. Baum pictured the environment vividly when he noted that in each could be found "a diabolical pianist, a gratey violinist or a discordant harpist. The noise of loud laughter and angry disputes issues from the opening doors to greet the passer-by in common with the stench of liquors, beer, tobacco, onions, and the like, conglomerated into one powerful odor impossible for pen to describe" (*ASP* 5 April 1890).

Sessions axle grease: When Brown County Republicans chose Henry C. Sessions of Columbia as their candidate for the party's nomination for United States congressman, Baum predicted that his name "will be used as a leverage, and in that way may accomplish some good" (*ASP* 16 August 1890). It might have worked that way if the rest of the delegation had been content to accept the state auditor position, but a multiplicity of aspirations and expectations, along with Sessions's early withdrawal from the race, clogged the smooth operations of the

Brown County organization. Sessions had always been an unlikely candidate. The former mayor of Columbia had "no control of the offices nor of the machinery of the party nor adherents won by official patronage." Rather than political savvy, he possessed a well-known generosity. A farmer and banker, he had personally lobbied the Ancient Order of United Workmen for the relief of farmers in the spring of 1890, receiving almost $9,000 for seed and feed for destitute Dakotans. Dispensing this largesse in "a quiet, unostentatious way," the Michigan native and Civil War veteran had won the respect of Brown County residents (*ADN* 24 August 1890), but it would not be enough to earn him a congressional nomination.

Sherman House: A huge frame structure that opened with a grand ball on 4 November 1881, the Sherman House was the most important of the early Aberdeen hotels. Under its proprietor, James Ringrose, and his four sisters, the hotel had a regional reputation for hospitality. Ringrose declared it "the largest hotel west of Minneapolis" when a brick addition was added in 1887 (*Brown County History*, p. 283). The owner's daughter later recalled that the menus were designed to "please the sophisticated palates of early residents who had come from the East" (quoted in *AAN* 2 February 1969). One of these early pioneers, Father Robert W. Haire, a Catholic missionary priest from Michigan, referred to the hotel as "a lighthouse on the coast of hell" (quoted in Murray, *A Church Grows on a Tree Claim*, p. 12). Boarders reportedly preferred to stay there because they could use silver knives rather than steel. The building had balconies on two sides, providing covered sidewalks and political platforms. From one of these elevations James H. Kyle gave the famous Fourth of July speech that propelled him into the fall 1890 election and then the United States Senate as one of the first Populist senators in the nation. Unofficially, the Sherman House also served as headquarters for the Brown County Democratic Party. *See also* Jimicrat central committee

Shields, Dan: "Good natured, jolly, whole-souled" Daniel L. Shields, as Baum referred to him on 12 April 1890, had his humor severely tested during the 1890 Republican state convention. City alderman from the first ward and Brown County delegate to the convention, Shields took a great deal of pride in Aberdeen's business enterprises and the county's position as the third largest in South Dakota. He had been among the loudest of those who predicted victory for the Brown County nominations. When congressional candidate Henry C. Sessions withdrew before the convention even began, Shields had not yet left Aberdeen. "Dan went away very hot and undoubtedly kept growing hotter all the way down" to Mitchell, the *Aberdeen Daily News* reported on 28 August. As the convention continued and Brown County failed to secure anything, businessman Spencer W. Narregang telegraphed Shields, querying, "Has the Brown county delegation reached Mitchell yet? Please answer." Shields shot back, "The Brown county delegation is sidetracked. We got what you got in the fourth ward caucus" (quoted in *ADN* 29 August 1890). When not preoccupied by politics, Shields worked as a collector of farm machinery loans.

Sill: Herbert L. Sill clerked at the United States Land Office and worked as city editor of the *Aberdeen Daily News*. Representing "the dignity of the *News* in the night time," Sill had reported the drunken doings of late-night visitors from Warner, a Brown County town straight south of Aberdeen (*ADN* 4 February 1890). His account of the Warner boys' midnight revels earned him a harsh reprimand from Fred Kile, the young editor of the *Warner Sun*. The local press, Baum among them, ribbed Kile in turn for his naiveté. In March 1890 Sill moved to Dubuque, Iowa, to become city editor of the *Daily Herald*.

Silver bill: Baum first addressed the silver question in the *Aberdeen Saturday Pioneer* in late July after the passage of the 1890 Silver Purchase Act, which provided for government purchase of the domestic output of silver. Local newspapers were predicting an inflation of values and a resulting boom, but Baum thought the profit from increased production of silver would "go into the pockets of our silver kings" and that any coming boom would be "healthful and honest and wholly independent of the new silver bill." In addition, Baum failed to see "how an increased coinage of silver can throw more money into circulation unless the government has some way to expend that money amongst our people." Though acknowledging that "something is wrong when agricultural products realize only 6 per cent on the value of land and labor employed in their production, while money rules at 12 per cent," he suggested that any new money generated would "go into our already over-laden treasury, and the evils the silver bill was presumably made to counteract, will still exist" (*ASP* 26 July 1890). Nevertheless, as the election neared that fall, Baum declared the silver bill a good measure insofar as it would keep America from playing "into the hands of foreigners who have been for years buying our silver at low prices and using it against us in the grain markets of the world" (*ASP* 4 October 1890). A Republican president and Congress had passed the bill; therefore, although it might not bring a boom, it had its benefits, and he urged his readers to vote Republican.

Sioux Falls: Not only could Sioux Falls claim to be the biggest city in South Dakota in 1890, with a population of 8,000 to 12,000 people; it could also boast that it was one of the oldest, having first been sited in 1856. Baum consistently approved of the "rustlers" from Sioux Falls who brought industry and business into their city, while the hapless Aberdeen Club built a clubhouse and limited its membership to the social elite. Sioux Falls, however, had some advantages in climate and location that Aberdeen did not. Situated on the banks of the Big Sioux River about two hundred miles closer to Chicago and Omaha, Sioux Falls sat atop rich rock quarries among farmlands that received adequate moisture in most growing seasons. In the fall and winter of 1890, as Aberdeen lost businesses and residents, town boosters may have nursed a hope of keeping the state fair in the Hub City another year, but the State Board of Agriculture awarded the prize to Sioux Falls for 1891.

Skilman, Phil.: Phil Skillman, a prominent lawyer, had offices in the Northwestern National Bank building. He served as mayor in 1883 and again in 1886–87, making ten dollars a year as the town's highest elected official. The *Aberdeen Daily News* noted that Skillman was "widely known as a well read, clear headed and eloquent lawyer" (*ADN* 24 February 1888). During August 1890, as drought withered crops for the second year in a row, Skillman and his family moved to Olympia, Washington.

Skip. *See* Salisbury, Skip; Salsberry's

Slosser: In 1883 George Schlosser migrated from Lodi, Wisconsin, to Blunt, Dakota Territory, where he ran the *Blunt Advocate* and managed the *Pierre Journal* for its owner, Governor Nehemiah Ordway. In the fall of 1888, just a few weeks after Baum's arrival, Schlosser moved to Aberdeen, where he managed the *Dakota Ruralist*, "a weekly Agricultural Paper, devoted to Farm, Stock and Home Interests" (*ACD* p. 10). In June 1889 Schlosser bought a controlling interest in the Aberdeen Daily News Company, becoming both part owner (with Edwin Torrey and other stockholders) and business manager of the *Aberdeen Daily News*. In this capacity, he could have refused to pay Herbert L. Sill, his city editor, for his "mistreatment" of Fred Kile (15 February 1890). As the election of 1890 approached, Schlosser had just been reelected secretary of the South Dakota Press Association, but the office did not prevent him and his Republican newspaper from printing all the dirt on the Independents. Baum must have chuckled gleefully as he demoted the state press association secretary to paperboy in his 31 January 1891 column. Nevertheless, the joke carried a distinct edge, for as business manager of the *News*, Schlosser had just thrown up stiff competition against Baum's newspaper in an attempt to survive the hard times. Before long, as Baum probably knew or suspected, Schlosser would lose his interests in the *News* as a result of the Hagerty & Company bank failure, but the enterprising Schlosser took no backward career steps. By 1892 he had purchased the *Warner Sun* and started the Publishers Printing Company, which he eventually merged with Edward Randall's Dakota Newspaper Union, moving the plant to Sioux Falls in 1896.

Smithereses; Smithers, Miss: Miss Smithers and her "hired lady" or "hired gal," like Miss Jenkyns, are undoubtedly fictional constructs, but they refer to a working class of women definitely present in Aberdeen. In his 8 February 1890 column Baum spoofed the detailed listings of ladies' gowns that appeared in some society papers. Apparently a boardinghouse keeper, Miss Smithers herself appeared in Baum's 15 November sketch when the columnist poked fun at society reading clubs.

Spitler, Zach: In March 1890 Zachariah Spitler worked as a law clerk in the office of Charles N. Harris. Born in Indiana in 1855, Spitler taught school and farmed before receiving his law degree from the University of Michigan. In 1882 he moved to Brown County, practicing in Frederick before associating with Harris in Aberdeen. Baum's 8 March column implied that Spitler had become restless, and, indeed, the lawyer took on the more "excitin' " task of collecting debts for the Deering Harvester Company in May.

Sponge: Mrs. Bilkins's hired girl, like other 1890s bread bakers, had to mix part of her flour with yeast or other leaven and allow it to ferment until a light, porous "sponge" formed (30 August 1890). This sticky mass was then added to the rest of the ingredients to make a light-textured, coarse-grained bread.

Stanley, King, o' Africa: Sir Henry Morton Stanley, world famous explorer of Africa, had been featured on the front page of Baum's 3 January 1891 issue. Under the headline "Stanley in Elegance," the boiler-plate item declared that the explorer had filled his ten-room South Kensington flat with skins, antlers, and the mounted heads of animals he had shot on journeys through Africa from 1871 through 1887. To Baum, Stanley in his London elegance obviously suggested a king in his court, where the Aberdeen band could be called to perform (31 January 1891).

Stearnes; Stearns, Ben: Elected as a city alderman in April 1888, Benjamin F. Stearns became mayor of Aberdeen on 8 August of the next year when regularly elected Anson W. Pratt resigned. Though a Republican himself, Stearns inherited a largely Democratic city council as well as Democratic appointments for city printer and auditor, among others. As manager of the Prairie City Manufacturing Company, a patent medicine plant, Stearns was an antiprohibitionist (patent medicines were heavily alcohol based), a position compatible with that of most Democrats. After the passage of prohibition, however, other Republicans would not tolerate such a stance, and in March the Republican governor accepted Stearns's resignation from the state board of pharmacy. In Aberdeen, Baum and his fellow Republican editors frequently accused the mayor of aiding and abetting the saloon and liquor interests. But the main complaint leveled against Mayor Stearns concerned his prodigal hand with civil projects. During his short tenure, sewers were built, water mains laid, sidewalks graded, and street signs put up, thereby making "a metropolitan city of a straggling village and at the same time [keeping] many men busy" when employment was scarce, the Democratic paper pointed out (*AER* 10 April 1890). Republicans, however, objected to the high expenditure of public money in lean times, and Baum accused the mayor of trying to win the laborers' vote by providing for them "against the earnest protests of the property holders" (*ASP* 15 March 1890). In April 1890 the political situation led the Republican Stearns to seek reelection on the "People's ticket," a predominantly Democratic slate. Roundly defeated in the municipal election, Mayor Stearns quickly faded from public view.

Strauss, Dave: David Strauss came to Aberdeen in 1887 to establish the Golden Eagle One-Price Clothing House, which specialized in men's garments. Fourteen years in the clothing business in Chicago had taught him the details of the trade, from materials to manufacturing. In the 1890s, however, business in Aberdeen was not booming. "I recall," Strauss said years later, "fitting out four farmer boys — their ages were from six to thirteen. Each got a suit, overcoat and cap — the entire purchase amounted to $16.85, and then their dad thought that was rather steep" (quoted in *Brown County History*, pp. 292–93). In spite of depressed prices, Strauss's careful and conscientious business practices allowed him to survive the hard times. His contemporaries lauded him as a leading citizen who was "always ready to put his shoulder to the wheel and help a good cause along" (*A&BC*), as Mrs. Bilkins found out on 15 February 1890.

Stroupe, Mat: Matthew P. Stroupe, a real estate and insurance agent, was mentioned as a potential Republican candidate for mayor in March 1890.

Susan B. See Anthony, Susan B.

Taub; Taubman: Edward T. Taubman, a Republican lawyer, had moved to Aberdeen from Iowa in 1883. In 1888 the people of Brown County elected him their state's attorney. As such, it became his job to interpret the state's new prohibition law and to prosecute offenders, even though, like Baum, he had not supported the legislation initially. Baum's constant ribbing and at least one source (Torrey, *Early Days in Dakota*, pp. 214–17) seem to suggest that Taubman was himself a denizen of the bars, where he sat in on the all-night poker games. After the United States Supreme Court ruling on interstate commerce allowed the shipping of liquor in original packages in May 1890, Taubman visibly scrambled to determine what it would mean to enforcement efforts in Aberdeen. By August his earlier advocacy of licensing liquor as a method of controlling it had made his efforts suspect to the local enforcement league, whose members took it upon themselves to track his record in closing saloons. A state attorney general's investigation would ultimately find that Taubman did as well as he could, given the uncertainties of the law, but temperance advocates were not satisfied. As Baum implied, prohibitionists blamed the failure of the legislation on Taubman rather than on the shortcomings of the law itself. With the political climate turned against him, Taubman did not run for reelection in 1890, but he became embroiled in the contest when Independent candidate Simeon Cranmer hired him to contest his loss to Republican Samuel Kennedy. Taubman won the case for Cranmer in court, but when the Brown County commissioners balked at authorizing Cranmer's bonds and confirming his position, Cranmer accused Taubman of conspiring with the commissioners to keep the job for himself. There matters stood when Baum wrote his 31 January column. As the bond issue dragged on through February, William E. Kidd entered the fray, branding Taubman "a standing disgrace to the bar of Brown county" and "devoid of professional honor" (quoted in *ADN* 17 February 1891). Taubman promptly slapped the *Republican* editor with a libel suit, in which Cranmer served as Kidd's attorney. *See also* Cranmer

Thompson, Clayton: Clayton B. Thompson, another New York state native, was part owner of Thompson and Kearney, Groceries and Crockery. Baum remarked cryptically on 15 March 1890, "If Clayton Thompson really wishes to learn the art of printing, we believe he can secure a more experienced teacher than the one he now studies with." Thompson, who was reportedly an excellent bookkeeper, may have been seeking a new line of work with one of the many newspaper or ready-print businesses in Aberdeen. Instead, Thompson bought out his partner in May and ran the grocery on his own through the summer. During the fall, stiff competition from the Fair and other grocers, as well as economic depression, forced the business into receivership when Thompson could no longer collect from customers. In November, Thompson took a position with the Keystone Mortgage Company.

Thompson & Kearney: Thompson and Kearney, Groceries and Crockery, a main-street business, was "always alive, always making some worthy change and always catching the public eye" (*ADN* 23 March 1890). Owners Clayton B. Thompson and William H. Kearney told customers that they aimed "to make our store the Center of Your World" because nothing could "affect you as much as the market price of your groceries" (*ACD* p. 1). In April 1890 the truth of their advertising came home to them in a pricing war among Aberdeen grocers that seriously affected their own ability to be competitive. The Fair, a newly established grocery concern, began to underprice them on many items, especially tea. Fighting back, Thompson and Kearney boasted, "We sell a tea for 30 cents as good as that for which he, the Fair man, charges 35 cents, and . . . our 20 cent tea is equal to his 25 cent tea." They further asserted that the Fair's claim to sell goods at 10 percent profit constituted "a positive deception upon the public," and they offered "a reward of $100 for proof to the contrary" (*ADN* 17 April 1890). The competition and struggling economy proved too much for Kearney, who sold out to Thompson the next month and accepted a "lucrative position with a large house in Chicago" (*ADN* 4 May 1890). When Thompson went bankrupt in October, however, Kearney returned, bought the stock at assignee sale, and reopened the business with a new partner.

Toothpicks. See Wendell, Nat

Uncommon council: The Common Council of the City of Aberdeen consisted of the mayor and two aldermen — elected every other April — from each of four wards. When Baum began his newspaper in January 1890, the council was solidly Democratic, but a Republican administration won the offices that spring. August Witte, who spent many years as both alderman and mayor in the 1880s and 1890s, recalled: "All of the city officials in those days took a personal interest in every city project and often we had to shed our coats and do work now delegated to laborers. The mayor then was paid but $10 per year, while the alderman received $5." Because they often had to dip into their personal funds to make projects work, they gave such public matters as sewers or street signage "the same attention as if they were private [concerns]," and, Witte recalled, "you can depend on it, we counted the dollars and cents." Because commercial clubs and chambers of commerce were still in their infancy, elected officials also took responsibility for promotion schemes. They were "willing to do this double duty," Witte explained, "because we believed that Aberdeen was to be a great city and we realized that its growth and development rested entirely with us" (quoted in *AAN* 31 January 1929). Baum, as satirist, found much to complain of in the early city administration, especially when it was Democratic. On 15 February 1890 he expressed his criticism in rhyme: " 'I really can't see / For the life of me,' / Said the mayor in deep cogitation, / 'Why they kick like a steer / On the administration here / When there really is *no* administration!' " After Charles Howard took a seat on the council in April 1890, the columnist frequently found the brash young alderman's activities a source of humor.

Updyke farm: The fictional Updyke farm, created by the *Aberdeen Daily News*, symbolized the potential of modern technology and predicted a future in which all farming and housework would be done with electrical appliances. The *News* was suggesting that artesian wells, though extremely expensive to drill, had multiple uses and would change the drought-prone nature of Dakota. Like "modern" Updyke, future South Dakotans would attach to their wells "a water motor and a dynamo to generate electricity" (*ADN* 16 December 1890). Readers were intrigued. "Yum, yum," wrote the *Redfield Observer*. "It makes one regret that he was not born a hundred years later, and is rather confirmatory of that theological notion that this earth regenerated is to be the heaven of scripture" (quoted in *ADN* 2 January 1891). Using his gift for inventive humor and satire, Baum pushed his rival newspaper's speculation a little further in his 3 January column. In the process he glimpsed the potential of technology for entertainment and, through Mrs. Bilkins's concern for her mental privacy, briefly hinted at electricity's potential for misuse — a concept he later explored in his juvenile science fiction novel *The Master Key: An Electrical Fairy Tale* (1901).

Vroom, Sam: Clarence S. ("Sam") Vroom, assistant secretary of the Abstract Company of Aberdeen, worked as a clerk in the register of deeds office. With the return of the county offices to Columbia in 1889, Vroom apparently moved to that community, at least for the court season of January and February 1890. His "exile" was temporary, however, and he usually made it back to Aberdeen in time for the evening socials. The *Aberdeen Daily News* referred to him as "a masher" and "social star" on 23 January, and on 9 February it remarked, "C. Sam Vroom, the beautiful dude and statesman from Columbia, is spending the Sabbath with Aberdeen admirers." Echoing this appellation in his 15 February column, Baum called him "the brittle statesman," perhaps referring to a dance in Columbia at which Vroom "created a little diversion by suddenly throwing himself at full length on the floor, where he instantly bec[a]me the cynosure of all eyes" (*ASP* 15 February 1890). In his September column Baum alluded to Vroom not only as a fashionable man but also as a tall one. The *News* had called him "the attenuated abstract man" on 6 September, noting that his long legs nearly touched the ground on either side of a pony when an accident forced him to assume such an inappropriate mount. By putting Vroom at the helm of the airship that would connect Aberdeen with the world in 1895, Baum predicted his continued popularity, even though punctuality appeared to be missing from the young man's store of virtues.

Wallace, Fred: C. Fred Wallace, a young bachelor who worked in Frank Hagerty's branch bank in Claremont (a small Brown County town), regularly attended Aberdeen social events. On 5 April 1890 Baum reported that at a recent Women's Christian Temperance Union tea party the hostess "announced that the closing number would be a quartèt by Messers. Kyle, Cranmer, Culver, and Baum, with Mr. Fred Wallace as organist." When the time came, the men "walked gravely enough to their places, and stood in a row with opened music books while Wallace ground out a diabolical dischord on the organ that brought tears to all eyes. Then the leader counted, 'one, two, three,' and the four mouths opened wide simultaneously but silently, while a dawning recollection swept over the assemblage that it was April 1st." When Hagerty's Aberdeen and Claremont banks failed in October 1890, Wallace returned to his hometown of Pittsburgh, Pennsylvania, "to recreate" (*ASP* 25 October 1890).

Ward, Al.; Ward's: Alonzo LaRue Ward was born in Lima, Ohio, in 1861 and homesteaded in Beadle County, Dakota Territory, in the early 1880s. After proving up, he moved to Aberdeen and started a "lunch counter," which he gradually built into a good-sized restaurant, ice cream parlor, bakery, hotel (1897), and candy factory (1907). During the 1890 state fair he opened a second lunch counter and dining hall to serve the crowds attending the event. Ward was well known in Aberdeen for his integrity and generosity. "He was at all times a liberal giver to the charitable and public enterprises," one contemporary said. Another remarked, "He was strictly honest, and never beat a man out of a penny, if he did it was a mistake and he made it good" (quoted in GSB p. 229). Baum's 2 August column testified to Ward's soft heart and recorded one of his many generous deeds. Ward would marry Carrie Paulhamus in 1894, but in 1890 he was still an eligible bachelor who attended most Aberdeen social events. In the 8 March column, which dealt with the awarding of the city printing, Baum playfully accused the restaurateur of hoping to supply the city pies, a pun on the printing term (pi or pie) for mixed or spilled type. The columnist later recorded that an arid, windy July day of 110 degrees had "prostrated" the popular businessman (*ADN* 12 July 1890). In the dull business climate of January 1891, Ward began to buy butter from local farmers with the intention of starting a creamery, showing just the kind of rustle and enterprise that Baum admired.

Warner Schoolboy's Bugle: The editor of the weekly *Warner Sun*, Fred Kile, earned this slighting title (15 February 1890) for his newspaper as a result of his impassioned editorials against the *Aberdeen Daily News*. The young men of Warner, who had competed unsuccessfully with Aberdeen for location of the railroad hub, frequently hopped the train to the larger community for late night entertainment. After one or two of them were thrown in jail and the *News* reported the events at some length, the *Warner Sun* accused the *News* editor of implying that all Aberdeen drunks were from Warner. The press of the area laughed heartily, the *Ipswich Gazette* remarking that Kile "considers it hard that the Warner boys can't run up to Aberdeen for a little fun without the *News* giving the whole thing away" (reprinted in *ADN* 4 February 1890).

Waterman, Johnny: John B. Waterman, a Michigan native, was a clerk at the Brown Brothers bank and treasurer of the Hub City Band. Declaring the Aberdeen band to be "among the best musical organizations in the northwest," the *Aberdeen Daily News* of 22 August 1888 gave some of the credit to the cornet solos of young Waterman. "Mr. Waterman not only believes in blowing his own horn," Baum wrote on 24 January 1891, "but everyone else believes in letting him do it."

Weisbeer. See Ringrose, Jim

Wendell, Nat.: A native of Albany, New York, Nathan Howard Wendell moved to Aberdeen at age twenty in 1888. He first worked with the real estate firm of Fletcher and Fisher and later became credit manager for Jewett Brothers. In 1890 the young bachelor made the rounds of the various church socials, where he earned the nickname "Toothpicks," by which Mrs. Bilkins refers to him on 8 February 1890. In his news report of the Gleaners' weight social, an account that took the form of a biblical parody, Baum included this sketch of Wendell: "And after the evening was far spent they all prepared to wend their ways to their different homes, when lo! poor Wendellibus was discovered leaning gloomily against the wall of a corridor, his toothpick chewed to shreds, and in his clasped hand a lonely piece of silver of the value of fifty cents." Since the women were sold for fifty cents per one hundred pounds, Wendell had been hoping to buy a dinner partner. The scales, however, had been tampered with, so that "they spake not the truth," and all the women weighed at least 115 pounds (*ASP* 8 February 1890). In the fall of 1890 Wendell took leading roles in the plays performed during the state fair, displaying "a magnetism which impresses people at first sight" (*ASP* 20 September 1890). By 8 February 1891 the dull business climate had adversely affected even Wendell's magnetism, or so Baum suggested as he teased the popular businessman about his work habits.

West Hill: In 1883, Beard, Gage and Beard (the firm of Baum's brother-in-law T. Clarkson Gage) platted a rise of ground outside Aberdeen as an exclusive district, advertising it as the "highest and most desirable residence portion of Aberdeen" (GSB p. 143). Actually, it measured only twenty-three feet or so higher than Main Street. Though some pretentious homes were built there in the 1880s, most of them were later moved because a marsh made travel to and from West Hill difficult.

West Surperior; West Superior: A major entry in the series of boomtowns that drew Aberdeen money and citizens, West Superior, Wisconsin, gradually became popular for "foreign investments." When Baum's friend George Kimberly visited his relatives there in April and May 1890, he wrote back that he had bought a high-priced town lot but planned to return to South Dakota. He judged that his Aberdeen property "will bring me better returns in time than anything else" (*ASP* 10 May 1890), an argument that Mrs. Bilkins clothed in more earthy guise on 4 October. Baum's job printing foreman, C. W. Downey, had also checked out the place in early August but took a position with the *Pioneer* instead. Nevertheless, by the end of September, Aberdeen businesses and citizens were relocating to Wisconsin. On 24 September the *Aberdeen Evening Republican* reported that Jim Ringrose, whose brother now lived in the boomtown, had received a telegram authorizing him to employ fifty men at two dollars a day to work on civic improvements there. Baum attributed West Superior's healthy business climate to its drain of Aberdeen capital; if the same money had been spent at home, Aberdeen would boom instead.

Wiggins: A national weather forecaster of the period, Wiggins represented a group that Baum called the "weather prophets." He reported on 29 March 1890 the forecasters' prediction "that South Dakota is to have a regular Califo[r]nia rainy season this spring and summer. From April 10th to the 25th, heavy rainfalls will be in order. From May 20th to June 20th, there will be a season of unexampled wet." Such abundance, the editor asserted, would not destroy the crops "as it did on the shallow soil of the eastern states last summer." Baum continued, "If the weather prophets are only correct this time they may live forever after in houses of gold, built by the contributions of the opulent and grateful people of

South Dakota" (*ASP* 29 March 1890). Indeed, local weatherman Isaac Hirvaskari, better known as Ike Finn, who successfully predicted a number of rainfalls, got a triumphal ride in the Fourth of July parade for his efforts.

Wilcox, Ella Wheeler: Ella Wheeler Wilcox was the "most successful newspaper poet" of the 1870–1920 era, according to Russel Nye (*Unembarrassed Muse*, pp. 123–24). She wrote forty books in forty-six years, producing "a poem a day for syndicated distribution" after 1884.

Wilder: In puns on their last names, Baum referred to Frank Wilder and his political rivals in his 12 April 1890 column. Wilder, who was state master workman of the Knights of Labor and business manager of the organization's newspaper, had announced his candidacy for mayor on 10 April, just before the Republican caucuses. Some businessmen of the city had encouraged this printer and sometime employee of the Barnes and Persons Lumber Company to represent them, acclaiming him as "an industrious, safe and commendable citizen" (*ADN* 10 April 1890). In political maneuvering before the election, Wilder withdrew his name from the three-way race for the Republican nomination, leaving the contest to Robert Moody and August Witte. As a reward, in June 1890 the governor appointed him South Dakota's first commissioner of labor, allowing him to establish the Department of Labor and Statistics in Aberdeen until the fall election.

Williams, Hank: Henry S. Williams, Brown County treasurer, spent the winter of 1889–90 commuting to Columbia to transact county business. Joining the group that went to Harriman, Tennessee, in February 1890, Williams spent $2,200 for two lots. On his return he reported that he "had lots of fun . . . and made a few small investments from which [he expected] a good return in a short time" (*ADN* 8 March 1890). Later that year, after accepting the Republican nomination for state senator, Williams hosted a ball and reception in Columbia with other members of the "Court House Crowd," the Wednesday night soiree to which Mrs. Bilkins alludes at the beginning of Baum's 1 November column. In his sketch of a political Halloween party, Baum confidently implied that Williams would seal the fate of Democratic opponent John Firey. The unmentioned Independent candidate, James Kyle, emerged the victor on 4 November, however, giving Hank Williams one reason to groan even as late as 1895 — but especially in January 1891, as Kyle began his term in the state senate. The former county treasurer had also lost over $7,000 of county money in the Hagerty bank closing, which he and his bondsmen were forced to make good in late January 1891. Within a few weeks Williams had further cause to moan, as the state legislature elected Kyle to the United States Senate.

Winsor: Another young New York state native, Walter B. Windsor had homesteaded in Dakota in 1883 and started an insurance business after he became "satisfied that Aberdeen would become a prosperous city" (*A&BC*). By 1892, Aberdeen promoters were claiming that his business was the second largest in the state, making his a success story in spite of hard times.

Witte, August: Referred to as "the witty man" in the 12 April 1890 column, German-born August C. Witte commanded the unqualified respect of Aberdeen politicians. A well-known pioneer merchant, he and a partner had started a hardware store (Mueller & Witte) in Aberdeen in 1881. The citizens first elected him a city alderman in 1885, and he ultimately served twenty-five years in that capacity. Before the 1890 election his name was often mentioned as a Republican candidate for mayor, but in the end a political deal allowed Robert Moody to emerge from the Republican convention as mayoral candidate; two years later, however, Witte would be mayor. In the fall of 1890 Baum grouped him with other Aberdeen bachelors contemplating the coming social season during hard times. Although the same age as Baum, Witte did not marry until 1895.

Wolsey: Amid the bustle of extra printing jobs and theatrical activities in September 1890, Baum did turn down one job: he refused to print badges for the town of Wolsey, a new contestant in the South Dakota capital race. Located twelve miles northwest of Huron, Wolsey boasted two railroads and claimed that a million dollars backed its mid-August entry into the contest. Although serious investors may have temporarily supported a Wolsey bid, Huron and Pierre boosters accused each other of putting up the Wolsey candidacy. Baum, a Huron supporter, claimed that he had been asked to print five hundred Wolsey badges and send the bill to Pierre headquarters. When he requested a written order, the party canceled. "Pierre managers," Baum concluded, "are probably kicking themselves even yet to think that their emisaries [*sic*] were foolish enough to 'give away' the inward cussedness of the Wolsey plot by telling a Huron newspaper to collect Pierre money to pay Wolsey debts" (*ASP* 20 September 1890). The *Aberdeen Evening Republican*, a Pierre supporter, had asserted on 19 August that Huron was booming Wolsey in its "desperate effort to stop the land slide in favor of Pierre." Nobody seemed to take Wolsey's candidacy seriously, even though some hungry job printer did eventually print ribbons in its support.

Wright, Cholly: Charles Wright owned a hack stand at the Sherman House. Not surprisingly, since the Sherman served as the unofficial headquarters of the Democratic Party, Wright was a delegate to the convention of the "People's caucuses" in April 1890. Given Mrs. Bilkins's vivid account (19 April 1890) of election night, one wonders what his thoughts must have been as he hauled the celebrating Republicans about town.

Reference works used to compile the glossary but not cited anywhere in the text are
marked with an asterisk (*).

Aberdeen: A Middle Border City. American Guide Series. Aberdeen: South Dakota
 Writers' Project, Works Projects Administration, 1940.

Aberdeen SD. Dacotah Prairie Museum. L. Frank Baum Letters.

Aberdeen and Brown County, S.D., Illustrated (*A&BC*). Aberdeen SD: Aberdeen Sun,
 [1892].

*Aberdeen City Council. Proceedings, 1889–1890. Dacotah Prairie Museum.
 Aberdeen SD.

Aberdeen City Directory, 1889–90 (*ACD*). St. Paul MN: Chas. Pettibone, [1889].

Algeo, John. "The Names of Oz: Onomastics in the Fantasies of L. Frank Baum."
 In *From Oz to the Onion Patch*, pp. 130–46. Publications of the North Central
 Name Society, no. 1. DeKalb IL, 1986.

———. "Oz and Kansas: A Theosophical Quest." In *Proceedings of the Thirteenth
 Annual Conference of the Children's Literature Association*, ed. Susan R.
 Gannon and Ruth Anne Thompson, pp. 135–39. Kansas City: University of
 Missouri, 1988.

Allen, W. C. "Memories." *Aberdeen American-News*, 12 November 1939; *Aberdeen
 Evening News*, 16 November 1939.

*Anderson, Lee. "A Case of Thwarted Professionalism: Pharmacy and Temperance
 in Late Nineteenth-Century Iowa." *Annuals of Iowa*, 3d ser., 50 (winter 1991):
 751–71.

Anthony, Susan B., to Mrs. L. E. Wimans, 21 December 1897. State Archives, #86.22.
 South Dakota State Historical Society, Pierre SD.

Attebery, Brian. *The Fantasy Tradition in American Literature: From Irving to
 Le Guin*. Bloomington: Indiana University Press, 1980.

*Bassett, Charles W. *O Brave Soul! A Biography of Kate Kennedy Jewett, 1865–1937*.
 Aberdeen SD: McKeever, 1953.

Baum, Frank Joslyn, and Russell P. MacFall. *To Please a Child: A Biography of L. Frank
 Baum, Royal Historian of Oz*. Chicago: Reilly & Lee, 1961.

Baum, L. Frank. *Animal Fairy Tales*. Intro. Russell P. MacFall. 2d ed. [Escanaba MI]:
 International Wizard of Oz Club, 1989.

———. Clipping Files. Onondaga Historical Association, Syracuse NY.

———. Collection. Alexander Mitchell Library, Aberdeen SD.

———. Letters. Dacotah Prairie Museum, Aberdeen SD.

———. *The Marvelous Land of Oz*. Chicago: Reilly & Britton, 1904.

——. *The Master Key: An Electrical Fairy Tale*. Intro. Donald L. and Douglas G. Greene. Westport CT: Hyperion, 1974.

——. *The New Wizard of Oz*. Indianapolis: Bobbs-Merrill, 1903.

——. Papers. George Arents Research Library, Syracuse University, Syracuse NY.

——. *The Patchwork Girl of Oz*. Chicago: Reilly & Britton, 1913.

——. "Queer Visitors from the Marvelous Land of Oz: How the Ozites Met a Beauty Doctor." *Chicago Record-Herald*, 16 October 1904.

——. Scrapbook. Beinicke Rare Book and Manuscript Library, Yale University, New Haven CT.

——. "When McKinley Gets the Chair." *Chicago Sunday Times-Herald*, 12 July 1896.

——. "Yesterday at the Exposition (From the Times-Herald, June 27, 2000)." *Chicago Sunday Times-Herald*, 2 February 1896.

——. *The Wizard of Oz*. Ed. Michael Patrick Hearn. Critical Heritage Series. New York: Schocken, 1983.

——(as Edith Van Dyne). *Aunt Jane's Nieces on Vacation*. Chicago: Reilly & Britton, 1912.

——(as Laura Bancroft). *Twinkle and Chubbins: Their Astonishing Adventures in Nature-Fairyland*. Chicago: Reilly & Britton, 1911.

Baum, Robert S. "The Autobiography of Robert Stanton Baum, Part I." *Baum Bugle* 14 (Christmas 1970): 17–22.

Bellamy, Edward. *Looking Backward, 2000–1887*. Foreword Erich Fromm. New York: Signet, New American Library, 1960.

Benjamin Franklin, Writings. New York: Library of America, 1987.

*Big Stone Lake Assembly Association. Incorporation Papers, 26 March 1889. Office of Records Management, Bureau of Administration, Pierre SD.

Biographical Directory of the South Dakota Legislature, 1889–1989. 2 vols. Pierre: South Dakota Legislative Research Council, 1989.

*"Biographical Sketch of Max Bass." *Collections of the State Historical Society of North Dakota* 4 (1913): 96–97.

*Black, Doris L. *History of Grant County, South Dakota, 1861–1937*. Milbank SD: Milbank Herald Advance, 1939.

Bones, Marietta M. "A Duty, Not a Privilege." *Monthly South Dakotan* 1 (August 1898): 61–62.

Breedon, Jane Rooker Smith. Papers. MSS 19, State Archives. South Dakota State Historical Society, Pierre SD.

Brown County Directory, 1887–8 (BCD). Aberdeen, Dakota Territory: Aberdeen Publishing, 1887.

Brown County History. Aberdeen SD: Brown County Museum & Historical Society, 1980.

Burgess, Neil. *Neil Burgess' New Play, entitled Vim; or, A Visit to Puffy Farm.* [New York, 1883].

———. *The Widow and the Elder: A Farcical Comedy in Three Acts.* San Francisco: Frances, Valentine, 1880.

Carnes, Mark C. *Secret Ritual and Manhood in Victorian America.* New Haven CT: Yale University Press, 1989.

Carpenter, Julia Gage. Diary. Orin G. Libby Manuscript Collection # 520. Chester Fritz Library, University of North Dakota, Grand Forks ND.

Chamberlain, H. R. *The Farmers' Alliance: What It Aims to Accomplish.* New York: Minerva, 1892.

Cleworth, Marc M. "Twenty Years of Brown County Agricultural History, 1880–1899." *South Dakota Historical Collections* 17 (1934): 17–176.

Cloud, Barbara. *The Business of Newspapers on the Western Frontier.* Reno: University of Nevada Press, 1992.

*Clow, Richmond L. "The Lakota Ghost Dance after 1890." *South Dakota History* 20 (winter 1990): 323–33.

*Coacher, Le Ellen. "The Sherman." 1977. Dacotah Prairie Museum, Aberdeen, SD.

*Coursey, O. W. *Who's Who in South Dakota.* Vol. 4. Mitchell SD: Educator Supply, 1923.

Curry, Jane. Introduction to Marietta Holley, *Samantha Rastles the Woman Question.* Urbana: University of Illinois Press, 1983.

*"Dakota Images." *South Dakota History* 1–24 (1970–94).

*"The Dakota Metropolis [Sioux Falls]." *New England Magazine,* n.s. 4 (May 1891): 350–63.

Dictionary of American Biography. Ed. Allen Johnson. New York: Scribner, 1928–31.

Drake, John. Clipping File. Onondaga Historical Association, Syracuse NY.

Dregni, Michael. "The Politics of Oz: Dorothy Meets William Jennings Bryan." *Utne Reader,* July/August 1988, pp. 32–33.

Early History of Brown County, South Dakota: A Literature of the People by Territorial Pioneers and Descendants. Aberdeen SD: Brown County Territorial Pioneer Committee, 1965.

Erisman, Fred. "L. Frank Baum and the Progressive Dilemma." *American Quarterly* 20 (Fall 1968): 616–23.

**Eureka, 1887–1937.* Ed. Federal Writers' Project. Eureka SD: Eureka's Golden Jubilee Organization, 1937.

*Ewen, David. *The Life and Death of Tin Pan Alley: The Golden Age of American Popular Music.* New York: Funk & Wagnalls, 1964.

*Firey, Carl. "The Settler's Story." *South Dakotan* 7 (August 1904): 21.

First Presbyterian Church, Aberdeen, South Dakota, 1881–1956. [Aberdeen SD: First Presbyterian Church, 1956].

Ford, Alla T., and Dick Martin. *The Musical Fantasies of L. Frank Baum*. Chicago: Wizard, 1958.

*Fox, Lawrence K., ed. *Fox's Who's Who among South Dakotans*. Vol. 1, 1924–25. Pierre SD: Statewide Service, 1924.

Gage, Helen L. "L. Frank Baum: An Inside Introduction to the Public." *Dakotan* 5 (January/February/March 1903): 267–70.

———. "Like the Pale Face." *Syracuse Standard*, 20 July 1890. Clipping, Dacotah Prairie Museum, Aberdeen SD.

Gage, Matilda Jewell. "The Dakota Days of L. Frank Baum, Part I." *Baum Bugle* 10 (spring 1966): 5–8.

———. "L. Frank Baum before He Came to Aberdeen." Transcript of speech, 28 March 1974. L. Frank Baum Collection, Alexander Mitchell Library, Aberdeen SD.

———. "To the readers of *The Baum Bugle*." *Baum Bugle* 17 (autumn 1973): 16.

Gage, Matilda Joslyn, to Lillie Devereaux Blake, 15 November 1890. Harriet Jane (Hanson) Robinson and Harriet Lucy (Robinson) Shattuck Collection. Schlesinger Library, Radcliffe College, Cambridge MA.

Gage, T. Clarkson. Scrapbook (GSB). Alexander Mitchell Library, Aberdeen SD.

Gardner, Martin, and Russel B. Nye. *The Wizard of Oz and Who He Was*. East Lansing: Michigan State University Press, 1957.

Garlock, Jonathan Ezra. "A Structural Analysis of the Knights of Labor: A Prolegomenon to the History of the Producing Classes." Ph.D. diss., University of Rochester, 1974.

Genovese, Michael A. "Tin Men and Witches Feud over Populism in Allegorical Land of Oz." *Minneapolis Star Tribune*, 22 March 1988.

*Goodspeed, Weston A. *The Province and the States*. Vol. 7. Madison WI: Western Historical Association, 1904.

*Green, Charles L. "The Administration of the Public Domain in South Dakota." *South Dakota Historical Collections* 20 (1940): 142.

Greene, David L. "The Writing of Two L. Frank Baum Fantasies." *Baum Bugle* 15 (autumn 1971): 14–16.

Greene, David L., and Dick Martin. *The Oz Scrapbook*. New York: Random House, 1977.

Greenman, Frances Cranmer. *Higher Than the Sky*. New York: Harper, 1954.

A Guide to the Hagerty & Lloyd Historic District. [Aberdeen, SD]: Brown County/ Aberdeen Landmark Commission, 1990.

Hamer, David. *New Towns in the New World: Images and Perceptions of the Nineteenth-Century Urban Frontier*. New York: Columbia University Press, 1990.

*[Hauser]. "Mrs. Louise P. Hauser — 1882, Brown County." Pioneer Daughters Collection, State Archives. South Dakota State Historical Society, Pierre SD.

*Hearn, Michael Patrick. Interview with author. Pierre SD. 12 May 1992.

———. Introduction, notes, and bibliography to *The Annotated Wizard of Oz: The Wonderful Wizard of Oz by L. Frank Baum*. New York: Clarkson N. Potter, 1973.

———. "L. Frank Baum: Amateur Printer." *Baum Bugle* 30 (spring 1986): 11–18.

———. "L. Frank Baum: Chicken Fancier." *Baum Bugle* 30 (autumn 1986): 23–24.

*Heiman, Hazel L. "A Historical Study of the Persuasion of the Populist Impulse in South Dakota." Ph.D. diss., University of Minnesota, 1969.

*Hendrickson, Kenneth E. "The Public Career of Richard F. Pettigrew of South Dakota, 1848–1926." *South Dakota Historical Collections* 34 (1968): 143–311.

Historical and Descriptive Review of South Dakota's Enterprising Cities, Their Leading Business Houses and Progressive Men. Omaha NE: Jno. Lethem, 1893.

**History of Mitchell*. Mitchell SD: Junior High School, 1919.

**History of the Finnish Settlement in Brown and Dickey Counties of South and North Dakota, 1881–1955*. N.p., 1955.

Holly, Marietta. *Samantha Rastles the Woman Question*. Urbana: University of Illinois Press, 1983.

Holmes, Oliver Wendell. *The Autocrat of the Breakfast-Table: Every Man His Own Boswell*. New York: Hurst, n.d.

Humphrey, Seth K. *Following the Prairie Frontier*. [Minneapolis]: University of Minnesota Press, 1931.

Huntzicker, William E. "The 'Sioux Outbreak' in the Illustrated Press." *South Dakota History* 20 (winter 1990): 299–322.

*"The Intrepid Nellie Bly." *Women's History Newsletter* 1 (January/February 1990): 1–3.

Kidd, William E. "Address of William E. Kidd, People's Party Convention, Aberdeen, South Dakota." 26 July 1894. Dacotah Prairie Museum. Aberdeen SD.

*Kingsbury, George W., and George Martin Smith. *History of Dakota Territory* and *South Dakota: Its History and Its People*. 5 vols. Chicago: S. J. Clarke, 1915.

Koupal, Nancy Tystad. "From the Land of Oz: L. Frank Baum's Satirical View of South Dakota's First Year of Statehood." *Montana, the Magazine of Western History* 40 (spring 1990): 46–57.

———. "The Wonderful Wizard of the West: L. Frank Baum in South Dakota, 1888–1891." *Great Plains Quarterly* 9 (fall 1989): 203–15.

*Lamar, Howard R., ed. *Reader's Encyclopedia of the American West*. New York: Thomas Y. Crowell, 1977.

Lauterbach, Stewart E., ed. *First There Was the Prairie. . . . An Oral/Pictoral History*. Aberdeen SD: Dacotah Prairie Museum Foundation, 1988.

Leach, William R. "The Clown from Syracuse: The Life and Times of L. Frank Baum." In *The Wonderful Wizard of Oz by L. Frank Baum*. American Society and Culture Series. Belmont CA: Wadsworth, 1991.

*Lindell, Terrence J. "Populists in Power: The Problems of the Andrew E. Lee Administration in South Dakota." *South Dakota History* 22 (winter 1992): 345–65.

Littlefield, Henry M. "The Wizard of Oz: Parable on Populism." *American Quarterly* 16 (spring 1964): 47–58.

Luehrs, Robert B. "L. Frank Baum and the Land of Oz: A Children's Author as Social Critic." *Nineteenth Century* 6 (autumn 1980): 55–57.

Lyon, William H. "The Significance of Newspapers on the American Frontier." *Journal of the West* 19 (April 1980): 3–13.

Mellette, Arthur C. Papers. State Archives, H74.188. South Dakota State Historical Society, Pierre SD.

Memorial and Biographical Record: An Illustrated Compendium of Biography. Chicago: Geo. A. Ogle, 1898.

Memorial and Biographical Record and Illustrated Compendium of Biography . . . of Prominent Old Settlers and Representative Citizens of Central South Dakota. Chicago: George A. Ogle, 1899.

Miller, John E. "The Old-Fashioned Fourth of July: A Photographic Essay on Small-Town Celebrations prior to 1930." *South Dakota History* 17 (summer 1987): 118–39.

Moore, Raylyn. *Wonderful Wizard, Marvelous Land.* Bowling Green OH: Bowling Green University Popular Press, 1974.

Morris, Linda A. *Women's Humor in the Age of Gentility: The Life and Works of Frances Miriam Whitcher.* Syracuse NY: Syracuse University Press, 1992.

*Muller, Alice B., and H. P. Carson. "A History of the Department of South Dakota Grand Army of the Republic." *South Dakota Historical Collections* 16 (1932): 3–437.

Murray, Robert J. *A Church Grows on a Tree Claim: A History of Sacred Heart Parish, Aberdeen, South Dakota.* Aberdeen SD: Sacred Heart Parish, 1974.

Nelson, Paula. *After the West Was Won: Homesteaders and Town-Builders in Western South Dakota, 1900–1917.* Iowa City: University of Iowa Press, 1986.

Norlin, Dennis A. "The Suffrage Movement and South Dakota Churches: Radicals and the Status Quo, 1890." *South Dakota History* 14 (winter 1984): 308–34.

Nostwich, T. D. "Nellie Bly's Account of Her 1895 Visit to Drouth-Stricken Nebraska and South Dakota." *Nebraska History* 67 (spring 1986): 30–67.

Nye, Russel. *The Unembarrassed Muse: The Popular Arts in America.* New York: Dial, 1970.

Official Program of the Grand Celebration of July 4th, 1890. [Aberdeen SD, 1890.]

*Partridge, Eric. *A Dictionary of Catch Phrases, British and American, from the Sixteenth Century to the Present Day.* New York: Stein & Day, 1977.

*Penfield, Allen. *Aberdeen: A True Story of Brown County, Dakota*. Aberdeen, Dakota Territory: Williams & Waterman, [1886].

A People's History of Beadle County, SD. Dallas TX.: Taylor, 1986.

Pickler Family. Papers. State Archives. South Dakota State Historical Society, Pierre SD.

*Pratt, William C. "Socialism on the Northern Plains, 1900–1924." *South Dakota History* 18 (spring/summer 1988): 1–35.

Pulliam, Walter T. *Harriman: The Town That Temperance Built*. N.p.: By the Author, 1978.

Quinion, Harold. "James H. Kyle: United States Senator from South Dakota." *South Dakota Historical Collections* 13 (1926): 311–21.

Redfield College: Academic Year, 1889–90. [Redfield, Dakota Territory: Redfield College, 1889.]

Reed, Dorinda Riessen. *The Woman Suffrage Movement in South Dakota*. 2d ed. Ed. Nancy Tystad Koupal. Pierre: South Dakota Commission on the Status of Women, 1975.

Reese, M. Lisle. Letter to the author, 8 May 1992.

Remele, Larry. " 'God Helps Those Who Help Themselves': The Farmers Alliance and Dakota Statehood." *Montana, the Magazine of Western History* 37 (autumn 1987): 22–33.

Republican Circulars. State Archives, 75.158. South Dakota State Historical Society, Pierre SD.

Reynolds, Helen M., to Jane Breeden. 14 February 1898. Box 1, Folder 1, Jane Rooker Smith Breeden Papers. South Dakota State Historical Society, Pierre SD.

Robinson, Doane. "A Century of Liquor Legislation in Dakota." *South Dakota Historical Collections* 12 (1924): 281–96.

*———. *Doane Robinson's Encyclopedia of South Dakota*. Pierre SD: By the Author, 1925.

———. *History of South Dakota*. 2 vols. N.p.: B. F. Bowen, 1904.

*———. *South Dakota, Sui Generis: Stressing the Unique and Dramatic in South Dakota History*. 3 vols. Chicago: American Historical Society, 1930.

*Rorabaugh, W. J. "Alcohol in America." *Magazine of History* 6 (fall 1991): 17–19.

Sannes, Erling N. "Knowledge Is Power: The Knights of Labor in South Dakota." *South Dakota History* 22 (winter 1992): 400–430.

———. " 'Union Makes Strength': Organizing Teamsters in South Dakota in the 1930s." *South Dakota History* 18 (spring/summer 1988): 36–66.

Schuler, Harold H. "In Pursuit of Permanence: A Photographic Essay on the Capital of South Dakota." *South Dakota History* 19 (spring 1989): 26–55.

Shillaber, B. P. *Partingtonian Patchwork*. Boston: Lee & Shepard, 1873.

Shortridge, James R. *The Middle West: Its Meaning in American Culture*. Lawrence: University Press of Kansas, 1989.

South Dakota Commissioner of Labor Statistics and Census. *Census Report of South Dakota for 1895*. Redfield SD: Journal Observer Press, 1895.

South Dakota Department of History. *Second Census of the State of South Dakota Taken in the Year 1905*. Aberdeen SD: News Printing, 1905.

South Dakota Equal Suffrage Association (SDESA). Papers (Correspondence and Publications). Boxes 13, 57, State Archives. South Dakota State Historical Society, Pierre SD.

South Dakota Equal Suffrage Song Book. Huron: South Dakota Equal Suffrage Association, [1890].

South Dakota Weather Service. Tabular Summaries. State Archives, H88.56. South Dakota State Historical Society, Pierre SD.

South Dakota Writers' Project, ed. *L. Frank Baum's "Our Landlady."* [Mitchell SD]: Friends of the Middle Border, 1941.

A Souvenir of Aberdeen, the Railroad Hub of the Dakotas. 1907. Rpt. Ed. Don Artz. Aberdeen SD: Brown County Landmark Commission, 1992.

Spaeth, Sigmund. *Read 'Em and Weep: The Songs You Forgot to Remember*. Garden City NY: Doubleday, Page, 1927.

Steele, M. F. "Buffalo Bill's Bluff." *South Dakota Historical Collections* 9 (1918): 475–85.

*Tawa, Nicholas E. *The Way to Tin Pan Alley: American Popular Song, 1866–1910*. New York: Schirmer/Macmillan, 1990.

*Thrapp, Dan L. *Encyclopedia of Frontier Biography*. 3 vols. Lincoln: University of Nebraska Press, 1988.

Torrey, Edwin C. *Early Days in Dakota*. Minneapolis: Farnham, 1925.

———. "So. Dakota Is Proud of L. Frank Baum." *Minneapolis Journal*, 13 September 1902.

Tryon, Warren S. "Agriculture and Politics in South Dakota, 1889 to 1900." *South Dakota Historical Collections* 13 (1926): 284–310.

Twain, Mark. *Adventures of Huckleberry Finn*. Ed. and intro. Henry Nash Smith. Boston: Houghton Mifflin, 1958.

United Workmen of South Dakota. *Constitution, General Laws and Rules of Order of the Grand Lodge Ancient Order of United Workmen of South Dakota*. Huron SD: Daily Huronite Print, 1898.

Utley, Robert M. *The Lance and the Shield: The Life and Times of Sitting Bull*. New York: Henry Holt, 1993.

Vertical Files. Alexander Mitchell Library, Aberdeen SD.

Vogel, Carl S. "The Amazonia of Oz." *Baum Bugle* 26 (autumn 1982): 4–8.

Wagenknecht, Edward. *Utopia Americana*. Seattle: University of Washington Book Store, 1929. Reprinted in L. Frank Baum, *The Wizard of Oz*, pp. 142–57. Ed. Michael Patrick Hearn. Critical Heritage Series. New York: Schocken, 1983.

Watson, Elmo S. "The Last Indian War, 1890–91: A Study of Newspaper Jingoism." *Journalism Quarterly* 20 (September 1943): 205–19.

Webb, Daryl. " 'Just Principles Never Die': Brown County Populists, 1890–1900." *South Dakota History* 22 (winter 1992): 366–99.

Whitcher, Frances M. *The Widow Bedott Papers*. American Humorists Series. Upper Saddle River NJ: Literature House/Gregg, 1969.

White, Bruce M. "Indian Visits: Stereotypes of Minnesota's Native People." *Minnesota History* 53 (fall 1992): 99–111.

Williams/Watson Theatre Collection. Dartmouth College, Hanover NH.

Wittmayer, Cecelia M. "The 1889–1890 Woman Suffrage Campaign: A Need to Organize." *South Dakota History* 11 (summer 1981): 199–225.

*Wolff, Gerald W. Introduction to "The Civil War Diary of Arthur Calvin Mellette." *South Dakota Historical Collections* 37 (1974): 346–52.

WPA Writers' Project Collection. Richardson Archives, I. D. Weeks Library, University of South Dakota, Vermillion SD.

education, 240. *See also* school
superintendent
effete East, the, 79, 108, 142
election fraud, 135–36
electricity, Baum comments on, 15–16,
153–57, 189–90, 250
electric lights, in Aberdeen, x, 162, 225
elevator companies, 12, 42–43, 49–50,
61, 194, 231
Ellendale, Dakota Territory, 3
elopements, 85–87, 103–4, 213
Emerald City, 181–82
enforcement. *See* liquor laws
Episcopalians, in Aberdeen, 14, 19,
32–34, 46, 128, 201, 230
Episcopal Ladies Guild, 105, 185, 214,
215. *See also* Young Ladies Guild of
Saint Mark's Episcopal Church
equal rights. *See* woman suffrage
Equal Suffrage Association (ESA).
See Aberdeen Equal Suffrage
Association; South Dakota Equal
Suffrage Association
Erisman, Fred, 178
Eureka SD, 106, 210
Evans, Dennis M., 90–91, 149, 207, 210
Excelsior Block, 7, 82, 235–36
experience meeting, 97, 188
extracts, 45

Fair, Aberdeen, 56, 210–11, 227, 249. *See
also* McWilliams, R. A. (the Fair man)
Fair, Chicago, 4
fairgrounds bond, 97–98, 243
fantasy, in Baum's columns, 7, 15–16,
209. *See also* futuristic speculation
farmers, 217, 219, 221, 231, 235–36,
242, 245, 248; Baum's views of, 13,
150, 23, 49–51, 60–62, 78, 109, 133,
181; circumstances of, 5, 9, 12–13,

17, 41–43, 49, 59–60, 69–70, 92–93,
108–9, 142, 171, 226, 228–29, 244; of
the future, 153–57, 250
Farmers' Alliance, 6, 7, 12, 85, 118, 125,
165, 184, 193–94, 206, 221, 228–29
Farmers and Merchants' Bank, 225
fashion consciousness, 203, 230–31, 240,
251
Father Goose, His Book (Baum), 172
Fayetteville NY, emigrants from, 3, 196,
227
Federal Writers' Project. *See* South
Dakota Writers' Project
Feelyerpaw. *See* Fylpaa, John A.
Felch, Miss, 78, 211
Felch, Mrs. H. H., 211
female armies, 72–74, *116*, 193
female rustics, 8–9
feminine utopias, 178
Fielder, William, 44, 211
Fin, Ike. *See* Hirvaskari, Isaac
finance: Baum's journal on, 104, 169,
186–87, 190, 194; Loucks's lectures
about, 90–91
Finch, Eva, 128, 227
Finnish immigrants, 77, 211, 213
fire department, Baum criticizes, 17,
128–30
Firey, John H., 127, 132, 212, 254
First National Bank, 202, 225, 239
Fisher, Charles A., 40, 212, 252
Fisk, Clinton B., 217
flax-processing plants, 235–36
Fletcher, Charles C., 64–66, 212, 252
Flynn, Joseph, "Down Went McGinty,"
231
"foreign investments," 35–39, 109–10,
221, 243, 253
"For Mollie and Baby," 234
Fort Abraham Lincoln, 142